BUSINESS ETHICS

Events such as Trafigura's illegal dumping of toxic waste in Sierra Leone and BP's environmentally disastrous oil spill have highlighted ethical issues in international business at a time when business leaders, academics and business schools were reflecting on their own responsibilities following the global financial crisis. The scope and scale of the global operations of multinational businesses means that decisions taken in different parts of the world have far-reaching consequences beyond the national settings where employees are located or where firms are registered and, as such, an awareness of these responsibilities needs to be integrated into all levels and all subjects.

Using four guiding principles – a critical multilevel approach rooted in the tradition of European social theory, a comparative and international perspective, a global rather than European standpoint, and engaging with subject-specific issues – this book aims to 'mainstream' business ethics into the work of teachers and students in business schools. This comprehensive volume leverages contributions from a range of experts to move away from business ethics being a box to be ticked towards an integrated consideration across the business disciplines.

This impressive book brings ethical considerations back to the heart of the business curriculum and, in doing so, provides a companion for the progressive business student throughout their university career.

Patrick O'Sullivan is Professor and Head of Department of People, Organizations and Society at Grenoble École de Management, France.

Mark Smith is Associate Professor of Human Resource Management at Grenoble Ecole de Management, France.

Mark Esposito is Associate Professor of Organizational Behaviour and Leadership at Grenoble Ecole de Management, France.

'Ethical issues have moved to the forefront of public policy debate following a series of crises affecting business, finance and government over many years. These culminated most recently in the BP oil spill in the Gulf of Mexico, the American subprime crisis and the sovereign debt crisis in the Eurozone. Consequently this provocative and stimulating new book is a welcome diagnosis of the ethical issues underpinning a wide range of academic disciplines and subjects that bear on business finance and government in particular, but also a normative essay on what policies government, regulators and managers might pursue to avoid these ethical dilemmas in future. While business ethics has been a Cinderella subject in business schools, this collection of essays places ethical considerations centre stage for the first time and the acute analysis will stimulate debate through the innovative range of case studies at the end of each chapter. Every discerning business school, manager and bureaucrat should read this book and follow its wise prescriptions.'

Nigel F. B. Allington, Downing College and Centre for Economic and Public Policy Research, University of Cambridge

'The authors provide a lively reflection on contemporary business ethics theory and practice and an original multi-level critique that helps the reader questioning conventional beliefs in strategic management. They offer a constructive critique to rethink business models and the managerial mindset towards responsible capitalism.'

Simone de Colle, Dublin City University, Ireland

'The gist of this book is a challenge – a challenge to reflect on and to rethink the role of business in society. The authors of this book pose questions that are at once inspiring, intriguing, and compellingly urgent.'

Christina Garsten, Stockholm University, Sweden

BUSINESS ETHICS

A critical approach:
integrating ethics across
the business world

Edited by Patrick O'Sullivan,
Mark Smith and Mark Esposito

Routledge
Taylor & Francis Group

LONDON AND NEW YORK

First published 2012
by Routledge
2 Park Square, Milton Park, Abingdon, Oxon OX14 4RN

Simultaneously published in the USA and Canada
by Routledge
711 Third Avenue, New York, NY 10017

Routledge is an imprint of the Taylor & Francis Group, an informa business

© 2012 Patrick O'Sullivan, Mark Smith and Mark Esposito

British Library Cataloguing in Publication Data
A catalogue record for this book is available from the British Library

Library of Congress Cataloging in Publication Data
Business ethics: a critical approach integrating ethics across the
business world/edited by Patrick O'Sullivan, Mark Smith,
Mark Esposito. – 1st ed.
  p. cm.
  Includes bibliographical references and index.
  1. Business ethics. I. O'Sullivan, Patrick. II. Smith, Mark,
  1950 June 25– III. Esposito, Mark.
  HF5387.B86677 2012
  174'.4–dc23
  2011048331

ISBN: 978-0-415-66356-4 (hbk)
ISBN: 978-0-415-66358-8 (pbk)
ISBN: 978-0-203-11901-3 (ebk)

Typeset in Bembo and Stone Sans by
Florence Production Ltd, Stoodleigh, Devon

CONTENTS

List of illustrations   *ix*
List of contributors   *xi*
Acknowledgements   *xiii*

PART I
Introduction   **1**

1 Ethics as social critique   3
   Patrick O'Sullivan, Mark Smith and Mark Esposito

2 Levels of critique: a methodological framework
   for the study of ethics and morality in business   22
   Patrick O'Sullivan

3 The ethical management of ethics: fostering ethical
   behaviour in corporations   34
   Ion Copoeru

PART II
Organizational strategy   **47**

4 Corporate Social Responsibility, definitional
   paralysis and ambiguity   49
   Mark Esposito

5 The impact of ethics on the issues of organizational
congruence   60
Lloyd C. Williams and Mark Esposito

6 Ethical issues of reification and recognition in HRM:
a Critical Social Theory perspective   74
Gazi Islam

7 Private vices, business virtues? The institutional strategy
of legitimated online gambling in Italy   86
Carmelo Mazza

PART III
Finance and economics   **99**

8 The ethical and social dimensions of executive
compensation   101
Terence Tse, Khaled Soufani and Lucie Roux

9 The ethics of the banker: reflections on the banker's
economic and societal functions, or how history
requires us to reflect on the role of banks in society   118
Sandrine Ansart and Virginie Monvoisin

10 Islamic finance revisited: a brief review with the
Singapore example   134
Habibullah Khan and Omar K. M. R. Bashar

11 Ethical issues in the policy response to the 2008
financial crisis: moral hazard in central banking
and the equity of bailout   147
Alojzy Z. Nowak and Patrick O'Sullivan

PART IV
Organizational behaviour   **167**

12 Ethics and management: the essential philosophical
and psychological basis of ethical management
driven by a progressive company   169
Loïck Roche

13 Mindfulness as a mediator between the effective
    and the ethical manager   179
    Dominique Steiler and Raffi Duymedjian

14 A cultural appreciation of diversity of ethical
    strategies: examples from European business   191
    Taran Patel

15 Employee surveillance and the modern workplace   206
    Marko Pitesa

PART V
Marketing and innovation   **221**

16 Ethics and marketing   223
    David Bevan

17 Deeper into the consumer's mind: market research and ethics   238
    Caroline Cuny

18 Social and societal marketing: applications for
    public policy makers and companies   254
    Carolina O. C. Werle

19 Designing for a better world   267
    Josiena Gotzsch

PART VI
HRM and employee relations   **285**

20 'You take the high road . . .': analysing the ethical
    dimensions of high performance work systems   287
    Keith Whitfield, Rachel Williams and Sukanya Sengupta

21 Ethical challenges in business coaching   302
    Pauline Fatien Diochon

22 Ethical issues for international human resource
    management: the case of recruiting the family?   317
    Mark Smith and Christelle Tornikoski

23 Competency management: between managerial
development and ethical questioning 332
Pierre-Yves Sanséau

PART VII
The ethical future? **347**

24 Epilogue: towards an ethical future for business? 349
Patrick O'Sullivan, Mark Smith and Mark Esposito

ILLUSTRATIONS

Figures

1.1	The three levels of critique	8
9.1	Banking activities and responsibilities	124
9.2	Banking activities and responsibilities in the 2000s	130
11.1	Inflation in the Euro area (annual percentage changes, non-seasonally adjusted)	158
14.1	Ethical strategies of the four cultures proposed by CT	201
19.1	The plastic bags are selected on colour, cut open, washed and dried	278
19.2	In a next step the plastic bags are compressed in a thicker, flexible material	279
19.3	Conserve India handbags	280
19.4	The Chulha stove	282
19.5	Modular structure of the Chulha stove	282
21.1	Typology of clients' reasons for resorting to business coaching	305
21.2	Main 'ethical traps' in the three-party business coaching contracts	312
21.3	Main tensions in the three-party coaching contracts	312

Boxes

1.1	The UN Global Compact for Business	5
17.1	Examples of national marketing deontological codes	240

Tables

3.1	The connection between ethics-related control mechanisms and management control-system components	37
5.1	The boundaries of sustainability and congruence	61

7.1   Gross gambling turnover trend 2003–2010   90
7.2   Gambling tax revenues in Italy 2003–2010   95
9.1   What is the banks' role in the economy? The activities of a
      modern bank   121
9.2   What is the banks' role in the economy? Introduction
      of the idea of the societal role   127
11.1 Official financial support to the financial sector up to
      February 2009 (in % of GDP)   157
20.1 Godard's classification of high performance work systems   289
20.2 Boxall and Macky's classification of high performance
      work systems   290
22.1 A typology of recruitment and selection for international
      assignments   323

CONTRIBUTORS

Sandrine Ansart, Grenoble Ecole de Management, France

Omar K. M. R. Bashar, Swinburne University of Technology, Australia

David Bevan, China Europe International Business School, China, and Grenoble Ecole de Management, France

Ion Copoeru, Babeş-Bolyai University of Cluj-Napoca, Romania

Caroline Cuny, Grenoble Ecole de Management, France

Raffi Duymedjian, Grenoble Ecole de Management, France

Mark Esposito, Grenoble Ecole de Management, France, and Harvard University, USA

Pauline Fatien Diochon, Menlo College, California, USA, and University of Lyon, France

Gazi Islam, Grenoble Ecole de Management, France

Josiena Gotzsch, Grenoble Ecole de Management, France

Habibullah Khan, U21 Global, Singapore

Carmelo Mazza, IE Business School, Madrid, Spain

Virginie Monvoisin, Grenoble Ecole de Management, France

Alojzy Z. Nowak, Warsaw University, Poland

Patrick O'Sullivan, Grenoble Ecole de Management, France

Taran Patel, Grenoble Ecole de Management, France

Marko Pitesa, London Business School, UK, and Grenoble Ecole de Management, France

Loïck Roche, Grenoble Ecole de Management, France

Lucie Roux, ESCP Europe, London, UK

Pierre-Yves Sanséau, Grenoble Ecole de Management, France

Sukanya Sengupta, University of Warwick, UK

Mark Smith, Grenoble Ecole de Management, France

Khaled Soufani, Concordia University, John Molson School of Business, Canada

Dominique Steiler, Grenoble Ecole de Management, France

Christelle Tornikoski, Grenoble Ecole de Management, France

Terence Tse, ESCP Europe, London, UK

Carolina O. C. Werle, Grenoble Ecole de Management, France

Keith Whitfield, University of Cardiff, UK

Lloyd C. Williams, The Institute for Transformative Thought and Learning, USA

Rachel Williams, University of Cardiff, UK

ACKNOWLEDGEMENTS

The editors would like to express their gratitude for the continued support during the preparation of this work to all those colleagues at Grenoble Ecole de Management who in various ways contributed to facilitating our task. Special thanks go to Katiaryna Zhuk for her meticulous and punctual editorial support throughout the phases of the book and to George Room for his valuable help with the proofreading and the English translations.

We would also like to send our heartfelt appreciation to our families, for their support, encouragement, patience and love during these past two years. In particular, Patrick O'Sullivan would like to dedicate this work to Ola, Mark Esposito to his loves Alina and Frappy, and Mark Smith to Sarah, Sam and Isabella.

PART I
Introduction

1

ETHICS AS SOCIAL CRITIQUE

*Patrick O'Sullivan, Mark Smith
and Mark Esposito*

The critical spirit of the age

It is autumn 2011; three years after the dramatic collapse of one of the iconic investment banks that epitomized an all-conquering financial capitalism, Lehman Brothers. By now we know that the case of Lehman Brothers was just the tip of an iceberg, even if no other big banks have been allowed to fail outright. Moreover, the fallout from the financial crisis and the associated over-indebtedness of consumers, businesses and governments, and the retrenchment of spending that is indispensable if that debt burden is to be reduced, have been translated into an ongoing economic depression from which few corners of the world have been spared and that has struck particularly violently in those advanced countries that were the pin-ups of the rampaging financial capitalism of the 1990s: the USA, Britain and Ireland, as well as in certain countries whose governments had persistently failed to master spiralling public sector debt (Greece, Portugal).[1]

Not surprisingly, these dramatic economic events have led to a more deeply rooted questioning of the whole economic system and of the way in which businesses behave therein. On the one hand, there has been a real questioning of the moral acceptability of a whole range of business practices that have contributed to, or are associated with, the financial crisis: the manner, for example, in which subprime mortgages[2] were sold by brokers on placement commissions to individuals who realistically never stood a chance of successfully repaying the mortgages and so were in effect being set up for personal financial disaster; or the manner in which large bonuses were being paid to bank executives on the basis of positive short-term results and these bonuses continuing even after the crisis. On the other hand, the depression has prompted a more profound critical reflection on the merits of an untrammelled ultraliberal free market capitalism driven by the pursuit of profits above all else, priding itself on the self-regulatory capacity of markets and derisory of the state and its interventions in the economic system. It is no exaggeration to say that the period from 1990 to 2007 was characterized almost the world over by a stifling, almost universal, consensus around a politico-economic model of aggressive profits-driven finance-led free market capitalism in which regulation of business and state intervention in the economy were being dismantled with a quasi-religious fervour. This 'religion' had a name: the 'Washington Consensus'.[3]

None of this consensus today seems so certain. It is in the context of this spirit of the age to ask some more searching questions regarding business practices and even of the system itself that we are presenting a new book on business ethics whose approach is openly and systematically critical in intent. At many points the shibboleths of the overweening 1990s' consensus will be mercilessly called into question. We will be illustrating how the implications of this critical intent permeate right to the heart of the whole range of business disciplines; how the considerations of a truly critical approach to business ethics will challenge some of the central presumptions of strategic management theory, of financial management and corporate finance, of human resource management, of marketing and, of course, of political economy.

In addition to its challenge at a theoretical level across a whole range of disciplines traditionally taught in business schools, this more critical spirit of the contemporary age has also had a practical manifestation through the Global Compact of the United Nations. This Compact, dating from 2000, commits signatory businesses (and business schools) to implementation of a more ethical approach to business in practice (see Box 1.1 for details of the Compact). It is possible to be cynical about the degree of real impact that the Compact has had but its very existence is a sign of the times.

Methodology and levels of critique

Before embarking on this comprehensive critical tour it seemed important to stop to reflect in more detail on the methodological significance and imperatives of the approach we are proposing; this is also treated in Chapter 2 of the book, which examines the possible levels of critique within business ethics and their logical significance and implications in more detail, so here we present just a brief outline.

Although business ethics has been recognized as a separate discipline, at least in business schools since the mid to late 1980s, it is surprising how little attention has been paid to its methodological characterization; this is all the more so because of the presence therein of certain methodological features not found in most of the other business disciplines. These methodological peculiarities are centred on the role of business ethics as a critical social discipline, a role that we have just seen is central to the spirit of the age.

It is true that business ethics could confine itself to a purely descriptive study of the norms and rules that are, or appear to be, adopted to guide various businesses in practice. In logical terms, such an approach to business ethics would consist entirely of *positive* discourse; that is to say, of propositions that describe facts or relationships among ideas. Business ethics would simply be a specialist branch of

BOX 1.1   THE UN GLOBAL COMPACT FOR BUSINESS

The UN Global Compact comprises ten principles in the areas of human rights, labour, the environment and anti-corruption. Drawing upon the Universal Declaration of Human Rights, the International Labour Organization's Declaration on Fundamental Principles and Rights at Work, the Rio Declaration on Environment and Development and the United Nations Convention Against Corruption, the Compact asks 'companies to embrace, support and enact, within their sphere of influence, a set of core values in the areas of human rights, labour standards, the environment and anti-corruption'.

As active stakeholders in the business world, business schools across the world have also committed themselves to the Compact. In our view this commitment requires a proactive consideration of ethical issues across all disciplines and recognition that ethical challenges create tensions between stakeholders, nationally and internationally, that can be addressed by a critical perspective developed in volumes such as this one. The ten principles of the Compact follow.

Human rights

- Principle 1: Businesses should support and respect the protection of internationally proclaimed human rights; and
- Principle 2: make sure that they are not complicit in human rights abuses.

Labour

- Principle 3: Businesses should uphold the freedom of association and the effective recognition of the right to collective bargaining;
- Principle 4: the elimination of all forms of forced and compulsory labour;
- Principle 5: the effective abolition of child labour; and
- Principle 6: the elimination of discrimination in respect of employment and occupation.

Environment

- Principle 7: Businesses should support a precautionary approach to environmental challenges;
- Principle 8: undertake initiatives to promote greater environmental responsibility; and
- Principle 9: encourage the development and diffusion of environmentally friendly technologies.

Anti-Corruption

- Principle 10: Businesses should work against corruption in all its forms, including extortion and bribery.

For further details see www.unglobalcompact.org/.

anthropology or comparative cultural studies, and would be thus methodologically straightforward.

However, such a purely descriptive business ethics would fall far short of the ambitions of most that have studied, or will study, the subject in the present age. For if a purpose of the subject is to conduct a social critique, and if that critique is to yield any practical fruit for the improvement of the world, it will have to issue, in the end, recommendations for modification, if not revolution, in practical actions for businesses (and many others in society). Hence, business ethics perforce will have a *normative* character; it will embody significant elements of what logicians classify as normative discourse. Normative discourse outlines not how the world is but rather how it *ought* ideally to be, and so it is a statement of *ideals* in effect. The full logical import of this distinction of normative from positive discourse will be elaborated in Chapter 2.

But if business ethics is going to be critical and so normative in character, we may actually identify a number of distinct ways or levels at which the critique may be carried out.

Level 1

This is the first step beyond a purely descriptive anthropological-type study where, in addition to simple description of the rules that govern (or appear to govern) business activity and managerial decisions, we begin to ask questions of a critical nature about those rules: are they, in the end, morally acceptable and, if not, what ought to be the rules that govern business? At this first stage or level, the role that a business plays in society is not per se called into question: it is simply taken for granted and the focus is very much on ethical rules within the company, always geared ultimately to fulfilling the conventionally presumed social role of the business.[4] A corollary question is, of course, on what these normative assertions regarding how businesses and their managers are to behave are to be based? This will be discussed in more detail in Chapter 2 but for now let us note that the sources could be the conventional morality of a society (but what society?), religion or moral philosophy.

Level 2

Once we have embarked on a normative investigation as to the rules that govern how businesses and their managers *ought* to act and behave, an important distinction suggests itself. Normative business ethics could be concerned with the rules that ought to govern the activities of individuals within the business, and this was the main focus in the early years of business ethics and of American business ethics in particular. This we have in effect just defined as Level 1 critique. But one could also raise questions about the moral responsibilities of the company as a whole in relation to the society or societies in which it operates: this is the sphere of company social responsibility. If these reflections are truly critical in spirit they will involve calling into question conventional or orthodox views about the role that a company ought to, or should be expected to, play in a community where it operates. This brings us to a deeper level of critique whereby the role of the company in society, rather than being taken for granted or beyond question, is subjected to a searching critique, and so we find it useful to designate this as Level 2 of critique in business ethics. A whole host of interesting questions suggest themselves once we begin to question the social role and contribution of businesses and to probe the critical normative question of what that role ought ideally to be. Some idea of the breadth of this discussion (which goes right to the heart of political philosophy and political economy as well as of ethics) will be given in Chapter 2.

Level 3

There is a third type or level of critical moral reflection that we also think it useful to distinguish. Once we are dealing with moral issues in international business, whether at Level 1 (what country's rules are to be applied within a company that is doing business in several states) or at Level 2 (differences in the essential view of the role of business in society in different countries/political philosophies), we will be forced to consider, at the very least, different moral codes; and where a multinational company makes a decision in these circumstances it will have, at least implicitly, decided to apply one or the other of the competing codes (or perhaps, less likely, some compromise between them). In effect therefore, whether implicitly or explicitly, the business or its relevant managers will have made a comparison of codes and decided that for whatever reason one is superior to another and so is to be applied. What we describe as Level 3 of critique would make this comparative evaluation of codes fully explicit. Level 3 consists in effect of conducting a metaethical evaluative comparison, a critical morality of moralities. Here, in the pursuit of a daunting endeavour to develop some universal rational moral principles, we seek to evaluate the various different codes with a view to giving rational guidance as to which code to apply when codes conflict, rather than letting that decision (because implicit decision at the very least there inevitably will be) be based on arbitrary unthinking prejudices. Given its metaethical character, it will be evident that Level 3 is the deepest level of critique within the subject.

The three levels of critique can be represented diagrammatically as in Figure 1.1.

Business ethics and the tradition of Critical Social Theory

Having delineated this conception of the various levels at which the critiques of business ethics may be carried out, a parallel clearly suggests itself with the broader field of 'Critical Social Theory'; and we would see this work as fitting easily within this field as one of its subdisciplines. Put very simply, Critical Social Theory refers to an approach to theorizing in the social sciences that is inherently critical in intent to the extent that it sees social structures and modes of interaction not simply as

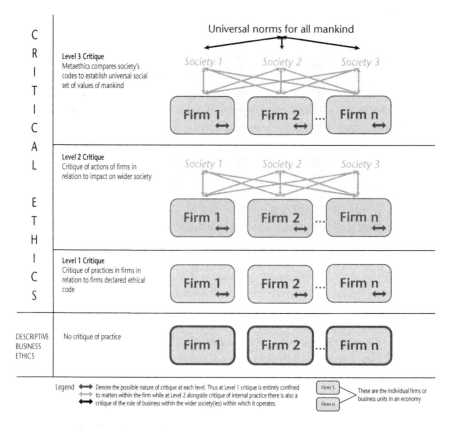

FIGURE 1.1 The three levels of critique.

given objective phenomena analogous to the natural objects and phenomena studied by the physical sciences but also as the carriers of, or as expressions of, deeply rooted human interests. As a result, it is never enough to understand social phenomena purely in objective terms because in so doing we will at best partially understand or at worst totally misunderstand them. We must at all times seek to unmask/discover the latent subjective dimension, the human interest or interests that they embody.[5] This unmasking of underlying human interests, to the extent that it invariably also lays bare the intricate power relations among individuals and social groups, becomes in effect also a critique of social processes. In the hands of its evident intellectual forebears, Karl Marx and his followers in social theory and political economy, this critique becomes a ruthless unmasking of ideology and false consciousness, from the ideological harnessing of social relationships and modes of interaction to buttressing the narrow dominating interests of ruling classes. Furthermore, in Marx the critique must issue ultimately (and indeed for Marx inevitably) in a social revolution in which the dominant class and its ideologies are overthrown decisively and new modes of social interaction introduced. (The point after all is to change the world![6])

However, Marx and Marxism, while certainly being the ultimate *fons et origo* of the tradition of Critical Social Theory, can today be seen in effect as an extreme expression of the approach. Contemporary Critical Social Theory does not harbour quite the same apocalyptic revolutionary flavour as Marx. Nonetheless, Critical Social Theory does still embody, to a greater or lesser extent, what we may call the 'transformational intent' of its Marxian forebears: the conviction that Critical Social Theory should culminate in at least insights or recommendations as to how the world *ought* to be improved. Put very simply, a critique that is merely negative or destructive, confining itself simply to showing up what is false or contradictory or immoral in social systems is stillborn: our social critique must also in the end be *constructive*, which is to say that it must put forth suggestions as to how the world can be changed and improved; in short, normative ethical and political recommendations for social transformation.

It will be evident that the critical approach to business ethics that we have outlined above, which through its three levels involves a deepening critique of business practices and is leading to normative recommendations in respect of these practices, lies squarely within this transformational tradition and may be conceived as a subfield of Critical Social Theory.

Ideology unmasked

One particular theme that has been central to all critical social theories is the unmasking of hidden ideologies. This theme will surface in a number of the chapters of the book and is its most subversive, or perhaps we should say Socratic, element.[7] Whereas in the past the unmasking of ideology and false consciousness has been largely a prerogative of what may loosely be designated left-wing critics of capitalism, in this book the critique of ideology will be more even-handed and it will be seen that both 'left' and 'right' harbour their own cherished ideologies and carefully ring-fenced areas of 'political correctness', shibboleths that are regarded as off limits to criticism.

It will be relevant to recall in a little more detail here the conception and role of ideology in Critical Social Theory and its relationship to what has come to be known as 'political correctness'. Tracing its origins to the works of Marx, ideology refers to sets of propositions constituting a systematic and internally coherent set of ideas/beliefs[8] that are presented as axiomatic or as beyond questioning and that are widely upheld by certain identifiable social groups. In Marx in particular, ideologies are seen as performing a key social function in defending the interests of a ruling class or group; they will be propagated by the ruling class and its media outlets as propaganda with a view to creating a 'false consciousness' in the oppressed groups or classes. The credo of liberalism or of the American dream has, from the time of Marx, been seen by many critical theorists as an ideology that serves the interests of the rich and powerful in capitalist market economies; it holds out a promise of the opportunity of freedom, material wealth and riches for all in a system in which these will be the prerogative of a select few and in which the children of the rich have a huge head start. But, equally, the credo of communism as propagated in the old Soviet system (and which ironically saw Marx as its inspiration) can be seen as an ideology that served merely to buttress the positions of power and privilege of the upper echelons of the Communist party and the KGB, and which inculcated a manifest false consciousness for the vast bulk of the impoverished population of the old Soviet empire.

Today, talk of ideology has somewhat receded in polite society but it has been replaced by a close and equally closed-minded relative: political correctness. Political correctness again refers to an internally coherent set of beliefs, usually regarding some rather narrower topic or set of topics than political ideologies; where once again there is the same unwillingness and even social sanctions against questioning these beliefs; and where some particular interest group would be seriously inconvenienced or discomfited by questioning of the beliefs. Precisely because it is isolated from any serious critical questioning within the society, the politically correct set of beliefs may in time also become a profound source of false consciousness. Hence, in the last analysis, positions of political correctness are little different from ideology as conceived within Critical Social Theory; about the only significant difference is that ideology is typically a wider set of beliefs constituting an all-embracing political credo, while political correctness typically refers to narrower, or often single, issue-sets of beliefs.

In this work, merely ideological claims or supposedly sensitive politically correct positions will be exposed for what they are, even if in some cases this may seem politically very *incorrect*; the spirit of our work is Socratic. No stone will be left unturned in the relentless pursuit of truth, even if we are fully in agreement with the great master – that finding and proving truth is fiendishly difficult. In the end, what other choice has any rational scholar or thinker?[9]

Examples of this unmasking of ideological positions can be found, for example, in Chapter 2, where the ideological function of the shareholder wealth maximiza-tion principle in strategic management literature is examined; in Chapter 4 on corporate social irresponsibility; in Chapter 16 on the abuse of language in market-ing, and in a sense also in Chapter 17, when the role of neurosciences in observation of consumers for marketing purposes is exposed.

How to use this book

One of the key aims of this volume is to promote the consideration and analysis of ethical issues across all disciplines and in a wider range of courses among business schools worldwide: in effect, to bring ethics 'out of the closet' and into all main-stream subject areas. Only by doing this do we believe that the ethical challenges facing business decisions in all functions can be imbued with the high standards called for by citizens disillusioned by the commercial behaviour of companies and as outlined in the Global Compact of the United Nations (see p. 5).

Each contributing author, or group of authors, was asked to provide a short case study or practical illustration to accompany their chapter. These case studies demonstrate the multidisciplinary nature of ethical challenges faced by businesses today and bring out one or more of the three levels of critique outlined in this chapter and developed further in Chapter 2. There is rarely a single answer to the ethical tensions set out in these case studies and it is possible to argue any number of a range of 'solutions'. The preceding text in each chapter will help locate the themes in the cases and provide a conceptual backdrop for the issues raised. The international nature of the authors drawn together for this volume provides a wide array of cases and illustrations that we hope will chime with the personal experiences of students and allow them to link the issues in the cases to elements of their own professional lives.

Using an approach recommended by Newell and Scarborough (2002),[10] we propose that students adopt a step-by-step approach to each case. Most of the cases are accompanied by a series of questions and these can be used to lead you through the case, or as points for further discussion. The four steps are:

1 Understanding the situation – clearly a good understanding of the issues raised in each case is vital and the chapter that precedes each case is written and structured in a way to complement the reading (and rereading) of the case materials.
2 Defining the problem – identifying the problem in each case is not always straightforward but is at the heart of developing potential solutions. Try to find supporting evidence in the case for the problem. The concepts developed in each chapter will help, as will the knowledge of other elements of the discipline.
3 Generating and evaluating solutions – in most case studies a single best answer is rarely available, and this is certainly the case in the materials developed by the contributors for this volume. Try adopting the different levels of critique, discussed in this chapter, as a tool to analyse your solutions and predict the reactions of various stakeholders.
4 Implementing solutions – generating a solution is only part of the way to completing the case, and implementation is not necessarily straightforward. Again, the competing views of stakeholders and the three levels of critique will help identify potential barriers and possible means to implement your ideas.

This step-by-step approach provides a structure for students to work through the material, as well as one for course leaders to plan the use of these materials and (we hope) integrate these ethical themes into their courses, whatever the discipline and whatever their experience of teaching ethics.

This brings us to a summary of the main themes to be covered in the chapters that follow. Most of the chapters are laid out with an initial essentially dialectical theoretical treatment of a specific theme followed by a practical illustration or case study that aims to bring the ethical theory or dilemma to life by showing how it can arise or has arisen in some very concrete situation for business or government. The volume does not aim to be a comprehensive treatment of every imaginable topic in business ethics and there are certain old or new chestnuts on which we have included nothing at all, for example corruption, whistle-blowing and environmental sustainability questions (although there will be some oblique reference to these). The range of topics we have chosen for inclusion has been dictated by another consideration that may be evident from a cursory glance at the table of contents. In response to a criticism that has increasingly been voiced in the past year regarding the teaching of business ethics, to the effect that teaching it as a standalone subject is rather pointless because students and later managers do not readily see its relevance to the conduct of everyday business, we have wanted to show how the themes of a critical business ethics, if taken seriously, will actually permeate into virtually all of the key managerial functions or areas of managerial decision making. Hence, there are chapters on the implications of ethics for strategic management, for finance and financial appraisal, for the conduct of the human resource management function and for the organization of operations, for the marketing activities of a company and even for design and innovation.

The work as a whole is unified by a critical methodological approach whose logical foundations are laid out in Chapter 2. Chapter 3 deals with the critical question of how a company's ethical policies should themselves be managed in action. Chapter 4 considers the degree of irresponsibility of which many contemporary companies are guilty as a way of gauging the importance of the ethical imperative, while Chapter 5 looks at the importance for the healthy long-term functioning of any business of achieving a congruence between the ethical values of the people who make up the business and those of the business as a whole as a social actor. Chapter 6 will press the critique further to examine and deconstruct the hidden presuppositions of much of the discourse of business organizations today to reveal how ingrained is the tendency to reduce human beings in a business context to being seen as mere objects or things, as human capital or human resource on a footing little different conceptually from capital equipment. Chapter 7 examines the role that state regulation can play in conferring moral acceptability to market activities that otherwise might be seen as morally questionable.

Chapters 8, 9 and 11 deal with a range of ethical issues in banking and finance that have been thrown up in sharp relief by the recent financial crisis and the state-sponsored bailouts it necessitated, while Chapter 10 looks at the age-old question of the morality of usury and the Islamic approach to finance with zero interest rates. Chapter 12, echoing to a degree Chapter 5, examines the importance of ethical leadership to the well-being both of the business and of the people working therein. Chapter 13 continues on this theme of well-being, focusing on the importance for people to have the space and time for reflection and, in particular, for ethical reflection within the context of their work life and activity. Chapter 14 looks at the difficulties of ethical decision making, which are posed in a specifically multinational business context, and the contribution that cultural theory can make to understanding these.

Chapter 15 examines the currently hotly debated moral issues surrounding privacy and the surveillance of employees in the workplace, a practice that has grown exponentially in recent years as a result of certain functional possibilities of information technologies.

Chapter 16 turns to the area of ethical issues in marketing with an investigation of the moral uses and abuses of language and communication in the marketing function, while Chapter 17 examines the morality of some of the uses of neuroscience that are currently being introduced in marketing and marketing research. Chapter 18 then looks at the whole field of social marketing, that is to say, the use of marketing techniques to promote socially or morally desirable practices by consumers or others. Chapter 19 looks at how ethical considerations can be introduced into product and service design alongside aesthetic and ergonomic considerations.

Chapter 20 turns to the moral issues surrounding human resource management (HRM) and poses the question in a bluntly critical manner of the degree to which the development of HRM, both in theory, and especially in practice, in recent years has been compatible with the well-being in the broadest sense of the workforce, or rather a major source of workforce stress. Chapter 21 examines the hidden dangers that lurk in the practices of executive coaching, and Chapter 23 looks at some of the ethical issues that can surface when HRM turns to a more competence-based approach. Chapter 22, having taken a general look at the manner in which ethical issues are central to the HR function, to the extent that it deals with human beings, looks at the key ethical issues surrounding recruitment practices, with particular reference to the international (expatriate) context. The rhetorical emptiness of much HR discourse will here be exposed.

Finally, since the ultimate aim of a critical approach is to provide recommendations as to how the world may be improved, Chapter 24 will ponder on the sort of world towards which the diverse critical reflections and normative recommendations of the volume are pointing.

CASE STUDY: SEIAGUSTUS LTD: IT STINKS

Alek Lychenko, captain of the large oil tanker *Petrograd*, registered under the Panamanian flag to the Russian shipping company Volganova Line, breathed a sigh of relief as his ship made its way into the open waters of the Atlantic Ocean leaving, by now many nautical miles behind, the port of Freetown in Sierra Leone. His ship was bound for Gdansk in Poland and its next assignment. He found himself hoping that his next assignment would be rather less of a depressing saga than that of the previous five months when the tanker had been under charter to Seiagustus Ltd, a little known and, as he had discovered, highly secretive UK-based company specializing in the trading and treatment of oil, chemical products and, especially, chemical waste. In fact, at many times in the previous months, while either he himself or his relief captain, Boris Myrgorodski, had been in command, they had found themselves harbouring serious misgivings about some of the commands that had come to them from Volgaline head office, but ultimately at the behest of Seiagustus whose cargo they had been carrying. Much of what they had been asked to do seemed to them shady and morally rather dubious, even if at no time were they ever asked to break any laws in the strictest sense. Of course, as seasoned captains, Alek and Boris had seen a lot and were all too aware of the ambiguities of what passed as international maritime law; so they had never hesitated to comply with the various orders regarding the Seiagustus cargo. But, nonetheless, they were both agreed that they did not feel quite right about the happenings and they hoped the next charter assignment would not involve Seiagustus or anything like it.

The saga had begun some five months previously when the *Petrograd* had picked up, from a Venezuelan refinery, a cargo consisting of coker gasoline (coker naphtha) which is a by-product of a process involving the pulverization of coke. This by-product is highly sulphurous but the coker naphtha can be transformed (sweetened) into a low-grade petroleum spirit that can be very profitably sold on as fuel oil in many developing countries, even if not in the EU or in other advanced countries. However, the chemical transformation requires the intensive application of caustic soda to reduce the sulphuric content of the coker naphtha and, both because of the risks associated with this potent chemical agent and the disgusting stink the process generates, such chemical transformation is rarely, if ever, permitted in any of the world's major ports or industrial zones. Moreover, the residues or 'slops', which would be the resultant, would contain a cocktail of highly sulphuric compounds and, in particular, high concentrations of hydrogen sulphide, a nauseous toxic gas. Hydrogen sulphide, if inhaled in small quantities, causes nausea, skin eruptions and respiratory problems; in higher quantities it is so repugnant that it can cause nervous system malfunction, coma and death. Nonetheless, Seiagustus' London-based traders had calculated that the profit margin on selling off the low-grade fuel oil after transformation of the cheaply available Venezuelan coker naphtha was huge, especially in the context of the then very high prices of fuel oil; each treated tanker load could bring a net return of some 4 million euros. So if the process could not be carried out on land, why not carry it out at sea, the brave boys at Seiagustus reckoned; and in this project they were actively encouraged by the company's gung-ho chief executive who fully endorsed their plans. The only trouble was that once the chemical transformation using caustic soda had been carried out on board there would be the 'minor matter' of disposing of the highly toxic slops. Lured by the huge profit margins, Seiagustus ordered the transformation of the coker naphtha at sea: they would sell the low-grade fuel at a fat profit and worry about disposal of the residue afterwards.

And so it was that the *Petrograd*, under the command of Boris Myrgorodski, made its way across the Atlantic to the Mediterranean where, far from prying eyes and in the balmy days of the Mediterranean summer, the coker naphtha was transformed into low-grade petroleum. The sulphur content of this low-grade petroleum would have been far too high to meet EU environmental standards for fuel oil but it could easily meet the typical African standards that permit ten times greater a sulphuric content in petroleum sold for general use. After three months at sea the low-grade petroleum was unloaded in Tunis and a handsome profit made by Seiagustus on the deal.

Boris had been told that under no circumstances should he reveal the detailed origins of the cargo and under no circumstances should he attempt to unload the slops in Tunis. So the *Petrograd* set sail into the Mediterranean without cleaning and a day at sea later came the order from Seiagustus via Volgaline to head for Antwerp in Belgium. Seiagustus had arranged for the slops to be unloaded and treated by an authorized local chemical waste disposal facility at the port. Boris was relieved as, although he did not fully understand their chemical nature, he wanted to get rid of these toxic and possibly unstable sulphuric slops from his ship as quickly as possible. Six days later the *Petrograd* tied up in Antwerp and began the cleaning process, pumping the slops ashore. However, some six hours into the cleaning process Boris received a message from an official of the Antwerp port authority to immediately stop the unloading of the slops. Puzzled, he passed on this message to Volgaline and Seiagustus who reassured him that all was in order. However, next morning the manager of the waste treatment facility at the port came on board accompanied by the port health and safety manager to question the captain about the exact nature and chemical composition of these slops. They told him that these were no ordinary slops, that they contained very high concentrations of caustic soda residue and hydrogen sulphide, and that instead of the usual treatment fee that had been negotiated by Seiagustus, a fee five times higher would have to be charged to treat these slops. A somewhat shocked captain relayed the message to Seiagustus who, after a 24-hour delay, declined to pay such a fee. The port authority, refusing to bargain over what they clearly saw as highly hazardous slops, ordered that the slops be pumped back aboard the *Petrograd* and that the ship should then be allowed to set sail.

Seiagustus soon sent word that the *Petrograd* should head for Tallinn in Estonia where it hoped that it would be able to arrange for cleaning of the ship's tanks and disposal of the slops, of whose extra toxic nature Boris was now all too aware. He did not hold out much hope for the cleaning being carried out in Tallinn if it had not been done in Antwerp, since Estonia was a member of the European Union, whose environmental regulations are not only the strictest in the world but also a supranational competence of the Union and so are applied as a common EU-wide standard. However, in Tallinn Boris was due to hand over command to his relief captain, Alek Lychenko, and while rather relieved to be leaving the ship Boris wondered what exactly to say to Alek, a longstanding colleague. Immediately upon docking in Tallinn Alek came aboard and, as was customary, they immediately set about the handover briefing in the seclusion of the captain's cabin. Boris had wondered how much he could or should tell Alek. After all, he had been told to maintain a strict secrecy about the off-shore conversion process of the coker naphtha that had been carried out in the Mediterranean and he was fairly sure that Alek would not have been briefed about this either by Volgaline or by Seiagustus. At the same time, he felt a duty of loyalty to his colleague and long-time acquaintance to let him know just how tricky the coming period of command was likely to be for Alek, what with the need to dispose of the ultra toxic slops whose real nature Boris had known since the call at Antwerp. While Alek expressed dismay, even as an old sea dog he was hugely grateful to Boris for having come clean with him about the nature of the slops; and when later Boris had gone ashore and left the ship for his leave period, Alek sat up late into the night in his cabin wondering what might be about to happen. He had an awful sense of foreboding of evil that he sought in vain to fight back.

That foreboding was borne out the next day as the Tallinn port authorities also declined to accept the *Petrograd* slops. After some days alongside, the order eventually came to Alek to set sail for West Africa. As the *Petrograd* made its way out of the Baltic, then into the North Sea and the English Channel and finally out into the Atlantic Ocean there was complete silence from Seiagustus and from Volgaline regarding the eventual destination in West Africa. As the ship passed abeam Dakar and the Cape Verde islands Alek decided to take the initiative and to ask for instructions from Volgaline as to where to head; meanwhile, he cut back on the engines and allowed the ship to proceed lazily at about 10 knots down along the West African coastline but in international waters. After two days the order came to sail towards Port Harcourt in Nigeria for a rendezvous off the Nigerian coast in that area with some barges that would take the slops and dispose of them in Nigeria. Alek wondered what might be their ultimate destination: dumping at sea by the barges or secretly in the already-polluted equatorial forest areas in the Niger delta. However, as the ship passed abeam Accra in Ghana, fresh orders came to make an about turn and to head back towards Freetown in Sierra Leone where arrangements were being made for discharge of the slops in the port of Freetown.

Seiagustus had indeed been active. The company had for many years been present in west and central Africa, involved in oil and chemicals trading there, and had built up a formidable network of political connections and privileges. Although it was whispered locally that its undoubted political influence and privilege were the result of the generous bribery of local politicians in these very poor states, Seiagustus was a highly discreet and secretive company, and no hint of such bribery had ever been documented or reported in Europe. Using its contacts and influence, Seiagustus had been able to arrange for a newly formed local waste disposal company, Teodoro CT, to take the toxic slops from the ship and dispose of them. When Alek was finally told a day later, when the ship was about 12 hours from Freetown, that the slops were to be transferred to a fleet of tanker lorries from Teodoro CT he was at first greatly relieved that he would at last be shot of them; but as the hours passed and the contours of the coastline became sharper on the approach to Freetown he could not but wonder what was going to happen to these slops once on the lorries. After all, in Antwerp, there had been a high-security disposal facility but even there they would only have been prepared to deal with the stuff for five times the normal rate. Alek shuddered to think of the degree of sophistication or safety precautions that might prevail in the disposal facilities in Sierra Leone, a very much less developed country than Belgium.

The *Petrograd* entered the port of Freetown and tied up at 16:30. Within 30 minutes, Babatunde Ogunoku, a local man and director of Teodoro CT, was on board together with the port Customs team to confirm that the fleet of lorries would be ready to begin taking the slops at 19:00. Alek was amazed at this uncustomary efficiency and zeal to get the job done in this part of the world but, given how keen he was to get rid of his toxic cargo, he was more than happy to go along, mustering his crew (who had rather been hoping for a night in Freetown after weeks at sea) for immediate discharge of the slops. And so it was that at 19:15 the first tanker lorries arrived to take the toxic slops. From the bridge Alek watched as the tanker lorries drove off into the night and away from the port area towards the city of Freetown. He was rather surprised, as he had expected that the lorries would be transferring the slops to some sort of facility in the port area, but not knowing much about the area he concluded that there must obviously have been some new chemical waste treatment facility elsewhere in the city or in its hinterland. At least, he thought to himself, the slops are being taken inland and there was no question of dumping them at sea – more than could be said of his fears of what might have happened if the slops had been offloaded onto barges off the Nigerian coast.

The first mate, Petru Popa, a gregarious and good-natured young Moldovan who had joined Volgaline two years before, asked Alek if he could leave the ship for a few hours to go into Freetown for a night out together with the second mate, Sergei Mihailova. Since they had been for weeks at sea, and as deck officers not directly required to oversee the discharge, and since Alek knew that he would be unlikely to sleep until the operation of discharge had been completed, he agreed to let the two men go up town. After all, he alone of the crew knew the dark secret of the truly toxic nature of the slops, so it would have not only been churlish but also suspicious if he had refused the request.

At 21:00, Petru and Sergei left the ship in high spirits and took a taxi from the port gates, asking the taxi driver to take them first towards some good local eating establishments, preferably in a lively part of town close to nightclubs so that they could treat themselves to some after-dinner rest and recreation. While sampling the local cuisine in a very basic eating establishment on the side of the street, the men could not but notice a growing disgusting smell that reminded them of rotten eggs, and this smell seemed to intensify when the wind blew. Having originally put it down to malfunctioning drains or sewers, they were puzzled as to why the stench increased when the wind blew. But this being a poor African country they did not give the matter too much thought and soon they were on their way to a local bar that had been recommended by the taxi driver for post-prandial relaxation. They were relieved to get inside the poorly ventilated bar with its strong smell of alcohol and human sweat and to escape the increasingly nauseous smell outside. In any case, as the local girls queued up to flirt with them in the dimly lit bar, all thoughts of the outside world receded. After some 30 minutes, a very tall lithe local girl whom Petru could not but notice came into the bar in an apparently very agitated state and made her way towards the toilets. When she emerged some three minutes later she huddled in a conversation with four of the other girls and two big local men whose role Petru could only assume was to protect the girls in the bar. After some five minutes of animated conversation one of the local men left the bar while the beautiful tall girl again went to the toilets. When she emerged, Petru noted to his delight that she had changed into brightly alluring clothes and had applied make-up. As she walked towards the centre of the bar she looked to him like a top European fashion model and he could not resist getting up and making his way to talk to her. She introduced herself as Soraya and allowed the charming Petru to buy her a drink.

Later, as they were relaxing and talking, Petru warmed hugely to this beautiful and very directly spoken local girl who told him of the poverty of her family, her mother and three younger siblings and how her bar work helped handsomely to feed and keep the whole family. So, without wishing to be too personal, he decided to ask Soraya why she had been so agitated when she had come into the bar earlier. She told him that she had had an extremely unpleasant experience earlier in the evening. In the slum area of the city where she lived with her family, at about 20:30 there had suddenly been an outbreak of an extremely foul and all-pervasive stink that had quickly led to extreme nausea and was affecting everybody in the slum area where she lived. Everyone was complaining of burning eyes and many people were vomiting; a few young children had apparently lost consciousness. It appeared, but Soraya could not be sure of this, that the stink was coming from a nearby open city rubbish dump. She said that this never smelled good but from 20:30 this evening the stink from the dump had suddenly become overpowering and totally nauseous. The slum dwellers were talking about some tanker lorries that had come to the dump just before the outbreak of the stink . . . Soraya said that the reason she had gone immediately to the toilets on arrival at the bar was that she herself had been so nauseated that she had had repeated vomiting attacks, including a last one in the toilets. Asked if the smell was reminiscent of rotten eggs Soraya confirmed this and Petru remarked that he and Sergei had noticed a similar smell outside earlier but nothing like as strong as it appeared to have been in Soraya's neighbourhood.

Some three hours later, Petru reluctantly left the beautiful Soraya and, having located his second mate Sergei, the men made their way back to the ship. There being no taxis available they decided to walk and, as they did so, that same nauseous rotten egg smell hung in the air. When they arrived at the ship Sergei asked to be promptly excused and went to his cabin where he was violently ill. Petru, on the other hand, who was not feeling quite so nauseous after the 45-minute walk back from town, went to announce his return to Alek to relay some of the evenings happenings to him. Without going into too much of the detail, he spoke of the smell and of the strange story of the open dump and immediate outbreak of nausea in the slum area that had been recounted by the lovely local girl, Soraya. Petru was struck by the grim impassivity of Alek's look as he told the tale. On other such occasions there would have been ribald exchanges about the delights and charms of the local girls, but this evening Alek barely managed a wry smile as Petru described Soraya. He concluded that this was not the time to talk to Alek, who obviously had something on his mind, and so Petru fairly quickly withdrew to his own cabin suffering by now from quite a throbbing headache that he put down to some of the local spirits he had been drinking before Soraya had engaged his whole attention. In minutes he was in a deep sleep . . .

Alek by contrast could not possibly sleep. He went up to the bridge to see how advanced was the discharge and noticed that there were still some of the tanker lorries of Teodoro CT taking the slops. He went onto the open-air bridge wing and sniffed the air. There in the port, and owing to the breeze blowing in off the ocean, the smell was predominantly of sea air mixed with diesel fumes but there was also an unmistakable hint of the rotten egg smell described by Petru, especially in moments when the sea breeze lulled. He paced the bridge for some minutes, then radioed the engineers on the decks below to ask how soon before the discharge and cleaning would be complete. A further three hours, they informed him. He curtly told them to expedite. He went to his cabin but there was no question of sleep: for Alek had by now understood more or less exactly what was happening. The toxic slops were being taken from the ship in tanker lorries and simply being dumped in open rubbish tips around Freetown. He was indignant, furious, outraged.

Thoughts raced through his mind. Should he call the harbour master to warn him of the dangers? Well, no, probably not, because in this part of the world the harbour master had almost certainly been paid off by Teodoro CT, if not by Seiagustus who had a reputation for discreet 'facilitation payments' and corruption in the region.

Should he call Seiagustus to protest? Hardly . . . given their track record they would probably just laugh at him and tell him to grow up. Or then again, they might offer him some money to keep quiet. But while Alek was not beyond taking a little sweetener to turn a blind eye on occasions, this was different: apparently serious and widespread human suffering was involved and it was not simply about payment to be discreet over some minor misdemeanour. So no use talking to Seiagustus.

He thought of calling Boris to tell him the turn of events, but what good would that do? What could Boris do?

He thought of calling Volgaline, but if he recounted a tale like this they would either take him to be drunk and delirious on some local opiate or, if they knew about the real nature of the cargo, they would probably relieve him permanently of command in the near future.

Alek even thought of calling his lovely Mexican girlfriend whom he had met on an earlier voyage and who always cheered him up; but tonight he would feel dirty if he called her, and what would she think of him if he told her what was happening.

Perhaps he could go to the press on his return to Europe out of a sense of moral duty to reveal the scandal of such open dumping of toxic wastes high in hydrogen sulphide on a poor unsuspecting and utterly unprepared population. The more he thought about it the more immoral and unconscionable the whole episode seemed. So, although if it were to come out that he was the one who had talked to the press he could expect at the least to lose his job with Volgaline, if not be in fear for his life, Alek resolved that once this voyage was over he would go to the press with the full story.

That resolution reached after an hour of struggle with his conscience, Alek felt slightly better. He even considered talking to the press straight away but he thought that that could point the finger too easily to himself as the source of the leaked information, and as the discharge of the slops was almost complete, the damage had by now been done.

Having made this internal decision, Alek fell into a deep but fitful sleep for about an hour, which was interrupted when Petru came to his cabin to say that the discharge and cleaning were complete and that they were ready to set sail for Europe. It was 07:00, just after sunrise. Petru looked pale and drawn and Alek asked if he was OK. Petru cursed the local alcohol, which he said had left him with a stinging hangover and vomiting during the night. Alek quipped about being a lightweight but Petru said that Sergei was apparently feeling equally bad. So Alek said that he would take command not only as the ship left port but also for the first part of the voyage up to 16:00, leaving Petru to recover in his cabin.

Alek now became almost hyperactive despite the short and fitful sleep he had managed just before dawn. He now wanted to be out of Freetown just as quickly as possible. He checked on the refuelling situation with the engineers who said that they could be ready for a 09:30 departure after bunkering. He contacted the harbour master and Customs to announce their imminent departure and somewhat to his surprise they were on board within 30 minutes signing the relevant pre-departure paperwork. He contacted Volgaline to announce their departure and this was promptly acknowledged with an order to proceed to Gdansk in Poland where Alek would be relieved of command and could go ashore on leave. By 09:45 the ropes were being let go and the *Petrograd* made its way as briskly as was feasible out of the port area of Freetown into the open waters of the Atlantic heading northwards towards Europe. Alek sat or paced pensively on the bridge, struck as never before by the purity of the deep blue of the tropical waters. He noticed the towering patches of cumulonimbus clouds that develop with the heat of the day as a backdrop, and which can produce the most spectacular of thunderstorms . . . The symbols tumbled through his mind: the purity of the ocean contrasted with mankind's pollution of the face of the earth, the thunderstorm of the reaction which his revelations to the press would cause. He was glad about the upcoming leave when he would at last have the chance to relieve himself of the moral burden he was secretly carrying by speaking to the press . . .

QUESTIONS FOR DISCUSSION ON THE CASE STUDY

1 Is it morally acceptable for advanced country businesses to exploit differences in local laws or in the application of local laws to reduce costs in the disposal of toxic wastes?
2 Seiagustus Ltd might well claim in its defence that despite having disposed of a fairly toxic cargo to cut costs in Freetown it had also in the past made a big contribution to the economy of the region through its activities in the materials extraction and trading sector. Is this a morally relevant defence of their actions?

3   If you think that there are morally unacceptable actions involved in the case study, whom do you think bears or shares the moral guilt for them?

4   If you were Alek Lychenko what would you have done?

Notes

1   As measured by real GDP for the last quarter of 2008 and the first three quarters of 2009, GDP growth rates as follows were recorded.
    USA: −1.7%, −1.2%, −0.2% +0.4%.
    Britain: −2.1%, −2.3%, −0.7%, −0.3%.
    Ireland: −4.8%, −2.5%, −0.3%, −0.2% (and −2.7% in the fourth quarter of 2009!).
Negative growth means outright contraction of the level of economic activity and so depression. Source: OECD Quarterly National Accounts statistics, http://stats.oecd.org/index.aspx?queryid=350 (accesssed 23/08/2010).

2   Subprime mortgages were mortgages sold to borrowers who hitherto (prior to 2000) would have been regarded as completely unworthy of credit, in some cases, NINJAs: no income, no job or assets. The phenomenon was widespread in the US but the UK and Ireland were not immune to it either.

3   So called because from the early 1990s certain leading world-level institutions based in Washington had come to a consensus view that economic development required a dismantling of extensive state regulation and a climate that would foster the development of indigenous business enterprise in poorer countries. This view is not without its merits, in particular given the evidence that trade (export-led growth) is in the long term more effective than direct aid; but encouraged by the fall of the Soviet system the position became a crusade against all forms of government intervention and state regulation.

4   In Western capitalist societies the role of business is supposed to be to make as much profit as possible as in so doing businesses are led 'as if by an invisible hand' (Smith, 1776) to promote the well-being of the society as a whole. On all of this, see Chapter 2, p. 26–27 and Adam Smith (1776), *The Wealth of Nations*, London: Methuen. See Book IV Chapter 2, p. 29.

5   For further elaboration on these themes there is a vast literature. On Critical Social Theory there is the whole literature of the Frankfurt School whose crowning achievement could be considered to be J. Habermas (1972), *Knowledge and Human Interests*, London: Heinemann. On the inescapable subjectivity of human action and interaction see Patrick O'Sullivan (1987) *Economic Methodology and Freedom to Choose*, London: Allen and Unwin, Chapters 4, 12 and 13; also the whole literature of Austrian economic methodology.

6   In Marx's famous phrase, 'Philosophers have sought to interpret the world: the point however is to change it'.

7   Socratic, because of course Socrates' dialectical method of constantly probing and criticizing received opinion in the relentless pursuit of truth was regarded in the end as highly subversive by the Athenians; the fact that Socrates was practising this method with the young and thus subverting them led eventually to his execution.

8   Ideo-logy means literally a logically related set of ideas; hence it is certainly internally coherent. The problem comes when the ideology is to be related to reality and when some of its axioms may prove to be unfounded or untrue.

9   On all of this see O'Sullivan, *Economic Methodology and Freedom to Choose*, Chapter 1. I have argued there in some detail that pursuit of truth is the only possible ultimate goal of rational enquiry, and that as academic scholars we cannot but be rational. After all, could you even begin to understand what I am writing and seeking to communicate if what I say were to be totally and systematically irrational?

10 Helen Newell and Harry Scarborough (eds) (2002), *Human Resource Management in Context: A Case Study Approach*. Basingstoke: Palgrave Macmillan.

2

LEVELS OF CRITIQUE

A methodological framework for the study of ethics and morality in business

Patrick O'Sullivan

In the introductory chapter reference has been made to the fact that when we speak of a critical approach in the study of business ethics this can be taken in a number of different ways. It can mean anything from a simple aim of reaching some normative as well as purely positive/descriptive conclusions regarding various practices of business to an in-depth critical evaluation of the role of business in society to a critical transcendental comparison of competing moral codes. The purpose of this chapter is to set out in a systematic manner these different levels at which a critique in the ethics and morality of business can be pitched. This is then intended to form a methodological framework within which the reflective essays in the rest of the volume will be developed.

There has for some time been an awareness that there are differences in the way in which the subject is viewed between theorists in different parts of the world. Crane and Matten[1] in their well-known textbook have pointed out a systematic set of differences between a North American and a European approach to business ethics. New writings in the subject from less developed parts of the world are also bringing new perspectives on old topics. This new kaleidoscope of perspectives, while certainly enriching the subject, has brought with it a range of methodological questions that to date have been barely touched upon in the literature of the subject. Many of these questions surround the level at which the critiques of business ethics are to be conducted. For example Crane and Matten[2] have noted that whereas North American business ethics has been very much concerned with the conduct of individuals (employees and managers) within companies, European business ethics has tended to focus more on the role and moral responsibilities of the company as a whole in relation to the society in which it is located and does business. The primary aim of this chapter is to set out the methodological issues as to levels of critique in a systematic fashion; to reflect upon them with a view to giving business ethics a critical methodological foundation; and then to investigate the implications of this critical methodology in a range of particular applications to business ethics issues and cases.

The starting point of our reflections on the differences in approach and on their methodological implications is, then, recognition that there are very different levels of critique, of critical reflection at which the study of business ethics may be conducted. We may begin therefore from a systematic outline of these different levels at which the critical reflections of business ethics may be pitched.

Level 1

At the most basic level there is the contrast between what may be called a positive and a normative approach to the subject in the sense of modal logic. In modal logic, positive discourse is that which simply records facts, states of affairs or relationships among ideas: for example 15 August 2009 was a Saturday, 2 + 3 = 5, etc. Normative discourse by contrast outlines how the world ought ideally to be; it is a statement of ideals. Normative discourse is thus centrally present in discussions of all ethics and political philosophy to the extent that both of these are concerned with views of how people ought ideally to behave for a better world to be possible. Hence in one very basic sense normative discourse will inevitably be encountered in business ethics to the extent that it will be concerned with questions of how businesses and/or people in business ought ideally to behave.

But if business ethics will be to a large extent a study about norms in business we can still recognize two quite logically distinct ways in which this study might be carried out: we could conduct a purely positive description and analysis of the norms that actually govern business actions in various companies and in various contexts; and from a methodological standpoint this would be a positive business ethics. Such an approach is entirely uncritical in relation to business practices and so in effect does not even begin to develop critique.

On the other hand, we could also envisage a methodologically normative approach to business ethics in which we investigate not so much the norms that actually govern the behaviour of businesses as the norms/ethical principles that ought to govern business activity, either in general or in particular contexts. It will be evident that this second approach begins to develop a degree of critique insofar as it is prepared not just to accept as given whatever may be the declared or supposed ethical principles that businesses proclaim but also to subject those principles to a searching critique.[3] This is what we shall label as the first level of critique (Level 1 critique in what follows).

A corollary question that arises if we say that we wish to conduct a methodologically normative business ethics is whence are the normative principles to come that we will use as the basis of deciding what ethical principles a business ought to adopt. The simple answer is that there are a variety of possible sources ranging from conventional shared moralities in certain societies through religious bases to humanism and moral philosophy. This last we conceive as the systematic academic study of moral principles. However, in moral philosophy we will often pass to a different level of critique (the critical morality of moralities), which will be dealt with below as Level 3 of critique. For now let us simply note that a business ethics that confined itself purely to the positive study of the ethical principles that companies supposedly follow would be relatively superficial and uninteresting by comparison with a methodologically normative study in which the ethical principles themselves and the behaviour of the business in respect of these are questioned in depth.

Level 2

A second key distinction in respect of the levels at which critique may be carried out in business ethics is that between the moral appraisal of the actions of individuals within a company, and moral appraisal of the actions and the stance of the company in relation to society at large or to the community(ies) in which a company is situated. This distinction is logically independent of the first level distinction just made, in the sense that we could envisage studying the actions of individuals within a company in either a positive or a normative way; and we could equally study the stance of a company in relation to the wider community in either a positive or a normative fashion. The distinction could be said to be more about the scope rather than level of critique; but since an approach to business ethics that combines a moral appraisal of the actions of individuals within a company with a simultaneous appraisal of the role of the company in relation to the community represents a much more searching critique in which, as argued below, far less is taken for granted, we have designated this distinction as also a distinction of level of critique. Therefore a critical business ethics that includes a critical discussion of the role that a company ought to play in relation to society we shall designate as Level 2 critique.

For many of the earliest writers on the subject, especially in North America, business ethics was essentially confined to a study of how individuals (both managers and employees) should behave within a company. Much ink was spilled on questions such as the ethics of pilfering, of internal whistle-blowing, of racial discrimination, sexual harassment and bullying, and on salary issues. The only parties outside the company who figured were the customers, insofar as there could be moral issues regarding how company employees dealt with or marketed to customers.

In this approach the role of the company as a collective entity in relation to the community is simply not questioned in any critical manner: in effect therefore it takes for granted as something beyond question the role that a business is playing within the society wherein it is located.

Continental European writers (and some of the more strident North American critics) on business ethics, by contrast, have been much more prepared to call into question the role that a business plays within a community and indeed to insist that the most important issues of business ethics concern precisely questions of the role of the business in the wider community.[4] The most obvious example of this latter of course is the concern for the ecological environmental impacts of business activity, but other themes such as cultural imperialism/insensitivity, responsibilities in respect of exploitation of labour (especially use of child labour), alleviation of poverty, adoption of 'corrupt' practices and the whole field of stakeholder theory may be mentioned.

If business ethics were to be confined purely to a positive study of the moral/ethical principles that actually appear to guide the actions of individuals within companies then it might be vaguely plausible to rule out consideration of the moral responsibility of a company in relation to the wider community in which it is located. But, as already suggested, such a purely positive business ethics, as well as being hopelessly uncritical, would be relatively uninteresting by comparison with a methodologically normative business ethics embodying at least Level 1 critique. But the moment we embark on a methodologically normative business ethics with Level 1 critique in relation to actual practices it is inevitable that this will culminate in a questioning of the most appropriate role for business in the community. Why should the critique necessarily stop, so to speak, at the frontiers of the firm?

In fact, for the theorists for whom any critique is thus stopped from consideration of the role that a business ought to play in society or the wider community, it is evident that the reason for this unwillingness to probe further is ultimately ideological in character; that is to say that these theorists are effectively presuming a certain predefined role or stance of business in relation to society as a sort of article of faith which it is not for business ethics to question or to criticize. Almost invariably this ideological stance is some form of unreconstructed faith in the beneficence of a capitalist market system whereby it is believed that by ruthlessly pursuing the company's own narrow self-interest (in turn interpreted as the maximization of profit for shareholders[5]) the business will thereby automatically be fulfilling the only social responsibility it has; it will 'as if by an invisible hand'[6] be contributing to the achievement of an end that was no part of its purpose, namely the well-being of the whole society.

Nonetheless, it would be easy to imagine an analogous stance in respect of the critique of business role in relation to society arising also in a centrally planned economy. Indeed, in such economies as have in practice been close to the centrally planned system there has been the very same unwillingness to call into question the prevailing fundamental ideological view of the appropriate role of business (or of production entities) in society in such a centrally planned system. The old Soviet communist system is a clear example; any serious critique of the prevailing economic system and of the role of state companies therein was discouraged and stifled.

Thus, ideological blinkers that prevent business ethics from carrying to its full and mature conclusion the normative critique of business practices are by no means the sole prerogative just of capitalist apologists on the one hand or of central planning apologists on the other: to a mature methodologically normative business ethics both positions are 'ideological' insofar as they shut down critique of the practices of business at a certain level and are unwilling to confront critical questions regarding the role of business in society.

It is emphatically our view in this work that the critiques of a methodologically normative business ethics must be carried through courageously to their fullest logical conclusion; no areas are to be fenced off from consideration of the probing critique for merely ideological reasons. Hence the critiques of business ethics will extend here to a questioning also of the most appropriate role for a business to play in a society; and the view of a company's social responsibility will go well beyond the idea that a company's social responsibility is entirely fulfilled through the maximization of profits (in a capitalist market system) or through the attainment of central plan targets (in a centrally planned context).

It may be useful already to make a brief reference to certain capitalist apologists whose views on this question have been highly influential throughout the high tide of faith in market systems during the period 1990–2008.[7] We may consider in the first place the pronouncements on this topic by Milton Friedman, particularly from his much-quoted 1970 article 'The social responsibility of a business is to increase its profits'.[8] Friedman's central thesis is clearly expressed in the title of the article: as he sees things, most businesses take the form of limited companies that possess a legal personality but are not to be considered as moral agents in themselves. The only moral agents are the individuals working within the company, in particular the managers who are charged with decision-taking; and their sole moral responsibility is identified by Friedman with their overriding legal responsibility to act in the best interests of shareholders. This in turn is interpreted at least by Friedman (but also by an extensive subsequent literature in management theory) as managers acting to maximize shareholder wealth; or since shareholder wealth will be a direct function of the expected profitability of a company, simple profit maximization.[9] That is then seen as the ultimate limit of the social responsibility of a company. It is not for the company to take upon itself caring about any other social problems; that is seen to be the job of elected politicians who may wish to apply certain regulations to the activities of business.

Friedman's views have been hugely influential especially in North American business schools and in American business practice. Yet, on reflection it can be seen to be highly challengeable on a number of key points. First of all, the idea that a company can have a legal personality but no moral responsibilities as a collective entity seems obtuse. One of the most fundamental principles of fairness in jurisprudence is that with rights go duties/responsibilities; hence a company can and indeed should have certain legal responsibilities. But if there are to be legal responsibilities why not also moral responsibilities?

Second, Friedman identifies the moral responsibilities with their legal responsibilities; yet it is well known that these do not necessarily coincide, otherwise how would it be possible to identify 'bad' laws, that is, laws that on moral grounds ought to be changed/different.

Third, there is the identification by Friedman of the interests of shareholders as profit maximization; and of this therefore as the sole and overriding goal and social role of any business. Here the nature of his position as a simple apologist for capitalism is laid bare. After all, who ever decreed morally that companies should be run exclusively for the benefit of, and in the interests of, shareholders? Simply to argue that this is legally the case is only to reveal all too obviously what Marx had understood a century before Friedman: that the legal system in a state is simply an apparatus to serve the interests of the ruling class. For let us be honest about this: why not have a system where businesses are run to serve the interests of consumers rather than shareholders or of workers rather than shareholders (as Marx had in effect argued); or even a system that legally (and morally) requires businesses to be run in the interests of a range of different stakeholder groups in a kind of simultaneous trade-off?

Finally, by way of critique of Friedman, it may be asked whether or not today's shareholders at any rate are exclusively interested in profits. It is patently obvious that this is true neither of individual or even of institutional shareholders; the phenomena of the ethical shareholder or ethical investment fund are very much with us and probably growing in importance if anything, even as there are also many high profile examples at the same time of investors consumed by material greed.

It is amazing that an article with so many obvious shortcomings and downrightly challengeable simplifications has continued to wield so much influence; perhaps this is the ultimate testimony to its ideological function in contemporary capitalism. But having once exposed its shortcomings here, one important line of attack against the position that we have taken up in this book regarding the level of critiques in business ethics is eliminated. The way is open to what we have labelled as a Level 2 critique, that is, to a consideration of the moral responsibilities of a company in relation to the wider community or society in which it is located, where this social responsibility is not seen as being exhausted in the simple maximization of profits.

A second set of pronouncements, which in a more subtle way ban any real Level 2 critique of the role that a business ought to play in a capitalist market economy, are those regarding 'strategic corporate social responsibility' (CSR) in the works of Porter and Kramer. Their thinking on strategic CSR has been outlined principally in two works written respectively in 2002 and 2006.[10] The essence in particular of their second article (2006) is that there has been a tendency to think of the pursuit of a socially responsible approach to business, the pursuit of CSR, as something entirely at variance with and incompatible with the pursuit of profits. Yet, they argue that especially in a world of increasingly critical and ecologically conscious consumers the deliberate pursuit of genuinely socially responsible policies may at the same time be very profitable for the company. They therefore urge companies to think of CSR not as a cost or drag, or even as cynical PR (as there has been a tendency), but rather as something that with a little imagination can be aligned with a firm's broader strategy for creating competitive advantage. They therefore urge businesses to think of CSR as something to be integrated into their overall formation of strategy rather than thinking of it as an annoying afterthought.

Porter and Kramer's thesis is not without its merits and they certainly point to a much more fruitful and effective way for businesses to integrate considerations of CSR into their day-to-day activities. The trouble is that they implicitly seem to suggest that there can always be a happy convergence of what is profitable and what is socially responsible to give a 'win–win' outcome. This may be the case more often than has been thought in the past but it is hardly the case all of the time. One has only to think of such examples as the Seiagustus case outlined in the first chapter of this work, involving the cynical dumping of waste in less developed countries with more lax regulations and/or corrupt self-seeking bureaucrats; or the application of lower safety standards to operations in states where companies think that they can get away with it. These sorts of activity are clearly good for profits (by greatly lowering costs) especially if they can be kept quiet, even if clearly socially irresponsible. Hence Porter and Kramer's position is based ultimately on a somewhat naïve faith that profitability and socially responsible behaviour by a company will always (or nearly always) coincide. Moreover they urge companies in effect to concentrate exclusively on those areas of CSR that can simultaneously contribute to the firm's overall strategy, that is, to the firm's profitability.

In the end, therefore, their position, like Friedman's, adopts an ideological stance in respect of capitalism. The overriding importance of the pursuit of profit as the goal of the firm, hence of running the firm in the interests above all of the shareholders, is reasserted as something that is beyond question.

For Porter and Kramer there can be no in-depth questioning of the role that a company plays in society; they suggest indeed that the antinomy of company and society is pointless since companies are an integral part of society and so they see the idea that companies could act against the society as almost an absurdity.

Such a stance, if taken to its extreme conclusion, would imply that there cannot ever be dysfunctional ties in societies or communities and so nothing that happens in a society can ever be criticized. It seems to us that it is this latter position towards which Porter and Kramer seem to tend that is patently absurd. Hence we reiterate the importance for business ethics to be prepared to carry out a searching critique of the role that business plays in relation to the wider community or society in which it operates; and this we have described as Level 2 of the critical dimensions of business ethics.

Level 3

There is a third level of critique incumbent on a truly critical business ethics which is perhaps more abstract than the previously identified levels but which in our view is inescapable in an international business setting. We have already alluded to this on p. 23 above when we introduced the concept of a methodologically normative approach to business ethics but we will now develop this third level in detail. Our argument will be that this third level of critique is unavoidable in the globalized context of contemporary business.

Put very simply, a typical multinational business (even a small or medium-sized enterprise) that seeks to conduct its business in an ethical manner will regularly find itself in a position where a variety of ethical codes could plausibly be applied, and therefore where a decision will have to be made either collectively or at an individual level as to which of the codes to apply (in cases where the codes give different or conflicting recommendations as to action). Stated abstractly as above, this might seem a relatively hypothetical type of dilemma about which a real business will rarely have to trouble itself. Yet in fact contemporary international business throws up these sorts of problems on a regular basis. Examples would be the ethics of employing child labour in less developed states, the treatment of and opportunities for women in the workplace, the moral issues of interest and usury[11] and issues about the appropriate ecological stance to take in respect of a whole range of environmental matters such as disposal of waste. Many commentators have tended to trivialize this moral choice by adopting glib formulae such as 'do whatever is legally acceptable in the country where one is operating' or 'when in Rome do as the Romans do'.[12]

Taking each of these in turn, the first formula commits the very basic conceptual error of equating what is legally acceptable with what is morally correct. Laws are certainly influenced by the prevailing morality of a community but morality cannot be reduced to or equated with law. Apart from the fact that there are many laws that are entirely morally neutral (e.g. laws regarding on what side of the road to drive, etc.), if law and morality are coincident it would be logically impossible ever to speak of 'bad' law. An alternative interpretation of this position would be to say that it is simply an application of Friedman's formula whereby a company's (or to be precise for Friedman, the manager's) moral responsibility is solely to maximize profits within the limits of the law (rules of the game). The same criticism as just mentioned applies to this but, furthermore, for a Friedmanite in the context of multinational business there is the question of which country's law to apply when there is a conflict of laws. Of course, a Friedmanite would probably at this point fall back on 'when in Rome do as the Romans do', that is, apply local law. But let us be quite clear: that is itself a moral choice.[13]

This brings us in fact to a discussion of the second position, 'When in Rome do as the Romans do'. At least this does not confuse law with morality and it makes a clear moral choice: we ought to act in each community exactly as the local people act (or say they ought to act). While in many cases this formula has been put forward in a relatively unthinking manner it in effect enunciates the position known to moral philosophers as moral relativism. We will now consider this position as a prelude to introducing the idea of metaethics: namely, of a critical morality of moralities (which in essence is our Level 3 of critique).

Moral relativism has been a popular and much touted position among wide ranges of contemporary thinkers not only in moral philosophical circles but also over a whole range of sociological, cross-cultural and even economic studies. Enunciating as its central principle that 'there are no absolute or universal moral values; all moral values are rather culturally relative', moral relativism finds itself very much in sympathy with the broader constellation of theories and perspectives that have come to be known as postmodernism. This latter is in effect an attack on a whole variety of fronts against the great Enlightenment movements of thought deriving ultimately from Descartes, Leibniz, Locke, etc. and which are often labelled as modernism. The hallmark of modernism is its rationalist starting point (epitomized in Descartes' *Discourse on Method*[14]). All modernists in various ways shared Descartes view that by the rigorous application of reasoning human beings could reach an array of absolutely proven indubitable and so universal propositions, that is, knowledge properly so-called. Such absolutely proven propositions were epitomized by mathematical theorems that in turn were extensively applied by the modernists to astronomy, physics, chemistry, etc. But many modernists also held that universal truths should be sought in such fields as moral and political philosophy. The moral philosophies of Immanuel Kant or Bentham's utilitarianism spring to mind, or the political philosophies of Hobbes, Locke, Rousseau, etc. The intellectual edifice constructed by Hegel whereby the whole of human history is interpreted and explained as the march of Reason in the world is perhaps the crowning achievement of modernism.

Modernism began to fall from intellectual favour from approximately the 1920s as a number of initially unconnected attacks were mounted across an array of different disciplines on rationalist universalist approaches to thinking. Broadly speaking, the attacks began from the field of literary criticism and hermeneutics, spread out into anthropology, cross-cultural studies (where of course the diversity in what different people take to be absolute became painfully apparent) and eventually crystallized around Bertrand Russell's failed attempt to construct a logically perfect language[15] and Ludwig Wittgenstein's effective response to this: the philosophy of 'language games'. This latter philosophy proclaims in effect a universal epistemological relativism: every human cognition is relative in the sense that it forms part of a particular language game with its own specific rules. People can readily understand each other and there can be a rational exchange of views among people who play the same language game (share the same basic pre-sumptions/world view); but, among people who are playing in different language games, rational discussion becomes difficult if not in the end impossible. This relativist philosophy was applied particularly to the fields of moral philosophy and cultural studies where it came to be seen as a badge of tolerance and respect: in different cultural settings there are different moral value systems (often deriving from different religions) and they are all worthy of equal respect, etc. There are no moral absolutes.

Yet, upon closer examination, this moral relativism can become extremely dangerous and a licence for the total abandonment of all moral values. In an increasingly interdependent world, where ease of travel and communication have led to huge increases in the degree of interaction between people of different cultures and moral values, there can arise a whole array of practical cases where the different cultures/moral systems yield up different and often directly conflicting moral advice; and then what are we to do? Which system are we to follow? For a strict postmodernist relativist there can be no absolute or universal set of values to which appeal can be made in such cases; and so there can be no clear moral advice to give. Hence, moral relativism in a multicultural context degenerates very quickly into what can at best be called moral nihilism: the complete abandonment of any moral standards or compass. Even worse, as Milton Friedman, in a moment of passing insight in an article on economic methodology, once put it: 'about differences in fundamental values men can ultimately only fight'.[16]

We, however, as authors of this work, would firmly reject such a disheartening conclusion. First of all we would rather argue that the epistemological relativism of Wittgenstein on which moral relativism is ultimately constructed is incoherent. It asserts as an absolute that there are no absolutes and so is self-contradictory. Furthermore, for a proponent of the possibility of absolutes it is sufficient to show that there is at least one absolute truth to defeat the argument that there are no absolute truths.

We would, moreover, argue that a moral nihilism is not only thus logically indefensible insofar as it relies on an incoherent epistemological relativism, it is also highly undesirable. In response to Friedman's depressing conclusion just cited about differences in ultimate values leading only to violence, we would argue that disagreements among human beings in a civilized society ought to be resolved by reasoning rather than by violence – admittedly itself already an attempted universal value judgement.[17] There can for us therefore be no question of accepting moral relativism; for all its superficial aura of multicultural tolerance, it is in the international setting little more than an excuse for the annihilation of morality if not for a descent into a brutish 'war of all against all'.[18]

In this work we are prepared therefore to pin our colours to the mast. The search for some overarching set of universal moral values applicable in all societies and cultures is vital to the resolution of moral issues thrown up in an international context and in particular an international business context. It may be unfashionable because it is distinctly modernist in flavour; it may be extremely challenging to arrive at such a set of universal values (and we certainly have not got a ready-made full set we made earlier!); but it is indispensable in our view to the development of international business in a manner responsible to the various communities in which it is located and indeed to the responsible conduct of international affairs in general that we should seek to develop some such set of universal values.

This then constitutes the third level of critique in the work. Rather than taking existing moral codes of various societies at face value and throwing up our hands in despair when we encounter conflict of moral values between different communities involved in international business, we will seek to develop a 'metaethics'; that is to say we will seek to evolve a 'critical morality of moralities'.[19] This will involve conducting a critical rational appraisal of the codes of different communities when they are in conflict, with a view to evolving towards a relevant overarching universal moral value relevant to the situation/dilemma in question.

Proponents of multiculturalism may be horrified at such suggestions, but in the end it is here in metaethics, in our Level 3 critique, that the real intellectual challenges of business ethics are faced. We do not intend to shirk them!

Notes

1 A. Crane and D. Matten (2006) *Business Ethics*, 2nd edition. Oxford: Oxford University Press. See pp. 27–29.
2 Ibid.
3 There are even two sublevels here; one could study the declared ethical principles of a business and compare these with their actual practices, an exercise in which some sharp divergences could appear; for example, greenwashing. Or one could take the declared principles at face value assuming them to be followed in practice and ask the critical question, whether these are the most appropriate principles, the principles that a business ought to be following.
4 Perhaps the clearest example is Edward Freeman whose work in the early 1980s clearly set business ethics in the context of the moral responsibilities of the company to all of its stakeholders, among whom were the community at large in which a company operates. See R. Edward Freeman (1984) *Strategic Management: A stakeholder approach*. Boston: Pitman, *passim*.
5 The 'unreconstructed' capitalist market position assumes among other challengeable things that a company should be run for the benefit/interests of its shareholders. Yet, why not run a company, for example, for the well-being of the workforce while making an 'adequate' but not necessarily maximum profit for shareholders? In fact, the more one probes critically the unreconstructed position, the more its purely ideological function as a defence of the interests of the owners of capital/shareholders becomes nakedly obvious. This point will be expanded in more detail in the main text discussion of Friedman.
6 The reference is of course to Adam Smith's work. See A. Smith (1776) *The Wealth of Nations*. London: Methuen. See Book IV Chapter 2 (p. 29).
7 I say 'high tide of faith' both in the sense that this was a period characterized by an almost blind faith in market mechanisms over a whole range of areas including areas previously not thought suitable for markets (e.g. privatization of utilities, professionalization of certain sports), and also in the sense that this faith ebbs and flows. It was strong at certain periods in the eighteenth, nineteenth and twentieth centuries but much weaker at other periods in these centuries.
8 M. Friedman (1970) 'The social responsibility of a business is to increase its profits', *New York Times*, 13 September 1970.
9 An interesting mutation can be noted in the managerial economics literature from about 1980 onwards whereby good old brutal 'profit maximization' was replaced by the slightly more polite 'shareholder wealth maximization'. One is reminded of the distinctly Anglo-American tendency to mutate words in a way to smooth over and understate problems: rather like 'blind' becoming 'visually impaired'.
10 Michael E. Porter and R. Mark Kramer (2002), 'The competitive advantage of corporate philanthropy', *Harvard Business Review*, 80(12): 56–68.
   See also Michael E. Porter and R. Mark Kramer (2006) 'Strategy and society: The link between competitive advantage and corporate social responsibility', *Harvard Business Review*, 84(12): 78–92.
11 Let us simply recall that in Islam all taking of interest is regarded in effect as usurious and immoral (sin of *riba*) whereas in Catholic thinking it is only the taking of 'excessive' interest that is usurious and so immoral. Judaism presents apparently a further variation whereby it is immoral for a Jew to charge interest to a fellow Jew but quite acceptable to charge interest to gentiles (non-Jews).
12 In effect, this is the position of ethical/moral relativism that will be further discussed below. For a more detailed description of its manifestations in business ethics literature, see for example Crane and Matten (2006), *Business Ethics*, pp. 76–78; 252–256.
13 As Jean-Paul Sartre so elegantly reminded us, choices are inevitable at every juncture in human existence; indeed, not to choose is itself a choice. See J.-P. Sartre (1968) *Existentialism and Humanism*, London: Methuen, *passim*.

14 R. Descartes (1999) *Discourse on Method and the Meditations*. London: Penguin Classics. See the *Discourse, passim*.

15 B. Russell (1918) *The Philosophy of Logical Atomism*. London: Methuen.

16 M. Friedman (1953) 'The methodology of positive economics', contained in *Essays in Positive Economics*. Chicago, IL: University of Chicago Press, Chapter 1. This is by no means just a theoretical position. Just think of George Bush's thinking on clashes of civilization as the justification of certain wars, or the justifications of holy wars by a whole range of religions.

17 We do not blush at this since we have now shown epistemological relativism to be untenable: a core of absolute propositions is indeed indispensable to human communication. For a further elaboration of this refutation of relativism see P. O'Sullivan (1987) *Economic Methodology and Freedom to Choose*. London: Allen and Unwin, Chapter 3.

18 With apologies of course to Thomas Hobbes who used this phrase in a slightly different context. See T. Hobbes (1968) *Leviathan*. Harmondsworth: Penguin, p. 143.

19 I acknowledge the direct inspiration in using this term of the eminent British jurist H. L. A. Hart. Hart used the term in perhaps the slightly different context of the discussion of the relationship that law bears to morality but the drift is the same. See for example, H. Hart (1961) *The Concept of Law*. Oxford: Oxford University Press, pp. 176–180.

3

THE ETHICAL MANAGEMENT OF ETHICS

Fostering ethical behaviour in corporations

Ion Copoeru

'Management' and 'ethics' seem to have contradictory meanings. The concept to 'manage' presupposes to act on or dispose of someone else, while 'ethics' refers primarily to the part of the individual's behaviour that is or is supposed to be – at least to some extent – in his or her control. The idea that ethics should be managed creates the impression that the limits of its manipulability are extended and that such efforts are trespassing into the individual's intimacy. It would probably be more accurate to refer to the 'management of moral practices', if moral practices did not have precisely the meaning of objective recurrent behaviour, which cannot be submitted to one's discretion or executive power. It is therefore difficult to imagine that the entire public domain, namely, 'objective' moral habits, together with the judgements and feelings, etc. that are associated with it, as well as all the moral exchanges that take place among individuals in an organization, can be controlled from outside. But we must admit also that people sometimes change the way in which they think or act in moral matters and the use of some methods or techniques could promote or deter particular lines of behaviour.

Ethical issues are not exclusively internal to the individual; they can or should be solved by the self in his or her confrontation with the external (public) moral instances that are recognized as valid according to some broadly acceptable way of reasoning. Ethics have thus to be related not only to the individual's universe, but also to the individual's cultural environment. While dealing with moral issues, especially in the context of a corporation, the individual is pushed outside his or her limits and encouraged to take others' points of view into account. The individual therefore leaves for a moment his or her position and empathizes with other human beings. At a certain point, he or she might realize that the role of employee and manager, as well as all the other hierarchies and rules, written or not, are only social constructions, behind which are people – embodied subjectivities in an endless exchange of ideas and feelings, through which they are continuously reconstructing their living world.

When seen as practical (instrumental), the relation between the self and the others is far from being simple. Subjective (internal) abilities to build concepts, to judge, to interpret, to make a decision, to act according to it, to reflect upon your own behaviour and to change it, if necessary, are essential to solve, theoretically and practically, ethical problems; it is nevertheless also true that these operations are performed in a specific cultural environment and request an action from others, as well as bearing (and modifying) the action of the others upon yourself. Although it grows between the walls of someone's interiority, ethics cannot be kept there; it also has to do with the exchange between the self and the others. Therefore, the ethical management of ethics in corporations should not trespass on the reign of subjectivity, breaking the individual's interiority, while still consistently operating as a tool for enhancing moral practices in the respective organization.

From this perspective, the corporation is the symbolic place where the interest of the corporation's owners meets that of its employees, and it is also the place where the private interests come face-to-face with public interests. We can say that there are two sets of interests operating in a corporation, namely, those related to operational efficiency and corporate performance on the one hand, and those related to the well-being of the corporation's workforce. A corporation's ethos presupposes that the administrators promote both of these sets of interests and aim to find a balance between the opposite points of view or some kind of 'organizational justice'[1] (Eberlin and Tatum 2005).

This chapter takes up the challenge of exploring some aspects related to the concepts and practices that allow managers to tackle the ethical issues in their organizations and to foster ethical practices in the corporations. It insists on how business activities can be associated with moral goals (in first section) and on the strategies of linking management and ethics in business organizations (in the second section). At a more general level, this chapter reflects upon the productive ways in which contemporary professional practice can be reshaped by moral goals by focusing primarily on the moral responsibilities of various individuals within the company regarding the values and interests of both the company and the community in which a company is situated. In effect, this means that most of the discussion is located at Level 1 of critique as outlined in Chapter 2 but some elements of Level 2 critique will appear also to the extent that the basis of certain moral actions within the company derive from the wider social responsibilities of the company in the community.

Associating business with moral goals

In the 1980s, Robert B. Denhardt argued convincingly that the organizations that we've established to work for us have instead imprisoned us. For him, the 'ethic of organization' inhibits the individual's search for meaning. His strategy consists therefore of an attempt to enhance the individual's role in the organization, including his or her independence, expressiveness, creativity over discipline and regulation as well as obedience (Denhardt 1989). His approach is insightful in what concerns the development of an understanding of individuality in an epoch of proliferation of conformism, yet his central focus remained on how the individual can *oppose* (or transcend – in his terms) the organization, identified with 'the system'. This kind of approach focuses naturally on the leadership's key role in organizations, possible risks of allowing unexplored and new ways of framing the role of the employee in the corporation to develop, as well as the most adequate ethical methods required for 'humanizing' corporations.

Getting out of the shadow of the corporation requires that this type of interrogation shifts into one in which not the opposition, but the *participation* of the individual in the life and the goals of the corporation becomes the key concept. A deeper understanding of the nature of the corporation and of its dynamics and norms is necessary. In the past few decades, a variety of new approaches have emerged, much more favourable in associating business and other related activities with various kinds of instruments and expertise, which may lead to fostering an ethical behaviour in the business organizations themselves. Some authors, for example, give credit to the covenantal relationship in the organizations, which is a special form of a relational *contract* between an employee and the corporation, outside the incentives and control mechanisms, in the absence of which it is difficult to build trust within organizations (Caldwell and Karri 2005). Many advancements have been made in the exploration of moral behaviour within the corporation, even if they took apparently divergent paths, from reshaping competitive interests and adversarial ethics (Applbaum 2000) to what is called in the field of legal ethics 'collaborative practice ethics'[2] (Cochran, Jr. 2010).

When 'management' and 'ethics' are set to work together, the main question becomes whether particular business procedures can be associated with moral goals. At the very core of the management of ethics is the idea that the answer to this question is affirmative. Therefore, a lot of attention has been focused on identifying instruments that are supposed to enhance morally legitimate business practices by linking them to specific moral goals.

The primary instruments required by the United States federal law as set out in the Sarbanes-Oxley Act,[3] which stipulates the main standards for public company boards, management and public accounting firms with respect to corporate and auditing accountability and responsibility, include: financial reporting, CEO and CFO certifications, internal controls, risk management, the composition of audit committees, corporate codes of ethics, whistle-blower protection, and attorney conduct. Even though only a part of these instruments are specific ethical tools – for example, the corporate codes of ethics – the others play important roles in the management of ethics, although their ethical dimension is incorporated in other types of control mechanisms (legal or managerial).

If we focus primarily on the ethical as opposed to the legal dimension of controlling employees' behaviour, a more complete list of instruments would typically include codes of conduct, whistle-blowing systems, ethics committees, judiciary boards, employee training in ethics, ethics-focused corporate governance, and reward systems (Lindsay *et al.*, 1996, p. 395). Ethics-related control mechanisms are linked to management control-system components as shown in Table 3.1.

The extent to which these instruments are efficient, or the degree to which they are actually used in corporations, is the subject of a vast volume of literature. It is, however, outside the range of this chapter's focus to describe and assess their effectiveness in detail. Because each of them is supposed to fulfil some moral goal as they are incarnated by societal expectations at a given time, their task is *twofold*: to set ethical standards in the corporation and to increase efficiency in the corporation. This is the reason why the way in which they are articulated into the internal policies of the corporation and the modes of interaction with the specific management procedures are worth studying. However, comparing ethical tools and management control components is still a restrictive approach, for it belongs only to the internal point of view of the corporation and privileges the purposes related to efficiency. Ethical tools should also be assessed by embracing the external point of view and relating them in a more direct and explicit way to the social (transcendent) goals of the organization. Furthermore, distinguishing them into ethical and non-ethical might be misleading. Many, if not all managerial instruments have ethical dimensions or implications and it would be a loss if they are not investigated and assessed from an ethical point of view.

Let us consider, as an example, the *financial reporting tools* in their relation to extrinsic (societal) moral goals, as they are usually embedded in the concept and practice of corporate social responsibility. The distinction that Van Marrewijk made between corporate social responsibility and sustainability (Van Marrewijk 2003; Baumunk 2009) shows a subtle, but essential split in *orienting the interest of the manager* either towards the dialogue with the stakeholders or towards the value creation inside the company. The design of the tool – namely, sustainability reporting in this case – appears to direct the attention and the resources towards one purpose

TABLE 3.1 The connection between ethics-related control mechanisms and management control-system components

Components of an MCS	Ethics-related control mechanisms
Specifying and communicating objectives	Code of ethics
	Employee training in ethics
	Ethics-focused corporate governance
	Ethics committee
Monitoring performance (feedback/control)	Motivation by linking rewards to performance
	Whistle-blowing channels
	Judiciary board
	Ethics committee
Motivation by linking rewards to performance	Ethics-focused reward system

or another (Baumunk 2009, p. 3). For ethicists, there is a disturbing ambivalence of the goal, which can be both moral and instrumental. While this intermingling of moral and instrumental goals and tools might be uncomfortable, it may be an advantage for the manager. We should see here a noticeable effort to make ethics become more related to professional actions and to the life of the corporation. The management of ethics in corporations thus unveils itself as an attempt to find the adequate instruments that will drive business on a morally legitimate path.

Most certainly an ethicist will prefer to place the code of ethics in the centre of an assembly of ethical tools, which include ethical committees, training and education, as well as an ethical audit. This view entails that the company elaborate and implement ethical policies and be ready to make an investment for administering these policies. Owners and managers, however, are still reluctant to adopt this kind of policy, not only because it has a significant cost, but primarily because it creates the impression of an interference with the professional practice and operations within the corporation. They appear to care more about discipline and the public image of the corporation than about the moral violations themselves.

Associating business with moral goals therefore seems to be more a matter of *practice*, or the application of some ethical instrument, than a matter of *principle*, after all the research and the debates revolving around such issues. Some instruments are more related to the professional practice itself, while others, such as those related to the codification of behaviour, are imported from other spheres of life – for example, from the juridical or religious spheres. In any case, both the (self-) reporting tools and the codes of ethics, which can be seen as two major ideal types of instruments in the management of ethics, represent an attempt to associate business with extrinsic (moral) goals and to submit the business activities of which business usually consists to an external moral categorization and an internal efficiency assessment. This may be a reason why the implementation of ethics in corporations should rather be considered a case of what may be called a 'deeply embedded approach' (Garbellotto 2009). It is noticeable that, from the viewpoint of the manager who is interested in fostering a morally sound climate in the corporation, *the ambivalence of the tool* plays an important role. Regarding the interests that it serves, the tool is not neutral, as a common-sense view would say. On the contrary, it shapes them or is shaped by them. At the same time, it still 'inhabits' the respective professional practice, which it is supposed to enhance. Of course, this type of approach is not exempt from any risks and these tools can relate to a variety of goals, some of which aim to increase efficiency and the internal legitimacy of management, while others pertain to the broader purposes of the collectivity, such as for environmental or social purposes. This particular situation may let us think that *the tools can be misused*, that they can diverge from the original purpose and that the entire subset of activities built around them can be strategized, subverted and eventually oriented towards undisclosed purposes. At any moment, the manager as the main actor can claim that business practices create new ways of acting that can be judged only by the rules of that practice. Applbaum addressed this issue in terms of 'the argument of redescription' as an attempt to short-circuit the moral evaluation of both actions and actors by redescribing them in practice-defined terms (Applbaum 2000, pp. 76–110).[4]

Certainly, this can happen at any moment and it has actually happened in the past. Each major ethical scandal in corporations can be seen as an illustration of the moral ambivalence of the ethical tools, that some would consider – not entirely without reason – as a weakness. We must however, accept that in professional practice strategizing ethics is a legitimate risk.

Ethics and management – two strategies

In modern times various forms of positivism[5] succeeded in cutting off professional practice *sensu stricto* from the interference of external (transcendent) goals, focusing on efficiency and performance rather than the fulfilment of some ultimate conditions, rules or principles. 'Practice positivism' (Applbaum 2000, p. 98 *et seq.*) is a challenge for ethics in professional practice in virtually all corporate areas, from the legal practices and administration to managerial activities. In a more or less self-conscious attempt to counterbalance the rise of practice positivism, many academics and practitioners seek to make visible the conditions and consequences of their professional practices and the ways in which these contribute to the processes of social and organizational (re)production. They recognize the institutional pressures that subtend their field of expertise and then react to such pressures. The challenge at the moment is to manage it in an open way; while adapting the internal practices of the organization to the moral demands of the stakeholders, the demands related to efficiency and economic performance should not be left untreated.

Linking ethics and management is always a matter of strategy or, more precisely, *a twofold strategy*. The first strategic aspect will emphasize the role of the *employees* and will emphasize the ways in which they may recognize themselves as ethical subjects – the *employee's* approach.[6] The second strategy will take the starting point as the need for developing theoretical and practical frameworks of control by linking ethics tools to the primary components of *management* control systems – the *organizational* approach.

Reaching employees' hearts and minds

While focusing on the employees, the overall context of corporate values or the internal (subjective) means of each of the individuals in the corporation can be brought forward and invoked to find the morally acceptable solutions and to enhance the moral climate within the corporation. Under this approach it is assumed that an individual's level of *moral development and ethical sensitivity* are the primary sources of motivation affecting the ethical behaviour of workers. Corporate policies and procedures reflect efforts to appeal to the worker's sense of right and wrong, and to sensitize employees to ethical problems they might face in the corporation. Corporations do this in part by specifying and communicating ethical objectives through training and codes of ethics, devices viewed by many managers as the most effective way of promoting ethical behaviour within the corporation (James, Jr. 2000; see Metzger *et al.* 1993).

Researchers and practitioners are searching for valuable tools with the help of which the employees may be able to make reasoned decisions in various corporate ethical climates. One of the most popular approaches of this kind is based on Kohlberg's theories of moral development.[7] VanSandt and Neck underline specifically how the practice of self-leadership can be employed as an important means to improve moral action within the firm by concurring with the notion that the individual retains the ultimate moral agency for her actions, but also recognize the profound influence that the organization has over those actions (VanSandt and Neck 2003, p. 366). They also endorse Jones and Ryan's idea that the personal costs of failure to comply with organizational directives can be quite high and they try therefore to find ways to ameliorate the results in the effort to promote ethical behaviour in business organizations (VanSandt and Neck 2003, pp. 366–367). It is reasonable to assume that corporations would have an interest in retaining employees capable of higher moral reasoning. VanSandt and Neck (2003, pp. 371–372) propose two methods to elevate the ethical climate of the organization. The first method entails inculcating ethics into the very fabric of the corporate culture. A code of ethics, when implemented and embedded in the corporation's culture might be a valuable instrument, but the goal is not just to obtain conformity, but also to allow for individuals' sense of morality. Other tools, such as providing continuing education and training in ethics issues, making part of the compensation package and promotion policy dependent on adherence to ethical standards, and dealing effectively with ethical violations must complement in the long run the codes of ethics if the managers want to reinforce and assure their efficiency. The second method proposed consists of revising reinforcements to promote prosocial behaviour, that is, a formal system that measures, rewards and promotes employees' ethical actions (ibid.).

Relating ethics to the components of a management control system

In this section the idea of relating ethics to the components of a management control system will be examined. The basic presupposition is that the 'unethical actions of managers do not result from individual moral deficiencies alone, but are encouraged by the bureaucratic structure of modern corporations' (Lindsay *et al.* 1996, pp. 393–407). The perspective adopted by the authors of this study is that 'an organization's management control system can play an important role in directing and influencing employees to pursue ethical behaviour' (ibid., pp. 393–394).

According to the *organizational* approach, managers assume that individual behaviour is primarily affected by factors external to the individual. These may be informal structures, such as the corporate culture,[8] or formal, such as the structure of the corporation.[9] From this perspective, the efforts and resources of the corporation should be oriented first to an examination of the organization's formal structure because of the direct effect it has on employee behaviour and because it is directly controllable by business managers. That is, an examination of the ethical impact of the formal structure of organizations is necessary and, when combined with an appropriate corporate culture, will generally be sufficient in promoting the ethical behaviour of workers. To do this, managers must ensure that each aspect of the organizational structure is *balanced* with the organizational culture and *appropriate* to the economic environment within which the business organization operates. As shown below, organizational structure and culture are important, but for different yet complementary reasons. The primary way in which organizational structure promotes ethical behaviour is by *not undermining* the ethical sensitivities and attitudes of workers. This is why an analysis of the formal structure is necessary (James, Jr. 2000, p. 44).

There are two distinct trains of thought intertwined with this approach. The first affirms that the formal structure of the corporation induces a particular behaviour of the employees, while the second sees the inconsistent corporate structures as a potential danger for the corporate culture and the personal moral sphere of the employees and hence as an obstacle for the development of a moral climate in the corporation. A compromise of formal and informal factors that might affect the ethical behaviour of the employees seems to be preferable, from a practical managerial perspective, to any uncritical endorsement of one point of view or another.

However, this perspective certainly privileges the role of the business manager and aims at providing him with tools and methods necessary to encourage and reinforce ethical behaviour in the employees. Basically, these are the *organizational reward systems, the performance and evaluation processes* and the *decision-making rights and responsibilities,* (James, Jr. 2000, p. 43 *et seq.*), which are defining the type of control employees have over their actions' (James, Jr. 2000, p. 50). According to this view, the manager is in control, but the individual employee is compelled to adopt a position of resisting the channelling of her actions. Finally, the manager is aware that he cannot force workers to internalize ethical principles and adopt a more flexible attitude, which consists in removing corporate obstacles to ethical behaviour and creating and maintaining an ethically based corporate culture (James, Jr. 2000, p. 50).

When it is necessary to define, to initiate and to make work an *ethical* system infrastructure (White and Lam 2000), not only the means, namely, the corporate rules, policies and procedures, and the opportunity have to be taken into account, but also and primarily the motivation of the employees. This is why some authors are focusing on designing management control systems that are able to integrate a motivational dimension while pursuing the organization's goals. Neither of these two approaches – the employee's approach and the organizational approach – can be effective if it leaves the employee in the position of a simple receiver, who interprets the actions of the manager as fair or unfair, just or unjust, but who does not have the power or the capacity to participate in the decision-making process. If the ethical tools are just instruments for transmitting ethical commandments, their ethical character vanishes and they become just other control means. Since ethical decisions have a significant impact on employees' lives, it is essential that they be empowered to make such decisions.

Empowering employees to make moral decisions is in fact a way of recognizing that they have both obligations to the firm and rights as individuals (Kaptein and Wempe 1998). None of the ethical tools can be effective in enhancing moral behaviour in corporations if the rights and the obligations of *each individual* in the organization are not observed, and if the way in which the organization works does not allow their continuous exercise. The focus on the design of ethical tools and of their interrelatedness both with the moral sensitivity of the individual and with the main elements of the management control system should not distract us from paying attention to the importance of legal obligations in the corporation. These belong to the wider question of the corporation's broader responsibilities in relation to society (Level 2 of critique), which in fact supplements the perspective on individuals in companies and on their exercise of moral actions.

Final remarks

The new understanding of the nature of the organization and of the norms and regulations that are operating in it may lead us to be able to pay attention simultaneously to persons and to efficiency and to take advantage of their juxtaposition. What came to the forefront of reflection on corporations was the fact that real people with real purposes try to make these organizations work in a complex and challenging social and cultural environment.

In an epoch of institutionalization of ethics, the goals for performing corporations are tied up with that of promoting ethics in business, as well as in other spheres of the social life. The idea that employee engagement is influenced by ethical factors has become common knowledge, but the ways in which business activities can be associated with moral goals and the strategies of linking management and ethics in business organizations are still to be determined and refined.

Business ethics thus reveals itself both as a valuable practical and theoretical resource for exploring ways of improving managerial work in corporations capable of fulfilling the moral expectations of the collectivities in which they operate.

CASE STUDY

There are many attempts to create an ethical climate in business organizations and in various segments of the market. However, when it comes to introducing ethics into corporations, public opinion and researchers in the field of business ethics are much more inclined to think of the major scandals that shattered the business world in the past decades. That is why I wonder how many noticed this news: 'Jones Lang LaSalle named in 2010's "World's Most Ethical Companies" list by the Ethisphere Institute for the third consecutive year'.[10]

Although the radiography of an ethical scandal is revelatory for the management of ethics in a company (or for its absence), it is more helpful for the purpose of this chapter to analyse the theoretical background and the strategy of the corporation, which is highly determined both to motivate its employees to act ethically in their workplace and to involve the management in actively addressing ethical issues.

The Jones Lang LaSalle's 'magic formula' is unveiled by its CEO in a post from 25 March 2008 on the site of Ethisphere: 'If ethics isn't everywhere, it's nowhere.'[11] In fact, what JLL's management did is much more mundane. The senior management team, in association with the legal team, made clear to everyone that the company expects them to do the right thing each and every day. Their programme, called 'Ethics Everywhere' included:

- messages and training about the importance of integrity in every aspect of the employee life cycle;
- making new hires read and agree to the Code of Business Ethics, which has been translated into fourteen languages;
- the Ethics Officers (most of whom are drawn from the legal staff) attending business meetings and leading discussions with employees about ethical dilemmas;
- an annual all-employee survey including questions about the company's ethical culture;
- providing employees with an annual report about the operation of its ethics programme, including metrics on how many matters were investigated, the types of complaints received, and how many employees were suspended, terminated or occasionally even jailed as a result of unethical or illegal conduct;
- a worldwide performance management programme that requires employees, starting with the CEO, to commit to annual goals in writing through a uniform electronic process. To receive a bonus, everyone, including the CEO, is required to re-certify his or her commitment to the Code of Ethics.

Taking JLL's experience in enhancing the ethical climate in the corporation as a starting point, Lindsay Walker (2010) underlines the idea of a comprehensive effort when stating that there is no point investing in and implementing an ethics and compliance programme unless time is also spent integrating the programme into every aspect of the corporation.[12] Ethics should therefore be integrated at the top level, the middle level and at the lower level of the corporation.

This approach however, is not uncontroversial. Ethicists may worry about the 'legalization' of the ethics, while managers and shareholders could ask about the costs and the effectiveness of such an encompassing programme. The corporation is actually aware of this, admitting that 'even if you are successful in keeping significant ethical lapses away from your company, you can never really know whether you have been smart or just lucky'.[13]

Notes

1 Organizational justice refers to the fair and ethical treatment of individuals within an organization, according to their expectations. It is important because it has been linked to critical organizational processes such as commitment, citizenship, job satisfaction and performance. Recent literature suggests that there is a link between leadership style, decision-making and organizational justice (Eberlin and Tatum 2005, p. 1040 *et seq.*). Studies suggest that there is a relationship between social justice and both managerial performance (Tatum *et al.* 2003) and employee behaviours (Masterson *et al.* 2000).

2 Collaborative practice (CP) is a new process for the resolution of legal disputes. It is most frequently used in the family law area, but can be applied to any substantive area of law in which the parties want to reach a mutually beneficial settlement and avoid litigation. Although lawyers who engage in CP are governed by the legal professional rules in their state, CP differs greatly from adversarial dispute resolution practice. Therefore, collaborative professionals have developed their own standards to provide guidance for their members.

3 Federal law enacted on 30 July 2002. It introduced major changes to the regulation of financial practice and corporate governance and set a number of deadlines for compliance. The Sarbanes-Oxley Act is arranged into eleven titles. As far as compliance is concerned, the most important sections within these are often considered to be 302, 401, 404, 409, 802 and 906. (See www.soxlaw.com/)

4 The rules of the practice of business – he explains – might claim to redescribe the breaking of a promise so that it is no longer the breaking of a promise, but merely the non-performance of a contract (ibid.).

5 Positivism is usually associated with an epistemology that has 'scientific method' at its centre. It has had a great impact on modern life and affected practices in virtually all areas of activity. Deriving from Enlightenment thinkers, it was meant to replace metaphysics, i.e. any reference to an external transcendence. It is widespread in economics and a dominant philosophy in jurisprudence, where 'legal positivism' essentially rejects the idea that there is a law whose content is set by nature and that therefore has validity everywhere.

6 This means only that the main focus is on employees, on their ability to comply to moral rules or to participate in ethical decisions. It should be distinguished from what could be called *the point of view of the employee*, and consists of situating yourself in the position of the employee while not being actually in such a position.

7 Kohlberg (1984) hypothesized that 'in many cases the best approach to moral education is one that attempts to reform the moral atmosphere in which individual decisions are made.'

8 As illustration, Nash (1990) and Badaracco and Webb (1995) cite a number of cultural organizational pressures resulting in unethical conduct, including an emphasis on the bottom line ('performance is what really counts'), an overemphasis on short-term results, and problems employees face balancing conflicting obligations ('show us you are a team player'). Similarly, Cressey and Moore (1983, p. 74) explain how organizations 'encourage ethical behavior in the midst of [a] corporate organization that continues to discourage it'.

9 Brickley *et al.* 1994; Lindsay *et al.* 1996; Trevino and Nelson 1995.

10 Colin Dyer, 'If ethics isn't everywhere, it's nowhere', http://ethisphere.com/if-ethics-isnt-everywhere-its-nowhere/ (accessed 17 September 2010).
   Jones Lang LaSalle (NYSE:JLL) is a financial and professional services firm specializing in real estate. The firm offers integrated services delivered by expert teams worldwide to clients seeking increased value by owning, occupying or investing in real estate.

11 http://ethisphere.com/if-ethics-isnt-everywhere-its-nowhere/ (accessed 17 September 2010).

12 Lindsay Walker, 'Integrating Ethics and Compliance Into the Entire Organization', FCPA Compliance and Ethics Blog, 27 July 2010. Available online at http://tfoxlaw.word press.com/2010/07/27/integrating-ethics-and-compliance-into-the-entire-organization (accessed 17 September 2010).

13 Colin Dyer, 'If ethics isn't everywhere, it's nowhere', http://ethisphere.com/if-ethics-isnt-everywhere-its-nowhere/ (accessed 17 September 2010).

References

Applbaum, A. I. (2000) *Ethics for Adversaries: The morality of roles in public and professional life.* Princeton, NJ: Princeton University Press.

Badaracco, J. L. and Webb, A. P. (1995) 'Business ethics: A view from the trenches', *California Management Review*, 37(2): 8–25.

Baumunk, J. A. (2009) 'Sustainability reporting and XBRL'. Available online at SSRN: http://ssrn.com/abstract=1620567 (accessed 17 September 2010).

Brickley, J. A., Smith, Jr., C. W. and Zimmerman, J. L. (1994) 'Ethics, incentives, and organizational design', *Journal of Applied Corporate Finance*, 7(2): 20–30.

Caldwell, C. and Karri, R. (2005) 'Organizational governance and ethical systems: A covenantal approach to building trust', *Journal of Business Ethics*, 58(1–3): 249–259.

Cochran, Jr., R. F. (2010) 'Legal ethics and collaborative practice ethics', *Hofstra Law Review*, Forthcoming. Pepperdine University Legal Studies Research Paper No. 2010/7. Available online at SSRN: http://ssrn.com/abstract=1605305 (accessed 17 September 2010).

Cressey, D. R. and Moore, C. A. (1983) 'Managerial values and corporate codes of ethics', *California Management Review*, 25(4): 53–77.

Denhardt, R. B. (1989) *In the Shadow of Organization.* Lawrence, KS: University Press of Kansas.

Dyer, C. (2008) 'If ethics isn't everywhere, it's nowhere'. Available online at www.us.am. joneslanglasalle.com/UnitedStates/EN-US/Pages/NewsItem.aspx?ItemID=18904 (accessed 17 September 2010).

Eberlin, R. and Tatum, B. C. (2005) 'Organizational justice and decision making: When good intentions are not enough', *Management Decision*, 43(7/8): 1040–1048.

Garbellotto, G. (2009) 'XBRL implementation strategies: The deeply embedded approach', *Strategic Finance*, November. Available online at http://glg.iphix.net/?p=406 (accessed 17 September 2010).

'A Guide to the Sarbanes-Oxley Act', available online at www.soxlaw.com/.

James, Jr., H. S. (2000) 'Reinforcing ethical decision making through organizational structure', *Journal of Business Ethics*, 28: 43–58.

Kaptein, M. and Wempe, J. (1998) 'Twelve gordian knots when developing an organizational code of ethics', *Journal of Business Ethics,* 17(8): 853–869.

Kohlberg, L. (1984) 'Moral stages and moralization: The cognitive-developmental approach'. In L. Kohlberg (ed.) *Essays on Moral Development, Vol. II: The psychology of moral development.* New York: Harper and Row, pp. 170–206.

Lindsay, M. R., Lindsay, L. M. and Irvine, V. B. (1996) 'Instilling ethical behavior in organizations: A survey of Canadian companies', *Journal of Business Ethics*, 15: 393–407.

Masterson, S. S., Lewis, K., Goldman, B. S. and Taylor, M. S. (2000) 'Integrating justice and social exchange: The differing effects of fair procedures and treatment on work relationships', *Academy of Management Journal*, 43: 738–766.

Metzger, M., Dalton, D. R. and Hill, J. W. (1993) 'The organization of ethics and the ethics of organizations: The case for expanded organizational ethics audits', *Business Ethics Quarterly*, 3(1): 27–43.

Nash, L. L. (1990) *Good Intentions Aside: A manager's guide to resolving ethical problems.* Boston, MA: Harvard Business School Press.

Tatum, B., Eberlin, R., Kottraba, C. and Bradberry, T. (2003) 'Leadership, decision making, and organizational justice', *Management Decision*, 41(10): 1006–1016.

Trevino, L. K. and Nelson, K. A. (1995) *Managing Business Ethics: Straight talk about how to do it right*. New York: John Wiley & Sons.

van Marrewijk, Marcel (2003) 'Concepts and definitions of CSR and corporate sustainability: Between agency and communion', *Journal of Business Ethics*, 44(2–3): 95–105.

VanSandt, C. V. and Neck, C. P. (2003) 'Bridging ethics and self leadership: Overcoming ethical discrepancies between employee and organizational standards', *Journal of Business Ethics*, 43: 363–387.

Walker, L. (2010) 'Integrating ethics and compliance into the entire organization', FCPA compliance and ethics blog, 27 July. Available online at http://tfoxlaw.wordpress.com/2010/07/27/integrating-ethics-and-compliance-into-the-entire-organization (accessed 17 September 2010).

White, L. P. and Lam, L. W.(2000) 'A proposed infrastructural model for the establishment of organizational ethical systems', *Journal of Business Ethics*, 28(1): 35–42.

PART II

Organizational strategy

4

CORPORATE SOCIAL RESPONSIBILITY, DEFINITIONAL PARALYSIS AND AMBIGUITY

Mark Esposito

$C SR$

Corporate Social Responsibility: an evolving concept and practice

It is a fact that in today's corporate world, a large number of companies, across sectors and industries and moreover geographical locations, are racing to achieve the highest possible marks on goodwill and Corporate Social Responsibility (CSR) initiatives of all sorts, with relatively little attention to the phenomenon outside of its more commoditized boundary of philanthropic good behaviour. We tend to notice that this race seems to have equal relevance to Western companies as well as to companies in emerging economies. This is mainly owing to the strong profile that CSR has managed to acquire as a modern interface for business.

In this regard, Corporate Social Responsibility has gone beyond the old philanthropy of the past, even from a seamless conceptual dimension, to embrace a much larger array of activities, transcending significantly the money donations to good causes – and has instead developed an enlarged role within business organizations, beyond mere seasonal tastes, to the proliferation of best working practices within the spectrum of the activities of the firm; thus, their engagement in their local communities, sense of collective value versus individual value and capacity to stand for an evolved uniqueness (price strategy, employee relations, internal marketing) has synthesized into communal, economic and environmental dimensions (Porter 1999).

In a nutshell, CSR has become the new strategy on how the science of risk taking and risk managing converges into a new paradigm of maximization of benefits (namely economic, social and environmental) while preserving an aggressive minimization of the risks (Carroll 1979). This same environmental emphasis is what can be easily traceable on main corporate trends in organizations located in BRICSA countries (Brazil, Russia, India, China and South Africa), as evidenced by a number of corporate surveys that indicated an increased amount of CSR reporting from the emerging economies (Mullen 1997).

Evidences of CSR reporting also support this increasing trend (Corporate Register 2010), with an exponential increase of report-based activities in developed countries as well as developing countries since 1992 until today. Brazil and South Africa, namely, have reported growth of CSR reporting on a steady level for the past two decades, thus aligning themselves with the major trends of European and North American companies.

While the above may be considered a given, it is relevant to remember that 'the fundamental idea behind and around Corporate Social Responsibility is related to the assumption or thesis that business entities have an obligation to work for social betterment' (Frederick 1986, p. 4 in Jones 1999, p. 164), while Wood's work (1991, p. 695) concentrates on the fact that 'business and society are interwoven rather than distinct entities'; therefore, as much as organizations should be held to a specific expected behaviour, societies at large have clear and sound expectations for appropriate business conduct and outcomes. This situates these discussions clearly at Level 2 of critique as outlined in Chapter 2.

The operationalization and/or concretization of this definition remains, however, largely hypothetical and has generated little by way of practical fieldwork on how organizations implement these principles into their daily modus operandi.

To find a first attempt to close the incongruity of thought versus action, we need to look a bit more closely to Davis (1973, pp. 312–313) where the original idea of corporate responsibilities is timidly announced a few years before Carroll would draw the map of what CSR has since become.

Davis asserts that 'It is the firm's obligation to evaluate in its decision-making processes the effects of its decisions on the external social system in a manner that will accomplish social benefits along with the traditional economic gains which the firm seeks'. This was quite a progressive statement for the period in which it was written, and it clearly identifies a relational link (between business and society) which in effect makes Davis' statement the prototype of '*Business IN society*', which is not only a very contemporary topic but also implies that social responsibility begins where the law ends. To delve deeper into this concept, Ackerman introduced the conceptual mapping of where the legal dimension stands and recognized social responsibility as an attitude and aptitude that goes 'one step further. It is a firm's acceptance of a social obligation beyond the requirements of the law' (Ackerman 1973).

While Ackerman recognizes with some hesitation social obligation as ancillary to legal requirement, in some current examples of emerging companies we can find a stronger symbiosis of legal compliance, intrinsic to the concept of social mandate (Victor and Cullen 1988).

The complexity of a clear and given definition of CSR can also lead to a confusion that can extend into inaction (Esposito 2009) with the creation of a multitude of definitions, evidences, approaches and methodologies. While this diversity can expand acceptance of the need of CSR, it can dilute at the same time the efficacy and consistency of the chosen definitions. This has led to different perceptions of the core meaning of CSR in a number of different societies across the world (Hull and Rothenberg 2008), although some of the definitions have become applicable in a larger number of shared practices, through their being adopted by multinational companies that operate simultaneously in established as well as emerging markets.

Definitions vary drastically from 'CSR being about the capacity to build for sustainable livelihoods', to those that see in the harmonization of cultural differences its true message, to the creation of new business opportunities through the utilization of better qualified and educated employees, to the establishment of a healthy relationship between companies and government, to the conversion of the societal input aimed at the corporate output back into society.

A slightly more integrated approach among definitions can be found in what Lord Holme and Richard Watts (World Business Council for Sustainable Development) define as 'Making Good Business Sense', which continues into a new definition that reads 'CSR is the continuing commitment by business to behave ethically and contribute to economic development while improving the quality of life of the workforce and their families as well as of the local community and society at large'. This definition and the efforts behind its description want to open the possibility of a new holistic assumption of responsibilities, conducted concomitantly by individuals, organizations and societies to the betterment of the platforms in which the diversity of human action can be encountered.

Although extremely powerful in its positioning, Holme and Watts' definition still lacks the visualization of more concrete practices and it leaves the concept of 'responsibility' undefined and arguably circular (since CSR is described as 'behaving ethically'). Arising from this lack of concreteness in the notion of Corporate Social Responsibility, there is a sense of *immobilism*, which translates to irresponsibility of action (Esposito 2009); thus, our need to move further in our definitional efforts to consider such aspects as the measurement of effective versus ineffective approaches, re-establishment of indicators and elevation to social performance, community capital and poverty reduction, etc. as operated by organizations.

Corporate Social Performance (CSP) or Corporate Financial Performance (CFP)?

In the first part of this chapter, we dealt essentially with the definition of Corporate Social Responsibility, while noting working and inhibiting factors that constitute overall the determination of success within society of the CSR movement. We concluded that the significant emphasis on the definition of the concept, rather than the implementation thereof, has created the need to observe best practices and determine which specific decisions tend to generate the highest level of CSR performance.

According to Orlitzky (2000), any organization's performance is normally affected not just by their explicit or implicit strategies, or by the market dynamics but also by external factors (both market driven and consumer driven) that help the creation of the operational ground for each company. Porter defined this as the opening towards the 'outside' (Inside-Out, vs Outside-In) (Porter and Kramer 2006), which is the new nest where the nexus of competitive advantage dwells.

In this context it becomes crucial to develop, in addition to the well-established measures of financial performance, some practical indicator of the real concrete social performance of businesses. This can be termed as Corporate Social Performance (CSP), and it will consist of a dual or multi-criterion index that combines the classic financial performance indicator (profitability, essentially) with other ethically inspired appraisals of corporate performance.

It is important to grasp the full and far-reaching significance of a broadly based indicator of CSP, although the concept of CSP has been around for quite some time. Historically, to an unreconstructed Friedmanite, CSP was reducible simply and solely to profitability; one has only to recall the title of Friedman's highly influential 1970 article 'The social responsibility of business is to increase profits' (M. Friedman, *New York Times Magazine*, 13 September 1970). That narrow conception of social responsibility of business and consequent narrowing of CSP measures to CFP in effect has had an abiding influence on much of the literature and teaching of Strategic Management.

In 1991, Wood defined CSP as 'a business organization's configuration of principles of social responsibility, processes of social responsiveness, and policies, programs, and observable outcomes as they relate to the firm's societal relationships' (Wood 1991, p. 693).

The key thesis of CSP relates to the fiduciary obligation while performing duties, adhering to the ethics of corporate conduct, promoting competitiveness for economic performance, creating a sustainable competitive advantage through core competences, while complying with the regulatory and legal frameworks, with the purpose of contributing effectively towards the preservation of a healthy, favourable business landscape and perhaps above all to a more harmonious society.

While the definition and applicative endeavour Wood describes points towards an inclusiveness of a wider range of activities (while continuing to maintain a number of more conservative criteria of measurability), CSP could become the inspiration for an entirely new and socially progressive view of the business value chain (Williams 2002) that would constitute the presence of a paradigm shift.

Coupled with its strong 'invisible' educational power, CSP mobilizes the organization in its entirety – the organizational structure, corporate culture, resources, political, technological and human capital (acquisition of new competences for instance), all aligned to service the creation of a newly adapted organizational knowledge (at times referred to as knowledge management) that pilots the organization towards higher social performance in a complex and dynamic market (Barney 1991; Russo and Fouts 1997; Wernerfelt 1984).

This trend lends itself towards a standardization of processes, aimed at the acquisition of Financial Performance, which can be easily encountered in today's corporate practices across the globe (Williams *et al.* 2007). This same trend seems to provide us with evidence that CSR, regardless of its maturity, can transform itself easily into performance measurements, which can be considered common ground to the world of business in general, irrespective of the location.

According to Shrivastava (1995), CSP would also change the reaction times in which the managerial response would occur, by de facto shifting the corporate responsiveness strategically towards preventive, anticipatory and proactive measures, against more traditional reactive ones. This would not only create a new fluid and dynamic managerial style, but it would also lead to a greater organizational preparedness for external fluctuations, market turbulence or crises (Majumdar and Marcus 2001).

This is also known as *institutional orientation*: a pattern of response by a corporation to its external environment is characterized by either avoidance and reactivity, or responsiveness and proactivity. This orientation is usually embedded in the corporate culture and closely associated with the organization's belief system and ideology. Institutional orientation is a crucial component of any Corporate Social Performance attempts because it builds on the assumptions about the actions that need to be endorsed by a business, and its role in the society.

As a positive side effect of these transactional and transnational efforts, other external positive outcomes could be yielded by this refreshed organizational structure and approach to CSP, including such 'cosmetic' factors as brand image and reputation (Adams and Hardwick 1998; Waddock and Graves 1997). Overall, many external stakeholders' dimensions, historically not contemplated by businesses' internal strategies and organizational adjustments, would become synergistic to the benefit of the larger operating network and platform that is constituted by the *stakeholders* of the business.

This same idea, studied thoroughly by several scholars, has been nicely formulated in terms of the contemporary *Weltanschauung* by Fombrun and Shanley, who see the business landscape as populated by an array of external parties such as investors, customers, suppliers, funding institutions, communities, clubs – all of which constitute the backbone of the parties who have a stake within a given organizational context. This approach could portray the company's level of CSP, not only as an internal measurement exercise but also as a measure of performance in relation to all of these outside parties and their interests and which may in addition help to nurture a positive image (Fombrun and Shanley 1990).

The theories from these authors tend to explain why organizations with high CSP ratings (if such a thing can be considered viable and reliable) may have an edge in relations with fundraisers and investors, thus facilitating the flow and access to capital, to attract and retain the best human capital and, at the same time, show good financial performance. This ultimately leads us to conclude that CSP is tightly linked to a positive Corporate Financial Performance, both because good performance on CSP can contribute reputationally and also of course in the very basic sense that the funding of socially responsible initiatives can be greatly facilitated by a good financial performance (what Friedman in his 1970 article would see as 'stealing from shareholders'). This synthesis between performances would combine, almost paradoxically, the need for economic performance, supported and yielded directly from human and social performance.

In full alignment with the above approach, Carroll identified the concept of Organizational Knowledge as operating through continuous learning and vision through the different lenses (political, economical, social, technological), thereby enhancing operational efficiency (Carroll 2000).

The key aspects of corporate or business social performance include competitiveness, responsibility, legality and legitimacy (Peery 1995). Peery explains that in order to show good economic performance there has to be good *competition*; ethical corporate performance requires *responsibility* in attempting to do what is right, *legality* requires business compliance with laws and regulations that are relevant to the business situation and *legitimacy* requires sensitivity to the political context of the business environment so that the right balance in the creation of a favourable business environment is maintained at all times (Romano 2005).

By introducing these four dimensions, Newman Peery (1995) offer a four-dimensional model for analysing social performance, or a framework that can be used as a benchmark to assess the level of CSP present in an organization.

According to this model, successful performance requires developing and achieving goals along all the above four dimensions in a cogent and consistent manner, leading to a congruent view between action and being (Williams 2002: Williams' notion of congruence in organizations is also discussed in more detail in Chapter 5 of this book).

When digging more deeply into any corporate incidents of improper behaviour and conduct (any recent scandals could serve the purpose of showing this), it becomes evident that failure in one of these four dimensions leads to the dismemberment of the organizational values that are the fundamental pillars of any company's social performance. A good example of the aforementioned is the Enron scandal, known for having used a relatively sound business model, capable of creating stability in the energy markets through the fraudulent exploitation of social issues to successfully obtain waivers and exceptions to norms and standards of the industry, from three major government audit agencies (Carroll 2000).

Some years afterwards, Carroll developed his pyramidal hierarchy of social responsibility (Carroll 2000) where both the Brown and Perry (1995) and Peery (1995) approaches are merged into the identification of the agents who will be responsible for ensuring performance on the various dimensions through the model, namely the business leaders. These latter are seen as the gatekeepers of the decision-making process within most organizational backgrounds and their capacity to act ethically towards the establishment of priorities, complexities, business dilemmas and uncertainties represents the link between the needs for CSR, the elevation to CSP through CFP and the establishment of ethical roadmaps within the business organizations.

Further to the above hierarchy, the cultural values of business leaders are known to have a strong influence on their response to non-market issues, and numerous authors (e.g. Bennis, Goleman) have spent time on the description of the individual leadership skills and their crucial roles in the definition of societal imperatives within the more economic and financial perimeters (Jones 1995).

In conclusion, businesses that take a proactive approach and download a culture around the four dimensions that Newman Peery describes, tend to introduce to the organization a sensor to the environment and its social expectations, while we note that when CSP builds on the principles of social responsibility, it leads itself into the formulation of a new hybrid model, known as Corporate Social Responsiveness.

Lessons learned

In this chapter, we have managed to demonstrate how CSR has become a worldwide practice, mainly because of its measurements rather than its mere philosophical output. The direct relationship between CSR and CSR reporting has created the operational ability for organizations to invest in CSR efforts, often driven by clear financial benefits. The idea of irresponsibility emerges as the ability of the organization to truly invest in CSR strategically but not cross-functionally, with the consequent risk of the creation of negative impacts generated by the side effects of short-term CSR policies, targeting short-term financial gain.

The broad and vague definition around CSR lends itself to ad hoc interpretations that may serve narrow economic scopes, rather than societal ones. This is supported by the increasing latent tendency of CSR to be transformed into CFP, rather than remaining as a genuine social *responsiveness* to society at large.

While the literature still supports the benevolent nature of Corporate Social Responsibility per se, the need for a rising concern on the 'industrialization' of CSR policies throughout the main global economies needs to be addressed. This can be a reason of generic concern, although the example on the BRICSA countries mentioned in this chapter seems to demonstrate a reductive role of CSR, guilty of procuring benefits of financial wealth, rather than being a social incubator of innovation prosperity and genuine social responsiveness. It is this tendency conveniently to reduce CSR to being just another form of CFP (rather than being genuine corporate social responsiveness) that I would label in effect as *Corporate Social Irresponsibility*.

References

Ackerman, R. W. (1973) 'How companies respond to social demands', *Harvard Business Review*, 51(4): 88–98.

Adams, M. and Hardwick, P. (1998) 'An analysis of corporate donation: UK evidence', *Journal of Management Studies*, 35: 641–654.

Austin, D. and Sauer, A. (2002) *Changing Oil: Emerging environmental risks and shareholder value in the oil and gas industry*. Washington DC: World Resources Institute.

Barney, J. (1991) 'Firm resources and sustained competitive advantage', *Journal of Management*, 17: 771–792.

Bennett, O. (2006) 'Healthy, wealthy and wise inc. "Sustainability" used to be just for hippies. In America, it's now big business', *The Daily Telegraph*, 25 October: 8.

Bright, C. (2000) 'Anticipating environmental "surprise"'. In L. R. Brown, C. Flavin and H. French (eds), *State of the world 2000: A Worldwatch Institute report on progress toward a sustainable society*. London: Earthscan, pp. 22–38.

Brown, A. S. (2009) 'CONFLICT on the green', *Mechanical Engineering*, 131(3): 42–45.

Brown, B. and Perry, S. (1995) 'Focal paper: Halo-removed residuals of fortune's "responsibility to the community and environment" – a decade of data', *Business and Society*, 34(2): 199–215.

Button, K. and Taylor, S. (2000) 'International air transportation and economic development', *Journal of Air Transport Management*, 6(4), 209–222.

Byrne, J. (1992) 'Towards a political economy of global climate: Energy, environment and development in the greenhouse'. In *Energy and Environment: The policy challenge*. Energy Policy Studies, Vol. 6. New Brunswick, NJ and London: Transaction publishers.

Carroll, A. B. (1979) 'A three-dimensional conceptual model of corporate performance', *Academy of Management Review*, 4(4): 497–505.

Carroll, A. B. (2000) 'Ethical challenges for business in the new millennium: Corporate social responsibility and models of management morality', *Business Ethics Quarterly*, 10(1), 32–42.

Daly, H. E. (1992) *Energy, Economics and the Environment: Conflicting views of an essential interrelationship*. AAAS Selected Symposium 64. Westview Press, Inc.

Daly, H. E. and Cobb, J. B. Jr. (1993) *For the Common Good*. Boston, MA: Beacon Press.

Daly, H. E. and Townsend, K. N. (eds) (1993) *Valuing the Earth: Economics, ecology and ethics*. Cambridge, MA: MIT Press.

Davis, K. (1973) 'Can business afford to ignore social responsibilities?' *California Management Review*, 2(3): 70–76.

DiGeorgia, J. (2008) editor and publisher of the *Gold and Energy Advisor Newsletter*. Available online at www.goldandenergyadvisor.com and the author of the popular book, *The Global War for Oil*. 21st Century Investor Publishing.

Dinica, V. (2006) 'Support systems for the diffusion of renewable energy technologies: An investor's perspective', *Energy Policy*, 34(4): 461.

Dixon, J. A., Scurra, L. F., Carpenter, R. A. and Sherman, P. B. (1994) *Economic Analysis of Environmental Impacts*. London: Earthscan.

Drucker, P. F. (2002) 'Discipline of Innovation'. August. Available online at HBR.org.

Duchin, F. and Lange, G.-M. (1994) *The Future of the Environment: Ecological Economics and Technological Change*. New York: Oxford University Press.

Dumiak, M. (2008) 'Climate change prompts strategic thinking', *American Banker*, 118(12): 35. Available online at www.americanbanker.com/magazine/118_12/-3680 (accessed 8 September 2009).

Ehrlich, P. (1981) *The Limits to Growth*. New York: Ballantine Books.

Esposito, M. (2009) *Put your Corporate Social Responsibility Act Together!* Mustang, OK: Tate Publishing.

Ewing, K., Hutt, J. and Petersen, E. (2004) 'Corporate environmental disclosures: Old complaints, new expectations', *Business Law International*, 5(3): 459–515.

Flavin, C. (1996) *Power Surge, Guide to the Coming Energy Revolution*. The Worldwatch Environmental Alert Series. New York: W. W. Norton.

Fombrun, C. J. and Shanley, M. (1990), 'What's in a name? Reputation building and corporate strategy', *Academy of Management Journal*, 33: 233–258.

Frederick, W. C. (1986) 'Toward CSR: Why ethical analysis is indispensable and unavoidable in corporate affairs', *California Management Review*, 28(2): 126–155.

Frederick, W. C. (1999) 'From CSR1 to CSR2: The maturing of business-and-society thought'. Working paper no. 279. Pittsburgh, PA: Graduate School of Business, University of Pittsburgh.

General Electric Company, Fairfield, Connecticut 06828. *GE Citizenship Report 2007– 2008*. 'Investing and Delivering in Citizenship'. The *2007 GE Annual Report*. Available online at www.ge.com/annual07 (accessed 9 September 2009).

Goldernberg, J., Johansson, T. B., Reddy, A. K. N. and Williams, R. H. (1988) *Energy for a Sustainable World*. New Delhi: Wiley Eastern Limited.

Gordon, P. J. (2008) 'The writing on the wall: Your 10-year road map for environmental innovation and trends', *Manufacturing Business Technology*, 26(7): 43.

Hawken, P., Lovins, A. and Lovins, H. (1999) *Natural Capitalism: Creating the next industrial revolution*. New York: Little, Brown and Company.

Hochbaum, D. S. (2009) 'Dynamic evolution of economically preferred facilities', *European Journal of Operational Research*, 193(3): 649.

Howard-Grenville, J. and Hoffman, A. (2003) 'The importance of cultural framing to the success of social initiatives in business', *Academy of Management Executive*, 17(2): 7–84.

Hoyer, K. G. (2000) 'Sustainable tourism or sustainable mobility? The Norwegian case', *Journal of Sustainable Tourism*, 8(2): 147–160.

Hull, C. E. and Rothenberg, S. (2008) 'Firm performance: The interactions of corporate social performance with innovation and industry differentiation', *Strategic Management Journal*, 29(7): 781.

Intergovernmental Panel on Climate Change (IPCC) (1996) *Climate Change 1995: Economic and social dimensions of climate change*. Contribution of Working Group III to the Second Assessment Report for the Intergovernmental Panel on Climate Change. Cambridge: Cambridge University Press.

Jones, M. (1999) 'The institutional determinants of social responsibility', *Journal of Business Ethics*, 20(2): 163–179.

Jones, T. M. (1995) 'Instrumental stakeholder theory: A synthesis of ethics and economics', *Academy of Management Review*, 20: 404–406.

Lovins, A. B. (1991) 'Least-cost climate stabilization', *Annual Review of Energy and the Environment*, 16: 433–531.

Majumdar, S. K. M. and Marcus, A. A. (2001) 'Rules versus discretion: The productivity consequences of flexible regulations', *Academy of Management Journal*, 44: 170–179.

Malone, T. (2004) 'Bringing the market inside', *Harvard Business Review*, April: 107–114.

Mitchell, J. (1994) 'What is the energy security problem?', *International Journal of Global Energy Issues*, 6(6): 293–300.

Moran, M., Cohen, A., Swem, N. and Shaustyuk, K. (2005) 'The growing interest in environmental issues is important to both socially responsible and fundamental investors', *Portfolio Strategy*, August 26: 5. Goldman Sachs.

Mullen, J. (1997) 'Performance-based corporate philanthropy: How "giving smart" can further corporate goals', *Public Relations Quarterly*, 42(2): 42–48.

Norgaard, R. B. and Howarth, K. (1992) 'Economics, Ethics and the Environment'. In J. M. Holland (ed.), *The energy–environment connection*. Washington DC: Island Press.

Orlitzky, M. (2000) Research Brief: 'Corporate social performance: Developing effective strategies'. Sydney: UNSW, Australian Graduate School of Management.

Pacala, S. and Socolow, R. (2004) 'Stabilization wedges: Solving the climate problem for the next 50 years with current technologies', *Science*, 305(5686): 968–972.

Pearce, D. W. (1993) *Economic Values and the Natural World*. Cambridge, MA: MIT Press.

Pearce, D. W. and Turner, R. K. (1990) *Economics of Natural Resources and the Environment*. Baltimore, MA: The John Hopkins University Press.

Pearson, P. (1989) 'Proactive energy environment policy strategies: A role for input-output analysis?' *Environment and Planning*, A 21: 1329–1348.

Peery, Jr., N. S. (1995) 'Business, government, and society: Managing competitiveness', *Ethics and Social Issues*, 9: 257.

Pezzey, J. (1989) *Economic Analysis of Sustainable Growth and Sustainable Development*. Washington DC: World Bank.

Phills, Jr., J. A., Deiglmeier, K. and Miller, D. T. (2008) 'Rediscovering social innovation', *Stanford Social Innovation Review*, 6(4): 34–43.

Porter, M. (1999) 'UK Competitiveness: Moving to the next stage', DTI Economics Paper No. 3.

Porter, M. and Kramer, M. (2006) 'Strategy & society: The link between competitive advantage and corporate social responsibility', *Harvard Business Review*, December 2006.

Romano, R. (2005) 'The Sarbanes–Oxley Act and the making of quack corporate governance', *Yale Law Journal*, 114: 1521–1523.

Russo, M. V. and Fouts, P. A. (1997) 'A resource based perspective on corporate environmental performance and profitability', *Academy of Management Journal*, 40: 534–559.

Senge, P., Smith, B., Kruschwitz, N., Laur, J. and Nicholas, S. S. (2008) *'The Necessary Revolution': How individuals and organisations are working together to create a sustainable world*. London: Brealey Publishing.

Shrivastava, P. (1995) 'Ecocentric management for a risk society', *Academy of Management Review*, 20: 118–137.

Siegel, J. (2008) *Investing in Renewable Energy*. Toronto: Angel Publishing.

Smith, J. (2005) 'The implications of the Kyoto Protocol and the global warming debate for business transactions', *NYU Journal of Law and Business*, 1(2): 511–550.

Solar and Wind Technologies for Hydrogen Production: Report to Congress. Department of Energy. December 2005, p. 38.

The Center for Social Innovation at the Stanford Graduate School of Business launched the *Stanford Social Innovation Review* – 2003.

Turner, J. A. (2004) 'Sustainable hydrogen production', *Science*, 305(5686): 972–974.

Victor, B. and Cullen, J. (1988) 'The organizational bases of ethical work climates', *Administrative Science Quarterly*, 33: 101–125.

Waddock, S. A. and Graves, S. B. (1997) The corporate social performance–financial performance link,' *Strategic Management Journal*, 18: 303–319.

Warren, S. (2006) 'DuPont warns high energy costs will hurt profit', *The Wall Street Journal*, January 12: A6.

Wernerfelt, B. (1984) 'A resource-based view of the firm', *Strategic Management Journal*, 5: 171–180.

White, L., Lee, G. J. (2009) 'Operational research and sustainable development: Tackling the social dimension', *European Journal of Operational Research*, 193(3): 683.

Willard, B. (2005) *The Next Sustainability Wave*. Gabriola Island: New Society Publishers.

Williams, L. (2002) *Creating the Congruent Workplace*. Westport, CT: Quorum Books.

Williams, L., Ecimovic, T., Esposito, M., Flint, W., Haw, R. and Mulej, M. (2007) *Sustainable Future of Mankind*. Maribor: Boris Editions.

Wilson, M. (2006) 'Chain store age: Staples aims for a greener planet', *New York*, 82(13): 60–63.

Witzel, M. (2008) 'The business case for more sustainability', *Financial Times*, London: 3 July, p. 16.

Wood, D. J. (1991) Corporate social performance revisited', *Academy of Management Review*, 16: 691–718.

World Commission on Environmental Development (WCED) (1987). *Our Common Future*. Oxford: Oxford University Press.

5

THE IMPACT OF ETHICS ON THE ISSUES OF ORGANIZATIONAL CONGRUENCE

Lloyd C. Williams and Mark Esposito

Creating a context for dialogue

This chapter explores the factors that block the creation of congruence in people and organizations and explores strategies that can simultaneously and congruently move people and organizations to a path of sustainability.

Developing a short treatise on ethical congruence and sustainability may be seen as a daunting task. Daunting in the eyes of many because, on the surface, the two thoughts – ethical congruence and sustainability – can be seen as anathemas to one another when trying to discuss healing and connected actions between people and organizational systems. Yet, our overarching purpose is to demonstrate the connection and pathway for understanding people in the world of work and play, and to give a congruence perspective for the development of sustainable thought and action in the lives of all.

Congruence and sustainability are two terms that are often viewed as 'apples and oranges'. Congruence focuses on the ability of people and systems to align perfectly, ensuring that words, actions and thinking match (Williams 2002). Sustainability has historically been viewed as the tenuous balance in nature to ensure that life and nature are balanced for the long term. Yet, when viewing these two concepts holistically, what has been considered anathema – the human being versus the natural world – actually represents the true connectivity of humanity and nature.

In *Creating the Congruent Workplace* (Williams 2002), congruity and the process of becoming congruent was defined as the creation and embracing of balance, alignment, integration and transformation as the key anchors in understanding and reframing who we are, how we think, when we act and what context drives our personal and professional development – our being if you will – versus the compartmentalized contents and sound-bite processes that drive living and corporate survival (p. xvii). The perspective from the definition focused on the thoughts and actions that often drive performance. When people in an organization are asked to narrow their approach, provide their professional history in one page, give information in bullets, think only as the team thinks, dress only as the organization perceives, look like the predominant culture, each component of the required actions progressively stifles human personality in its uniqueness.

Sustainability is a system concept relating to the continuity of economic, social, institutional and environmental aspects of human society, as well as the non-human environment (Williams *et al.* 2007). Sustainability is a means of configuring civilization and human activity so that society, its members and its economies are able to meet the needs of people today while preserving the biodiversity and natural ecosystems, and planning and acting for the ability to maintain these ideals into the very long term.

Contextually, boundaries are created when dialogues occur on sustainability and congruence. Table 5.1 details boundaries that frame dialogues on the two concerns.

When one considers Table 5.1, there is a natural tendency to think that there is a competition between the two; nothing could be further from what is intended.

TABLE 5.1 The boundaries of sustainability and congruence

Sustainability boundaries	Congruence boundaries
Addressing cautiously risk, uncertainty and irreversibility	Clarity in all thoughts and actions
Ensuring appropriate valuation, appreciation and restoration of nature	Collaboration as the baseline of self with others
Integration of environmental, social and economic goals in policies and activities	Complements or anchors that ensure balance in thought and deed
Equal opportunity and community participation	Choices that effectively utilize beliefs and values to remain balanced and in sync with self
Conservation of biodiversity and ecological integrity	Constants that create synergy and comfort with choices and decisions
Recognizing the global dimension	Consequences that drive adherence to personal and communal values and beliefs deemed critical
A commitment to best practices	Change practices that adhere to underlying beliefs and values
No net loss of human and natural capital	Capacities that drive pathways for movement to expand and grow
Adhering to the principle of continuous improvement	Culture that sets the baseline for thinking and action, ensuring that beliefs and values are culture centred
Good governance	Congruence that all the characteristics that drive harmony are centred in the person as an internal reference point
(Williams *et al.* 2007)	(Williams 2002)

The table represents the framework, end points and conflictual stances that often occur when one considers the challenges to be sustainable or congruent. Congruence requires clarity, collaboration, complements, choices and complexity to address the connectivity that emerges within a congruent organization or a congruent person. Equally important is the necessity of becoming sustainable to engage uncertainty, assure valuation and appreciation of nature or what exists, integration of sustainable goals, equity in all aspects of planning, implementing and evaluating life and performance, sensing the global arena for all actions and commitment to follow through on choices.

The most poignant realization becomes the foci of the dialogues. Explicitly, congruence seems to focus on the internal referencing of humanity from an inside-out perspective, while sustainability's focus is on the external referencing of society and culture. Unfortunately, dialogues that occur among business, educational, government and community leaders often focus on the external concerns of sustainability without the inclusion of congruence, the essential characteristics of human interaction and human sustainability. To that end, the dialogue occurs here because the challenge is often impacted by the challenges of ethics.

Balancing sustainability and congruence

As the dialogues that historically and currently occur among business, education and governmental decision makers, when issues of ethical congruence and sustainability arise, focus on the external factors of human and organizational performance, rarely is completeness a result of the discussion. This is not an indictment of the concept of sustainability, rather, the short-sightedness of the decision makers. The process of creating ethical, congruent, sustainable change, personally and organizationally, is about the understanding and creation of reasoned balance and alignment, a strategy that we call congruence building. This process explicitly focuses on creating a metanoic shift – a change in thinking and acting – that establishes different outcomes for the work, growth and change within organizations and among people. The Society of Human Resource Management says, 'employees will spend more than 70% of their year at work in the United States and somewhat less in Europe and more in Asia'. If that assessment is true, then organizations and their leaders are challenged to create a more balanced life that is aligned with the long-term, sustainable needs of the employees, the community in which they reside, and the networks essential to healthy communal living, as well as attending to the critical issues of organizational success and sustainability through ethical thought and action. What blocks that movement is often the thinking and practice paradigms of organizations, leaders and stockholders. What would the shift look like? How would one shift their thinking? Where could one explore honouring self and others? Where would one develop a sense of culture and society? What is the key to understanding these issues? The key is congruence building – a new approach to personal, organizational and business systems development.

Many people continue to believe that we can separate what we do at work from who we are in the privacy of our lives. What we achieve instead is (1) lack of clarity about who we are and what we do, (2) an inability to effectively collaborate with one another because the rewards of individuation outweigh the nuances and enlightenments of joint or collaborative efforts and ventures, (3) a lack of awareness of the complements in our lives that create effective anchors for risking the development of change, (4) a retreating from creativity and change, (5) an abdication of personal and professional choice that creates co-dependency and systemic moroseness and the desire to make life and work simple, (6) an inability to understand and embrace complexity that enriches and challenges us to go beyond the known and conscious to the unknown and unconscious to bridge the past, present and future, to be fully present in our personal and professional lives. What organizations have lost is their direction, their connectivity to the entrepreneurship that created them, and to their ethical responsibility to their partners – the people. What we have lost and need to create is ethical congruence in our personal and professional lives, the seventh paradigm, and in so doing we create the capacity to develop ethical sustainability in our lives and in our work. We ensure that organizations, governments, communities and individuals all focus on the concepts of ethical sustainability and ethical congruence, both essential for human and societal development. What we have not recognized is that organizations and people operate from psychological schemas – perspectives of how things should be – that drive what we choose to do, when we do them, where we engage, who is important and what is necessary. If our schemas are misaligned, incongruent, then the outcomes are in jeopardy regarding the impact we initiate and often institutionalize in organizations.

One might ask what this focus on congruence and sustainability has to do with business and organizational development, with governmental success and societal cohesion. Paradigmic thinking is critical to business and people development. Whatever the personality type that emerges from the particular company paradigm – be it classical (no chaos, tight boundaries, company person), scientific dynamic (cause-and-effect driven, blame and shame – not my fault type of person), communication cybernetic (data driven to the point of no decision – give me more information to get it right type of person), field (test processes for decision making – prove it to me/show me type of person), evolutionary (change for change's sake – change now – change every day type of person) or process thought/emotive driven (a balance and alignment in thought and action to the outcomes necessary – if it works and if it moves me and others type of person) – the underlying thought process impacts, empowers, influences and directs the actions of organizations (Freire 1973; Gibb 1978; Williams 1996, 2002). When that thinking is compartmentalized, controlled, boxed, when that thinking is designed to protect and limit, rather than understand and grow, the process of imbalance, misalignment and incongruence, leading often to unethical actions, occurs and people and organizations are the ultimate losers!

As stated earlier, congruity and the process of becoming congruent is the embracing and creation of balance, alignment, integration and transformation as key anchors to the understanding and reframing of who we are, how we think, when we act and what context drives our personal and professional development, our being if you will, versus the compartmentalized contents and sound-bite processes that drive Western living and corporate survival and, unfortunately more and more, global living and corporate survival. When one is asked daily to narrow one's approach – provide one's professional history in one page, provide all information to the leaders in 'bullets because they will not read', think only as the team will think, dress only as the organization perceives appropriate dress, look as Europeans or Americans look in order not to offend or threaten – we are continually participating in strategies that dishonour the uniqueness and the congruence of each person for the sake of an ideal or belief that has little place in a world of global diversity and global differences. Everyone is being asked to create more imbalance and misalignment in their lives and the cost is the loss of the critical congruence essential to the fluidity and flexibility essential to organizational and business growth and development. Organizations and individuals are sustained by their ability to move in concert with their underpinning values; organizations become more ethical when the ability of the organization embraces fluidness and flexibility as a core underlying and guiding principle of what it means to BE in a world of difference. Recalcitrant action, sticking to a one-size-fits-all strategy or a strategy that no longer works, becomes the downside of organizational performance. When employees are afraid to challenge the stance of the organization, the actions of the manager, the thinking of the leader when they sense an unethical strategy – often an unethical approach is set in place – organizations lose the opportunity and capacity to heighten and enhance ethical performance because of the restrictiveness that exists within the organization; employees lose the ability to risk, collaborate and make choices, and being more ethical is stifled through the fear within.

The need for change

Each and every day, organizational leaders report difficulties in their quest to create strategies that work without an increase in dysfunction among employees of the organization (National Bureau of Professional Management Consultants (NBPMC) 1999–2010 Annual Reports). The issues cited that seem to contribute to the plethora of problems or barriers that haunt organizational leaders include:

- a lack of understanding of the organizational strategies by managers, thus impacting the comfort levels of the employees charged with performing the strategies;
- development of strategies that focus on one part of the organization without recognition of their impact on other areas of the company, creating problems that formerly did not exist;
- continuation of unresolved issues, or one-way decisions, that only favour the organization, creating areas of mistrust and discomfort that prevent managers from effectively planning or developing strategies to resolve the organizational and human issues;

- differing mindsets between executive managers and descending levels of accountability within the organization, creating tangents in strategies that veer off track from plans of the leaders; and
- unclear or unsafe strategies that set employees up to fail, creating strategies for protection of employees rather than success of a product or service (NBPMC 1999–2010 Annual Reports).

Each issue seems to impact the healthy, sustainable and ethical development of organizational strategies. In addition, numerous theoretical concerns recognized at least since the works of Karl Marx, Max Weber and Emile Durkheim regarding the role of the distribution of labour versus the needs of organizations impact on the successful development of balance strategies within organizations. The initial understandings in our society of how and why division of labour should exist emerged from their writings, setting both the stage and the standards for modern-day thinking. However, there has been a continual ethical division between people and organizational systems that continues even as this writing is being penned.

What is the real issue before us? What makes it hard for employees, managers and leaders to embrace one another to create strategies for success and sustainability? Somehow, there is a perspective that there is no tangible connection in the minds of managers, leaders, employees or even theorists, that connectivity must occur between the actions and thinking of people and between the strategies and structures of systems. That is the underlying premise of this ethical dialogue on human and organizational congruence and sustainability.

In the book *The Congruence of People and Organizations: Healing dysfunctions from the inside out* (Williams 1993), the focus began on the issues of connectivity between people and systems. To address that connectivity, the issue was approached through the underlying values and belief systems that are created within organizations and societal systems, demanding an ethical approach. In *Organizational Violence: Creating a prescription for change* (Williams 1994) a strategy was presented to address the actions and thinking of organizations that create separation among employees. The premise of the book is that inconsistency of thought and action of organizational leaders creates an unethical sub-paradigm of systemic violence impeding the ability of employees to act, thus reducing the effectiveness of the organization as a whole. In *Business Decisions, Human Choices: Restoring the partnership between people and their organizations* (Williams 1996) the focus is on the integration of people and systems to create an effective, ethical pathway for change and development.

The book introduced the trinity system (the connection of people, business systems and congruence characteristics) and focused on the integration of context, content and process as ethical strategies for change among people and organizational systems.

What has grown out of years of consulting practice, research and publication efforts is the belief that unethical behaviour and thinking occurs, and incongruity occurs between people and organizations and among people within organizations instilling a less than sustainable strategy for long- and short-term performance of people and systems. When there is inconsistency between role prescription and role behaviour in the organization setting, both the organization and the person become disconnected, disjointed and dysfunctional – unethical and incongruent. Such inconsistencies create historical and systemic dysfunction in organizations.

To test this belief, a Congruence Development Model was developed in Williams' *Business Decisions, Human Choices* in 1996. The model is a dual-process paradigm that requires the utilization of business and human characteristics to create effective alignment of thought and action in organizations, their leaders and managers. The model consists of six characteristics in each of two paradigms that create opportunity and capacity for people to sense completeness in their decisions, and the implementation of those decisions. The two paradigms in the Williams' Congruence Model are referred to as the Business Process Paradigm and the Human Process Paradigm (Williams 1996). The purpose of the paradigms was to establish connection points for thought and action in business and human behaviour that create the emotional and systemic tensions necessary for change. The more connectivity between thought and action, the more congruence between people behaviour and organizational performance, the more sustainability occurs between societies, governments and people.

Statement of the problem

Lived experiences of employees within organizations are often discounted as valid expressions of meaningful information that can be used by organizations and leaders to create change, movement and direction within an organization. Executive decisions are most often based on quantitative data provided by departments on performance and research within organizations. There are, however, other sources of information available to organizations as they prepare strategies for change, growth and development. These information sources include e-mails, memos, reports, retreats, focused discussions and other records of interactions within an organization. Organizations historically rely less, if at all, on these records of interactions to provide a lens of understanding about what happens within the organization. As a result, valuable qualitative data, generated from the lived experiences of managers and executives, often takes a back seat to more traditional quantitative data.

Every employee has a source for data collection. They are the conversations, coffee breaks, rumours, family experiences and dialogues that inform and shape thinking while impacting the actions taken by people in work and play. These informal, non-scientific data sets often influence the direction and actions of people more than the quantitative information that is available. Consider the number of times people have said: 'They can make numbers say anything; I don't trust their data; they didn't ask me, so they don't consider what I have to say as important.' In those statements is embedded the power of phenomenological inquiry – lived experiences – that are often not used in organizational choices. Effectually, when numbers alone are used, the opportunity for organizations to be unethical escalates to an immeasurable level.

Within every organization, phenomenological (lived experiences and appearances) and hermeneutic (biased interpretive) data exist that can impact the ethical thinking and actions of managers. What is often discounted is the utilization of these data to enrich and streamline the actions of organizational leaders in the decisions before them. These data were often suspect, and therefore, were considered anecdotal – not for business consumption. Safety was generally the norm and quantitative information was generally the answer to data required for decision making, structural development and environmental happiness or manager/employee satisfaction. Yet organizational leaders continually 'skew the data', creating opportunity for unethical action to occur.

Corporations, governments and non-profits – in fact most organizations – are continually faced with struggles to develop ethical approaches to achieving outcomes defined by organizational leaders and stakeholders without destroying the employees and managers charged with accomplishing those outcomes. Research (Burke 1997; Maier 1997; Mallinger 1997; Jennings 1998) suggests that some strategies of organizations may create unethical disruptions in the behaviour and thoughts of employees and managers, thereby reducing the effectiveness of that organization. Burke's research focused on ethical issues; Mallinger's, on decision making; Jennings', on gender and employee performance; and Maier's research focused on organizational transformation and its challenges in corporate strategy. Each researcher stated that there was a central core missing in creating organizational effectiveness. The missing link was and remains organizational and human congruence – the ethical stance.

Questions abound regarding the causes of organizational failure from Senge, Covey, Burke, Bennis, Sommerville, Goldsmith and numerous other researchers and writers. These questions centre on development of a core understanding of what creates organizational and employee success. Each speaks of the need for alignment of people with organizational outcomes; none state what that sense of alignment or balance must look like. As this discussion among theorists continues to evolve, it is believed that focusing on the concept of balance and alignment – congruence – will generate the necessary strategy frame for how managers and organizations can create a better path for ethical organizational and managerial success. It has been learned, through years of consulting, that the lived experiences, stories and accounts of employees are an important vehicle for discovery. Even with that belief, however, developing a perspective to identify or describe the issues without numbers was difficult.

The challenge in such an application is determined by the definition of terms used to frame the issues for exploration and discovery. The challenge in this writing has been the exploration of a concept of ethical congruence and sustainability applied to the development of more effective managerial and organizational performance through the use of a thematic analysis methodology. The challenge was predicated on the assumption of a gap between organizational and people development postulated by Daniel Goleman in his book, *Emotional Intelligence* (1995: xiii–xiv), where he said:

If there is a remedy [to the dysfunctions of people], I feel it must lie in how we prepare for life. At present we leave the emotional education of our children to chance, with ever more disastrous results . . . I can foresee a day when education will routinely include inculcating essential human competencies such as self awareness, self control, empathy, the art of listening, resolving conflicts and cooperation.

In the *Nicomachaen Ethics* (a philosophical enquiry into virtue, character and the good life), Aristotle's challenge is to manage our emotional life with intelligence. Transposing this into the terms and situation of the modern workplace means that our passions, when well exercised, have wisdom; they guide our thinking, our values, our actions and our survival. The question of appropriate emotion is essential to effective being in the workplace, in society and in our own lives. Somehow we have lost that connection, and in that loss we have removed from our thinking and acting the necessity of emotion in our decisions and in our practice.

In effect, ethical congruity and sustainability become the connection for thinking, feeling, acting and becoming.

Goleman's research and statements were explicitly directed at the actions of individuals; however, organizational leaders and managers are also confronted with the issues of human emotion, competencies, group and team awareness, team and individual control, and the resolution of conflict. Goleman's statement speaks of the relationship between the structure and functioning of the human brain and human emotions and, thus, the consequences (of this relationship) for human behaviour and development as individuals and as groups. By implication, Goleman asserts that individuals, teams, businesses, governments, societies and cultures have a lack of understanding of this relationship and its ethical impact on human learning and behaviour. Further, Goleman asserts that one's lack of understanding of the brain/emotion relationship and its impact on, or consequences for, group and individual development and behaviour is the missing piece of our definition of human intelligence, thus causing an ethical deficit in the education of the young. It seems fitting, therefore, to use Goleman's analogy to support the direction of this chapter's argument. If there is a connection between the human brain and emotion, can there be effectiveness in organizations without ethical congruence and sustainability – as an analogy to Goleman's perspective? Can there be movement in the world of business through compartmental actions – disconnected actions – or does real movement require some level of understanding of both the concept of congruence and congruent actions and the strategy of sustainability and sustainable actions in the creation of ethical strategies for change and development? Can ethical congruence occur within organizations if only the needs of the organization are met? If the needs of employees are also essential to the success of the organization, how might the organization ensure the balance and alignment of the employees and the organization to create effective, ethical sustainability? Can analysis of lived experiences yield the necessary information that governs the ethical future of organizational change and development?

Similarly, can individuals achieve personal, ethical congruence where they sense that their sustainability in the workplace is based on acting like everyone in the workplace, when they do not perceive themselves as being themselves? What happens to personal/individual contribution in the workplace when one must operate through a personal façade – an unethical lens? If, to take a simple example, one's family operates from a communal value set, yet the workplace focuses on individuation, what happens to one's ability to contribute?

A 2000 study conducted by the American Society for Training and Development (and again in 2009) examined the average annual training expenditures of more than 500 US-based publicly traded firms. The study concluded that firms in the top half of the group (i.e. firms that spent the most on training) had a total stockholder return 86 per cent higher than firms in the bottom half – and 46 per cent higher than the market average. Studies such as this revealed that the right kind of investment in people can generate exponential returns. Yet, what happens each time the stock market hiccups? Look at any paper from any city, state, country or international marketplace and one will discover massive layoffs from corporations, and at the same time increases in the compensation for executives because they cut people. When is there an ethical review of the strategy? When does the concept of ethical congruent and sustainable action drive the decision making of organizational leaders? Businesses, governments, educational institutions, service organizations and corporate entities are at that ethical crossroads and the economic upheaval of the years since the financial crisis, the distillation of the unethical actions of banks, investment firms, leaders throughout the world, reveals the importance of ethical thought and action on the actions of the globe.

Creating greater sustainability and congruence

Given the aforementioned perspectives, one might consider exploring strategies that can move people and systems towards greater ethical sustainability and congruence.

First, one begins with an exploration of the internal and external referencing factors in one's life and actions. People across the globe are used to the external references that guide their actions and thoughts. From educational institutions to governmental actions, others consistently state what is appropriate and right in the lives of human beings. These external references become ingrained to the extent that often people are unaware of what truly drives their thinking and feelings, their being. In Cuba, the external reference points of Fidel Castro and his perspective of Communism drive what is allowable in the minds, feelings and actions of the citizens of Cuba. In Africa, tribal edicts dictate what people of nations can consider as appropriate thinking. In America, the religious right and the conservative agenda work diligently to force Americans to see the world through an extremely conservative lens and often establish punitive outcomes for those with a more liberal or socially minded ideology. Throughout the world, addressing global warming through the lens of countries and nations that believe that nothing is proven, thus nothing is wrong, rather than adhering to the internal voice of each person who believes that what is seen represents a departure from sustainable action are all examples of external referencing. In the business world, group think (Janus) and a focus on the leaders and the strategy that demand that all appear and act the same is another form of external referencing. To move towards ethical congruity and sustainability, one understands the external influences of a leader, boss, organization, government or family history, yet balances that external reference with internally referenced thoughts. The concept of individuation – thinking for oneself, thinking according to guiding principles, living by one's values and beliefs, acting ethically, congruently where who one is matches what one does – are all internal references that can make a difference in how one proceeds in a world that often seeks to block uniqueness and individuation.[1]

Second, one seeks clarity – to understand what is clear and unclear about the life one experiences. Where is the confusion, the dissonance, the discomfort, the unspoken that creates disruptions in the thinking and feeling? Where has the process of gaining clarity fallen short of one's expectations and was the shortfall based on fear of consequences or the lack of data that were required for clarity to emerge. In delving further, were the actions, behaviours, expressions of thought consistent with the intellectual, emotional, social and spiritual realms that have heretofore appeared congruent? Were the actions too misaligned? What bargains have been agreed to that add to the obfuscation?

Third, if the old adage of 'no man is an island' holds true, are actions and strategies focused on the creation of collaborative actions between self and others; or is collaboration an ideal, not a planned requirement for success? In today's business environment, teamwork is increasingly heralded as laudable and even as essential. Teams are seen as the *coup de grâce* of successful business. In family businesses, family sustainability holds that same place of honour and cruciality. The underlying perspective is that strength and wisdom are uplifted when more than one person, one ideal, one value is tested by the internal and external reference perspectives of members of a team, a family, a group or a community.

Fourth, complements or anchors must be identified to ensure that when stressed to the point of abdication of a point of view that is central, one does not falter and lose the footing essential to self-identity. One is often unsure of critical anchors that govern a perspective and belief. For some it is religion, for others family, for still others, past experiences; yet the concept of a complement allows one to stay on a path of sustainability or congruence.

Fifth, choices are essential to personal and systemic ownership. Just because one business wants to 'rape critical minerals', it does not mean that all businesses must follow suit. Sustainable and congruent action is always about the choices made and the perseverance that drives that choice. Too often, choice does not come into the decision processes because organizations and their leaders have overcommitted to an idea or strategy, even when they recognize that the return on investment is less than desirable.

Sixth, and critical for the levels of understanding is the concept of constants. Reliance on a perspective that some things will remain the same is essential to the risking nature of being congruent or acting in a sustainable manner. Reliance on values and beliefs represent constants that govern how one engages the world, thus if justice and duty, the aeratic and deonic principles of ethics, are constants, then one can conceive of using one's constants to drive personal and organizational action, cultural and societal choices. The idea of constants is also the forgotten or overlooked perspective in some fields of sustainability. To be sustainable, constants help us focus on what has existed; how one strays from that existent process, and what one uses as a point of reference to make decisions, implement actions and evaluate outcomes is often governed by the constants in one's life.

These six perspectives drive the context analysis that one considers when seeking to create congruent and sustainable actions from an internal and external reference system. Whether institutional, economic, financial or ecological sustainability, the analysis along congruent theoretical strands becomes essential to the concepts of sustainable thought and action, congruent thought and action. The two perspectives are irrevocably connected to one another and live collaboratively in the process of business and social development.

Understanding context analysis alone as a method of creating sustainability and congruence is insufficient to reach success that lasts. Content analysis is required to ensure the balance that is necessary for sustainable and congruent thought and action. Content, for the purposes of this dialogue, focuses on the specific factors that often alter and derail strategies planned by organizations, families, communities and leaders because attention to these areas are costly, time consuming and often of critical concern that inhibits performance and strategic direction.

Areas of concern for content analysis are consequences, change, control, capacities and culture. Consequences represent the actions that interrupt planned action when individuals and organizations make choices to operate 'outside' of the congruent values, beliefs and assumptions that maintain the balance of congruence and sustainability. Change, in the content arena, focuses on the inappropriate actions and thoughts instituted by leaders to gain the antithesis of change – control, where boundaries are strictly created to ensure that everything remains as it has been, allowing no growth and development within the system or among the people. Capacities represent the opportunities that exist for individuals, groups, teams, organizations, societies and cultures to expand the sacred cows and totems to build new directions and expansions of existing knowledge. Culture represents the histories and traditions that frame the world – the usually implicit viewpoints that drive thought and action. The process of congruence and sustainability requires explorations of both context and content analysis to frame and identify pathways that allow for growth and movement, balance and alignment, movement from stagnation for people and systems.

Recognizing these characteristics and factors will allow organizations and people to focus on the development of relationships that build new world views that can shape new futures, new realities and new pathways for understanding and relationships.

The future

The crossroads where a wrong turning can lead to incongruence have now been identified. Each person has the opportunity to create ethical newness in his or her work and play. Each organization has the opportunity to identify the steps critical to ethical sustainability. The realization of ethical sustainability and congruence is based on the risks and challenges that one, not all, can take to be fully present with self and others. Ethical congruence – the balance of what one is with what one does – is always available. Our challenge is to be personal and systemic simultaneously. Each of us, all of us are challenged to engage *ourselves*, our choices, our actions and discern the level of congruity that we create or discard to be in this world. Our challenge is to explore the choices that we make regarding where we work, what we choose to do at work, what we acquiesce to in the actions of our leaders and managers. If *people* make the organization, then it is *people* who must challenge the actions of the organization, the decisions of the organizational leaders, the actions that are unethical, inappropriate and harmful to people and societal systems. Only through challenging what is, can one discover what can be. The challenge is up to all of us!

Note

1 Some of these themes have been developed in great detail in existentialist phenomenology, notably by Maurice Merleau-Ponty in Merleau-Ponty (1964) *The Primacy of Perception, and Other Essays on Phenomenological Psychology: The philosophy of art, history, and politics*. Evanston, IL: Northwestern University Press.

Bibliography

Aristotle, *Nicomachaen Ethics*.
Barrett, R. (1998) *Liberating the Corporate Soul: A values-driven approach to building a visionary organization*. Boston, MA: Butterworth-Heinemann.
Barton, L. (1998) *Ethics: The enemy in the workplace*. Darby, PA: Diane Publishing Co.
Bowie, M. E. (1998) *Business Ethics: A Kantian perspective*. Oxford: Blackwell Publishers.
Burke, R. J. (1997) 'Save the males: Backlash in organizations', *Journal of Business Ethics*, 16(9): 933–942.
Costa, J. D. (1998) *The Ethical Imperative: Why moral leadership is good business*. Boston, MA: Addison Wesley Longman, Inc.
Cowton, C. (ed.) (1998) *Business Ethics: Perspective on the practice of theory*. Oxford: Oxford University Press.
DeGeorge, R. T. (1998) *Business Ethics*. Upper Saddle River, NJ: Prentice Hall.
Freire P. (1973) *Pedagogy of the Oppressed*. New York: Continuum and Seabury Press, pp. 12–13.
Getz, D. (1998) *Business, Ethics and Society*. Philadelphia, PA: Ginn Press.
Gibb, J. (1978) *Trust: A new view of personal and organizational development*. Los Angeles, CA: Guild of Tutors Press.
Goleman, D. (1995) *Emotional Intelligence*. New York: Bantam Books.
Hartman, E. M. (1996) *Organizational Ethics and the Good Life*. New York: Oxford University Press.

Ingram, L. C. (1995) *The Study of Organizations: Positions, persons and patterns*. Westport, CT: Praeger Publishers, Greenwood Publishing Group.

Jennings, M. (1998) *Case Studies in Business Ethics: The case of buffalo pioneering*. Cincinnati, OH: South-Western College Publishing.

Kumar, B. and Steinmann, H. (1998) *Ethics in International Management*. Berlin: Walter De Gruyter Inc.

Maier, M. (1997) 'Gender equity organizational transformation and challenger', *Journal of Business Ethics*, 16(9): 943–962.

Mallinger, M. (1997) 'Decisive decision making: An exercise using ethical frameworks', *Journal of Management Education*, 21(3): 411–417.

Newton, L. H. and Ford, M. (1998) *Clashing Views on Controversial Issues in Business Ethics and Society*. New York: McGraw-Hill Higher Education.

Shaw, W. H. (1998) *Business Ethics*. Belmont, CA: Wadsworth Publishing Company.

Werhane, P. and Freeman, R. E. (1998) *Blackwell Encyclopedia Dictionary of Business Ethics*. Oxford: Blackwell Publishers.

Williams, L. (1993) *The Congruence of People and Organizations: Healing dysfunction from the inside out*. Westport, CT: Quorum Books.

Williams, L. (1994) *Organizational Violence: Creating a prescription for change*. Westport, CT: Quorum Books.

Williams, L. (1996) *Business Decisions, Human Choices: Restoring the Partnership between People and their Organizations*. Westport, CT: Quorum Books.

Williams, L. (2002) *Creating the Congruent Workplace*. Westport, CT: Quorum Books.

Williams, L. Ecimovic, T., Esposito, M., Flint, W., Haw, R. and Mulej, M. (2007) *Sustainable Future of Mankind*. Maribor: Boris Editions.

6

ETHICAL ISSUES OF REIFICATION AND RECOGNITION IN HRM

A Critical Social Theory perspective

Gazi Islam

Chapter overview

In the early twentieth century, Georg Lukacs proposed the idea of reification in order to describe a particular kind of perspective promoted in capitalist societies. Under reification, people begin to see the products of their labour as 'thing-like', independent of the social processes that created them, and as having an autonomous existence outside of society. The process of reification spreads to social relations, where people come to see each other as means to ends, rather than as free, conscious actors, in breach of key principles of modern ethical thought. Finally, reification extends to workers' own views of themselves, such that they begin to consider their own traits, attitudes, capacities and skills as 'human capital', bundles of resources that can be traded for material benefit. To Lukacs, the process of reification was a false view of society and social relations that was promoted by contemporary capitalist relations in the workplace and in consumer markets.

Although the reification concept fell largely out of use in more contemporary discussions of worker well-being, it has recently been revived in Axel Honneth's discussion of recognition theory. Honneth clearly establishes a link between modern forms of social life under capitalism and the process of reification, arguing that this concept is as useful today as ever. Further, he enriches the concept by linking it to recognition-theoretic foundations that stand at the cutting edge of Critical Social Theory, giving the concept a wide purview and divorcing it from the more orthodox Marxist foundations upon which the earlier concept had rested. Thus, using the ideas of recognition and reification can support current critical theories of business without becoming beholden to particular ideological foundations, allowing these ideas to make an important contribution to thinking in the field of Human Resources Management (HRM).

This chapter will give a brief overview of recognition theory and reification as they apply to the workplace, and discuss the contributions of these notions to ethics in HRM. Ethical perspectives in HRM attempt to unpack the human consequences of employment relations, and how such relations can avoid exploitation and promote social well-being. While some perspectives focus primarily on particular principles, codes of ethics or rules for employee treatment, other perspectives more critically examine the work relation itself, suggesting that this relation may contain elements that are inherently unethical. For example, no matter how much utilitarian benefit work may provide employees in terms of salary or other benefits, if the work relation compromises fundamental values of human dignity, autonomy or respect, it may be ethically problematic. Such 'deontological' views, often overlooked or ignored in classical liberal approaches to market relations, lead to macro-critiques of employment relations as a whole, rather than critiques of particular workplace practices, such as unsafe workplaces, low pay or long work hours. Workplace practices are sound, critical perspectives emphasize, when they reflect conceptions of human beings that acknowledge their dignity and humanity, notions that are linked to, but not identical with, material benefits.

Next, this macro-critique will be explored more fully, asking what it means for HRM to 'use' people unethically. I will discuss the conceptual tools that allow us to understand how such practice is promoted in organizations, why it is problematic, and how we can begin to imagine alternative practices. First, the discussion will explore the recognition-theoretic bases of contemporary critical theory before turning to the problem of reification understood as a problem of recognition. After contrasting recognition and reification perspectives on work, the chapter will conclude by weighing the advantages and disadvantages of a recognition approach to HRM.

Recognition theory and the workplace

Recognition, according to the theory, involves a basic social acknowledgement of human worthiness that underlies forms of social participation. Honneth predicates recognition theory on the premise that people's well-being is founded on a social acceptance of their presence as a member of a community. Garnering philosophical argumentation and empirical results from developmental psychology, Honneth argues that such acceptance is a *sine qua non* of self-esteem and healthy psychological functioning.

Although few would disagree that people depend to a large extent on those around them to provide emotional support and a sense of belonging, the idea of recognition has some subtleties that make it conceptually more complex. First, Honneth claims that recognition contains an affirmative or positive social regard for actors. Affirmation, however, is different from agreement, and for Honneth it is possible to hold fundamental disagreements with others and still recognize them socially, begging the question as to what exactly the affirmative stance is an affirmation *of*. Second, and relatedly, recognition is considered a precognitive basis for social relations, implying that it precedes particularistic judgements about others' opinions and behaviour. Following a long tradition of critical philosophy, affirmation of human dignity arises from one's nature as a human subject and a participant in society rather than from the position one inhabits in society. Resulting from this, a third aspect of recognition follows that recognitive bases underlie most if not all forms of social relations, a claim to universality that gives recognition its power and also, as we will see, creates difficulties for the theory.

Applied to the workplace, recognition implies a willingness to view colleagues as meaningful contributors to an organizational community, what Honneth and Margalit describe as a 'motivational readiness' to take other people seriously. Related constructs that are well researched in the organizational literature include organizational identification, value alignment or prosocial attitudes. However, recognition is somewhat different because, while these concepts all involve some kind of substantive sharing of attitude features among organizational members (e.g. identity roles, values, objectives), recognition only requires a mutual willingness to exist together. In this sense, recognition might be thought of as necessary but not sufficient for a wide array of other prosocial constructs studied in the workplace.

Recognition theory serves as a corrective for its predecessors in the critical theory tradition, most notably the discursive position of Jürgen Habermas, whose theory of communicative action had been criticized for being overly cognitive. For Habermas, society involved functional distinctions between those elements that were primarily instrumental, constituting a 'system' governed by the 'steering mechanisms' of money and power, and those elements where the intersubjective seeking of truth and justice were privileged as parts of a discursive 'lifeworld'. The distinction between system and lifeworld was useful for constructing a critical theory, because enlightenment ideas of truth and democracy were threatened when the instrumental system began to colonize the lifeworld space, undermining democracy and reason. However, the sphere of instrumental action itself, which presumably includes the corporations and most market institutions, was immune from criticism because its function was profit maximization and not public reason.

By locating recognition at the basis of social systems, Honneth allowed inroads to understanding business ethics because the functional distinction between system and lifeworld was no longer tenable. Because the basis of social ties was not cognitive but affective (and precognitive), the functions of spheres of society was not the fundamental element constituting these spheres; instead, recognition was necessary across social spheres. Conversely, the encroachment of instrumental reason on the lifeworld process was no longer to be critiqued but, on the other hand, instrumental action itself was not immune to critique by being outside of society. Rather, recognition was to be rescued from within instrumental action itself, with market actors no longer able to claim that their goals were inconsistent with humane treatment.

This aspect of recognition theory makes it ideal for applications in business ethics, because it brings the workplace back into the sphere of ethical action. Under recognition theory, the workplace is a sphere of instrumental action, where actors attempt to reach goals, make deals and maximize profits. However, it is also an ethical sphere with existential stakes, where people are engaged as free autonomous human beings, whose actions require acknowledgement as such. Since collective instrumental behaviour is not seen as precluding recognition, but finds its ground in recognition, the question for critique becomes how such recognition becomes lost or neglected in the day-to-day activities of organizations, or in Honneth's terms, how we 'forget' recognition.

Reification, human resources and the forgetfulness of recognition

Because, as discussed above, recognition theory assumes that recognition underlies social relations, the theory essentially supposes that members of social groups have already, in a sense, agreed to recognize each other, but that they may, owing to ignorance or distraction, renege on that commitment or neglect the bases of sociality. Work processes may be based on recognition while simultaneously promoting habits of thought that undermine recognition. Scholars have noted that workplaces often contain implicit models regarding employee agency and the products of work behaviour, and that these models can shape how people view their work, their colleagues and their own identities. Honneth gives the name of 'reification' to those practices that essentialize work processes, making them appear as thing-like or law-like, rather than as social products, and can thus produce a kind of alienation from work.

Reified social interactions, as mentioned above, affect employees along various dimensions. Following Honneth, actors at work begin to see their environments as composed of objective products that are only useful as units of exchange. In addition, they begin to see their social relationships as opportunities for gain and loss, and other actors at work as transaction partners or as competitors for goods or benefits. Finally, they begin to see themselves as bundles of 'human capital', useful to the organization based on their ability to provide tradable value and not for their intrinsic worth as community members. Each of these dimensions reinforces the others, until employees develop a sense of themselves as disembodied and isolated, foreign to both their colleagues and themselves.

Applying the notions of reification and recognition to the workplace would entail exploring the mechanisms by which work processes thus come to stand apart from their social bases in recognition. HRM theory and practice depend on implicit or explicit conceptions of human behaviour in order to focus attention on certain types of productive behaviour and task-related coordination; some scholars have argued that these implicit theories have promoted 'human capital' perspectives and thus create an environment that calls attention away from its social recognitive features. For example, Foss describes human capital as 'a capital asset like any other which may be more or less specialized to specific uses and/or users',[1] a perspective that clearly illustrates a reified view of organizational members.

Organizations promote these kinds of views through particular practices involved in selection, evaluation, incentive and measurement. For instance, by specifying work capacities in terms of individualized, discrete traits and personality profiles, organizations promote views of behaviour that are decontextualized from social processes. Views of human personality are often seen as the result of innate, stable potentials that facilitate a view of human beings as predetermined and similar to 'products' that can be allocated to tasks based on their intrinsic qualities (c.f. the discussion of ethical issues in respect of competences of workforce members in Chapter 23 of this work by Pierre-Yves Sanséau). These qualities, rather than outcomes of people's existential struggles to find meaning and value in the world, are considered as a form of asset specificity, thus negating the intentional and autonomous quality of personality. Research in industrial psychology attempts to 'discover' and taxonomize such qualities in order to best formulate selection and allocation systems. As Honneth argues, the administration of 'talents' through objective measurement may contribute to a culture of observation and surveillance, where individuals are objectified and submitted to a kind of alienating organizational gaze that is typical of reification (the moral issues in this latter tendency to surveillance are discussed in Chapter 15 of this book by Marko Pitesa).

In addition, organizations routinely implement measurement systems geared towards linking employee incentives with performance on the job. While rewards linked to good performance can send messages about employee value and competence, ample empirical research demonstrates that when such rewards are framed as controlling or directing behaviour, they can lead to decrements in employees' intrinsic pleasure on the job. This is because controlling rewards, rather than valuing rewards, sends the message that employee behaviour is being 'bought', rather than rewarded, reflecting a commodified view of employee behaviour. Several scholars have linked such an economic framing of employee work processes to a lack of employee trust and autonomy, as well as a feeling of loss of dignity.

The distinction between reifying and non-reifying reward systems is important because recognition theory acknowledges the potential use of rewards and incentives as signals of social recognition. Honneth argues, for example, that recognition can involve a 'principle of achievement', whereby recognizing successes and competence can instil a sense of social worth among employees. However, it is the symbolic function of incentives as communicating approval (rather than compensating for lost time or effort at work) that constitutes recognition. Organizations that do not recognize this subtle but key difference may promote cultures of reification unwittingly.

Beyond the relatively traditional workplace practices of the individualization and separation of work into specific traits and capacities, and the measurement of performance outcomes linked to economic incentives, recent changes in the world of work also may promote reified perspectives on the part of employees. Sociologists of work have noted the increase in contingent forms of work, such as temporary or part-time work, shortened organizational career tenures and other forms of precariousness at work. Such changes in the structure of the world of work can not only have psychological costs on workers owing to decreased security, but may also promote reification by reconfiguring the 'psychological contracts', or sets of mutual expectations, that people hold at work. Research in the area of psychological contracts suggests that 'relational contracts', which involve a feeling of community and connection between employer and employees, are being increasingly replaced by 'transactional contracts', which involve a view of work as simply an economic exchange with no further expectations for psychological or social support. If this is true, it means that the economic, utilitarian aspect of work is coming to be the implicit expectation within organizations, and the focus on recognitive aspects of work may be increasingly ignored.

Although not exhaustive, the above examples are meant to illustrate some of the ways in which discrete organizational and work practices can promote reification, although they do not, as Honneth emphasizes, determine or cause reification in a direct way. Based on recognition theory, contemporary workplaces (as well as most forms of market exchange) do contain as implicit terms a recognition of human autonomy and dignity, although some forms of social life might be richer in recognition than others. The critique of market exchanges in recognition theory is that they often do not acknowledge these implicit terms, and thus, rather than failing to conform to an outside standard of moral rectitude, they are internally inconsistent with their own premises. To quote Honneth: 'reification has not eliminated the other, non-reified form of praxis but has merely concealed it from our awareness'.[2] Thus, the critique of modern workplaces launched by recognition theory is an internal critique (often referred to as *immanent* critique) aimed at consciousness-raising about our own practices, not an attempt to change fundamental values behind these practices. What does this mean in terms of real changes in the workplace? Accepting the critique of reification, what can actors do to promote recognition?

Social acknowledgement: recognizing the existential engagement of work

The attempt to maintain instrumental, goal-directed behaviour in the workplace, promoting the full use of workers' capacities and talents, without reducing workers to the sum of these capacities, would be the key issue in promoting recognition at work. Simply decrying, as some critical theorists have done, a focus on instrumental action is to deny the possibility of collective production, since such production by definition involves instrumentality. Rather, instrumentality should be understood within a context of mutual recognition and respect that ultimately undergirds collective instrumental action, and thus takes analytical priority over instrumentality.

In its current form, recognition theory does not provide many specific solutions to the problem of 'remembering recognition'; the majority of space devoted to the topic has concerned diagnosing and explaining recognition. Perhaps this is not surprising, since the internal nature of the recognition critique means that current workplace practices, in principle, should be consistent with workplace respect, and thus there is no set of specific behaviours that institutionalize recognition rather than reification. This element of recognition theory has led to criticism that it is an essentially conservative theory, not promoting deep or revolutionary change.

I believe that such critiques are important, but also somewhat misguided. Common sense tells us that *how* something is said (i.e. respectfully or disdainfully) is perhaps just as important as *what* is said (i.e. the semantic content of the words). The same workplace prize can be seen as a manipulative ploy or as a sign of respect, and it is this duplicity of organizational practices that recognition theory helps us to acknowledge. By remembering recognition, what is important is to create a workplace atmosphere where the social bonds holding people together are acknowledged, so that workers recognize the importance of their work in the lives of others, and vice versa. Thus, a recognition solution, at its best, would involve less of a revolution in the workplace (unlike the earlier, Lukacian solution for reification, based on an orthodox Marxism) than a consciousness-raising policy. Although recognition theory has not offered particular organizational policies with regard to such consciousness-raising, keeping in mind the nature of the attentional deficit involved in reification, some initial directions could be proposed.

For example, as discussed above, incentive systems have the potential to both recognize and subvert employee autonomy and respect.

Some research suggests that unexpected rewards that are nevertheless important to workers do not undermine intrinsic motivation and interest in tasks. Such rewards, rather, are considered spontaneous shows of esteem and lead employees to see work as valued, rather than coerced. In this sense, an astute manager would attempt to develop a sense for rewards that, in addition to the predictable, standardized incentive system, would 'top off' such a system with signals of value, potentially changing the ways that employees interpret their incentives in general.

In addition, some literature on recognition in business ethics suggests that cultivating a culture of diversity and inclusion can increase recognitive attention in organizations. Rather than traditional notions of diversity, which take a 'diversity capital' approach by viewing diverse workers as sources of new information and skills, these views frame diversity culture as a matter of finding solidarity across social groups. Where groups may be driven apart by social stereotypes, within the organizational space they are able to build ties of solidarity by working together on meaningful projects, thus promoting a social bond that could potentially carry over into other spheres of society. Although such an outcome might sound idealistic, the key would be to emphasize a bond of solidarity through inclusion of diversity, rather than a focus on diversity as difference.

In these examples, the actual changes made to organizational practices may be small and often mostly symbolic. For example, in their discussion of solidarity, Pless and Maak recommend exchanging the term 'human relations' for '*human resources*' to emphasize the relational bases of recognition at work.[3] Such a change in terminology would only be effective to the extent that it sent a convincing message to organizational members about management's views of their relationship. However, the importance of this message should not be underestimated, and emphasizing this importance is a key contribution of recognition theory.

Concluding discussion

Business scholars and managers are increasingly becoming aware of the ways in which organizations affect personal and social well-being, and are looking for ways to think about work that recognizes these effects. Critical theory has a long tradition of analysis of the work role, and recognition theory is perhaps the state of the art in the critical theory tradition. Thus, the relative lack of treatment of issues of recognition in the organizational and business ethics literature is somewhat surprising. On the other hand, some works have appeared, and there is reason to think that this area is ripe for future development.

Because work is still one of the most central categories in people's lives, taking up most of their waking hours and demanding much of their physical and mental energy, finding ways to ensure the workplace is a proper forum for personal and social flourishing is a critical task. The recent precarization of the workplace does not make this task easier, nor does the increasing conception of work in terms of market transaction over relational connection. The most urgent task for recognition theory is to combine its observations about the key role of recognition and social esteem in personal development with the seemingly eroding bases of recognition in the macro environment.

While earlier views of reification saw the only solution to this seeming dilemma in proletarian revolution, and the final transcendence of capitalism, Honneth's theory allows space for improvement within the status quo, a feature that may be seen as either an advantage or a disadvantage of the theory. For those who would like to see radical change, recognition theory might seem at best a palliative to please workers while the fundamental machinery of exploitation continues unhindered. For recognition theorists, however, the issue of exploitation was always symbolic as well as material, and material benefit only aids in human flourishing when it becomes embedded in people's life worlds. To expect increased salary and benefits to make employees happy at work would be itself, from this perspective, to concede to a reified and disempowering view of workers.

Other criticisms of recognition theory have viewed as idealistic its assumptions about a basic affirmative bond at the basis of social relations. Although Honneth defines such affirmation very broadly, allowing recognition to coexist with negative emotions and hostile behaviour, some critics have claimed that some social relations may be, in essence, rotten to the core, based on exploitation and domination. As Judith Butler argues, for example, some relationships are abusive and exploitative, not because their members forgot their original reason for being together, but rather as their reason for being, for example, in patriarchal or slave relationships, in cases of domestic abuse or bullying at work. Individuals may enter such relationships in order to exert power over or exploit others. To call such cases 'forgetfulness' may not do justice to the wide and often disturbing range of human relationships.

That said, much of the validity of such criticisms depends on how one interprets recognition theory's framing of the primary bond of recognition. The wider it is framed, the more it is able to take into account the diversity of human social arrangements. On the other hand, to the extent that recognition is consistent with exploitative or abusive behaviour, it loses its force as a normative compass and comes to look like an abstract formalism.

The task of research in recognition theory at work is thus, at the theoretical level, to better specify how social bonds operate in the workplace, and empirically to examine how such bonds can be ignored or neglected. Simply beginning such a discussion, in this author's view, can direct attention to areas needed to raise consciousness about recognition. Thus, perhaps for scholars to affirm the sociality and connectedness of human beings, even in the most instrumental areas of the workplace, has some value in itself, redefining in a more humane way processes that we previously took to be purely instrumental.

CASE STUDY: PERFORMANCE, DIGNITY AND TRUST AT SCOTT PAPER MILL[4]

The Scott Paper Corporation is a US-based manufacturing corporation whose production is based in paper products. As one of the oldest US paper companies, Scott had a long tradition in product innovation, being among the first companies to market now universally accepted products such as roll-based paper towels and toilet paper, among other paper products. Scott had built a reputation for a wide variety of high-quality products, which one plant manager described as 'the best paper in the world'.

As an industry, Scott workers were highly unionized, under the United Paper-workers International Union (UPIU), which included carpenters, machinists and other technical operators involved in the industry. Scott had built a reputation on strong relations with workers, and its labour relations were considered one of its competitive advantages, leading to higher-quality products and a relatively stable accord between management and labour. This stability was, in part, a result of the relative inelasticity of the paper products Scott produced, allowing generous benefits to be accorded to workers without losing the consumer market.

Just as with many other US-based manufacturing companies in the 1970s and 1980s, Scott began to feel pressure from foreign competition, and began to experiment with 'Japanese'-style manufacturing techniques and other efficiency-raising practices, known collectively as 'high performance work practices'. These practices are marked by high levels of interdependence, as well as increased job responsibilities and flexible job categories. Replacing older, 'Taylorist' forms of factory work, high performance work practices necessitate high levels of organizational trust and commitment, and a willingness of workers to adapt to flexible working conditions.

The adoption of high performance work systems in the US tested the robustness of worker–management relations in many industries across the manufacturing sector. The flexibility and interdependence involved in these systems meant that traditional job roles were flexibilized, creating uncertainty among organizational actors. As in many manufacturing industries, the success of high performance work systems depended on the establishment of strong ties between workers and management, and a feeling of plant-wide solidarity, mutual respect and teamwork. On the other hand, lacking a strong sense of the basic respect of management for worker well-being and competence, the high performance work practices could appear as ways to do away with traditional forms of work and labour–management interaction, including traditional forms of job seniority and worker stability, that provides stable social identities to the workers. These forms of social well-being and interaction had been forged over decades of hard struggle and would not be given up without an acknowledgement that changes were being made in collaboration *with* workers, not *to* workers.

When Scott Paper Corporation attempted to implement high performance systems in its paper mills, it adopted a 'Jointness' paradigm to try to spur increased cooperation among the workers and management in the different factories, attempting to avoid provoking union resistance. Jointness involved labour–management teams that were organized at the plant level, who, with the aid of outside consultants and experts, would find ways to develop organizational trust, and develop employee skills and human capital. The trust workshops would go hand-in-hand with the flexibilization of work processes in the plant, systems of quality improvement to improve earnings, which had been stagnating at Scott. The trust workshops served to brace the workers psychologically for the impending changes in work design. The idea was, in part, to give back to the employees through skill development and community building what they were losing in job security and stability.

The Jointness programme was generally considered a success, and the transition to high performance work systems was relatively smooth in most plants. The UPIU viewed the relatively large economic concessions given by Scott to its workers as examples of good practice, and were willing to negotiate and reciprocate on their side. However, in the Westbrook and Hinkley Mills in Maine, workers resisted the changes, rejecting the notion of Jointness as inauthentic. What were the differences between their reaction and the wider union reactions that made the concessions offered by Scott relatively unattractive?

First and foremost, the mills that were least responsive to Scott's changes were those where the employees read economic ulterior motives into the labour concessions. In other words, for many mills where strong community and solidarity ties were present, receiving benefits such as extra paid days off were not compelling when they saw that each mill was being treated as an independent profit centre, with unproductive mills being closed down. Even though these mills were high performers, the instrumentality implied in this strategy corroded trust and reframed work as purely economic. In one of the mills, where a particular paper line was being closed, one worker complained not because of the economic implications, but because he thought that no one else would be able to produce paper of such high quality, and the product would be lost to the world. This type of pride in a product was anathema to a human capital approach where workers trade or lease their skills for products that do not express their personal and social ties.

On the other hand, the mills that were most responsive to the changes were those that were able to create a shared sense of purpose between management and workers, sensing a common threat in the increased competitiveness from opening markets. Rather than Scott closing down its mills, they viewed their task as an attempt to make Scott competitive and thus preserve the well-being of both managers and employees. Although the economic environments of these firms may not have been any different, their workers viewed a common purpose between managers and employees, and were able to flexibly switch roles when necessary to preserve the organization.

The situation at Scott exemplifies how assumptions regarding solidarity and social recognition within the workplace can change people's willingness to work with colleagues and sacrifice for the organization, independently of economic factors. Although such cooperation may improve organizational performance and outcomes in the long run, such performance, it has been argued, is best seen as a side effect of good practice, and not as an end in itself. Competitiveness, in some cases, may paradoxically depend on its taking back seat to solidarity.

CONCEPTUAL QUESTIONS

1   Under what conditions does reification characterize a work relationship?
2   Why does reification consist in a 'forgetting' of recognition? What is being forgotten exactly?
3   Does agreement have to exist between parties in order for recognition to take place? Can recognition exist if there is *no agreement whatsoever*?
4   What is the difference between instrumental action and reification? Is it possible to treat employees instrumentally without reifying them?

CRITICAL QUESTIONS

1   If all social bonds presuppose interpersonal recognition, is this also true of social relationships involving abuse or exploitation?
2   If exploitation is nothing more than a misrecognition, does this mean that those who exploit others do not understand what they are doing? Can this really always be the case?

Notes

1 N. J. Foss (2008) 'Human capital and transaction cost economics', *SMG Working Paper No. 2*, Copenhagen Business School Working Paper Series, p. 8.

2 A. Honneth (2008) 'Reification and recognition: A new look at an old idea'. In M. Jay (ed.), *Reification: A new look at an old idea*. Oxford: Oxford University Press, p. 31.

3 N. M. Pless and T. Maak (2004) 'Building an inclusive diversity culture: Principles, processes and practice', *Journal of Business Ethics*, 54: 129–147.

4 The following case study is drawn from M. G. Hillard (2005) 'The failure of labor-management cooperation at two Maine paper mills: A case study', *Advances in Industrial and Labor Relations*, 14: 127–171.

7

PRIVATE VICES, BUSINESS VIRTUES?

The institutional strategy of legitimated online gambling in Italy

Carmelo Mazza

Chapter overview

Which principles ought to govern business practice? Some contributions in this volume meaningfully address this key question concerning normative business ethics. However, this question brings along another one, which is the key topic of my contribution: How do the principles that ought to govern business practice change? Old debates in political philosophy, starting from de Groot (1625/2002), assume that what ought to govern society is stable or changes very slowly. Empirical observations apparently support this assumption when we examine the evolution of societal values, religions, international relations, etc. Does it apply to business? Empirical observations and the large stream of research on institutional change (for an overview, see Dacin *et al.* 2002) seem to suggest that the speed of evolution of normative standards for business is more controversial.

By looking at the *Harvard Business Review* supplement on 75 years of management ideas (Sibbet 1997), we can notice how principles that ought to govern business practice have changed several times. The same observation underlies the seminal piece by Barley and Kunda (1992), which outlines the two waves of normative and rational control shaping managerial practices. From a more pragmatic perspective, Abrahamson's (1996) arguments on management fashion coincide with the idea that principles governing business practice are expected to change quite often: from scientific management, to rational approaches, cultural views, economic maximization, etc.

From the business ethics' perspective, it is therefore interesting to understand how principles governing business practice change. In particular, it is interesting to analyse how business practices, once perceived as borderline from the ethical viewpoint, may later become widespread. Institutional theory has fruitfully investigated how practices become diffused and dominant from several theoretical angles ranging from cultural persistence (Zucker 1977) to agency dilemmas at the micro organizational level (DiMaggio 1988).

In order to contribute on such a stream of investigation, I selected a peculiar case showing how what is accepted and legitimized by the State as an ethical practice may deeply change in very few years and pave the way for the birth of a profitable industry. This is the case of the wave of gambling regulation from 1999 to 2011, turning Italy from an almost protectionist country to the Continental Europe market with the widest legal gambling portfolio (Tani 2010). The opening of the gambling market has been accompanied by the emergence of principles reinforcing the ethical acceptance of gambling. In this sense, the case is of particular interest in revealing how the role of the State and the business community to promote legitimated practices could shape the perception of what principles should govern the business, finally framing what is ethical, even for a critical 'borderline' industry. In other words, the case shows us how, by creating legitimated business practices and claiming their compliance to high ethical standards, the *private vice* of gambling has become, in less than one decade, a *business virtue*.

The chapter is structured into three sections. First, the theoretical lens, looking at the dynamics leading to the acceptance of the selected gambling practices outlined. Second, the case of the regulation of gambling in Italy is analysed by emphasizing which principles have emerged to govern the business. Finally, discussion and conclusion are reported on the case focusing on how the concept of ethical business practice has been shifting along with the opening of the legal gambling market. Since in effect the chapter will be looking at the interaction between, and evolution of, competing moral principles and philosophies that may at various times be thought to be the normative basis that ought to govern gambling practice, it is in effect at Level 3 of critique as outlined in Chapter 2 above (metaethics). This is true even if much of the focus here will be on how institutional factors in effect influence the evolution of moral principles rather than on the critical rational debate itself between competing moralities.

The rise of ethical practices: an institutional perspective

Institutional strategies have been largely investigated from the perspective of organizational actors adopting business practices (Westphal *et al.* 1997; Scott *et al.* 2000) and looking for legitimacy in the field (Singh *et al.* 1986; Mazza *et al.* 2005; Lawrence *et al.* 2009). Approaches differ upon two main assumptions: 1) strategies are shaped by the timing of adoption, distinguishing early *vs* late adopters (Tolbert and Zucker 1983; Kennedy and Fiss 2009) and 2) strategies depend on the pressure coming from the competitive and institutional environment (Oliver 1991; Goodstein 1994).

In these frameworks, the relations among institutional strategies and ethical norms have remained largely unexplored. Institutional strategies emerge and are selected within the domain of legitimized practices; in other words, institutional strategies are typically intended to avoid the emergence of legitimacy crises. The ethical implications that underpin the rise and adoption of institutional strategies are basically dealt with by assuming institutional strategy alignment with taken-for-granted or conventional norms as a way to ensure full ethical compliance. Of course, this approach leaves open the question about the validity of the conventional norms assumed.

The tight link, almost a reduction, of ethics to taken-for-grantedness or mere conventions brings two important logical consequences. First, ethics is dependent on the environment and environmental change taking the role of the revisited iron cage suggested by DiMaggio and Powell (1983) even for ethics. Second, by assuming that organizations may positively affect what becomes taken for granted (Oliver 1991), organizations themselves are able to set up the practices that later ought to govern business in an ethical way. The Habermasian stance holding that we (re)produce what in turn constrains us (Habermas 1981), as well as Perrow's (1986) suggestion that we have met the environment and it is us, simply describe the way ethical principles arise and spread.

From the ethical perspective, as well as from the organizational one, these approaches leave unaddressed several key questions. The most relevant one is the question on how ethical dilemmas in decision making emerge and are solved. If conformity to the environment, to prevailing conventions, is the key to understand what ought to govern business, it is unclear how dilemmas may emerge (other than in very clearly multicultural societies that may lack any well-defined set of moral conventions taken for granted by all). On the contrary, if interest and agency, as suggested by DiMaggio (1988) and, recently, Battilana and D'Aunno (2009), shape the way the environment is enacted, ethical dilemmas, as we normally think of them, constantly arise. More interestingly, bringing interest and agency back into the dynamics creating the principles that ought to govern business allows us to understand how the interplay among institutional actors with divergent interests may generate ethical clashes.

By using the concept developed by Lawrence and Suddaby (2006) and Lawrence *et al.* (2009), the description of the institutional work organizational actors put in place in order to execute their institutional strategies sheds light on several ethical clashes as well as on the rise of those practices accepted as ethical. In particular, by delving into the agency nature of institutional strategies, the concept of institutional work also allows us to shed light on the ethical profile of organizational actions when regulatory issues and public/private interplay are key. In these cases, ethics directly involves State organizations that have to cope with both the intent to legitimize a field and the obligation to prevent the promotion of unethical behaviours in society.

Institutional work is an increasingly adopted concept to look at field and organizational transformations. It enables researchers to dig into the micro dynamics of institutional change by bringing an agency perspective back into the institutional picture (Lawrence *et al.* 2009). This has not been the first attempt to link action with institutional dynamics. Similar attempts were made by introducing an actor-network perspective into the institutional approach (Czarniawska and Sevon 1996) and by outlining how strategic action emerges from the possibility of challenging institutional pressure (Oliver 1991; White 1992).

All these attempts converge in dealing with strategic action as a factor for institutional transformation. However, these approaches have not underlined the implications of an action view of institutional dynamics on ethical considerations. In particular, action is seen as shaping the institutional landscape by framing a coalition and clashes of actors as well as creating the condition for practices and views to emerge (Zilber 2009). Accordingly, action – namely, institutional work – shapes what are expected to be the legitimated practices in a field. Lawrence and Suddaby (2006) reveal the underpinning connection between institutional work and legitimacy; institutional work defines, based on a daily effort, what is in the process of being legitimated or de-legitimated. Looking at institutional work patterns is therefore a useful perspective to understand what practices are accepted and what they result from.

Accepted practices are those expected to govern business. One legacy of the institutional theory is in fact to assume that institutions, that is, taken-for-granted practices, are perceived as 'the way things are' (Zucker 1977). From the institutional perspective it is therefore consistent to make ethical practices and institutionalized practices converge. As a matter of fact, from this perspective, to study what is ethical is therefore to study what is taken for granted. Since it can be argued that although persistence is a key trait of taken-for-grantedness, institutional transformations are ongoing (Lawrence *et al.* 2009) and it is important to look at how taken-for-granted conventional practices are shaped and changed by the purposeful action of organizations and networks of actors. Changes in conventional moral principles may be a reflection of changes of business practice and thereby of the ethical principles that ought to underpin business practice.

This is the core of the narrative on the development of regulations for online gambling in Italy and its diffusion throughout most of Europe. In the next section, I will give a close look at the Italian gambling development in recent years. The reported case will provide the empirical evidence for the following discussions and conclusions over the way the principles that ought to govern business change and how they may rapidly change. It describes how the regulatory effort, by creating a new set of rules to institutionalize, has deeply changed what was considered taken for granted about gambling. In particular, the assumption of what is illegal in gambling has been questioned and transformed. At the end of this stage, gambling emerges as a legitimated field and several practical principles are outlined to govern this specific business, constructing the ethical norms to apply to a previously unethical domain.

THE REGULATION OF GAMBLING IN ITALY 1999–2011

The growth of gambling in Italy is a phenomenon raising a wide interest in Europe. As reported by important actors in the industry (Agipronews 2011), France, Denmark, Hungary and Sweden have undertaken ongoing discussions with the

Italian Regulatory Agency in order to define a successful regulatory path. The last gaming portfolio opening, according to the Law no. 88/2009, has turned the Italian online gambling market into the largest regulated one throughout the world, apart from the UK. In 2010, gross gambling turnover[1] in Italy reached €61 billion (AAMS 2011) (see Table 7.1). Online gross gambling turnover in Italy has almost reached €5 billion, still not including the new products defined in the Law no. 88/2009, some of them (cash poker and casino games) launched on 18 July 2011. Gaming Tax revenues for the Italian State reached almost €10 billion in 2010 (AAMS 2011). In 2003, a parliamentary investigation on gaming in Italy (Italian Senate 2003) estimated the whole Italian market as about €36 billion; more than half of this gross gambling turnover originated from illegal, unregulated gambling activities. In the same year, legal gross gambling turnover amounted to about €15 billion.

This evolution is the effect of a process involving the regulatory and the business side, the role of EC regulatory stances and the narrative of responsible gaming that provided constant reference for all business communication and regulatory initiatives. First, actors have followed different action paths, although all of them were protecting very well-defined interests. Second, the effort to regulate has been shaped by the constraints coming from EC legislation on gambling. To pass EC control over the regulation is still a key success for all the regulatory authorities. Finally, the narrative of responsibility and compliance has been in these years much more visible than the pure business success narrative. Accomplishments in terms of responsible gambling have been widely communicated by key actors. The regulation enforcing responsible gambling has been largely supported by customers and related associations.

From a law perspective, gambling in Italy is illegal. This simple statement does not imply it is forbidden; it only implies that only the State can, by law and consequent applied regulation, decide to allow gambling. As a matter of fact, gambling

TABLE 7.1 Gross gambling turnover trend 2003–2010

Segment	2003	2004	2005	2006	2007	2008	2009	2010
Lotto	6,938	11,689	7,315	6,588	6,177	5,852	5,664	5,232
Superenalotto	2,066	1,836	1,981	2,000	1,940	2,509	3,776	3,524
Lotteries	282	594	1,546	3,970	7,955	9,274	9,434	9,368
Pool games	497	443	359	304	229	175	144	99
Sport betting	1,123	1,304	1,489	2,281	2,591	3,909	4,026	4,396
Horse race betting	2,962	2,903	2,775	2,908	2,748	2,272	1,981	1,730
Bingo	1,257	1,542	1,553	1,755	1,726	1,636	1,512	1,954
Gaming machines	367	4,474	11,470	15,436	18,827	21,685	25,525	32,004
Poker (skill games)	–	–	–	–	–	242	2,348	3,146
TOTAL	**15,125**	**24,786**	**28,487**	**35,243**	**42,192**	**47,554**	**54,410**	**61,453**

Source: Corte dei Conti (2011)

in Italy is a State monopoly (like tobacco sales). So, in principle, any gambling activity that is not explicitly allowed and regulated by the State is illegal and forbidden. Owing to this legal approach, shared by many European countries, the story of the development of gambling in Italy is mainly the story of State law and regulation. Following the institutional approach, it is a story of how new principles are adopted by the State and later spread into the business community (Dobbin *et al.* 1993).

Legal gambling activity was already present in Italy after the Second World War. Pool games on football matches – the highly popular Totocalcio, existing in similar versions in Spain (Quiniela) and France – started on 6 May 1946, managed on behalf of the State by a private company. At the same time, betting on horse races was permitted within horse race tracks and in authorized dedicated shops. Horse race betting was highly popular in Italy although restricted to a group of highly loyal punters. Lotteries spread during the 1970s, also as a result of the development of TV-related shows. A form of yearly Christmas lottery – similar to the Loteria de Navidad diffused in Spain – with the final draw taking place the night of 6 January (the night of 'La Befana') was very popular until the early 1990s and is still offered nowadays. The TV show on the night of the final draw reached an audience comparable to top football matches of the national team.

Starting from 1999, fixed odds betting was introduced in the legal gambling portfolio to be offered in horse race betting shops and later, in 2000, by licensed betting shop owners. Along with the authorization of bingo halls at the end of 2000, they represented the first important opening of the legal gambling portfolio in Italy. This opening was primarily the result of the State interest in facing the decline of Totocalcio revenues, which were funding the Italian sport movement. At that time, the perception of a wide illegal gambling activity in Italy was very diffused, partly because of the scandals on football (soccer) match fixing that had hit Italian Serie A credibility since the early 1980s, even involving well-known top football players, team managers and CEOs.

As a matter of fact, the mounting evidence of large illegal gambling activities and likely criminal organizations' implications provided the rationale for a deep parliamentary investigation that took place in 2001/2002 (Italian Senate 2003). Direct parliamentary intervention put the definition of a strategy to face illegal gambling on the agenda of public administration and gambling companies. This led to the operational definition of the role of the Amministrazione Autonoma dei Monopoli di Stato (AAMS) as the regulatory authority for gambling. AAMS was given responsibility to undertake all the needed initiatives to reduce the size of illegal gambling and increase the tax revenues on the industry.

At that time, the industry consisted of three main Italian companies active in betting and lotteries, and many small gambling entrepreneurs running their own betting shops or small networks. Besides that, licensed owners of bingo halls were active in this specific segment, including foreign companies specialized in bingo operations, mainly in Spain and Latin America where this game was very popular. At the same time, the largest portion of illegal – because unregulated – gambling was in gaming machines, 'videopoker', diffused in bars and small gaming locations, and in illegal betting. The choice made by AAMS and finally supported by the government was to start the process of an extensive gambling regulation.

Based on the analysis of regulatory law and decrees, regulation looked to be based on three main premises: a) the presence of a State-owned system to track all the gambling operations; b) the detailed definition (called 'typification') of legal gambling products; and c) the adoption of a multi-licensee scheme – with the exception of lotteries – allowing the introduction of degrees of competition in each of the gambling segments. The presence of the State-owned system brings several consequences in terms of IT requirements for those who aim to get a licence. Italy was the first large market to introduce the real-time ongoing data exchange between gambling infrastructure and State-owned systems. After Italy, all the regulated online markets are adopting similar solutions. The impact has been twofold: on one side, the enforcement of State control created an entry barrier for those companies unable or unwilling to change their operating systems already working outside Italy. On the other hand, it meant that gambling companies were therefore acting also as providers of IT services for those who were willing to enter. Thus, IT practices intended to increase State control ended up creating further business opportunities.

The typification was a key move shaping all Italian regulation. From this approach viewpoint, games were not generic labels (poker, sport betting, etc.); legal games were carefully defined by the State along with their key parameters (tax rates, minimum payout, maximum winnings, minimum and maximum bets, etc.). By defining what is a legal bet or a legal poker, laws and decrees were shaping the field of what was ethically acceptable. In other words, betting was still illegal unless it precisely met the State definition. Under these premises, it was possible to define the principles that ought to govern betting business. Many of them were already reported in the law and decrees typifying legal games (for instance, customer protection, customer information, responsible gaming, self-exclusion rules as well as the use on all games images of the logo of AAMS reporting the label 'Gioco Sicuro' – safe gambling). Typification appears to be a trademark of Italian regulation and had a big influence on the definition of new gambling regulations in other countries such as France, Denmark and Spain.

Finally, the regulatory framework largely adopted a multi-licensee scheme for online gaming, betting, bingo and gaming machines. Unlike several existing regulations, and previous Italian experience, monopolies only remained for lotteries. This choice resulted in a significant change; the regulating authority, AAMS, was now part of a system where several players were interacting. Competition first emerged in land-based betting and bingo around several local operators. After 2007, fierce competition arose in the online gambling segment where all the main gambling MNCs operate.

These three premises have been reinforced by the new regulations issued in the last two years mainly on online gambling. In particular, recent regulation has focused on responsible gaming and on transparency of ownership structure. Interestingly, all the regulatory initiatives are generating additional costs to gambling companies but they are expanding the industry size and increasing tax revenues. Regulation consistency has emerged as a goal for AAMS, implying that a workable regulation is the basis for a growing industry. Recently, the entry of investment funds in the ownership of gambling firms and the increasing interest on the links of gambling with occupation have revealed how the gambling industry is little by little coming to resemble well-institutionalized sectors with ethical implications no longer questioned.

Discussion and conclusion

The story of the development of gambling in Italy reveals several interesting elements from the business ethics viewpoint. In 2003 in Italy gambling was mainly illegal and, where legal, gambling business was perceived as unethical. The stigma of gambling as unethical was represented, among other symbolic events, by the prosecution of top Italian football players in 1980. The coexistence of the perception of gambling as unethical and the progressive institutionalization of gambling business practices poses a question to be addressed in the discussion of the case: what if a misalignment between critical ethical principles and taken-for-granted practices emerges?

Our arguments stand on the assumption that institutional dynamics work to ensure that such misalignments are temporary. From the institutional approach perspective, misalignments may emerge during a deinstitutionalization stage, when previously taken-for-granted practices are in the process of being replaced by others (Davis *et al.* 1994). Institutional theory has first hypothesized this as a temporary and extraordinary condition, since institutional pressures effectively work to ensure persistence of conventional principles and taken-for-granted practices. This is the core of the 'iron cage revisited' argument by DiMaggio and Powell (1983).

Today, a significant stream of institutional research has shown how the creation and re-creation of institutionalized practices is constantly in progress. Boxembaum and Strandgaard (2009) have shown how in the domain of academia institutionalization and deinstitutionalization processes are constantly under way. In a similar vein about management practices, Abrahamson and Fairchild (1999) did show that legitimized management practices emerge and disappear all the time. So it can be argued that, within the business domain, taken-for-grantedness is always *in process* and misalignment between what is generally and conventionally accepted and what ought ideally to be may emerge at any time.

What happens when such misalignments are in place? Three answers are possible. First, ethical principles that ought to govern business practice are those expected gradually to become taken for granted. In other words, ethics is supposed to be institutionalized and become dominant. This is a positive view, where finally ethical practices are established over time since there is an underpinning consistency between ethics, social norms and value driving institutionalization processes. It can be argued from the case that regulation drafting has been a process involving actors and including conflicting interests. The convergence among ethical principles and institutionalized norms did not occur spontaneously.

However, evidence of tensions between ethical principles and business practices, as discussed in a variety of other chapters in this volume (see, for example, the case study in Chapter 1), reveals how a second answer is possible: ethics and legitimated business practices may not converge. Critical views of business ethics argue that ethical clashes are the result of these distinct institutionalization processes. Coming back to Barley and Kunda's (1992) seminal paper, waves of rational and normative control may explain why at a specific point in time, rational (economic) drivers of business practices may prevail over normative (ethical) drivers of business practices. Barley and Kunda's (1992) arguments on waves of organizational control suggest that competing institutionalization processes are common in the business domain. As a consequence, competition and clashes between business practices and ethical principles are not the temporary outcome of acute institutional changes but the ongoing outcome of the production and reproduction of social norms. The development of the gambling regulation in Europe is now part of a general process of regulation of this industry promoted by the EU. When Italy started the process it is easy to see the impact of the parliamentary investigation into evidence of illegal gambling. However, rather than being an effect of an overarching regulatory process, gambling regulation was seen at least in part as a way to increase tax revenues (see Table 7.2) in a time of State budget downsizing.

A third perspective is, however, possible. Building on narrative organizational approaches (Czarniawska 1997), it can be argued that misalignment among taken-for-granted practices and ethical principles that ought to govern business might reflect the presence of different narratives of ethics and business. Narratives of business are not always reflected by taken-for-granted practices. Current narratives of success and innovation tend to overcome institutionalized practices. Narratives of clashes between what is successful and 'the way things are' are reported as signs of good innovativeness and fruitful creativity. This may encourage the misalignment and generate a positive view of the misalignment itself. According to this view, narratives supporting new principles that ought to govern business practice emerge, changing the perception of what should be an ethical practice. An example in this sense is the current emphasis on energy saving compared with previous emphasis on the research of top performance – namely speed and acceleration – cars. The diffusion of online gambling is a similar example: the narrative of gambling as a human attitude and as pure entertainment points towards new principles looking at responsible gambling and customer protection. A few years ago, gambling prohibition and full State control over limited legal gambling operations were just 'the way things are' in many European countries, while the UK, with its widespread fixed odd betting tradition, private gambling firms (bookmakers) and bingo halls, was seen as an almost unique peculiarity.

The description on how principles that ought to govern may change reveal how a concept is tightly coupled with ethical practices: legitimacy. In the recent story of gambling in Italy, legitimacy is the joint effect of three factors: State regulation, the acceptance of these rules by gambling companies and the diffusion of gambling. Using Suchman's (1995) framework, State regulation provided the basis for *moral* legitimacy by defining legal practices. Interestingly, typification was intended to define practices rather than legal principles. Regulation does not define the rules for legal gambling but the specific practices to be adopted can be morally legitimated, such as the format of game accounts, the rules for customer information (AAMS decree 2006), the obligation to IT certification (AAMS decree 2011). Unlike other regulatory approaches in Europe, Italian regulation aimed at defining the principles to govern gambling business or, at least, most of them.

Acceptance by gambling companies provided the basis for *pragmatic* legitimacy. Practices created by regulation have been the result of a complex process where State and operators have worked together. Practices of business require a large support from the industry. The State involved operators in order to find a balance of two competing interests: the State interest on regulation and customer protection, leading to higher tax revenues, and the self-interest of operators aiming at higher profits. The outcome of this balance is the trend of tax revenues from gambling, showing a reducing tax rate but a significant growth in absolute terms (see Table 7.2).

The diffusion of gambling provided the basis for cognitive legitimacy, based on comprehensiveness and taken-for-grantedness (Suchman 1995). Similar success is confirmed by the wave of regulation inspired by Italy already launched in France and on its way in Spain, Greece, Denmark, the Netherlands and Germany. Recent data by AAMS published in January 2011 report that in Italy there are 1.4 million euros of game accounts only for online gambling. The diffusion of gambling and the related business practices turn gambling into a taken-for-granted field. Gambling companies are no longer hiding and are getting more visible by increasing advertising expenses and sponsorships of sport activities. Following the regulation framework, lotteries are financing cultural events and renovations.

So, by the process of legitimating business practices, the State has been able to turn gambling into an accepted activity even though higher standards of security and regulation are asked by the parliament and no-profit associations. What is interesting for the purpose of this chapter is to show that the trigger has been to understand that industry legitimacy was intertwined with the creation of the principles that ought to govern the gambling business. In other words, AAMS understood that the industry was not in the condition to develop these principles out of pragmatic legitimacy. Industry actors need to receive support by sharing the generation of principles with the regulatory agency that provides moral legitimacy.

TABLE 7.2 Gambling tax revenues in Italy 2003–2010

Segment	2003	2004	2005	2006	2007	2008	2009	2010
Tax revenues	3,457	7,298	6,157	6,718	7,195	7,747	8,793	8,734
Avg. tax rate	22.9%	29.4%	21.6%	19.1%	17.1%	16.3%	16.2%	14.2%

Source: Corte dei Conti (2011)

The resulting institutional process was able to create principles to govern business practice that can be later made explicit to society at large to make them accepted. This is the case, for example, of responsible gaming, with self-exclusion as well as with the full visibility of the AAMS 'Gioco Sicuro' brand on every gambling device, online and land-based.

The main concluding remark is that gambling in Italy is a successful story of the creation of principles to govern business, which are now taken for granted. Taken-for-grantedness is achieved by an intense institutional process involving the key industry actors and AAMS, as well as other actors involved in the regulation. First it might be interesting to explore cases where success is not so clear or when conflicts among actors have prevented the institutional process from succeeding. Second, the way ethical standards emerge out of previously unethical activities deserves more scholarly attention. In the Italian gambling case, new ethical standards emerged with the creation by the State (AAMS) of new principles to govern gambling practice; in other industries, ethical standards may emerge from competing interests and actors' networks. Cases of competing standards may help understand where the rise of business ethics is concretely rooted.

Studying ethics out of gambling may look a provocative choice and, indeed, it is to a certain extent. Nevertheless, it is important to notice how ethics is not made of quasi-immutable values. Ethics in business reflects the volatility of the environment and the ongoing social work that institutions and organizations daily undertake. This chapter is an attempt to bring such works and the related dynamics into the business ethics picture; what is observed on gambling, from the ethical perspective, does not look that far from other more mainstream economic sectors.

Note

1   By gross gambling turnover, it is here intended the amount of money actually played, including the winnings that players play again. Gross gambling turnover represents a rough indicator of the market size and should not be confused with market profits for the gambling company.

References

AAMS (2006) 'Misure per la regolamentazione della raccolta a distanza delle scommesse del bingo e delle lotterie'. *Decreto direttoriale n. 2006/7902/GIOCHI/UD Mar 21, 2006.*

AAMS (2011) 'Decorrenza degli obblighi relativi alla raccolta del gioco a distanza, attuativo dell'articolo 24, commi da 11 a 26, della legge 7 luglio 2009, n. 88'. *Decreto direttoriale n. 2011/190/CGV Feb 8, 2011.*

Abrahamson, E. (1996) 'Management fashion', *Academy of Management Review*, 21: 254–285.

Abrahamson, E. and Fairchild, G. (1999) 'Management fashion: Lifecycles, triggers, and collective learning processes', *Administrative Science Quarterly*, 44: 708–740.

Agipronews (2011) *Serve una visione politica più generale per il settore; Agenzia dei giochi fondamentale.* Roma, 24 May.

Barley, S. R. and Kunda, G. (1992) 'Design and devotion: Surges of rational and normative ideologies of control in managerial discourse', *Administrative Science Quarterly*, 37: 363–399.

Battilana, J. and D'Aunno, T. (2009) 'Institutional work and the paradox of embedded agency'. In T. Lawrence, R. Suddaby and B. Leca (eds), *Institutional Work: Actors and agency in institutional studies of organizations*. Cambridge: Cambridge University Press, pp. 31–58.

Boxembaum, E. and Strandgaard, J. (2009) 'Scandinavian Institutionalism – A case of institutional work'. In T. Lawrence, R. Suddaby and B. Leca (eds), *Institutional Work: Actors and agency in institutional studies of organizations*. Cambridge: Cambridge University Press, pp. 178–204.

Corte dei Conti (2011) *Rapporto 2011 sul coordinamento della finanza pubblica*. Roma, 18 May 2011.

Czarniawska, B. (1997) *Narrating the Organizations: Dramas of institutional identity*. Chicago, IL: The University of Chicago Press.

Czarniawska, B. and Sevon, G. (1996) *Translating organizational change*. Berlin: De Gruyter.

Dacin, T., Goodstein, J. and Scott, W. R. (2002) 'Institutional theory and institutional change: Introduction to the special research forum', *Academy of Management Journal*, 45: 43–56.

Davis, G. F., Diekmann, K. A. and Tinsley, C. H. (1994) 'The decline and fall of the conglomerate firm in the 1980s: The deinstitutionalization of an organizational form', *American Sociological Review*, 59: 547–570.

De Groot, H. (1625/2002) *De Iure Belli ac Pacis*. Paris: Buon.

DiMaggio, P. (1988) 'Interest and agency in institutional theory. In L. G. Zucker (ed.), *Institutional Patterns and Organizations: Culture and environment*. Cambridge, MA: Ballinger, pp. 3–21.

DiMaggio, P. and Powell, W. W. (1983) 'The iron cage revisited: Institutional isomorphism and collective rationality in organizational fields', *American Sociological Review*, 48: 147–160.

Dobbin, F. J., Sutton, R., Meyer, J. W. and Scott, R. W. (1993) 'Equal opportunity law and the construction of internal labor markets', *American Journal of Sociology*, 99: 396–427.

Goodstein, J. D. (1994) 'Institutional pressures and strategic responsiveness: Employer involvement in work–family issues', *Academy of Management Journal*, 37: 350–382.

Habermas, J. (1981) *Theorie des Kommunikativen Handelns*. Frankfurt am Mein: Suhrkamp. Trans. in *Teoria dell'agire comunicativo*. Bologna, Italy: Il Mulino (1986).

Italian Senate (2003) *Indagine conoscitiva sul settore dei giochi e delle scommesse*. Roma: VI Commissione permanente del Senato.

Kennedy, M. T. and Fiss, P. C. (2009) 'Institutionalization, framing and diffusion: The logic of TQM adoption and implementation decisions among US hospitals', *Academy of Management Journal*, 52: 897–918.

Lawrence, T. B. and Suddaby, R. (2006) 'Institutions and institutional work'. In S. R. Clegg, C. Hardy, T. B. Lawrence and W. R. Nord (eds), *Handbook of Organization Studies*, 2nd edn. Thousand Oaks, CA: Sage Publications, pp. 215–254.

Lawrence, T. B., Suddaby, R. and Leca, B. (2009) 'Introduction: Theorizing and studying institutional work'. In T. Lawrence, R. Suddaby and B. Leca (eds), *Institutional Work: Actors and agency in institutional studies of organizations*. Cambridge: Cambridge University Press, pp. 1–28.

Mazza, C., Sahlin-Andersson, K. and Strandgaard, P. J. (2005) 'European constructions of an American model', *Management Learning*, 36: 471–491.

Oliver, C. (1991) 'Strategic responses to institutional processes', *Academy of Management Review*, 16: 145–179.

Perrow, C. (1986) *Complex Organizations: A critical essay*, 3rd edn. New York: McGraw-Hill Publishers.

Scott, W. R., Ruef, M., Mendel, P. J. and Caronna, C. A. (2000) *Institutional Change and Health Care Organizations: From professional dominance to managed care*. Chicago, IL: University of Chicago Press.

Sibbet, D. (1997) '75 years of management ideas and practice', *Harvard Business Review*, September/October Supplement, 75: 2–12.

Singh, J. V., Tucker, D. J. and House, R. J. (1986) 'Organizational legitimacy and the liability of newness', *Administrative Science Quarterly*, 31: 171–193.

Suchman, M. (1995) 'Managing legitimacy: Strategic and institutional approaches', *Academy of Management Review*, 20: 571–610.

Tani, N. (2010) 'In Italia al gioco non si rinuncia'. *Italia Oggi*, 4 Jan.

Tolbert, P. and Zucker, L. (1983) 'Institutional sources of change in the formal structure of organizations: The diffusion of civil service reform, 1880–1935', *Administrative Science Quarterly*, 28: 22–39.

Westphal, J. D., Gulati, R. and Shortell, S. M. (1997) 'Customization or conformity? An institutional and network perspective on the content and consequences of TQM adoption', *Administrative Science Quarterly*, 42: 366–394.

White, H. (1992) *Identity and Control: A structural theory of social action*. Princeton, NJ: Princeton University Press.

Zilber, T. (2009) 'Institutional maintenance as narrative acts'. In T. Lawrence, R. Suddaby and B. Leca (eds), *Institutional work: Actors and agency in institutional studies of organizations*. Cambridge: Cambridge University Press, pp. 205–235.

Zucker, L. (1977) 'The role of institutionalization in cultural persistence', *American Sociological Review*, 42: 726–743.

PART III
Finance and economics

8

THE ETHICAL AND SOCIAL DIMENSIONS OF EXECUTIVE COMPENSATION

Terence Tse, Khaled Soufani and Lucie Roux

The financial crisis in late 2008 witnessed the end of the housing boom and closedown of the credit markets in many parts of the world as well as the downfall of many financial services titans such as Lehman Brothers and Bear Stearns in the US and the Royal Bank of Scotland (RBS) and Halifax Bank of Scotland (HBOS) in the UK. Commentators of the crisis have analysed the different aspects of this watershed event. One aspect that has attracted public attention is that banks, in their relentless pursuit of profitability, seemed to have neglected the social roles that they were supposed to play (Jenkins 2010). Many governments across the world had to resort to taxpayers' money to rescue their respective banking systems. The moral hazard problems resulting from such bank bailouts are explored elsewhere in this volume. In this chapter, we are concerned with the ethical dimension of executive compensation, particularly those in the financial services. Executive incentive packages have caused significant public outcry, not only because the substantial amount of remuneration staggers people who are unfamiliar with the payout practice of this sector but also because executive compensation in the financial industry was perceived to be conducive to banks (especially those of retail) taking excessive risk, the consequence of which could have led to the financial crisis. Indeed, this view was shared among the members of G20 when they jointly announced that 'excessive compensation in the financial sector has both reflected and encouraged excessive risk taking' (Leaders' statement: The Pittsburgh Summit 2009). The Financial Services Authority (FSA) in the UK has also listed remuneration structures as one of the possible driving forces behind excessive risk taking when it claims that it would appear that in many cases the remuneration structures of firms may have been inconsistent with sound risk management. It is possible that they frequently gave incentives to staff to pursue risky policies, undermining the impact of systems designed to control risk, to the detriment of shareholders and other stakeholders, including depositors, creditors and ultimately taxpayers.[1]

The issue has become even more controversial, as at the same time many governments in the world injected astronomical sums of capital into their respective economies to avert further damages, bankers continued to pay themselves huge monetary rewards. For example, as Murphy (2009) points out, Merrill Lynch and AIG paid substantial year-end bonuses to their respective employees after being bailed out by the US government. Various UK banks followed similar actions despite the fact that they were rescued and became partially, if not fully, owned by the British government.

Viewing from this vantage point, it appears that the consequence of the crisis was borne less by the financial services sector and more by the rest of society. Indeed, as an aftermath of the financial crisis, unemployment has increased while consumption that is vital to fuelling economic growth has decreased. In addition, having used public money to save collapsing banks, impoverished governments have cut funding previously allocated to services that are critical to social cohesion and welfare. A recent example is the UK government's decision to raise university tuition fees. The rise is not so much about providing further funding to higher education as making up the shortfall in the budget originally earmarked. Students have taken to the streets as a result. Perhaps the sentiment among these students is best captured by Porter (2010) when he writes:

> Our fight is not just an issue of policy, but one of principle. The government has blamed the financial crisis and told us (the public) there is no alternative. The first people who will pay these astronomical fees were aged just 13 when the banks fell. They didn't cause the crisis but they are becoming its victims.

Against this backdrop, this chapter aims to examine some ethical and social aspects of executive compensation. In light of the crisis, this subject matter is flourishing in the domain of business ethics (e.g. Kanagaretnam *et al.* 2009; Moriarty 2009; Walsh 2008). This is an important development as the financial crisis highlights an unethical quandary in which individual managers are perhaps (generously) rewarded at the expense of the general public and society. The difficulty in developing such an appropriate compensation package is that it not only has to incentivize top managers to run their firms effectively, thereby creating value for shareholders; it should also be designed in a way that the incentive would not encourage managers to pursue self-serving purposes that could lead to undesirable consequences to the shareholders, and, as the financial crisis shows, to society as a whole.

This observation highlights two important issues. First, a generous incentive package to executives is necessary to generate good results. This implies that generous compensation is seemingly acceptable as long as companies are performing well. This notion may originate from the belief that individual performance is highly correlated with pay level. However, a number of studies such as Bogle (2008), Groom (2010) and Walsh (2008) have shown that the pay–performance relationship is not as strong as was previously claimed. Second, even if an optimal incentive structure can be designed for an executive, whose own interest is *not* placed first, we must ask whose interest this executive is supposedly serving: should it be that of the shareholders or all the stakeholders including society as a whole? It is in this respect that the chapter will operate at levels 1 and 2 of normative critique as outlined in Chapter 2. We consider both the potential impact of executive compensation on managerial behaviour (Level 1) and the possible relationship between executive compensation and the welfare of society (Level 2). It must be noted at this juncture that it is virtually impossible to observe a direct causality between executive compensation and the adverse behaviour of executives, let alone whether incentive packages are related to ethics. However, if we follow the fundamentals of economics, that incentives influence managerial behaviours (Liber8 2010), it is highly probable that there are some links between remuneration to executives and their ethical responsibilities to society. We therefore operate on the assumption that compensation could modify the ethical behaviours and responsibilities of executives, whose actions, in turn, could lead to various (unintentional) social damages.

The aim of this chapter is to probe deeper into this issue by opening up the different ethical and social aspects of executive compensation for examination. To do so, we first provide a general discussion on the harms inflicted upon society by the crisis. This is necessary because it can offer a sense of magnitude to the damages done. The subsequent section looks at whether high pay to executives vis-à-vis the general public is justified. Indeed, we ask a fundamental question: is it right to pay some managers so much? The chapter then proceeds to examine the potential adverse managerial behaviour that can be caused by executive compensation. If incentive packages may lead to such behaviour, is it possible to mitigate it? Drawing from observations made in the Canadian banking system, the following section offers three recommendations to companies, policy makers and future researchers on how adverse managerial behaviour can be potentially moderated. The final section offers some concluding remarks.

The social harm of the crisis

According to Aristotle, the purpose of business activities is to simultaneously create wealth, be ethical and be happy (Nielsen 2010). Yet, far from such an ideal, as Nielsen (2010) notes, the latest economic crisis has clearly demonstrated that business activities in the past decade are 'not about creating wealth and bettering ourselves and the world, but, instead, the massive destruction of wealth and allowing some to get very rich at the expense of others' (Nielson 2010, p. 300). One of the greatest social harms brought by the crisis is significantly weakened economies. The recapitalization of financial institutions has effectively shifted wealth and income away from ordinary people, causing some cross-sections of society to suffer. For example, those who live on fixed incomes and depend on imports (especially food and energy) have seen a drop in their purchasing power as interest rates and currencies fall in value (Nielson 2010). Weakened economies have also made it difficult for companies to increase their revenues, making headcount reduction a very attractive, if not the only, alternative to sustain profitability (Nadler and Spencer 2009). Personnel retrenchment has attracted further public criticism when it appears that banks in the UK have been conducting rounds of lay-offs (of low-level staff) to lower costs, while paying bonuses to senior executives.

Unemployment, in turn, has led many people to reduce spending and become more reliant on debt. While it may be a good idea to curb conspicuous consumption, this happens at exactly the time when governments depend on consumer spending to fuel business activities and boost economic growth. Overburdened with debt, many families have failed to make mortgage payments and lost their homes, at the time when governments have trimmed public spending, which has further hurt the vulnerable in society. At the same time, banks had overladen themselves with debt through excessive leverage before the crisis (see below for a more detailed discussion). In an attempt to repair their balance sheets (and also because they belong to taxpayers), banks have become very cautious with lending, resulting in a reduction of credit available to consumers and businesses. As a consequence, small and medium-sized enterprises (SMEs) have been struggling to obtain the financing necessary for further growth, if not for survival. Lending to British SMEs by the dominant high street banks, which traditionally provide 90 per cent of the banking services to these companies, has been declining across the economy since early 2009 (*The Economist* 2010a). Continental Europe also suffers from similar problems (Milne 2010). Since SMEs accounted for a majority of the value added and job creation in the EU (Schiemann 2009), reduced credit liquidity could have impacts on the long-term prosperity of European countries.[2]

Is it right to pay executives so much?

Some observers such as Keller and Stocker (2008) identify poor executive incentive schemes as one of the most fundamental causes of the financial crisis. Initially, executive compensation was one of the primary targets of public concern and criticism; later, it became a way that regulators and policy makers reacted to the crisis. Managerial pay turned itself into a visible target partially because the absolute pay levels had ballooned dramatically in the past few decades. For instance, the CEOs of the largest 1,000 corporations in the US in 2005 collectively made nearly the equivalent of Bolivia's GDP (Walsh 2008). The combined compensation of the top 100 CEOs totaled $2.1 billion in 2011, the rough equivalent of the estimated annual economic output of Sierra Leone.[3] Others such as Agarwal (2010) find that compensation of CEOs went up from 40 times that of the average employee in the 1960s to nearly 200 times in 2002, usually with no apparent justifications for such a stellar increase. The rises in total compensation were particularly significant in the manufacturing and financial services sectors, where CEOs have historically received above-average pay (Gabaix and Landier 2008). Indeed, Kaplan (2008a, 2008b) has contested that CEOs are perhaps *underpaid*. Compared to other high earners such as 'superstar' athletes and venture capital investors, CEOs deserve even better pay if the stress and pressure of the role as well as the fact that a CEO job is becoming 'increasingly difficult and less pleasant' (2008a, p. 17) are taken into account. However, others would argue that the 'stellar' pay of certain top footballers is just as 'obscene' as that of top executives in the financial sector, and is indeed in danger of ruining that sector financially.

Controlling excessive executive pay, especially that at financial institutions, has become part of the measures employed by many governments to respond to the crisis. The FSA in the UK now controls both the structure of compensation and the time period over which the incentive pay is distributed. In the US, limits have been set on the compensation payments to executives at companies receiving Troubled Asset Relief Program funds (Faulkender *et al.* 2010). Germany, on the other hand, has set an absolute upper limit to pay and bonuses (Sabiwalsky 2010).

The ever-increasing executive compensation has led to a proliferation of research in the field in recent years, 'rivalled only by the growth of executive pay itself' (Bruce *et al.* 2005, p. 1493). Many of these studies view executive compensation to be the central underlying mechanism of corporate governance. Ever since Friedman (1962), academic literature has been stressing that the ultimate goal of company managers should be creating value for its owners. Using the capital advanced by these shareholders, managers should invest in those projects that generate the maximum value for these fund suppliers. Nevertheless, effective incentivizing and monitoring mechanisms must be put in place because shareholders and managers have different access to firm-specific information as well as broadly divergent interests and risk preferences (Fama and Jensen 1983; Jensen 1986). As a result, it is necessary to have a well-designed remuneration scheme that can align managerial incentives with those of shareholders when making investment decisions (Jensen and Meckling 1976). In other words, given the strong relationship between performance and pay, generous incentive packages can serve as an effective mechanism for value creation (Kaplan 2008a, 2008b).

While such a Friedmanite view underpins a plethora of concepts in finance and corporate governance, it has been critically challenged in the last two decades (Desjardins and McCall 2005). Specifically, it has been argued that executives should act on the interest of not just the shareholders but also other stakeholders (Clarkson 1995; Donaldson and Preston 1995). The problem with this view is that it is often deemed impractical for several fundamental reasons. First, managing multiple stakeholder relations implies the need to have multiple constituencies and simultaneously juggle several goals – having more than one objective is potentially confusing for some less competent managers (Sundaram and Inkpen 2004). Second, there remains a lack of tools and techniques available to monitor and incentivize benefits to all stakeholders (Grant 2009). Third, it is unclear as to who (and indeed what) should be counted as stakeholders. Despite the fact that the term stakeholder appears to include all the parties affected, it means different things to different people owing to its conceptual breadth (Phillips *et al.* 2003). Past literature has suggested that stakeholders can range from those who wield power over firms (Frooman 1999) to non-human entities such as trees (Starik 1995) and the deity (Schwartz 2006). Therefore, until these three fundamental issues are adequately addressed, it is likely that businesses will continue to resort to pay for performance measured somehow in terms of profits as the main form of motivation mechanism and the basis of executive compensation.

Arguably, the relationship between pay and performance should not represent the only way to assess whether executives are overpaid – we should seek another point of reference. Walsh (2008) suggests that it is necessary to adopt the viewpoint of what 'normal' people from different facets of society earn. Even though, admittedly, such assessment was not scientific, it raises a very important point: the general public do not care if executive pay is sensitive to performance. Instead, people care about fairness – why do executives earn so much whereas others so much less? According to *The Telegraph* (2010), the fifty best-paid CEOs in the UK received on average a total compensation of £8 million in 2009. At the same time, the median pay for nurses was £29,431(*The Guardian* 2009). Comparing them, one might ask if it is fair that nurses, who dedicate their work to the benefits of the public and society, are paid so much less than executives whose primary constituency is often the shareholders. Indeed, one might further question why an executive, who could engage in actions and decisions that, if they result in a negative financial outcome and losses, can cause potential widespread societal damage, can be so much better paid than a nurse, who is unlikely to create social harm of similar magnitude. The issue of pay fairness can be further interrogated when it is observed that the average household gross income in Britain (£23,244) is insufficient to cover utility bills and mortgage payments (£24,100) and leaves no money to pay for other living expenses including petrol and clothing (Butterworth 2010). Taking all these into account, we would like to ask the same question posed by Walsh (2008): what is to become of a society in which the very rich do not share a common destiny with the vast majority of the population? Is it fair that, as the chairman of the House Committee on Oversight and Reform in the US once said, '[Dick Fuld, the CEO of Lehman Brothers] can walk away from [the firm] a wealthy man who earned over $500 million. But taxpayers are left with a $700 billion bill to rescue Wall Street and an economy in crisis'? As Walsh (2008) reminds us, our norms of fairness are no less important than economic gains. The legitimacy of executive pay should have as much to do with such norms as the link between pay and performance.

Does executive compensation lead to adverse behaviour?

Blinder (2009) points out that one of the fundamental causes of the crisis is the perverse incentive built into the compensation plans of many financial firms. In their study of the relationship between compensation structure and risk choices, Hagendorff and Vallascas (2011) find that CEOs who received substantial bonuses for completing acquisitions are more likely to engage in risk-inducing takeovers. They see it as a support to the argument that incentive packages can drive CEOs to increase the default risk of their institutions, resulting in the current crisis. Before the crisis, many financial services companies engaged in excessive borrowing and securitization without prudence because these firms could make more money from short-term commissions and fees for advising, structuring financing and trading debt products than they could otherwise make on long-term assets such as traditional lending (Kane 2008; Nielsen 2008). Executives, bankers and traders in turn received their compensation in the forms of bonus and commission in the year the profits were realized, without taking into account whether such profits obtained could cause long-term damage to the firms and the wider societies (Bebchuk and Fried 2006; Nielsen 2010). In short, there were enormous incentives to hold a short-run view and maximize the current gains – perhaps all in the name of enhancing shareholders' wealth – which can lead to different forms of opportunism that stretch the ethical responsibility of executives.

Existing studies have suggested that opportunistic executives can engage in manipulative activities in relation to earnings such as timing of disclosures, accounting restatement and earning management in order to enhance their own personal gains (Bergstresser and Philippon 2006; Burns and Kedia 2006; Faulkender *et al.* 2010; Gao and Shrieves 2002). Furthermore, past literature has also suggested that managers can at their discretion distort earnings so as to boost the value of their compensations (Aboody and Kasznick 2000; Yermack 1997).

If remuneration could indeed lead managers to deliberately misreport or manipulate firms' accounting, does compensation encourage them to assume more risk? This has been a central question in many current debates as well as academic studies. On the one hand, some past academic evidence suggests that executive compensation may offer managers strong incentives to *avoid* taking excessive risks (Eisenhardt 1989; Kale *et al.* 2010; Low 2008; Milgrom and Roberts 1992). On the other hand, a plethora of studies have reached contradictory conclusions. For example, studies conducted by Rajgopal and Shevlin (2002), Chen *et al.* (2006) and Sanders (2001) find that compensation could lead executives to greater risk-seeking behaviour. In the financial crisis, bank executives were perceived to have overexposed their organizations to risk related to leverage as these banks were hungry for extra returns, the capture of which in turn, by logical extension, can boost their remuneration to the top executives.[4] For instance, RBS increased its debt–equity ratio from 60.1 per cent to 86.2 per cent in the period between 2005 and 2008 (RBS annual report 2008). Similarly, HBOS raised its debt from 7.5 times to 10.6 times its equity between 2004 and 2007. In the case of Northern Rock, the first UK bank to be nationalized, its retail deposit accounted for 60 per cent of the bank's liabilities when it demutualized in 1998. However, by 2007, it had dropped to only 23 per cent, with the funding gap made up of securitized debt and borrowing (Shin 2009). Just before its collapse, Lehman Brothers' debt level rose from $484.3 to $668.6 billion (a difference of $184.3 billion) between 2006 and 2007. During this time, its level of equity only went up from $19.2 to $23.5 billion, representing a mere $3.3 billion increase (Lehman Brothers annual report, 2008). Bear Stearns, the first financial services firm to collapse in the crisis, had as much as $42 of debt to every $1 of equity. As the former CEO later admitted, 'in retrospect, in hindsight, I would say leverage was too high' (Corkery and Johnson 2010, p. C3).

If we are right to assume that the compensation structure encourages a short-term view and pay increases with performance (as measured by the increase in return on equity), then it would not be difficult to imagine that incentive could influence risk-taking decisions. As Bebchuk *et al.* (2010) estimated, between 2000 and 2008, the CEOs of Bear Stearns and Lehman received cash from bonuses and share sales of about $388 million and $541 million respectively, with the aggregate cash of about $1.4 billion and $1 billion to the top five executives in each firm, respectively. The authors conclude that the firms' performance-based compensation failed to produce a sufficiently tight alignment of executives' interests with long-term shareholder value. Rather, the design provided executives with substantial opportunities to take large amounts of compensation based on short-term gains and retain it even after the drastic reversal of the two companies' fortunes. This setting has effectively provided executives with incentives to seek improvements in short-term results even if it means maintaining an excessively high risk of an implosion at some point in the future.

It should be noted that compensation is often not only confined to the form of salaries and bonuses – managers may also be tempted to gain power and prestige. Bebchuk and Fried (2006) suggest that executives have an excessive incentive to expand the company, most likely through acquisitions, to achieve these non-monetary rewards. At the same time, the increased difficulty of running a firm after an acquisition enables the executives of the enlarged companies to demand additional compensation. Malmendier and Tate (2009) show that some CEOs reap personal benefits from achieving 'superstar' status at the expense of the shareholders. Furthermore, they find evidence that 'superstar' CEOs have a greater tendency to manage the earnings. It is therefore probable that the desire to attain fame and reputation could lead to adverse managerial behaviour.

What can be done to moderate the adverse behaviour potentially resulting from generous executive compensation?

The above discussion has shown that while executive compensation can align the interests of managers with that of shareholders, it can potentially lead them to engage in behaviour that creates a negative impact on their firms as well as society. The key to deal with the downsides of the incentive package is therefore not to abandon it entirely, but instead fix its structure and use (Martin 2011). So, the question is: how can we maintain the positive effects of compensation yet simultaneously reduce the potential opportunistic behaviour that can harm society and reinforce business ethics? This is an important question because if executives could reinforce negative business ethics, it would probably lower the probability of another financial crisis in the future. With this in mind, we attempted to answer this question by focusing our discussion on observations made in the financial services sector.

One of the primary causes of the crisis is that banks have deviated from their traditional role (see Chapter 9 of this work for the argument of Ansart and Monvoisin on the transformation of the concept of the role of the professional banker; also see De Grauwe 2009), which is to act as a financial intermediation between loan borrowers and depositors (Diamond 1984). Depositors provide the funds lent to borrowers, with the bank being in the middle assessing the quality and creditworthiness of the borrowers. While this can reduce the risk exposure to the capital suppliers including the shareholders, a potential problem with this business model is that it may not be very profitable. This is because banks must hold costly shareholders' funds to meet the minimum level of capital required as a guarantee. In order to boost returns, banks became ever more involved in growing outside the traditional commercial activities in the so-called 'shadow banking' (Adrian and Shin 2009; Gertler 2010; Gorton and Metrick 2010). In this banking system that is parallel to the traditional one, banks engaged in a range of activities involving riskier – and hence more profitable – instruments. Among these activities, securitization of loans not only enabled banks to gain higher returns, it also allowed them to avoid holding costly capital by effectively turning themselves into underwriters that could originate loans but then sold them off to others. At the same time, executives and bankers were keen to undertake these activities because their remuneration packages were tied to the good performance of the banks. Consequently, in this way, banks became intermediaries between borrowers and investors, as opposed to borrowers and depositors (Acharya *et al.* 2009a). The digression into shadow banking and significant securitization activities eventually became major causes of the financial crisis (Acharya *et al.* 2009b; Faten and Okongwu 2009).

Among the best survivors that emerged from the financial crisis are Canadian banks. Indeed, the Canadian banking system has remained relatively intact after the crisis about which Paul Volcker, the former Federal Reserve chairman, advised U.S. lawmakers seeking to overhaul rules governing the biggest U.S. bank to 'learn from Canada's banking system' (Whitman 2010). Compared to their US and UK counterparts, Canadian banks were found to be more restrained with risk taking, as a result of being (unfairly) branded as 'boring'. However, Krugman (2010) argues that being 'boring' is good and, like Volcker, further suggests that Canadian banks should be considered the role model for financial institutions worldwide because this can keep banks safe. So, what is the secret of Canadian banking? In their study examining why the Canadian banking system showed greater resilience by comparison to those in other parts of the world, Ratnovski and Huang (2009) find that Canadian banks clearly stood out in terms of funding structure. These banks depended much less on wholesale funding and much more on the traditional deposits to fund their loans. The fact that these banks financed most of their lending activities through their captive deposit base meant that there was an absence of significant securitization. In other words, banks in Canada have adopted a more conservative mindset by adhering more to the traditional commercial model of banking and the low-risk funding structure. A similar scenario can be found in a number of other countries that were not affected (or only to a very limited extent) by the crisis. A conservative policy in respect of mortgage lending, securitization and the holding of various risky derivatives on banks' balance sheets applied by regulators and central banks in such countries as Lebanon and Poland insulated these countries almost entirely from the crisis. Moreover, in states with Islamic banking systems where much stricter rules about lending conditions are applied and where outright speculation (such as in short selling) is prohibited by Shariah law, the effects of the financial crisis have also been minimal.

An important implication of a conservative approach to banking on pay–performance is that such a context and environment can be effective to discourage some executives from taking excessive risk in their pursuit of greater personal gains. It is highly probable that if banks can adopt a corporate culture that modifies individual opportunistic rent-seeking behaviour, they can collectively promote safer and more stable systems, which, in turn, lessen the moral hazard problem discussed above and in the later chapter. Therefore, we would like to make the following suggestion:

> *Recommendation 1*: Take a more conservative approach to business. This is especially paramount for financial services companies as the failure of this sector has widespread and long-term social implications. Being conservative at least in finance is being forward thinking.

Changing the corporate mindset alone is perhaps insufficient; executive pay needs to be structured in a way that takes into account the long-term effect of today's decisions. At the same time as taking a more prudent approach to fund their businesses with retail deposits, Canadian banks also demonstrated themselves better at managing their loan assets. As Booth (2009) points out, Canadian banks suffered from lower loan losses because the maximum loan-to-value was 80 per cent (compared to, for instance, the UK, in which borrowers could take out a mortgage of more than 100 per cent of the value of the underlying property) and there were no NINJA loans.[5] These loans were almost always kept on the banks' books, instead of being moved off-balance sheet (Booth 2009). Canadian banks also engage in less securitization (Davies 2009). In contrast, the increased use of securitization, notably in the US and UK, has led financial institutions to become large and increasingly complex and opaque in their activities. A prime example is the use of collateralized debt obligations (CDOs), which can be highly complicated; it has been suggested that a proper understanding of a typical CDO would have required reading 30,000 pages of documentation (*The Economist* 2010b). Yet, banks rushed to trade these instruments (Sheth 2008). The reason that banks were so enthusiastic about them was probably owing to the pay structure: in the period leading up to the financial crisis, bankers were increasingly paid through short-term cash bonuses based on volume and immediately realized profits on securitization (Acharya *et al.* 2009c). Nevertheless, this arrangement produced at least two negative consequences.

1   *Maximize gains by taking excessive risk.* Such incentive schemes encourage bankers to actively search for excess returns by taking 'tail risks', which produce a steady positive return most of the time in exchange for a rare but very significant loss (Rajan 2008). In this way, bankers benefited from the so-called 'fake alpha' – generating a great deal of huge returns without giving much thought to the enormous underpinning risk (Sharfman *et al.* 2009). Rajan (2008) argues that since there are only a few sources for creating alpha, many bankers could only justify their pay by investing in tail risks.[6] This perhaps may not be an issue if the employing banks can separate genuine and fake returns when designing remuneration packages, yet many banks failed to make the distinction. Indeed, Sharfman (2009) argues that large bonus policies can encourage the pursuit of fake alpha. For example, in a report produced for its shareholders explaining the asset write-downs, the Swiss bank UBS (2009) recognized this problem when it pointed out that the employee incentivization arrangements in place did not differentiate between returns generated by skills in creating additional returns and returns made from holding subprime positions (a fake alpha activity). In other words, bankers were paid for their performance regardless of how the excess returns were attained. While this observation may suggest that the Swiss bank had failed in structuring an appropriate compensation scheme, Foster and Young (2010) argue that it is indeed very difficult to devise performance-based compensation that rewards genuine creation of excess returns while filtering out the unreal ones.

2   *Ignore potential long-term problems.* An aftermath with rewarding bankers based on immediate results is that there is no incentive for them to take into account the quality or the sustainability of the profits made from their 'bets'. Again, the case of UBS provides a telling illustration. Acharya *et al.* (2009c) report that for every $1 of CDO held, the bank booked the premium as immediate profit. In turn, every dollar of current 'profit' booked, the members of the CDO group received correspondingly high bonuses. Consequently, the members of the group were motivated to hold as many CDOs as possible, as their bonuses were tied to instant profits with no recognition of any risk. This finding seems to be substantiated by UBS (2009) when the bank admitted that its compensation structure generally made little recognition of risk issues. For instance, there were incentives for the CDO structuring desk to pursue concentrations in Mezzanine CDOs, which had a significantly higher fee structure than High-Grade CDOs. All these observations reveal that such compensation structures are likely to motivate executives, bankers and traders to engage in opportunistic rent-seeking behaviour, yet are insufficiently linked to the potential longer-term negative impact that such positions could create.

One way to address these problems is to tie pay to long-term performance rather than short-term achievements (Bebchuk and Fried 2010). Rajan (2008) suggests significant portions of compensation be held in escrow, paid out only long after the activities that generated the compensation occur. Others such as Fried and Shilon (2011) and Sharfman *et al.* (2009) argue that excess rewards should be clawed back when losses materialize. Another possibility is to change performance measurements (Fried and Shilon 2011). Acharya *et al.* (2009a) point out that measures should be designed on a risk-adjusted basis. For example, a traditional accounting measure such as return on equity dismisses the risk resulting in high leverage.

> *Recommendation 2*: Executive compensation should be structured over a longer-term horizon. Bonuses should be tied to long-term results and not paid out to reward immediate 'achievements'. Employees should be required to return the extra pay received if the long-term results turn out to be negative; at the very least there should be some sort of risk-sharing mechanism in place whereby the executive suffers a serious negative pay penalty when long-term investment/lending results turn out to involve serious losses.

While we argue that it is important for companies to adopt a conservative mindset and to structure pay by linking to long-term results, they alone may not be sufficiently effective without the support of strict regulations. A more stringent regulatory environment is likely to be conducive to discouraging managers from taking excessive risk. For example, governments can perhaps better regulate the use of off-balance sheet accounting (which was used extensively by Bear Sterns and led to its eventual demise) as well as the speed of financial innovation. Ratnovski and Huang (2009) argue that the fact that Canadian banks emerged from the financial crisis relatively unscathed was partly owing to its regulatory environment including the imposition of the minimum capital requirements significantly above those demanded by Basel II. Furthermore, it has been suggested that the Canadian government plays an important role in ensuring stability of the banking system as it continuously renews and monitors the banking market (Booth 2009; Davies 2009).

An important insight that can be drawn from these findings is that governments offer the possibility to coordinate the efforts made by different financial institutions to mitigate the adverse effects on executive compensation. Financial risks at these institutions are now increasingly concentrated in the hands of a few 'high performance' profit centres. Executives, bankers and traders running these centres have skills in creating, packaging and repackaging, marking to market and hedging financial securities (Acharya *et al.* 2009c). Since such skills are largely fungible across institutions, these employees possess enormous bargaining power in their institutions and in obtaining highly attractive, short-term compensation packages that provide significant cash bonuses for short-run performance (Sharfman 2009). The problem with this arrangement is that no one institution can change the compensation expectations alone. If a single employer applies new and more appropriate incentive packages together with stronger risk-control management, it is likely to lose their best bankers to the competitors (Acharya *et al.* 2009c; Sharfman 2009).[7] The inefficiency is thus the result of a coordination problem between financial institutions. In this case, the society can benefit most perhaps from having the government derive common policies that aim at assisting individual financial institutions to become safer, which, in turn, lowers the risk of negative social impacts resulting from financial instability.

> *Recommendation 3*: Governments should try to create a more stringent regulatory environment, perhaps by drawing on the experience of the Canadian banking system. Policy makers should seek to tighten the regulations that allow for the creation of a setting that enables and encourages financial institutions to structure compensation appropriately and to better manage risk.

Concluding remarks

Executive compensation is a complicated subject. The ethical and social aspects of executive compensation are even more complex. We are fully aware of the fact that we may have raised several questions without answering any. However, we hope that this chapter encourages future researchers to branch off from examining the link between pay and economic performance and to delve into the ethical and social implications of executive compensation. Only then can we develop a more complete picture of the impacts of managerial incentives on all the stakeholders, including society. In this way, we can be better informed as to how we can simultaneously create wealth, be ethical and be happy, as Aristotle suggested some 2,500 years ago.

Notes

1 FSA letter to CEOs of financial firms regarding remuneration policies, 13 October 2008. Available online at www.fsa.gov.uk/pubs/ceo/ceo_letter_13oct08.pdf
2 In this case, banks that were nationalized by governments find themselves getting stuck between a rock and a hard place. On the one hand, they need to be prudent with the loans made in order to protect taxpayers' money. On the other, these banks are under pressure to make more lending available and accessible so as to aid economic growth.
3 *The New York Times* (2012) 'In executive pay, a rich game of thrones', 7 April 2012. Available online at www.nytimes.com/2012/04/08/business/in-chief-executives-pay-a-rich-game-of-thrones.html?_r=2 (accessed 2 May 2012).
4 This effectively creates a situation, as demonstrated by the government bailouts in the financial crisis, in which one gambles: if he wins, he gets all the gains; if he fails, the losses are borne by the others. This moral hazard issue receives a fuller treatment in Chapter 11.
5 NINJA stands for 'no income, no jobs or assets'.
6 Sharfman (2009) argues that it is possible that some or most executives, traders and investment bankers who pursued fake alpha did so without the intent to deceive. If so, they thought they were actually pursuing genuine alpha, but in reality they were just pursuing fake alpha with no real expectation of excess returns.
7 Cukierman (2009) further suggests that high turnover of skilled financial individuals has encouraged the short-term view.

References

Aboody, D. and Kasznik, R. (2000) 'CEO stock option awards and the timing of corporate voluntary disclosures', *Journal of Accounting and Economics*, 29(1): 73–100.

Acharya, V., Cooley, T. and Richardson, M. (2009a) 'The new banking model of manufacturing tail risk', *Foundations and Trends in Finance*, 4: 247–325.

Acharya, V., Philippon, T., Richardson, M. and Roubini, N. (2009b) 'The financial crisis of 2007–2009: Causes and remedies', *Financial Markets, Institutions and Instruments*, 18(2): 89–137.

Acharya, V., Cooley, T. and Richardson, M. (2009c) 'How did we get there?', *Foundations and Trends in Finance*, 1(4): 253–272.

Adrian, T. and Shin, H. (2009) 'The shadow banking system: Implications for the financial regulation', *FRB of New York Staff Report*, No. 382.

Agarwal, A. S. (2010) 'Motivation and executive compensation', *The IUP Journal of Corporate Governance*, 9(1/2): 27–46.

Bebchuk, L. A. and Fried, J. M. (2006) 'Pay without performance: Overview of the issues', *Academy of Management Perspectives*, 20(1): 5–24.

Bebchuk, L. A. and Fried, J. M. (2010) 'Paying for long-term performance', *University of Pennsylvania Law Review*, 158: 1915–1960.

Bebchuk, L. A., Cohen, A. and Spamann, H. (2010) 'The wages of failure: Executive compensation at Bear Stearns and Lehman 2000–2008', *Yale Journal on Regulation*, 27: 257–282.

Bergstresser, D. and Philippon, T. (2006) 'CEO incentives and earnings management', *Journal of Financial Economics*, 80: 511–29.

Blinder, A. E. (2009) 'Crazy compensation and the crisis', *Wall Street Journal*, 28 May. Available online at http://online.wsj.com/article/SB124346974150760597.html (accessed 2 November 2010).

Bogle, J. C. (2008) 'Reflections on CEO compensation', *Academy of Management Perspectives*, 22(2): 21–25.

Booth, L. (2009) 'The secret of Canadian banking: Common sense?' *World Economics*, Jul/Aug, 10(3): 1–17.

Bruce, A., Buck, T. and Main, B. G. M. (2005) 'Top executive compensation: A view from Europe', *Journal of Management Studies*, 42(7): 1493–1506.

Burns, N. and Kedia, S. (2006) 'The impact of performance-based compensation on misreporting', *Journal of Financial Economics*, 79: 35–67.

Butterworth, M. (2010) 'Average household bill higher than average salary', *The Telegraph*, 21 July. Available online at www.telegraph.co.uk/finance/personalfinance/7903432/Average-household-bill-higher-than-average-salary.html (accessed 12 December 2010).

Chen, C. R., Steiner, T. L. and Whyte, A. M. (2006) 'Does stock option-based executive compensation induce risk-taking? An analysis of the banking industry', *Journal of Banking and Finance*, 30: 915–945.

Clarkson, M. B. E. (1995) 'A stakeholder framework for analyzing and evaluating corporate social performance', *Academy of Management Review*, 20: 65–91.

Corkery, M. and Johnson, S. (2010) 'Bear: Leverage was too high', *Wall Street Journal*, 6 May, C3.

Cukierman, A. (2009) 'The limits of transparency', *Economic Notes, Banca Monte dei Paschi di Siena SpA*, 38 (1–2): 1–37.

Davies, P. (2009) 'The way of the north', *Region*, September, 23(3): 30–53.

De Grauwe, P. (2009) 'Lessons from the banking crisis: A return to narrow banking. *Journal of Institutional Comparisons*, 2(7): 19–23.

Desjardins, J. R. and McCall, J. J. (2005) *Contemporary Issues in Business Ethics*, 5th edn. Belmont, CA: Thomson/Wadsworth.

Diamond, D. W. (1984) 'Financial intermediation and delegated monitoring', *Review of Economic Studies*, 51(3): 393–414.

Donaldson, T. and Preston, L. E. (1995) 'The stakeholder theory of the corporation: Concepts, evidence, and implications', *Academy of Management Review*, 20: 65–91.

Eisenhardt, K. M. (1989) 'Agency theory: An assessment and review', *Academy of Management Review*, 14: 57–74.

Fama, E. and Jensen, M. (1983) 'Agency problems and residual claims', *Journal of Law and Economics*, 26: 327–349.

Faten, S. and Okongwu, C. (2009) 'How did we get here? The story of the credit crisis', *Journal of Structured Finance*, Spring, 15(1): 53–70.

Faulkender, M., Kadyrzhanova, D., Prabhala, N. and Senbet, L. (2010) 'Executive compensation: An overview of research on corporate practices and proposed reforms', *Journal of Applied Corporate Finance*, 22(1): 107–118.

Foster, D. P. and Young, H. P. (2010) 'Gaming performance fees by portfolio managers', *Quarterly Journal of Economics*, 125(4): 1435–1458.

Fried, J. M. and Shilon, N. (2011) 'Excess-pay clawbacks', *Journal of Corporation Law*, 26: 722–751.

Friedman, M. (1962) *Capitalism and Freedom*. Chicago, IL: University of Chicago Press.

Frooman, J. (1999) 'Stakeholder influence strategies', *Academy of Management Review*, 24: 191–205.

Gabaix, X. and Landier, A. (2008) 'Why has CEO pay increased so much?' *Quarterly Journal of Economics*, 123(1): 49–100.

Gao, P. and Shrieves, R. I. (2002) 'Earnings management and executive compensation: A case of overdose of option and underdose of salary?', working paper, University of Tennessee.

Gertler, M. (2010) 'Macroeconomics in the wake of the financial crisis', *Journal of Money, Credit and Banking*, September 2010, Supplement 1(42): 217–219.

Gorton, G. and Metrick, A. (2010) 'Regulating the shadow banking system', *Brookings Papers on Economic Activity*, Fall: 261–312.

Grant, R. (2009). 'Shareholder value maximisation must be used appropriately'. *Financial Times*, 18 March. Available online at www.ft.com/cms/s/0/0ede1ee8-135f-11de-a170-0000779fd2ac.html.

Groom, B. (2010) 'Executive pay rises out of line with results', *Financial Times*, 5 July, p. 3.

Hagendorff, J. and Vallascas, F. (2011) 'CEO pay incentives and risk-taking: Evidence from bank acquisitions', *Journal of Corporate Finance*, 17(4): 1078–1095. Special Section: Managerial Compensation.

Jenkins, P. (2010) 'Remuneration still the big sticking point', *Financial Times*, Special Report, 18 November 2010, pp. 1–2.

Jensen, M. C. and Meckling, W. H. (1976) 'Theory of the firm: Managerial behavior, agency costs and ownership structure', *Journal of Financial Economics*, 3: 305–60.

Jensen, M. C. (1986) 'Agency costs of free cash flow, corporate finance, and takeovers', *American Economic Review*, 76: 323–329.

Kale, J. R., Reis, E. and Venkateswaran, A. (2010) 'Promotion incentives and corporate performance: Is there a bright side to "overpaying" the CEO?' *Journal of Applied Corporate Finance*, 22(1): 119–128.

Kanagaretnam, K., Lobo, G. and Mohammad, E. (2009) 'Are stock options grants to CEOs of stagnant firms fair and justified?' *Journal of Business Ethics*, 90(1): 137–155.

Kane, E. J. (2008) 'Regulation and supervision: An ethical perspective'. In P. Molyneux and J. Wilson (eds), *Oxford Handbook of Banking*. New York: Oxford University Press.

Kaplan, S. N. (2008a) 'Are U.S. CEOs overpaid?' *Academy of Management Perspectives*, 22(2): 5–20.

Kaplan, S. N. (2008b) 'Are U.S. CEOs overpaid? A response to Bogle and Walsh', *Academy of Management Perspectives*, 22(3): 28–34.

Kaplan, S. N. (2010) 'Should bankers get their bonuses?' *Finance and Development*, March: 42.

Keller, C. and Stocker, M. (2008) 'Executive compensation's role in the financial crisis', *The National Law Journal*. Available online at www.law.com/jsp/cc/PubArticleCC.jsp?id= 1202426091714.

Krugman, P. (2010) 'Good and boring', *The New York Times*, 31 January 2010. Available online at www.nytimes.com/2010/02/01/opinion/01krugman.html (accessed 11 May 2011).

Leaders' statement: The Pittsburgh Summit (2009). Available online at www.treasury.gov/ resource-center/international/g7-g20/Documents/pittsburgh_summit_leaders_statement_ 250909.pdf (accessed 2 May 2012).

Lehman Brothers (2007) *Lehman Brothers 2007 Annual Report*, Lehman Brothers inc., New York.

Liber8 (2010) 'Executive compensation and market risks'. Available online at http:// liber8.stlouisfed.org/newsletter/2010/201002.pdf (accessed 2 November 2010).

Low, A. (2008) 'Managerial risk-taking behavior and equity-based compensation', *Journal of Financial Economics*, 92(3): 470–490.

Malmendier, U. and Tate, G. (2009) 'Superstar CEOs', *Quarterly Journal of Economics*, 124(4): 1593–1638.

Martin, R. (2011) 'Recasting executive compensation: From gamesmanship to authenticity', *Rotman International Journal of Pension Management*, Spring, 4(1): 6–10.

Milgrom, P. and Roberts, J. (1992) *Economics, Organization and Management*. Englewood Cliffs, NJ: Prentice Hall.

Milne, R. (2010) 'Business: The cogs are clogged', *Financial Times*, 15 February. Available online at http://cachef.ft.com/cms/s/0/0e5c21aa-1a6a-11df-a2e3–00144feab49a.html# axzz1LxRBcCWz (accessed 11 May 2011).

Moriarty, J. (2009) 'How much compensation can CEOs permissibly accept?' *Business Ethics Quarterly*, 19(2): 235–250.

Murphy, K. J. (2009) 'Compensation structure and systemic risk', *USC Marshall School of Business Working Paper No FBE 34–09*. Available online at http://ssrn.com/abstract= 1461944.

Nadler, M. and Spencer, J. (2009) 'Leading through a crisis', *Viewpoint*. Available online at www.mmc.com/knowledgecenter/viewpoint/Leading_Through_a_Crisis_The_Basics.php.

Nielsen, R. P. (2008) 'The private equity-leveraged buyout of finance capitalism: Ethical and social issues, and potential reforms', *Business Ethics Quarterly*, 18: 379–404.

Nielsen, R. P. (2010) 'High-leverage finance capitalism, the economic crisis, structurally related ethics issues, and potential reforms', *Business Ethics Quarterly*, 20(2): 299–330.

Phillips, R., Freeman, R. E. and Wicks, A. (2003) 'What stakeholder theory is not?' *Business Ethics Quarterly*, 13(4): 479–502.

Porter, A. (2010) 'After tuition fees vote, students will ensure politicians are the biggest losers', *The Guardian*, 10 December. Available online at www.guardian.co.uk/commentisfree/ 2010/dec/10/tuition-fees-politicians-biggest-losers (accessed 10 December 2010).

Rajan, R. (2008) 'Bankers' pay is deeply flawed', *Financial Times*, 9 January. Available online at www.ft.com/cms/s/0/3d0ad046-be6e-11dc-9932–0000779fd2ac.html#axzz1MbIe PmGI (accessed 17 May 2011).

Rajgopal, S. and Shevlin, T. (2002) 'Empirical evidence on the relation between stock option compensation and risk taking', *Journal of Accounting and Economics*, 33: 145–171.

Ratnovski, L. and Huang, R. (2009) 'Why are Canadian banks more resilient?' *International Monetary Fund Working Paper*, WP/09/152.

RBS (2008) *Annual Report and Accounts 2008*, The Royal Bank of Scotland Group plc., Edinburgh.

Sabiwalsky, R. (2010) 'Executive compensation regulation and the dynamics of the pay-performance sensitivity', *SFB 649 Discussion Papers*, HU Berlin, 22 October 2010.

Sanders, W. M. G. (2001) 'Behavioral responses of CEO to stock ownership and stock option pay', *Academy of Management Journal*, 44(3): 477–492.

Schiemann, M. (2009) 'SMEs were the main drivers of economic growth between 2004 and 2006', *Eurostat*. Available online at http://epp.eurostat.ec.europa.eu/cache/ITY_OFFPUB/KS-SF-09-071/EN/KS-SF-09-071-EN.pdf (accessed 2 November 2010).

Schwartz, M. S. (2006) 'God as a managerial stakeholder', *Journal of Business Ethics*, 66(2–3): 291–306.

Sharfman, B. S. (2009) 'Enhancing the efficiency of board decision making: Lessons learned', *Delaware Journal of Corporate Law*, 34(3): 813–851.

Sharfman, B. S., Toll, S. J. and Szydlowski, A. (2009) 'Wall Street's corporate governance crisis', *Corporate Governance Advisor*, January, 17(1): 5–8.

Sheth, D. (2008) 'The fall of the giants', *Business Today*, 16 October. Available online at http://businesstoday.intoday.in/story/the-fall-of-the-giants/1/7637.html (accessed 16 October 2008).

Shin, H. S. (2009) 'Reflections on Northern Rock: The bank run that heralded the global financial crisis', *Journal of Economic Perspectives*, 23(1): 101–119.

Starik, M. (1995) 'Should trees have managerial standing? Toward stakeholder status for non-human nature', *Journal of Business Ethics*, 14(3): 207–217.

Sundaram, A. K. and Inkpen, A. C. (2004) 'Stakeholder theory and "The Corporate Objective Revisited": A reply', *Organization Science*, 15(3): 370–371.

The Economist (2010a) 'The mother of invention', 30 September. Available online at www.economist.com/node/17151365 (accessed 12 December 2010).

The Economist (2010b) 'Betting on the balance sheet, repent on leisure: A special report on debt', 26 June 2010, pp. 8–9.

The Guardian (2009) 'What do people get paid? The latest salary survey results', 12 November. Available online at www.guardian.co.uk/news/datablog/2009/nov/12/pay-salaries-survey-ashe-ons (accessed 12 December 2010).

The Telegraph (2009) 'Executive pay report 2010: Share boost puts CEOs' pay at new high'. Available online at www.telegraph.co.uk/finance/jobs/7729304/Executive-Pay-Report-2010-Share-boost-puts-CEOs-pay-at-new-high.html (accessed 12 December 2010).

The Telegraph (2010) 'Profile: David Baker', 14 April. Available online at www.telegraph.co.uk/finance/newsbysector/banksandfinance/7587024/Profile-David-Baker.html (accessed 13 December 2010).

UBS (2009) 'Shareholder report on UBS's write-downs', 18 April. Available online at www.ubs.com/1/ShowMedia/investors/agm?contentId=140333name=080418Shareholder Report.pdf (accessed 18 May 2011).

Walsh, J. P. (2008) 'CEO compensation and the responsibilities of the business scholar to society', *Academy of Management Perspectives*, 22(2): 26–33.

Whitman, J. (2010) 'Volcker lauds Canadian banks', *The Financial Post*, 2 February 2010. Available online at www.financialpost.com/story.html?id=2514580 (accessed 2 May 2012).

Yermack, D. (1997) 'Good timing: CEO stock option awards and company news announcements', *Journal of Finance*, 52(2): 449–476.

9

THE ETHICS OF THE BANKER

Reflections on the banker's economic and societal functions, or how history requires us to reflect on the role of banks in society

Sandrine Ansart and Virginie Monvoisin

Chapter overview

At the time when the banking sector is experiencing an historical crisis and a succession of financial scandals, questions are beginning to rise among both the public and analysts about bankers' practices.

This paper seeks to clarify this evolution of banking practices, referring mainly to the development of the banking profession throughout past centuries. Thus, the deep changes relating to risk and to risk taking in bankers' daily activities correspond to a transformation of the banks in respect of their responsibilities to the economy and society, and thereby to a change in values for the bankers themselves. We show that these mutations are at the origin of disastrous economic consequences and the adoption of questionable practices.

Introduction

The numerous scandals that have come to light in the financial sector over the last few years seem to have become ever more serious, provoking increasing condemnation by the general public. On the one hand, obvious disparities between the rewards and enrichment are considered more than extravagant, even improper. And, on the other hand, the severe difficulties being constantly aggravated by the current economic crisis put the financial system, its actors, and specifically their behaviour, at the heart of questions about ethics.

At the forefront of this activity, one of these financial actors attracts a great deal of attention – the banks. Singling them out seems to be all the more necessary as a good proportion of them – and in a number of countries – were supported by the State and public money in 2008 and early 2009. Thus, they recorded colossal profits and paid extravagant bonuses in the second half of 2009. Worse still, for a number of years, they arguably no longer fulfil a key role for which they are responsible – they are no longer offering the financial intermediation service required by the economic sector. This is seen for example by the implementation in France of credit mediators[1] who seek to prevent any bank's unjustified refusal for credit. This environment, which is already critical of banking practices, worsens even further when the recent frauds perpetrated by Kerviel, Madoff and Goldman Sachs are included. Without stating that these frauds are a common banking practice, banks today are well and truly in the line of fire.

In fact, the crisis has shown how bankers' practices, and even more their business, have changed over recent years; professional references are no longer the same – because the sector has developed so fast – so questions about ethics are now being asked. But what approach to ethics and what questions does the banking business provoke?

The banking sector has few specific characteristics: it has a *role in society*. The importance of the banker's role in the economy can be gleaned from the intervention by different States – of whatever nationality – and the size of their intervention during the events of 2008: States joined their forces and rushed to intervene in order to prevent a string of bankruptcies by banks and in the banking system in order to maintain a payment and financial structure essential to economic activity. The authorities had learned from the crisis in the 1930s. They therefore believed – and reminded everyone – that banks fulfil a real mission for society, that they are responsible for a true societal activity, they have *a real responsibility to society*.

Passet (2003) explains that any company generates four types of impact – on nature, on agents within the company, on agents outside the company and on society – and each impact can become the object of a responsibility and therefore the implementation of ethics. The 1929 crisis not only showed the possible impact of banks on society but also the extent of this impact. Following the crisis in the 1930s, the authorities set up financial regulations designed to avoid such a crisis ever happening again.

Thus, any reflection about the ethics of the banker (which represents Level 1 of analysis in the terms of Chapter 2) must take into account this societal role; it is the cornerstone for new regulation. It means creating a regulatory method devoted not only to stability and risk management, but also to supporting the societal role of the bank – namely, *regulations for ethics*.

We therefore propose to develop our demonstration in two parts. The first part will discuss banking practices over the centuries in order to determine the role – and therefore the business – that the banks are engaged in with other players in society, thus underlining *the economic role of banks*. The second part will go beyond this economic activity to discuss the existence of a *responsibility towards society*[2] that the banks should have, referring to the 1930s crisis and the more recent period leading to the present crisis.

Our approach includes the banks' and bankers' responsibilities to society in a collective sense and therefore in a macroeconomic sense, corresponding to Level 2 of analysis shown in Chapter 2. This does not mean covering Corporate

Social Responsibility in a general way by referring to the different ways of integrating social and environmental aspects that the banks could implement in the same way as other firms. We propose rather to examine the banks' specific economic functions as an essential dimension of the economy and of society.

We will therefore define a certain number of conditions that arise from an analysis of economic history and that today seem to lead to ethical and regulatory requirements for banks. To demonstrate this, we would particularly quote on the one hand the rejection, or at least the disbelief, of the general public about banking practices and, on the other hand, the challenges concerning the new standards to be implemented for financial regulation.

The historical core business of the banker's profession: skills in risk assessment

It appears difficult to assert that there is a clear definition of the banker's profession and his role in the economy that is universally accepted in the world of economics (see Ansart and Monvoisin 2012). Some use the vocabulary of the financial broker without realizing that the specifics of banking mean both generating payments and participating in the process of creating money.

Thus, to try to create this definition, we propose going back to the banker's profession and how it has developed over the ages. Defining the banker's profession, without at this stage referring to the theoretical framework of economics, leads us to construct this definition using the three main categories of operations undertaken by the banks. These are in fact the same operations that French banking laws have adopted since 1984 to characterize the banks, and that later inspired European banking laws in the 1990s. They are:

- collecting deposits
- granting credit
- managing procedures for payment.

In order to catalogue the banker's activities and determine whether these fall mainly in the categories above, we propose covering the period from antiquity to that between the two world wars.[3] Having completed this first step, we can outline the characteristics of the banker's profession and, specifically, his skills – namely, risk assessment and management. So whereas monetary theory can be discussed more or less scientifically around the five main ideas about banking operations and activities, our views will complete what is sometimes only a partial approach to banking and bankers (see Table 9.1).

The banker's role: accompanying economic activity

It may seem superfluous to reflect on the history of banking solely to insist upon how much bankers are involved in accompanying and supporting economic

TABLE 9.1 What is the banks' role in the economy? The activities of a modern bank

Profession	Operations	Economic functions
Skills: risk assessment	Deposits	Financial intermediary
Result: accompany the activity	Credits	Creation of money
	Means of payment	

activity. This could be considered as being well covered already. Nevertheless, based on the conduct and the deviations that have developed during the present crisis, and particularly the ever-growing implication of bankers in operations concerning stocks and, more and more, in derivatives, it appears both necessary and justified to remember what the banker's profession represents. Two main periods can be identified: until the seventeenth century; and then from the eighteenth century when the industrial revolution and the growth of economic activity strongly influenced the population's need for banking services.

This principle of accompanying production activities continued mainly *until the seventeenth century* through the management of procedures for payment, and less significantly for credit as such. Monetary functions – units of account, means of payment and store of value – explain both its use by, and its direct link to, the development of trade. During this period, the services offered by bankers concerned *the management of means of payment*: the diversity of monies – as a result of both the variety of cities issuing them and the physical characteristics of each form of money – positioned the banker as a type of 'exchange agent'.

Throughout the Middle Ages, trade grew through fairs, steering a course between places and periods that were more or less stable, and influenced too by the crusades. The banker's profession thus remained closely linked to both national and international trade. 'The bill of fair, then the bill of exchange were methods for payment at a distance, without physically moving money' (Descamps and Soichot 2002, p. 25). 'As drawing interest was forbidden,[4] the merchant bankers' income was based on these foreign exchange spot and forward transactions which disguised actual credits' (Descamps and Soichot 2002, p. 26).

The banker thus manages means of payment and, by offering advances against future payments, he sustained production activities by supplying a service. He managed both risk in a given area and risk over a given time against payments from sales made, thereby supporting production that had already been initiated.

From the eighteenth century onwards, in addition to these operations for the management of payments, which obviously became more and more complex, credit activities in the widest sense of the term grew together with the banker's profession. This is in the context of the boom in industry based initially on the first industrial revolution, and then on the second. The first banking development was the arrival of the 'High Banks', which were the forerunners of 'investment banking'. Both were mainly devoted to financing firms. At the end of the nineteenth century, the first major long-term deposit banks appeared alongside investment banking. The banker's profession, with his skills in granting credit, evolved initially with companies. There was no question at the time of offering credit to families. It represented *production that was financed*.[5]

This supposes a close bond between the banker and his customer. The banker, who needs information and guarantees,[6] establishes an almost family relationship with his creditor or debtor.

The banker – his implication and his responsibilities: a certain type of link to economic risk

The inventory of bankers' operations during a number of centuries leads us to understand how their activities were intimately related to production, by initially being responsible for *means of payment* (remittances) to shore up the sales of that which was produced – that is, production – and then by indirect or even direct *financing* of the production itself, through the purchase and occasional resale of securities. Banks financed private activities and public activities – certain of the latter may even include wars. As *the banker's responsibility* consists of accompanying the individual's, the company's or public credit and deposits, *the banker fully assumes this responsibility* because it is his core business.

For the period being reviewed here, it does not seem that the main operations and the associated responsibilities that the banker assumes have been greatly modified – credit, deposits or means of payment always remain within his field of activity. The reason for this is very simple: no other economic agent is able to exercise this very specific type of accompaniment which is not directly productive but essential for production and which has its own status. In general, responsibilities and the profession have both developed only marginally over the centuries.

However, it appears that a change did in fact occur that produced major upheavals. This did not concern the banker's profession or his missions as such; it was in a key element – that of the approach to risk that was used by the banker until the end of the nineteenth century. More specifically, this association with risk was based on:

- the banker's participation in using his own resources for a large part of his activities
- the closeness, the proximity – in the familiar sense – that existed between the banker and the entrepreneurs that he financed, and whom he often followed on an almost daily basis.

It so happens that, until the end of the nineteenth century, it was above all the bankers themselves with their close family and business relations that were the agents capable of supplying finance. The banker was thus involved in economic activity in two ways: as a financial intermediary and as a key actor because of his ability to finance activities.[7] The financial resources thus made available to the banks –

even if a part of them could then be used to finance securities – came mainly from the banker's own equity, as well as that of his family, his friends and/or from his professional network.[8]

This important share of the banker's and his relations' own assets in the volume of capital managed by our banker leads one to suppose an *entrepreneurial behaviour*, that is, engaging in risk activities. This adoption of risk does not mean 'too much risk' or 'not enough risk', but an awareness of risk considered 'acceptable', even 'just the right amount of risk', '*responsible risk*', in an activity related to production as it concerned methods of payment, short- and medium-term credit, buying securities or trade and arbitration. The fact that the banker was personally involved in the funds invested encouraged him to adopt a *certain approach to risk*.

Let us also add that this approach to risk can be even more motivating when the banker himself comes from a commercial or industrial sector: certain of them were initially at the head of a trading company,[9] others wanted to create their own bank, such as the Credit Lyonnais – today the LCL – founded in 1863 by businessmen in the Lyon area who came from the metal industry in the Loire and from gas and silk firms in Lyon. Not only may the banker himself initially be an entrepreneur in the industrial sector – he also maintains an important personal role in the management of companies (Demourgues 1988, pp. 111 and 118).

This role as an entrepreneur demonstrates his significant involvement in productive activities and therefore a *skill* – even an understanding – in the constraints, the challenges and the difficulties facing him every day. It is thus possible to speak of the banker's true proximity, even familiarity, with those engaged in production activities.

This proximity can be explained notably by the preponderance of short- and medium-term credit granted by the banks for financing firms. These credits, which were first and foremost agreements for overdrafts (Bonin 2000, p. 94) required bankers to be particularly close to the company that they were financing in order to appreciate the fluctuation in its activities and assess the risk to which they were exposed. This was more than ever necessary in view of the many uncertainties and variables to which the companies were subjected at that time.

Thus bankers – by exercising their profession – took over *a true role of accompanying productivity at the societal level* by both managing means of payment and deposits, and making credit available. It appears that during this period, it was possible to say 'accompanying production' in view of the bankers' financial and managerial involvement. Bankers obviously did not support every activity, but chose on the basis of the skills that they were thought to have, that is, *assessing and managing risk*. By selecting some projects and refusing others, one can assume that the bankers created a *certain form of risk control* at the economic level.

These practices lead us to recognize certain key characteristics in the earlier bankers' approach to risk. We refer here to the high percentage of the banker's (and/or his family's) assets in the volume of capital managed by the financial intermediary, and its proximity to those involved in production. One can therefore suppose that (i) particular attention is paid to the risks involved and (ii) through the banker's significant participation in projects for the production of goods and services, he becomes in effect an *entrepreneur*.

It should be emphasized that the banker 'is involved' rather than 'has invested'.

The regulation of risk thus exercised by the banker also relied on the fact that the banker – investing for himself and/or his family – first evaluated the risk of integrating and keeping a *portfolio of assets*. The approach to risk is then much more based on his evaluation – a primary and constant evaluation – than on his management. Risk management at that time consisted of continuously evaluating the risk – through direct implication or very regular, close monitoring – and integrating it in a strategy of diversification of assets, possibly selling them if necessary. Management did not rely on the active recourse to various techniques for protection against risk or for disposing of the risk.

This analysis therefore allows us to define a banker's ethics based on his 'ancestral' practices where the banker was clearly responsible to society and his customers for fulfilling a specific mission at the economic level (see Figure 9.1): accompanying production by making available methods for payment and financing.

We should also emphasize that his legitimacy was rarely contested because his status – rich, industrial or notable personality – encouraged and authorized him to 'create and do business'. As an entrepreneur, he took risks and knew how to evaluate them. His wealth built up over time; always envied but rarely questioned.

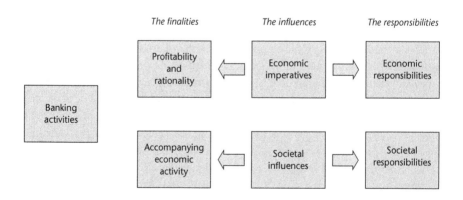

As for every company, the bank is faced with two obligations, sometimes contradictory. The first relates to its own profitability which depends on economic imperatives which are known and acknowledged by economists and managers (see R. Passet). The second concerns its impact on society in the widest sense (on production, consumers, society and nature). For the bank, the main element of this societal influence is that the bank accompanies economic activity. This social responsibility remains very poorly identified.

FIGURE 9.1 Banking activities and responsibilities.

The banks' societal role: a revelation through the crisis of the 1930s and that of 2008

We have clarified bankers' ancestral practices to define and explain the nature of their profession: accompanying production by making means of payment available, receiving deposits and granting credit while managing risk. It is this reference point that allows us to question current banking practices. As for any profession, that of the banker has seen and still experiences major changes, together with those in society and technology, described as adaptation and even crucial adaptation. But can one state that this profession has changed fundamentally? Even if its areas of influence have expanded, its basic operations remain indispensable for the reasons stated above – these operations can only be assumed by the banks. The basic definition of the banker's profession remains valid.

How then can one judge the role in the banks' accompaniment of production today when their implication is more and more dependent on financial markets and the pursuit of activities such as primary securities and derivatives? Or how can one judge their management of risk in the light of the banks' stated recourse to securitization – one of the mechanisms that contributed to the 2008–2009 crisis – when this process is known to allow a bank to free itself of any risk?

It so happens that these periods of crisis allow the economic role of bankers, combined with their truly societal role, to be highlighted. To do so, we will revert to the 1930s crisis and that of the first decade of the present millennium.

The crisis of the 1930s and the recognition of the banks' specific responsibility in the economy

Reverting to the 1930s is not just a way to offer yet another series of comparisons between that crisis and the one of today. It was during the crisis of the 1930s that, firstly, most of the dangers relating to State intervention in difficult times were revealed and, secondly, that the societal role of the banks justified these interventions.

The crisis as a revelation of the pertinence of economic policies

The 1929 crisis arose at a time when economics appeared to have found its defining, fundamental principles, both theoretically and politically. Since the end of the eighteenth century, it seemed to be accepted that only the market and its unrestrained activity would in effect constitute an optimal economic policy. Although shaken by the social movements of the nineteenth century and monetary turmoil, laissez-faire reigned supreme. This was justified by an economic theory showing that the market regulates the economy and leads to an optimum – a true optimum outside monetary phenomena – and, more anecdotally, by an approach in which only the real phenomena are pertinent, money being simply a 'veil'.[10]

The violence of the 1929 crisis obliged politicians and economists to radically rethink their position. Although Hoover initially tried to get out of the crisis by favouring the market and the business world, Roosevelt initiated a policy of major public works and recovery, thus turning his back on two centuries of economic theory and practice. The era of the State of providence and interventionism then began in all sectors of the economy, and the banking and financial sectors were no exception.

The United States introduced the Glass–Steagall Act in 1933, which separated the activities of commercial banks from those of investment banks in order to avoid the former losing money on the capital markets, thereby provoking a run on the commercial banks. The objective was clearly to dissociate banking activities from speculative, market activities and to be able to anticipate any default in the banking system that had paralysed the economy.

It should be noted that the Glass–Steagall Act was repealed in 1999. After the McFadden Act in 1990, which forbade banks to locate outside their State of origin, the distinction between commercial banking and investment banking simply evaporated, ending with the liberalization of the banking sector. The growth of competition then reached the banks. Competition, synonymous with lower profitability, justified the introduction of products such as subprimes in 2001, which permitted both benefiting from the housing bubble and keeping the market share.

The crisis exposes the banks' economic responsibility

Thus, in 1929, the banking sector also became the object of regulations and legislation, even though monetary phenomena were previously considered as insignificant! How was this possible? To answer the question, it is necessary to return to the role of the banks during the crisis, which highlighted their societal function.

The 1929 and 2008 crisis scenarios are remarkable for their similarity, and particularly in the course of their events. Let us remember the conditions that existed.

- A real estate and mortgage crisis and grossly excessive debt – involving the banks, property developers and households – weakened the banking system.
- The virtual or real threat of bank failures provoked a restriction on credit because banks faced a liquidity and solvency crisis and cut back on loans.
- The reduction in credit turned out to be catastrophic for businesses who no longer had any financial resources and in turn found themselves weakened and in great difficulty.

Nevertheless, the lessons of 1929 had been learned and the authorities in 2000 were able to avoid a number of pitfalls; remember that between 1931 and 1933 some 9,000 American banking institutions went bankrupt, that is, 15 per cent of deposits in the banking system. At that time, the authorities had given the market its freedom and therefore the banks threatened with bankruptcy were not bailed out. The closure of the banks, dramatic for customers who saw their deposits and savings disappear, was even more disastrous for businesses that not only met the same fate but also had no possibility of financing themselves.

It is necessary here to understand that financing through lines of credit not only involves business investments, it also supports working capital, supplier credit, etc. Without credit or overdraft facilities, firms simply cannot operate. We have seen that the banking activity has many particularities that no other economic agent can assume. But it was necessary to await the arrival of the 1929 crisis for the importance of the banks' economic role to finally appear. Apparently it was necessary to await the arrival of the 2008 crisis for the importance of the banks' societal role to finally appear.

The present crisis and the revelation of the banks' societal role as regulators of risk

If the 1930s crisis allows us to emphasize the specific role of banks as an essential part in an industrial market economy, it is the present crisis that leads us to define this societal role, namely, a function of *regulating risk* (see Table 9.2). This is shown by referring to the practices of risk management that developed among the banks over the last ten years and that are at the heart of the mechanism of the crisis.

A new relationship towards risk

The banks' approach to risk has changed both in its assessment and its management. It is particularly this change in management that has made major advances and led bankers to adopt a new approach to risk. Three major developments can be observed that, when examined closely, highlight the evidence of a new approach to risk by bankers: the development of securitization, more and more recourse to collateralized debt obligations (CDOs) and collateralized default swap (CDS) and the reconciliation of two sectors, banking and insurance, which lead to referring more and more to 'bankinsurance' and a certain endorsement of a method of risk management through mutualization.

TABLE 9.2 What is the banks' role in the economy? Introduction of the idea of the societal role

Profession	Operations	Economic functions	Societal function
Skill: risk assessment	Deposits Credit	Financial intermediary	Regulation of risk
Result: accompanying economic activity	Means of payment	Creation of money	

Since the start of the 1980s, the importance of securities as both a bank's assets and liabilities has grown. What interests us here is mainly the process of securitization of banking assets. The classic intermediary has given way to an 'originate and distribute' model that takes into account the credit securitization process offered by the banks. Banks thus extract from their balance sheets the credits that they have initiated. These operations are all the more interesting as they extend the capacity for banks to lend because of credit securitization; these credits are no longer taken into account in the calculation of international ratios – the Basel agreements – as the commitments are transferred to the bank's equity. As a result of these operations, the banks:

- free themselves of the risk
- participate in the distribution of this risk through various financial products
- modify their approach to risk, as it is no longer in their portfolio
- build up outstanding credits for which the risk is not correctly appreciated.

This tendency towards securitization has found two financial instruments particularly harmful for the approach to risk by the banks – these are CDOs and CDS. CDOs are bonds secured by a group of assets generally consisting of bank credits, bonds and CDSs, combining different qualities of credit within the same fund. Overall, this creates a number of tranches of assets, the first tranche benefiting from maximum liquidity, ranked AAA by the rating agencies; the other tranches carry all the risk but offer higher returns. These funds were issued notably by financial institutions to cover risks related to loans with variable rates of interest, which represented 91.6 per cent of US mortgages in 2006.

These instruments were largely involved in the securitization process over recent years, allowing banks to remove debts from their balance sheets and to combine them in a specific fund (Special Purpose Vehicle). Dupuy (2008) clearly emphasizes that this concerns the transfer of risk within the financial profession: loans granted by agents were temporarily left in the hands of undercapitalized 'mortgage' banks and then resold in a block to the investment banks – hence the problems of Lehman Brothers – who restructured the loans and then, following their rating, sold them on to institutional investors. Participants in each link in this 'value' chain were thus motivated by the profits earned from bank charges.

This excessive securitization led to the development of many other innovations, including the infamous CDS. The appearance of these contracts resulting from credit defaults is the major innovation of recent years. In 2005, they represented US$426,000 billion, that is, the equivalent of private housing assets in the US, compared to US$18,500 billion in stock exchange capitalization and US$4,500 billion in treasury stocks. These CDSs simply allowed one to protect against risk of defaulting.

In other words, CDOs and CDSs offered banks new opportunities for managing risk. This method of management is particularly characterized by the possibility and especially the development by banks to no longer hold portfolios of credit –

credit initiated by the banks themselves. Thereafter, the stakes involved in the initial valuation of the risk at the moment it was created by the bank were considerably reduced. First, the securities had every chance of not remaining in the bank's portfolio; then its removal from the bank's balance sheet was facilitated by the opportunities for integrating doubtful debt into packages for which there was a high demand because quality and high returns were being offered. This was made all the more possible *in fine* because the new financial products were able to guarantee against risks of default.[11]

A new conduct in the face of its responsibilities

The bank, supposed to assume the risk when accompanying the entrepreneur, no longer does so and renounces responsibility for it. The older approach to risk that we have presented, including both the evaluation and management processes, is completely sidetracked. Management no longer means monitoring the initial risk that the bank considered 'acceptable' and that it therefore agreed to, once the evaluation process becomes biased and subject to influence, including in particular the assessment that led to the credit being granted in the first place. The close relationship between the banker and production activities that existed during previous centuries has little or no reason to survive. Risk evaluation activity is now positioned elsewhere: it concerns above all the evaluation of risk for secondary securities and not primary securities – those that are directly linked to the accompanying production activities.

Let us add to this the movement towards the reconciliation of the banking and insurance sectors over the past few years and we find here another argument for emphasizing this development of the approach to risk by the banks. Even if it is generally agreed that the common element between these two sectors lies in the management of risk, their approach and therefore their professions are not the same. For insurers, risk management relies on two basic principles – the relative probabilities of risk and the mutualization of risk across the population.

It appears here again that bankers' practices are evolving and in some ways are coming closer to this method of managing risk, which was not a part of their tradition. The instruments used by the banks for covering risk rely on their assessment of the probability of the risk maturing. By disseminating risk the securitization process, notably with the CDOs and CDSs, creates a de facto mutualization of the risk. One thus finds oneself considerably removed from the approach to risk that the banks adopted during the last century.

The banks, who are supposed to be experts in evaluating risk, accepting it or refusing it, making funds available and then managing them, are an essential regulator of risk for the economy – when they exercise their traditional profession. It would seem that the evolution of their activity has led them to abandon this regulatory function and, even worse, to be the originators of new risks (see Figure 9.2).

Certain observers, including Jacques de Larosière, speak of 'losing the sense of risk'.[12] No doubt some of these cases, as some commentators have highlighted,

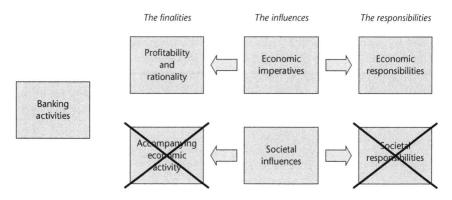

FIGURE 9.2 Banking activities and responsibilities in the 2000s.

remain occasional incidents that can be considered as 'mistakes'. Few refer to these 'mistakes' as being symptomatic of deeper problems within the banking profession and the approach to risk as it is seen and practised today. Bankers no longer assume their societal responsibility for regulating risk because they no longer assume their economic and societal roles. Their values – as 'references' or 'principles' – have changed:

- It is no longer necessary to fulfil the internal economic constraints – now they have to be maximized.
- It is not only about maintaining financial profitability but also about finding all the possible effects of leverage in the capital markets.

This leads bankers to become involved in activities generating risk, that is, *the opposite of their initial responsibility*.

This deviation is seen in the general public's opinion of the banking sector. The public is deeply shocked by bankers' remunerations, by both the amounts involved and the apparent ease and speed with which they create their own fortunes.[13] The perception of this loose and careless behaviour is reinforced by the attitude of the banking sector and the increasing number of scandals that seem to strengthen the argument that bankers are only concerned with their own profitability.

Thus, major changes have occurred and continue today:

- As a result of banks' detachment from production activities in both their own interests and those of third parties, an increasing part of their net banking returns comes from activities and arbitraging relating to securities and derivative products.
- Serious questions have arisen about risk regulation activities at the economic level as banks no longer have the same restrictions for evaluating risk because they now manage it differently.

- Beyond the reduction in risk regulation activities relating to the overall economy in general, banks are themselves becoming producers and distributors of risk: they are actively participating in a risk-mutualization process and no longer fulfil their primary mission. So who manages risk? Who has the skills for managing risk?

Thus, what about the banker's ethic regarding those mutations and breaches? Bankers claim to assume perfectly their responsibilities concerning agents inside and outside the bank. For example, they all run projects for sustainable development and corporate societal responsibility and describe themselves as 'ethical' – like the Crédit Coopératif in France. Publicity campaign or real concern, the use of 'ethical' seems here irrelevant.

In fact, these projects relate to secondary activities of banks and not its fundamental activity. The banker's ethic for banking operations and for his societal responsibilities does not exist. An ethic for the shareholders, for the employees or for ecological matters has been rising for years – especially since the financial crisis. An ethic for the banker's profession, per se granting credit or accompanying production, is still to define.

Conclusion

The economic and societal roles of banks are extremely important. We have seen that they have accompanied economic activity since the beginning. Banks first existed to accept methods of payment and sustain trade. They then supported production by granting credit. Some may even say that the economy could not function without them. Their skills, the heart of the banking profession, consist of assessing and managing risk – the risk of means of payment and credit.

The recent developments in the banking and financial sector have altered the profession very considerably and the banker's trade, as he exercised it since time immemorial, seems to have been abandoned. Banks prefer to concentrate their main activities in other fields, often financial and above all more profitable. This has its consequences.

First, the economic consequences: the crisis has shown us that the banks' failure to support firms – an economic role – had disastrous results! Then the social consequences: by relinquishing their mission to evaluate and regulate risk – the societal role – bankers forced the economies into grave difficulties as no other player can replace the banks without in turn becoming a bank; this societal role is the very basis of banking activity.

To be even more precise, the bank has turned away from the risk related to the customer's activity in order to focus on the risk generated by its own activity, mainly in the stock markets. For a long time, the banker's ethic was not questioned. Bankers assumed their economic and societal responsibilities; the sector's morals were neither suspected nor 'suspicious' because bankers appeared to be legitimate in both their functions and their positions. Today, not only do bankers' practices invite many questions but they also distance the banks from their first responsibility as regulators of risk. And bankers appear to have less and less moral legitimacy in their professional and societal positions because they have abandoned their classic functions and responsibilities, even their duties towards society.[14]

While politicians and economists work to produce new banking rules, the question of the sector's responsibility and ethics becomes more and more important. As a regulator of risk, bankers should respect ethics that are appropriate to the profession. Simple rules are not applicable here, particularly as their main theme consists principally of managing financial agents' risks and not those of the overall economy; only full legislation would allow both the recognition of the societal role and its control. The introduction – or restoration – of banking ethics needs to come from legislation aimed at controlling banking practices in accordance with their economic and above all social responsibilities.

Notes

1　Oséo saw its activity explode over the last two years and is increasing the number of its regional centres to forward the monitoring of requests for credit to the banks.

2　The term employed here has no direct relationship to Corporate Social Responsibility as generally understood. See the following paragraph.

3　We exclude from this return to the past the more recent period from the end of the Second World War, for two reasons. The end of this war was noted for the State takeover of channels of credit in order to meet the overwhelming needs for reconstruction and particularly for long-term financing. Since then, this statutory situation can be considered as introducing a bias in the nature of the banker's 'trade'. Also, the process that followed for liberating controls is much better understood than for the previous periods, and will be discussed in part during the analysis of bankers' current professional practices.

4　We can perhaps consider the Church's ban on charging interest.

5　This financing was available through two main channels: '*rural, seasonal*' credit, or short- and medium-term credit, that assisted companies for their cash flow, and *medium- and long-term* credit, through the subscription by these banks in large volumes of shares. Banks are the key players: they are both the institution that organizes the issue of shares and their subscription, and who then manage the comprehensive written records of these operations. These financing activities through shares were very considerable at the time.

6　As we will see later.

7　The banker invested his personal assets in various activities. These can include:

- during the Middle Ages, personally taking risks related to the 'spice trade' in international commerce and development in foreign countries: trade in precious metals, money, spices, carpets and furs, merchant vessels, development of distant countries, local artisans and financing new activities (Demourgues 1988, p. 111);
- in the nineteenth century, merchant banks particularly devoting an important part of their activity to taking major personal risks through the creation of new companies, in exchange for sharing in the decision-making process in these companies (Demourgues 1988, p. 118);
- at the same time, the 'High Banks' and then merchant banks, supported by the deposit banks (for investing in an increasing volume of shares), being major actors in share investments by the issuing of syndicates for which they are mandated, take major personal risks as they commit to buying unplaced assets for their own account (Bonin 1992, pp. 109–110).

8 Let us remember that banks had a relatively limited number of deposit customers until the nineteenth century; thereafter, this clientele consisted above all of large fortunes often resulting from the development of economic activity, as was the case for the middle class from whom the banks sought to attract the cash resulting from their daily activities.

9 The most notable example is Worms, which moved from trading in coal to become a bank (Bonin 2000, p. 61).

10 Here, theoreticians consider that money is neutral, that it has no influence on the economy.

11 Despite possible parallels with the idea of moral hazard (cf. Chapter 11 of this work), we would point out that his idea falls within a regulatory framework and describes practices for avoidance. Here, we describe practices that were freely adopted.

12 Jacques de Larosière notes particularly that 'a certain number of financial institutions wished nevertheless to increase their revenue by granting risky credit with higher margins. In order to attract investors – by securitizing these credits – they offered them returns above the customary low interest rates; many financial institutions encouraged them to take excessive risks' (de Larosière 2008, p. 12).

13 Greed and excessive desire for material goods are in fact considered by most moral codes as cardinal sins. If we refer to the level of moral criticism identified in Chapter 1, it is a strong criticism of the banker as an individual.

14 This implies a Level 2 moral criticism (Chapter 2), i.e. a criticism of the role and contribution of the financial system for the harmonious operation of society. It can even lead to questioning the entire current financial system.

References

Ansart, Sandrine and Monvoisin, Virginie (2012) 'Le métier du banquier et le risque : La dénaturation des fonctions de financement du système bancaire'. *Cahiers d'Économie Politique*, forthcoming.

Bonin, Hubert (1992) *La banque et les banquiers en France du Moyen-âge à nos jours*. Paris: Coll. Références Larousse Histoire, Larousse.

Bonin, Hubert (2000) *Le monde des banquiers français au XXème siècle*. Paris: Edition Complexe.

Bourguinat, Henry (1992) *Finance Internationale*. Paris: Presses Universitaires de France.

de Larosière, Jacques (2008) 'La crise financière actuelle. Pourquoi le système a-t-il déraillé? Réflexions sur la titrisation'. *Revue d'Économie Financière*, no. Hors-Série Crise financière: Analyse et propositions.

De Mourgues Michèle (1988) *La monnaie. Système financier et Théorie monétaire*. Paris: Economica.

Descamps, Christian and Soichot, Jacques (2002) *Économie et Gestion de la Banque*. Colombelles: Coll. Management & Société, Editions EMS.

Dupuy, Claude (2008) 'Crise financière 2007-2008: les raisons du désordre mondial / Entretien avec Claude Dupuy'. *La Documentation Française*, www.ladocumentation francaise.fr/dossiers/crise-financiere-2007-2008-index.shtml (consulté le 10 janvier 2010).

Passet, René (2003) *L'émergence contemporaine de l'interrogation éthique en économie*. Paris: United Nations Educational, Scientific and Cultural Organization, Économie Éthique no. 2

10

ISLAMIC FINANCE REVISITED

A brief review with the Singapore example

Habibullah Khan and Omar K. M. R. Bashar

Chapter overview

Islamic finance has been growing rapidly over the years. Although it was not fully immune from the global financial crisis (GFC) of 2008 and the subsequent economic downturn, it was viewed more favourably mainly owing to its lesser exposure to speculative investments. This chapter briefly examines the concepts and principles behind various Islamic finance products. Although religions, particularly the more organized ones such as Islam, generally impose strict ethical standards on both individuals and business firms, it is often difficult to specify what exactly should be construed as a 'socially responsible business practice'. The UN Global Compact launched in July 2000 plays a significant role in this regard as it clearly states ten universally accepted principles in the areas of human rights, labour standards, environment and anti-corruption (for details see United Nations Global Compact 2008) that need to be embraced by companies for sustainability and responsible business operations. Some conservative Muslims have, however, raised questions about whether business entities engaged in '*haram*' activities (prohibited in Islam) could be treated as socially responsible. We believe that a 'moderate' stance is beneficial for peaceful coexistence of Muslims and non-Muslims in today's globalized world and both will benefit from businesses that follow the framework laid out in the UN Global Compact, even though some of these businesses are not truly Islamic. Singapore, for example, although not an Islamic country, aims to promote itself as a centre for Islamic finance in Southeast Asia. The city-state republic offers various Islamic finance products alongside conventional banking and finance products as part of its strategy to become an international financial centre.

The chapter is organized as follows: after introducing the concepts and principles of Islamic finance, we discuss the ethical issues involved in Islamic finance. A case study of Islamic finance in Singapore is then presented and we conclude the case study with a summary of the main points and closing remarks. Since, as we shall see, Islamic finance involves a detailed set of rules for how businesses should behave in respect of borrowing and lending, speculative activity and distribution of wealth, the discussion clearly involves both Level 1 and Level 2 critique as outlined in Chapter 1 of this book. To the extent that one may be prompted to reflect on the overall impact of Islamic as opposed to other more conventional types of financing and to compare these as to their beneficence one will in effect be at the Level 3 critique: the comparison of different moral codes and their overall effects.

Introduction to Islamic finance

The operations and activities of the Islamic banking system or Islamic finance are fully governed by the Islamic or Shariah rules. The main factor that distinguishes Islamic banks (IBs) from conventional banks (CBs) is that all transactions are administered without involving any element of interest or *riba*. There is a general consensus among Muslim scholars that the word *riba* encompasses both 'interest' (a fixed rate paid against a loan or deposit) and 'usury' (exceedingly high interest rate) and all types of *riba* are considered illegal (*haram*) even if they are associated with productive loans or consumptions. The Muslim creditors are allowed only to demand the principal amount from borrowers and they are urged to deal justly and fairly with debtors. In the event that the debtor is unable to pay his/her debt, the lender can either extend the repayment or convert the loan to charity depending on the circumstances faced by the borrower. Besides, the IBs are based on principles such as a ban on speculation owing to uncertainty and lack of transparency (*gharar*), adherence to risk sharing as well as profit sharing, promotion of socially responsible and ethical investments that are conducive to the welfare of society, and asset-backing of all financial transactions.

A distinctive feature of Islamic finance is that it does not allow the creation of debt through direct lending and borrowing of money or other financial assets. The debts can only be created through the sale or lease of real assets through lease-based financing schemes (such as *murabaha*, *ijara* and *sukuk*). The asset that is leased or sold must be real (building, property or any other physical infrastructure) and the transaction must be genuine (approved by government regulators, as well as religious experts comprising the Shariah board) with the full intention of giving and taking charge, and the associated debt (risk) cannot be sold or transferred to someone else.

As a result of a strict discipline from religious as well as regulatory points of view introduced into the process of debt creation, the growth of Shariah-compliant financial (SCF) products can rise only in line with growth of the real economy. The system thus provides a self-protective device and curbs speculative transactions leading to excessive credit expansions. If economic growth fails to achieve the target or enters into a phase of contraction, Islamic finance institutions will suffer but they are unlikely to go bankrupt as borrowers are treated as joint owners and are liable to incur losses (and profits at times of high growth). From an individual investor's perspective, Islamic finance is usually considered a 'low risk, low gain' system that should satisfy the needs of those who subscribe to the basic principles of Shariah (which generally discourages greed and excessive wealth accumulation). The innocent and those who are not fully aware of the benefits (as well as associated risks) of financial investments are protected against any kind of fraudulent activities that may arise out of pure speculation or exploitation of ignorance.

Like conventional banks, Islamic banks also provide a wide variety of financial products, a brief description of which is given below:

- Profit-sharing financial products

    - *Musharakah* – all partners participate in terms of equity, investment, management and profit (based on pre-agreed ratio) and loss (based on equity contributions);
    - *Mudarabah* – one contributes capital, others provide entrepreneurship. Profit is shared on a pre-agreed ratio;
    - *Qard Hasan* – charitable loans that are free of interest and profit-sharing margins; repayment by instalments. A modest service charge is permissible;
    - *Wakalah* – a bank is authorized to conduct business on customers' behalf;
    - *Hawalah* – an agreement by the bank to undertake some of the liabilities of the customer in return for a service fee. The customer pays back the bank when the liabilities mature.

- Advance-purchase financial products

    - *Murabaha* – a contract between the bank and its client for the sale of goods at a price that includes a profit margin agreed by both parties;
    - *Istithna'* – a contract for acquisition of goods by specification or order, where the price is paid progressively in accordance with the progress of job completion;
    - *Mu'ajjal* – a sales contract that allows purchase with deferred delivery;
    - *Ijarah* – a leasing contract under which a bank buys and leases out for a rental fee equipment required by its clients;
    - *Sukuk* – a bond that prohibits the charging or paying of interest. Funds raised through the issuance of *sukuk* are invested in an underlying asset and trust certificates evidencing the holder's pro rata share of the ownership of the underlying assets are issued. The certificate holder is entitled to the benefits generated by that asset in proportion to his or her contribution.

- Deposit products

    Wadi'ah – deposits, including current accounts (*giro wadi'ah*). Under this safe custody principle, *hibah* (gift) in the form of dividends may be distributed to customers as a token of appreciation for depositing their money with banks in savings or term deposits. The rewards (gifts) may be in the form of cash bonus, or kind (air ticket for Haj, cars, carpets, etc.) or profit as announced by the bank;

- *Mudarabah* – in effect deposit products based on revenue sharing between depositor and bank, including savings products that can be withdrawn any time and time-deposit products;
- *Qard al-Hasanah* – unremunerated deposit products, usually for charitable purposes.

• Insurance products

- *Takaful* – Islamic insurance based on the principles of social responsibility, cooperation and mutual indemnification of losses of any of the participants. The *takaful* contract usually involves *mudarabah* (profit-sharing contract with one party investing capital and the other party providing specialist knowledge to invest and manage the capital), *tabarru* (to donate for the benefit of others), and mutual sharing of losses with a view to eliminate uncertainty.

Starting with the establishment of Mit Ghamr Savings Bank in Egypt in 1963, the international market for Islamic banking and finance has grown substantially over the years. Although the size of assets under Islamic finance tends to vary owing to different interpretations of Shariah, the latest data (see IFSL Research 2010) published by International Financial Services London (IFSL) shows that Shariah-compliant assets have grown from a meagre $150 billion in the mid 1990s to a staggering $951 billion at the end of 2008. Although the average growth rates have hovered around 10–15 per cent annually over the past ten years, the Islamic assets have seen strong growth in the years preceding the GFC. For example, total assets grew from $549 billion in 2006 to $758 billion in 2007 showing a 38 per cent growth in the year 2006–07, and the same assets grew from $758 billion to $951 billion between 2007 and 2008, registering a 25 per cent rise in 2007–08. Commercial banks account for the bulk of the Islamic assets (74 per cent) with investment banks and *sukuk* bonds accounting for another 10 per cent each, and Islamic funds and *takaful* making up the remaining 6 per cent. The top five countries for Shariah-compliant assets in 2008 were Iran ($293 billion), Saudi Arabia ($128 billion), Malaysia ($87 billion), UAE ($84 billion) and Kuwait ($68 billion). The UK, in eighth place, was the leading Western country with $19 billion of reported assets largely based on HSBC Amanah.

Despite the rapid growth of Islamic banking and finance in recent years, the factors contributing to its diffusion are still not well understood. A recent study by Imam and Kpodar (2010) concluded that factors such as the September 2001 terrorist attacks in New York and the quality of institutions did not play any visible role in the diffusion of Islamic banking. The study concludes that Islamic banking is a complement to CBs as devout Muslims want Islamic banking products that CBs are not supplying. Having a well-functioning conventional banking system already in place – through sharing of a common platform and human capital, helps spread Islamic banking, the authors argued (Imam and Kpodar 2010).

Indeed, Islamic banking, despite its rapid growth in recent years, cannot be seen as a substitute for conventional banking. Why? First, although it has been operating for long in the Gulf and Iran and there is also some evidence that IBs in Malaysia have performed better than CBs, the system is yet to be fully tested with a wider set of data and there is hardly any country (with the exception of Iran) that practises it exclusively. Second, the Muslim world is predominantly comprised of developing countries from the south (such as India, Pakistan, Bangladesh and Indonesia) and some poor African countries (such as Egypt, Nigeria and Sudan) and they are overly dependent on Western foreign aid and loans. As a result, these countries are tied to the conventional financial system and they cannot jeopardize their development efforts by implementing some other system. Third, Islamic finance is not opposed to capitalism (in fact all Muslim countries, including the rich Persian Gulf states, are capitalistic in nature and are characterized by huge concentrations of wealth and income disparity) and is therefore unlikely to support any radical transformation of the prevailing financial system.

Have IBs been affected by the GFC and the subsequent economic meltdown? Though not severely affected, the growth of Islamic assets was rather flat in 2009. Some banks suffered a higher rate of non-performing loans than CBs owing to their exposure to falling real estate markets. Revenue and profitability also suffered in both 2008 and 2009 and liquidity was a significant restraint for some banks. The *sukuk* market declined somewhat in 2008 but recovered quickly in 2009. A recent IMF study (Hasan and Dridi 2010) compared the performance of IBs and CBs during the recent global crisis and concluded that factors related to IBs' business model (the asset-based risk-sharing nature of Islamic finance) helped limit the adverse impact on profitability in 2008, while weaknesses in risk-management practices in some IBs led to a larger decline in profitability in 2009 compared to CBs. IBs' credit and asset growth performed better than did that of CBs in 2008–09, contributing to financial and economic stability. Large IBs have fared better than small ones. Better diversification, economies of scale and a stronger reputation might have contributed to this better performance. External rating agencies' reassessment of IBs' risk was generally more favourable. In sum, adherence to Shariah principles precluded IBs from financing or investing in the kind of instruments that have adversely affected their conventional competitors and triggered the GFC, the study claimed.

Ethical issues in Islamic finance

Islamic finance is based on the fundamental teachings of Islam that are contained in the verses of Holy Quran and the Hadith that carry guidelines and views given by the Prophet Muhammad. Besides, the views of Islamic scholars are also considered important particularly when instructions on certain issues are difficult to understand or cannot be easily found in the above. Shariah law sets out the guidelines for a Muslim to lead his/her life in the meaningful way that is required by Allah and it classifies things/activities into three categories:

- *halal* – lawful and encouraged
- *haram* – prohibited (e.g. alcohol)
- *makruh* – discouraged.

Although Muslims consider this worldly life as purely temporary they have been asked to work to earn a living (*rezeki*) by means of honest labour and economical use of the resources that Allah has bestowed upon them. Islam regards business as a preferred option for sustenance (in fact, Prophet Muhammad in his early life was a trader) but those who are engaged in business should be honest/righteous and must give to charity, as pronounced in the Quran through the following verse:

> Those who rehearse the Book of Allah, establish regular prayer, and spend [in Charity] out of what we have provided for them, secretly and openly, hope for commerce that will never fail.
>
> (Surah Fatir, verse 29)

The implication of the above verse is that a Muslim (Believer) businessman does not have absolute ownership of the property he possesses and he cannot reinvest the entire profit for business expansion as he has an obligation to allocate part of the property to paying *zakat* and offering charity. The business undertaken by the Believers will not fail as Allah has assured them the return. Business carried out in accordance with the teachings of the Quran and Hadith will not only lead to profits in this world but also in the next world.

Islam requires that men and women follow the path of life in light of the teachings of the Quran and Hadith. Any action that is based on Islamic philosophy is regarded an act or worship (*ibadah*) and this lays the foundation for ethics in Islam. The Islamic businesses (banks and financial institutions included) are not mainly profit motivated – rather they focus on betterment of the community at large. Islamic banks are expected to be particularly mindful about the needs of the Muslim society though they can extend their services to any other religious groups as well, promote social welfare programmes and activities and make more contributions to the poor and needy. Islam forbids the accumulation of wealth (hoarding) by individuals for self-interest and indeed such an act could create social imbalances (income inequality) and stifle economic growth. The holy Quran in the following verse strongly discourages such acts and warns of severe punishments for the violators and their businesses:

> And not let those who covetously withhold of the gifts which Allah hath given to them of His Grace, think that it is good for them: and, it will be worse for them; soon shall the things which they covetously withheld be tied to their necks like a twisted collar, on the Day of Judgment. To Allah belongs the heritage of the heavens and the earth; and Allah is well-acquainted with all that ye do.
>
> (Surah Ali Imran, verse 180)

Based on the fundamental principles of Islam described above, the ethical basis for Islamic businesses can be summarized as follows.

Role of firms

Islam encourages doing business; however, the activities of a business should be *halal*. Transactions or businesses involving interest, market manipulation, as well as risky transactions are not permitted in Islamic finance. Although there are some differences of opinion on the definition of interest and its applications, Islam clearly prohibits interest (*riba*) of all kinds. The main argument is that interest may create social problems by making the rich richer and the poor poorer. Moreover, there is always an element of risk in business (no matter how well run the business is) and a fixed amount of payment (interest) to creditors may put businesses in trouble, particularly in a situation when profitability declines or the economy faces a general slowdown of activities for reasons beyond control. Corruption and cheating are highly discouraged and all the stakeholders of the business should be treated fairly and with respect.

Consumer issues

Islam puts consumer welfare ahead of the producers or suppliers. Price fixing is prohibited and the price should reflect the market conditions and affordability of the customers. Islam is particularly mindful about the needs of the poor and discourages hoarding of any kind that may increase the prices. The supplier should adhere to the quality, weight and measures as quoted in the product disclosure. The following verse of the Quran clearly shows that Allah has given topmost priority to protection of consumer interests:

> Give just measure and cause no loss [to others by fraud]. And weigh with scales true and upright. And withhold not things, justly due to men, nor do evil in the land, working mischief.
>
> (Surah asy-Syura, verses 181–183)

Environmental issues

Islamic teachings are based on the notion that everything (that includes all natural resources) is created by Allah and the men and women are expected to maximize their gains through proper utilization of resources. Wastage of any kind and overutilization of resources are strongly discouraged in Islam. It also emphasizes the need for the protection of nature by preserving forests and jungles, water and mineral resources, birds, bees and animals (particularly those that are not harmful to humans), planting trees, using farmland cautiously so as to retain its fertility, and restricting land use for productive purposes only (while construction of housing, essential infrastructure and wage goods production by means of appropriate technology have been encouraged, building of unnecessary structures and production of hazardous goods that are harmful to the environment are discouraged).

Discrimination

Islam strongly encourages fair treatment; discrimination against minorities or people from other faiths is discouraged. It also emphasizes gender equality and respect for women in particular. In fact, the equitable distribution of income can be related with the concept of justice in Islam. Allah has assured that everyone would be able to enjoy bounties on earth (created by Allah) and the Quran particularly mentioned that all resources on earth have been created for human beings and that humans are the masters of the resources. There is also a provision for wealth redistribution (the compulsory *zakat* system) among the less fortunate in the Islamic system. The basic principle of equality is also clearly reflected in the Prophet Muhammad's Last Sermon:

> No Arab has superiority over any non-Arab and no non-Arab has any superiority over an Arab; no dark person has superiority over a white person and no white person has any superiority over a dark person. The criterion of honour in the sight of Allah is righteousness and honest living.
>
> (quoted by Williams and Zinkin 2005)

It is evident from the above that Islam has recommended high ethical standards for any business that includes banking and finance and violators are warned of serious consequences in this world and thereafter. Williams and Zinkin (2010) in a recent study made a meticulous review of the basic tenets of Islam and the ten principles of the UN Global Compact. They conclude that with the possible exception of Islam's focus on personal responsibility and the non-recognition of the corporation as a legal person, there is no divergence between the tenets of the religion and the principles of the UN Global Compact. The same authors in an earlier study (Williams and Zinkin 2005) also investigated the differences in attitudes towards corporate social responsibility (CSR) between Muslims and non-Muslims and found that Muslims are less concerned about CSR than non-Muslims and that these differences are not the result of demographic, socio-political or cultural factors. Thus, it is clear that Islamic teaching on business ethics is very much in line with CSR agenda and the IBs and financial institutions built in accordance with Islamic principles require high ethical standards from all stakeholders for their successful operation and long-term viability.

The issue that still remains to be resolved is whether Islamic teaching has created any 'confrontational' attitudes of Muslims towards the ethical behaviour of firms engaged in activities that are not approved by Islamic principles. For instance, Islam prohibits some activities that are *haram* (forbidden) but they are widely accepted as business activities in the non-Muslim world and even in parts of the Muslim world. It is therefore not surprising that some Muslims (particularly the more radical ones) would be concerned about those firms (engaged in *haram* activities) and their ultimate discharge of social responsibilities. However, if Islam's preference for a moderate stance is adopted (in fact, the Quran asked Muslims to avoid 'extremes' and follow the middle path), this issue can be resolved very easily. We believe that moderation is necessary for peaceful coexistence of Muslims and non-Muslims in today's globalized world and both will benefit from thriving businesses that are 'socially responsible' even though some of these businesses may not strictly follow the Islamic rules.

ISLAMIC FINANCE: A CASE STUDY OF SINGAPORE

For purposes of illustration of Islamic finance in practice we have chosen to look at the case of Singapore, with which the authors are closely familiar and which is an interesting example of an emergent new hub of Islamic finance that is not confined to or solely located in an Islamic state. The following is a brief description of Singapore's recent development in Islamic finance.

Regulatory treatment

In June 2006, the Monetary Authority of Singapore (MAS) gave its approval to banks to engage in non-financial activities, such as commodity trading, to facilitate *murabaha* transactions for clients' investments. Prior to this, banks had been forbidden to engage in non-financial activities such as trading, which is not normally associated with banking and finance. This move shows that MAS recognizes the fundamental characteristics of *murabaha* – a key form of Islamic financing in the Middle East. In 2009, MAS issued two regulations pertaining to the operations of Islamic banking – Singapore-based banks are allowed to enter into diminishing *musharaka* financing and spot *murabaha* transactions. It should however be mentioned that there is no separate regulatory framework for Islamic Banking in Singapore and the government approach is to keep the existing regulatory framework 'responsive and relevant' to the 'fast growing and ever-changing' Islamic finance industry. According to MAS, the major significant unique risk that IBs face is the Shariah-compliance risk and that is precisely the reason why Singapore has chosen not to put in place a separate regulatory framework for Islamic banking (MAS Staff Paper No. 49, December 2008).

Tax treatment

The Singapore government recognizes that, given the nature and structure of Islamic financial products, they tend to attract more tax than their counterparts. The overall policy approach has been to align tax treatment of Islamic contracts with the treatment of conventional financing contracts that they are economically equivalent to. In line with this policy, the Finance Ministry announced several changes in the 2005 and 2006 budgets.

In 2005, Singapore waived the imposition of double stamp duties in Islamic transactions involving real estate and accorded the same concessionary tax treatment on income from Islamic bonds that are applicable to conventional bonds. In 2006, income tax and GST (goods and services tax) applications on some Islamic products were further clarified. The government identified three Shariah-compliant products and ensured that they do not attract more taxes owing to the nature of their structuring. In addition, to level the tax playing field for *sukuk* (the Islamic equivalent of a bond), remission will be granted on stamp duty on immovable property, incurred under a *sukuk* structure, that is in excess of that chargeable in the case of an equivalent conventional bond issue.

Growth and development of financial products

In July 2001, Maybank, Malaysia's largest bank, started Islamic banking in Singapore with the introduction of the Singapore Unit Trusts Ethical Growth Fund, which complies with the principles of Shariah. In November 2005, the bank introduced a Shariah-compliant online savings account and a Shariah-compliant savings cum checking account. In January 2009, MAS launched a facility to issue *Sukuk* jointly with the Islamic Bank of Asia and Standard Chartered Bank (MAS *Annual Report 2008/09*). In September 2010, Maybank opened an Islamic banking hub in Singapore. As of the end of 2009, the bank had about a 1.3 per cent share of total Shariah-compliant assets and it ranks among the top twenty IBs worldwide. In 2006, the first Shariah-compliant term deposit in Singapore was launched by OCBC Bank.

Islamic insurance or *takaful* has also been successful in Singapore with over S$500 million *takaful* funds under management. For instance, HSBC (Singapore) launched the Takaful Global Fund in September 1995, while the Takaful Sinaran Fund was launched in May 2005. Returns from these funds are not subject to income tax. There were about S$2 billion Shariah-compliant real estate funds managed out of Singapore. Singapore has recently launched its first Shariah-compliant real estate investment trust (Reit), called the Sabana, and it currently holds about 850 million Singapore industrial properties.

Islamic equity index

In recognition of the increasing interest of Middle East investors in diversifying and tapping the growth opportunities in Asia, the first Shariah-compliant pan-Asian equity index was launched in Singapore in February 2006. This index serves as a benchmark for Shariah-compliant funds investing in Asian equities, and paves the way for the growth of Shariah-compliant funds seeking Asian exposures.

IFSB membership

MAS is a member of the Islamic Financial Services Board (IFSB). MAS joined the IFSB in December 2003 as an observer member and became a full member in April 2005.

MAS currently participates in the Islamic Money Market Taskforce, the Supervisory Review Process Working Group and the Special Issues in Capital Adequacy Working Group. MAS also organized the IFSB Summit in May 2009, the first time the event was being held in East Asia (MAS *Annual Report 2008/09*).

Education

Another significant move in the development of Islamic finance in Singapore has been the announcement by the Singapore Islamic Scholars and Religious Teachers Association (PERGAS) that some Islamic religious scholars would be trained in banking and finance to assist Singapore's aim of becoming a hub for Islamic finance. PERGAS also developed *Asatizah* (religious teachers) and a Shariah Advisers Training Programme with the same objectives in mind. In 2009, PERGAS established the Islamic Finance Consultation Unit (UKKI). These are timely moves as many Singaporeans (even the savvy investors) are still hazy about the world of Islamic finance and the various Shariah-compliant products, according to a recent report.

Exchange-traded fund

Singapore moved a step forward in the development of its Islamic finance industry with the first listing of a Shariah-compliant exchange-traded fund (ETF) on 27 May 2008. Daiwa Asset Management Co. Ltd.'s first ETF offers an investment channel into Japanese companies that fully complies with Shariah investment principles.

Conclusion

Islamic banking and finance operates under Islamic rules (Shariah) that are derived from the Quran and Hadith. In sum, the guiding principles are: (1) making money from money (through fixed interest payments) by saving deposits or lending is not allowed; (2) the saver/lender must share in the profits or losses arising out of business; (3) speculative activities are prohibited; (4) investments should only support practices or products that are *halal* (not forbidden); (5) while profit is allowed, the enterprises must perform social responsibilities (such as distributive justice and poverty reduction).

There are several advantages of the Islamic system over the conventional one: (1) the principle of profit–loss sharing is likely to channel investible funds to projects that have the highest expected profitability as opposed to an interest-based system where funds go to the most creditworthy borrowers whose projects may not necessarily be the most profitable ones; (2) the Islamic system will ensure 'economic efficiency' leading to optimality in production (if producers offer 'too much' of one product and 'too little' of another, the quest for profit would immediately alert entrepreneurs to the fact and provide incentives for them to change the line of production) and consumption (as price fixing is not allowed and special consideration is given to the needs of the poor); (3) the Islamic system promotes an 'integrated' development as it encourages the use of money for facilitating trade in goods and investment in productive capacity rather than creating money for the sake of money. Such a system is likely to be more stable and is less vulnerable to financial crisis that can be caused by speculative activities. Indeed, the impact of the GFC on IBs and financial institutions was somewhat muted, as we discussed in the chapter; (4) the Islamic system is welfare enhancing as it has special provisions for the poor and needy. In fact, Islamic principles enforce high ethical standards and create more responsible businesses, as we discussed previously.

Islamic finance is a relatively new concept in Singapore. The small domestic market and lack of public awareness do not offer strong growth potential for the Islamic finance industry within the Republic. Over the years, Singapore has revised its regulatory framework and tax structure and introduced various Shariah-compliant financial products. The city-state republic also faces strong competition from Malaysia in providing Islamic products regionally. However, the country can still find a niche market in Southeast Asia (particularly Indonesia), the Middle East and South Asia, given the reputation of being a regional financial hub and its overall attractiveness as a business location. Singapore's neutral stance to all religious beliefs and practices and its harmonious development of various race relations within the community at large has further added to its strength. Another important point is worth mentioning. Singapore is pursuing a strategy of integrated development of financial and real sectors as it believes that the two can reinforce each other. Singapore has just completed a free trade agreement (FTA) negotiation with the Gulf Cooperation Council (GCC) and this is likely to facilitate trade and investment between the two sides. With deeper trade and investment links, there will be greater opportunity for financial integration that could open new opportunities for Islamic finance and the related products.

CONCEPTUAL QUESTIONS

1 What are the main Islamic principles behind Islamic banking and finance?
2 What are the main financial products of Islamic finance?
3 What are the principles of the UN Global Compact? Do you think they conform to Islamic principles?

CRITICAL QUESTIONS

1 Can Islamic finance substitute conventional banking systems? Justify your views.
2 Islamic banking did not suffer as much as conventional banking during the recent global financial crisis. Do you agree? Explain the reasons for your answer.
3 Do you see growth prospects of Islamic finance in Singapore compared to other regional competitors, such as Malaysia and Indonesia? Justify your answer.

Further reading

Chia Der Jiun and Wang Yining (2008) 'Risks and regulation of Islamic banks: A perspective from a non-Islamic jurisdiction', *MAS Staff Paper No. 49*, Singapore.
Khan, H. and Bashar, O. (2008) 'Islamic finance: Growth and prospects in Singapore', *U21 Global Working Paper No. 001/2008*.

References

Hasan, M. and Dridi, J. (2010) 'The effects of the global crisis on Islamic and conventional banks: A comparative study', *IMF Working Paper No. 10/201*.
IFSL Research (2010), *Islamic Finance*, January. Available online at www.londonstock exchange.com/specialist-issuers/islamic/downloads/ifsl-research.pdf (accessed 30 April 2012).
Imam, P. and Kpodar, K. (2010) 'Islamic banking: How has it diffused?' *IMF Working Paper No. 10/195*.
Monetary Authority of Singapore (MAS), *Annual Report* (various issues).
Williams, G. and Zinkin, J. (2005) 'Doing business with Islam: Can corporate social responsibility be a bridge between civilizations?', working paper, Nottingham University Business School.
Williams, G. and Zinkin, J. (2010) 'Islam and CSR: A study of the compatibility between the tenets of Islam and the UN Global Compact', *Journal of Business Ethics*, 91: 519–33.

11

ETHICAL ISSUES IN THE POLICY RESPONSE TO THE 2008 FINANCIAL CRISIS

Moral hazard in central banking and the equity of bailout

Alojzy Z. Nowak and Patrick O'Sullivan

Chapter overview

This chapter will deal with some issues that are highly topical at present, at least in the advanced Western economies: the moral questions that surround the large-scale bailout of the banks and other financial institutions that has been mounted by central banks and by governments since September 2008. This may seem a very specific topic of interest only in passing during these years of crisis but in fact we will show that the issues are of perennial interest. Apart from the fact that the broadly capitalist-style financial system that today predominates in the world economy is inherently subject to bubbles and crises,[1] so giving perennial relevance to moral reflections on the policy responses to such crises, we shall show that some of the equity issues go right to the heart of the critique of contemporary capitalism as a socio-economic system. This locates the chapter very firmly in Level 2 of critique as outlined in Chapter 2 although some of the reflections on equity in particular will take us in effect to Level 3 of critique: the assertion of certain universal values in relation to the whole world financial system.

We will begin with a discussion of the problems of moral hazard in central banking and the conduct of the bailout before proceeding to a reflection on its size and the redistributional implications of what has occurred.

The notion of moral hazard

For a notion that is fairly widely used in contemporary discussions of finance and of insurance in particular it is remarkable how difficult it is to pin down a definition of the concept. A quick search via Google already yields the following variety of definitions:[2]

- the lack of any incentive to guard against a risk when you are protected against it (as by insurance); 'insurance companies are exposed to a moral hazard if the insured party is not honest' (wordnetweb.princeton.edu/perl/webwn);
- the tendency of a person or entity that is imperfectly monitored to engage in undesirable behaviour (www.unc.edu/depts/europe/euroeconomics/glossary. php).

While Wikipedia (not of course notorious for its high level of intellectual rigour or precision), offers:

- Moral hazard arises because an individual or institution does not take the full consequences and responsibilities of its actions, and therefore has a tendency to act less carefully than it otherwise would, leaving another party to hold some responsibility for the consequences of those actions (http://en.wikipedia. org/wiki/Moral_hazard [accessed May 1 2012]).

These definitions tend to focus on the temptation to dishonesty and so to immoral actions that can arise from the way in which certain types of risky interactions are set up, in particular in insurance. Some other definitions focus on the temptation to immorality in the manner in which various types of principal–agent situations are set up, in particular when governed by contract:

- moral hazard also arises in a principal–agent problem, where one party, called an agent, acts on behalf of another party, called the principal. The agent usually has more information about his or her actions or intentions than the principal does, because the principal usually cannot completely monitor the agent. The agent may have an incentive to act inappropriately (from the viewpoint of the principal) if the interests of the agent and the principal are not aligned (http://en.wikipedia.org/wiki/Moral_hazard [accessed May 1 2012]);
- the tendency of agents who are insured to behave more recklessly because of their insurance cover (wps.pearsoned.co.uk/wps/media/objects/2499/ 2559960/glossary/glossary.html);
- an example of information asymmetry where a contract or relationship places incentives upon one party to take (or not take) unobservable steps which are prejudicial to another party (www.dfpni.gov.uk/eag-glossary).

Clearly there is a fairly wide variety of definitions but, broadly speaking, the finance and insurance sector seems to be particularly prone to moral hazards, to judge by the range of definitions above. Our interest here is to focus first on those situations where the presence of a moral hazard may in itself be immoral or lead to serious immorality; to explain in what exactly this immorality consists; and then finally to investigate the degree to which such immoral moral hazard has been present in the bailouts that have been seen in the recent financial crisis.

The first thing to notice about the range of definitions is that some of the definitions speak only of incentives to 'reckless' behaviour.[3] Reckless behaviour is not per se immoral (that would at least depend on what one is reckless about) and so it follows that many of the phenomena that are described in the definitions as involving moral hazard are not in effect immoral. They may reflect certain inefficiencies of incentive systems in a principal–agent context or poor drafting of contracts but they do not involve immorality per se. Hence we need to define clearly when instances of moral hazard are immoral and in what the immorality consists.

We would argue that moral hazard becomes immoral when the incentive system that surrounds some set of transactions (and that may or may not be bound by a contract) involves an inducement (usually unintended) to one or more of the parties to act in an *immoral* manner. How to define what sorts of actions or omissions are immoral is of course another matter but that need not concern us here. All that matters for moral hazards to become a potential case of immorality is that either some of the parties involved or some external critic should view some of the induced actions as immoral. The classic examples come from travel insurance: given that the insurance will undertake to replace items that are lost during travel (usually upon submission of a simple police declaration of loss/theft), the traveller is certainly put in a situation where they may be tempted to 'lose' an item with a view to claiming and getting a nice new replacement. The traveller is faced with a degree of inducement to be downright dishonest and thus (in pretty much anybody's moral code) to being immoral. In this simple example of moral hazard it is easy to see the dishonesty of the insured person who makes a dishonest declaration of loss and one can no doubt moralize and sermonize about the immorality of the dishonesty. But what about the morality of the insurer who sets up contracts that could be an invitation to those of weaker moral fibre to act immorally? How morally acceptable is it deliberately to tempt people to be immoral? While of course the traveller who succumbs to dishonesty has certainly been immoral, we would be inclined to suggest that the party that tempts is also morally blameworthy. Put bluntly: it is immoral deliberately to put others in a situation where they will be clearly and strongly tempted to be dishonest (or in other clear ways immoral).

Moving to what has been described in Chapter 2 as Level 2 critique in this simple case of moral hazard in travel insurance, we can also ask the question as to whether the whole socio-economic set-up or system within which such insurance is offered might itself be morally questionable. Is the problem the whole insurance system per se? The answer in this particular case is almost certainly no: insurance could hardly be said to be immoral as a matter of principle. While insurance companies are in economic terms simple gamblers, insurance meets openly, and for the most part fairly, a very fundamental demand from risk-averse individuals or businesses to cover themselves with a view to avoiding large losses.[4] But one could possibly imagine other cases where upon conduct of a critique of certain types of moral hazard one might wish to conclude that there is some fundamental immorality inherent in the system as set up, in the socio-economic system design so to speak, quite apart from the immorality of the specific actors involved. To take a somewhat extreme example (which has little to do with moral hazard) one could argue that a system of international relations that allows for warfare among nation states as a way to resolve conflicts is inherently immoral in itself as a system, quite apart from the immorality of any of the individual actors involved in war.

What we now propose to argue is that, in the manner in which the contemporary Western financial system is set up, there is a veritable minefield of moral hazards present; and some of these could be put down to some serious defects of the system as a whole, as opposed to the moral hazards faced by the individuals involved.

Moral hazard in central banking and government policies

We will now seek to apply the above analysis of moral hazard to the case of government policies adopted in the face of the recent financial crisis and to the role of the central banks in particular (as controllers of macroeconomic monetary policies). It is well known and well documented how the various central banks and especially the US Federal Reserve faced a growing policy dilemma in the summer of 2008 as the real scale of the hole in banks' balance sheets as a result of the lending spree in the US (and UK and Irish) subprime mortgage and credit card markets began to be realized. To give some idea of the size of these in effect non-performing loans, in the US the value of subprime mortgages was US$1.3 trillion (of a total US$6.8 trillion mortgage loans [19 per cent of total US mortgage market at the time]) in the second quarter of 2007 while in the UK it was estimated in May 2007 as £30 billion (8 per cent of the total UK mortgage market). In very simple terms, the real value of the bank's assets was way below the real current value of their liabilities to customers (depositors) and, as this awareness spread, panic runs on banks inevitably followed in the US and the UK. The effects of this panic were felt far and wide because, as is well known, the low-quality loans had been repackaged by the financial institutions into various types of composite derivatives such as mortgage-backed securities and sold on to others than the originating institutions. Thereby the originating banks offloaded what they must have known were very low-performance assets with very high default risk and the attendant risks were thus spread out around the whole of the world's financial system. There were a few notable exceptions of countries that, through luck or judicious regulation, were less exposed because they bought much fewer of these derivatives (e.g. Poland, Lebanon), but the effects were widespread and reached far beyond the US, the UK and Ireland where the subprime lending spree had originated.

The case of Poland is interesting because of the curious concatenation of circumstances that shielded the Polish banking system and economy from the financial crisis. The Polish economy, almost uniquely in the EU, has barely been struck by the wider recession that resulted from the financial crisis. First of all, the good condition of the banks' balance sheets that – quite paradoxically – resulted from their conservative attitude towards expansion abroad, accompanied by relatively prudent lending policies at home by comparison with those of many other states insulated the Polish banks from the sort of collapse of confidence and the panic that affected the banks in so many other states, but especially in the US, the UK and Ireland. This fairly prudent approach of the banks was underpinned by the strategy and policy stance of the Polish central bank, the National Bank of Poland. The same cannot necessarily be said of the stance of broader government policy. The government in Warsaw behaved as if the Polish economy was immunized against external shocks. That strategy of playing down external impulses by relatively limited intervention brought some positive effects. In particular, as observed by some experts in social psychology, the crisis, while actually affecting Poland to a limited extent (e.g. through international trade impacts), has not become planted in people's minds. If the real crisis had been accompanied by that spreading in people's minds – as it was in Britain, the United States, Japan or France – according to experts, the situation could have indeed become dramatic.[5] Fortunately, in Poland no crisis of confidence occurred. Poles proved resistant to signals heard or read until such time as they felt an impact in their wallets or day-to-day spending possibilities and even then no signs of panic were seen. No matter how one evaluates the attitude of the Polish government, which perhaps should have done more in order to control the crisis, rather than wait for the story to unfold, one thing is beyond any dispute: Poland managed to largely defend itself against and overcome the global financial crisis and its consequences. It is telling that things went otherwise in a number of Eastern and Central European countries where the period of aggravation of the crisis was accompanied by weakening of business activity – the trend that in Baltic countries reached a truly dramatic scale that was partly a result of their approach to regulation in the banking sector.

The dilemma that faced the central bankers in September 2008 was a fairly basic one. Either they entered the market in their classic role as lenders of last resort to the banking system to lend funds to the banks facing runs (it should be remembered that with the general collapse of confidence even the interbank lending market had begun to dry up seriously), thereby preventing the collapse of banks suffering runs; or, in view of the patent recklessness of the subprime lending that had occurred, should they let some of these institutions face their just deserts and fail. Of course, among those who suffer in the event of a bank failure are the depositors as well as the managers, other employees and shareholders, and it is usually deemed to be unfair that the depositors should suffer for the mistakes of the others; hence, the moral argument is often swayed towards rescue of failing banks. Thus, even while central bankers might be tempted to let patently reckless institutions fail, if for no other reason than to set an example, governments at least are often under huge political pressure to prevent outright failures of financial institutions. Thus it was that, faced with the gaping holes in the asset/liability structures of whole ranges of institutions (and no very clear knowledge of how bad the situation was in many cases because of the camouflaged nature of the content of many derivatives), governments felt that they had no option politically but to step in, even where central banks preferred not to, with a view to injecting liquidity into the banks or other shaky financial institutions.

Prompt intervention on the part of governments and central banks made it possible, first, to maintain the financial liquidity of a lot of struggling commercial banks and financial institutions, which in practice offered a lifeline to many of them that otherwise would have faced prospects of imminent bankruptcy. Second, the interventions in the form of macroeconomic fiscal stimuli managed to maintain aggregate demand, thanks to government spending on collective consumption, personal services and infrastructural investments (e.g. construction of roads). In achieving this, the intervention managed to maintain overall aggregate demand of the economies at a certain level, despite the serious drop in demand by the private sector as a result both of a credit crunch and a general loss of confidence.

Third, consistent action of governments and central banks managed to maintain credit systems, thus preventing a massive drop in business activity and ensuring financing of the real economy with no major obstacles. Guaranteeing security of bank deposits, buyout of 'toxic' assets from banks, reduction of central banks' interest rates and more generous crediting of commercial banks were aimed – as mentioned above – at supporting business activity, aggregate demand, production and employment.

It should be immediately evident that the dilemma facing the central bankers and indeed also the governments was a clear-cut case of moral hazard. The central bankers who are charged with overseeing and regulating the whole of the banking and financial system with a view to making sure that it runs efficiently and in a manner that inspires the confidence of all (confidence being absolutely essential to the efficiency of any financial system and especially to a fractional reserve banking system) are also in that role required to stand ready to act as lenders of last resort, *in theory* only in emergency situations. However, with the deregulation of the financial sector and its internationalization, both pursued avidly since the early 1990s, the banks and other institutions embarked on a largely unsupervised wave of financial innovation that by the 2001–2010 decade had become a binge of ever more reckless lending and repackaging of dud loans. As a result, central bankers began to find themselves in a situation where they were being called upon to rescue in effect institutions that had simply been irresponsible rather than dealing with some sort of genuine emergency (as might result from war or natural disaster for example). They were in a classic situation of moral hazard whereby the very fact of being seen as a lender of last resort tempted many financial institutions into extremely reckless lending on the grounds that it was a one-way bet. If it worked out, the gung-ho bankers and brokers would look like financial geniuses, whereas if it all went sour, well, the central banks would ride to the rescue in the 'emergency' of a crisis; and of course the bigger the institution, the less the likelihood that it would ever be allowed to fail. In short, there was almost nothing to lose and a lot potentially to gain from downright recklessness in lending, especially for the bigger institutions. No doubt many of the individual actors in this drama, with little appreciation of economic history and ignorant of the theory of business cycles, believed that indeed the party could go on indefinitely; they were thus easy prey to the temptations inherent in the stance of central banks. But that is surely all the more a reflection on the seriousness of the moral hazard inherent in the position of the central bankers.

Of course, the central bankers were not entirely insensitive to the moral hazard inherent in their position and it was this that led to the debates of August and September 2008 regarding the advisability of letting some institutions fail just as a lesson; and, in the event, Lehman Brothers Investment Bank did fail in September

2008. However, the fallout from this failure in terms of financial panic was the complete freezing up of the interbank lending market (as banks suddenly began to suspect 'who next'; after all there was no clear picture of where the real risks lay because of the derivatives camouflage); and so, no further big high-profile institutions were allowed to fail.

Instead, quite aside from the central banks, governments began to indulge in an array of expensive confidence-building measures aimed to restore the equilibrium of banks' balance sheets and thereby to rebuild confidence. These measures included various kinds of liquidity injection, government purchase of (often majority)[6] shareholdings in banks, hiving off of the dodgiest assets into government-owned 'bad banks'.

We have witnessed so many unprecedented things in such a short period of time. In the US on 3 October 2008, President Bush signed the $700 billion bailout package. The US treasury secretary Henry Paulson said that this money would be used to buy distressed mortgage-backed securities from banks; $250 billion of the $700 billion bailout was going to be used to inject capital into the banks. The largest banks (Bank of America Corp., Citigroup Inc., Bank of New York Mellon Corp., JPMorgan Chase and Co., Merrill Lynch and Co. Inc., Goldman Sachs Group Inc., Morgan Stanley, State Street Corp. and Wells Fargo and Co.) were going to receive $125 billion from this package.

In November 2008, the US government announced a massive bailout of Citigroup, which was the largest bank in the world in 2007, worth over $300 billion. Citigroup was also considered to be 'too big to fail' and its bailout was nearly five times larger than AIG's.

In 2009, as the new president, Barack Obama anticipated another $750 billion bank bailout, a move that more than doubled the direct infusion of taxpayer money into the reeling financial sector. The White House's 2010 budget included a $250 billion contingency fund for 2009 that – if needed – could leverage three times as much in asset purchases from financial institutions in need of capital.[7]

We will be looking later in the chapter at the redistributional impact of these massive financial transactions of the governments but for now what we should note is that, by being so willing to ride to the rescue of the financial institutions, governments too have become involved in setting up a serious moral hazard for financial institutions and one that is closely analogous to that of the central banks (and indeed aggravates the latter). For today, not only do the bigger institutions in particular know that the central bank as lender of last resort will be unlikely to allow them to fail outright if their reckless activities go pear-shaped, they also know that governments are terrified of the potential consequences of a major financial collapse and so governments too stand ready to bail them out when things go badly wrong. The incentive to recklessness, and so the moral hazard, could hardly be greater than it is in the contemporary financial system.

But, as noted earlier, recklessness may not necessarily be immoral. So, is the clear moral hazard at the heart of the contemporary system also *immoral*? At the individual level of the actors involved in the sector (Level 1 critique in the terms of Chapter 2), it would be very difficult to argue that the actions of the bankers and the financiers in general is actually immoral. Certainly, they have been taking what in effect are huge gambles, very largely with other people's money. But the people who placed the money in their care did so knowingly and with a view to making large gains precisely from the risk-taking activity of the various banks and investment funds. Moreover, unless one takes a very strictly puritanical or strictly Islamic moral stance, gambling per se cannot be seen as immoral.[8] Once we say that the primary activity of the gambling engaged in by the bankers and financiers is not immoral we cannot say either that the regulators who oversee a system that tempts the financiers to take reckless risks are behaving immorally, since the inducement is to recklessness, not to some inherently immoral action. Hence at Level 1 of critique it is hard to see any immorality involved in the moral hazard that surrounds the role of central banks and governments as lenders of last resort or protectors of the financial system. There may be other attendant immoralities such as uncontrolled selfish greed on the part of financiers at an individual level (not to speak of the dishonesty of some such as Bernard Madoff)[9], or the regulators could be accused of negligence in respect of the way in which they allowed the recklessness to get out of hand; but neither could be accused of being involved in an *immoral* moral hazard by their actions.

In theory, Bernard L. Madoff Investment Securities LLC was meant to invest its clients' money in profitable business ventures. Actually, it never invested anything. The money was deposited in a bank account in Chase Manhattan Bank and the business operated like a classic financial pyramid. It was from fresh money brought by new clients that the interest was paid, or even the capital returned to those who chose to step back. A lot of clients preferred to reinvest their profit, so the company presented sham statements on the accounts. Bernard L. Madoff Investment Securities LLC created a vast accountancy department producing paper fiction to feed clients or auditors. The entire business could work as long as there was new capital flowing in. In the end the financial markets crisis made the inflow of fresh capital insufficient. The pyramid collapsed like a house of cards. It turned out that one of the world's largest investment companies was nothing but a giant fraud. In fact, while fishing out no less than US$65 billion from his clients' billfolds, Madoff fooled everybody: prominent personalities from cultural and political circles, reputable European and American banks as well as financial supervision institutions, not to mention the tax authorities. The list of those who were taken in by the Ponzi scheme is quite incredible and includes Banco Santander, Bank Medici, HSBC Holdings, BNP Paribas, Dexia, Credit Mutuel, Fortis Bank and many more, insurance companies – CNP Assurances, Groupama, Harel Insurance – a few investment funds, some charity foundations and of course many private individuals.[10]

However, as we know, there is also a Level 2 critique that may be pertinent to the moral assessment of moral hazards: is the whole banking and financial system as it is currently set up and regulated with the rampant moral hazards that we have seen in itself immoral? To answer that question would involve taking a view about the contribution of the contemporary financial system to the world economy and to world well-being. It is a vast question, which it is beyond the scope of this single chapter to answer. To answer it will inevitably take one into the realms of critical political economy and political philosophy. Although some might be tempted to try to answer the question in empiricist terms by pointing to the simple fact of the long-term economic growth made possible by the efficiency of the capitalist financial system with its free markets and fractional reserve banking, others might equally well point empirically to a system that has produced a damaging (and often brutally unfair) tendency to cyclical fluctuation and periodic financial crises. And of course there is always the question of how the world economy and society would have evolved had it been under a radically different form of *financial* system? While most would probably agree that a free market system is broadly beneficent, at least with appropriate regulation of monopoly power and externalities etc., it must be empha-sized that the specific form of capitalist *financial* system that has evolved in the West is by no means so self-evidently beneficent and, as we have just noted, has had an inherent tendency to produce periodically severe financial crises that are highly damaging to the 'real' economy. Hence, the ultimate beneficence or otherwise of the capitalist-style *financial* system as we know it is unlikely to be settled by empirical studies of its supposed link with long-term economic performance and so the debate is likely to be played out on the level of political philosophy. Fascinating certainly, but not perhaps the place for such a debate in this volume, so we shall content ourselves with simply having flagged up the issue.

We cannot leave the topic of moral hazards in the contemporary financial system without of course mentioning the rating agencies. These are the institutions such as Standard and Poor's, Moody's, etc. that allocate marks (grades) to various types of financial asset and instrument where the mark awarded is intended to be a reliable indicator of the potential risk of serious or total loss of the asset in question.

Already potentially problematic is the fact that the three dominant rating agencies are American and operate under American law – Standard and Poor's, Moody's and Fitch – and in effect have never been subject to adequate supervision in their operations. After all, their combined market share is around 90 per cent. It was only in late 2010 that the American government decided to amend imperfect provisions belonging to a larger financial act, the objective of which is to reform the way the rating agencies operate. The new legislation assumes that the Securities and Exchange Commission (SEC) will establish a special council to overview the activities of the agencies and to become an intermediary body between them and the businesses rated. Equally importantly, SEC will name the agency whose rating will be regarded the key one. These partial changes are delayed attempts to control the omnipotence of the three huge rating agencies in question. However, even facing these limited regulations, the Standard and Poor's spokesman argues that the new law may create an impression of the agencies being seriously dependent upon the government and that the measures will reduce competition among them. These sorts of arguments seem to totally abstract from the history of these agencies' operation.

These private sector agencies began their existence in a humble way as a type of specialist advisory or consulting service to investors but they have evolved as we know into highly influential institutions that, among other things, give marks to sovereign government debt, which in turn can seriously affect a government's ability to borrow on the open markets.[11] What is less well known about these agencies is the manner in which at least the biggest and most influential agencies radically changed their modus operandi in the early 1970s with the full acquiescence of the SEC. This change of business model has introduced a major moral hazard into the heart of their operations. Up to the early 1970s, the rating agency was paid an investigation fee by the *investor* and only by the investor. After that date, however, the system was changed to one where the *issuers* of financial assets/ instruments could ask for their product to be rated and would pay a fee for this service; this has transformed the business model of the rating agencies so that today the vast bulk of rating agency revenues comes from the fees paid by issuers. A good rating would clearly make it a lot easier for the issuer to place the asset/instrument with potential investors and in the case of bonds would permit for example a lower coupon rate to be given by the issuer. Hence, issuers of securities of all sorts may be prepared to pay high fees to get a (good) rating.

But a moment's reflection will reveal the huge moral hazard inherent in this revamped set-up. Issuers of securities being prepared to pay high fees to get their assets rated and, dare we say it, perhaps pay higher fees for even better ratings, especially in a market where the rating agencies are private firms in competition with each other . . . there will inevitably be a temptation for the agencies to give better ratings than merited. In short, the system as currently constituted harbours a major moral hazard for the rating agencies; the consequences of succumbing to this moral hazard on the part of the agencies in their rating of many of the new derivatives that appeared in the wake of the subprime lending binge and the lead-up to the financial crisis of 2008 may well have been a key contributory factor to the severity of that crisis insofar as high ratings lulled investors into a false sense of security regarding their holdings of what in reality were dud assets. It is worth remarking that, had the system of payment and the related business model not been overhauled in the US in the early 1970s, this moral hazard would just not have been present.

Unfortunately, this moral hazard we would argue also involves a temptation to immoral behaviour and not just recklessness. Put bluntly, it involves a temptation to the rating agencies to overrate securities; that is to say, to give a falsely high rating and so in effect a direct temptation to dishonesty.

A further moral issue: the equity of the bailouts

We have hinted above at some of the much wider political philosophical issues that are raised by a Level 2 critique of the moral hazards inherent in the role of the central banks and of governments in relation to the large-scale rescues and bailouts of various kinds that occurred in the financial crisis. While we have eschewed a detailed treatment of these political issues here as being well beyond the scope of this book, there is, however, one quite specific and essentially moral philosophical issue that must also be mentioned and examined in more detail: the question of the equity or fairness of the bailouts that have occurred.

The scale of the injections of government and central bank funds, whether in the form of loans, equity participation or other instruments has been gigantic by any measuring rod. Some idea of the scale of these bailouts has already been given above at p. 153 and Table 11.1 gives somewhat more detail of the size of the various governments' commitments to bailouts.

Central bank lending as last resort will inevitably expand the monetary base of the economies in question and so will contribute to a dramatic expansion of money supply unless banks decide to revise upwards their minimum cash reserve ratios (not implausible in a period of crisis). To give some idea of the scale of expansionary monetary policy (nowadays politely labelled as quantitative easing), cumulative liquidity easing programmes were worth close to 7 per cent of US GDP, 9 per cent of UK GDP and 5 per cent of Euro area GDP at the end of 2008.[12]

TABLE 11.1 Official financial support to the financial sector up to February 2009 (in % of GDP)

Country	Capital injection	Purchase of assets and lending by Treasury	Central bank supp. prov. with Treasury backing	Liq. provision and other supp. by central bank	Guarantees	Total
Australia	0	0.7	0	0	n.a.	0.7
France	1.2	1.3	0	0	16.4	19
Germany	3.7	0.4	0	0	17.6	21.7
Greece	2.1	3.3	0	0	6.2	11.6
Hungary	1.1	0	0	4	1.1	6.2
Ireland	5.3	0	0	0	257	263
Italy	1.3	0	0	2.5	0	3.8
Japan	2.4	6.7	0	0	3.9	12.9
Netherlands	3.4	2.8	0	0	33.7	39.8
Poland	0.4	0	0	0	3.2	3.6
Portugal	2.4	0	0	0	12	14.4
South Korea	2.5	1.2	0	0	10.6	14.3
Spain	0	4.6	0	0	18.3	22.8
Sweden	2.1	5.3	0	15.3	47.3	70
United Kingdom	3.5	13.8	12.9	0	17.4	47.5
United States	4	6	1.1	31.3	31.3	73.7
G-20 average	1.9	3.3	1	9.3	12.4	27.9

Source: OECD (2010) *The Financial Crisis: Reform and exit strategies.* Paris: OECD, pp. 75–76.

In the United States the Federal Reserve has taken its time with reining in monetary policy as this would present a blow for the weak recovery in the real economy. An increase of interest rates, or of reserve requirements, would not only result in more expensive credit for the economy, but would also threaten the strategies based upon borrowing low-interest dollars to invest them in risk assets. The problem is a little different in the case of China and India. In China in early 2010 the rates of reserve requirements were raised by 50bp to 15.5 per cent and in India by 75bp. China already has experience of the effects of unsound risk management in the banking sector, which may partially answer the question why the government this time chose to raise the rates earlier. At the beginning of this decade in the midst of the aftermath of the Asian financial crisis, the percentage of bad credits was so high that the banks affected would have to go bankrupt unless they had obtained state aid. In Europe the Executive Board of the ECB believed, in 2010, that the level of interest rates was still appropriate and so maintained them with no major changes; throughout the ongoing crisis the ECB has (famously) not seen any reason to make any drastic changes to its interest rate or broader monetary policy stance. (It is of course politically independent and required by its statute to focus above all on maintaining low inflation in the Euro area.) The chart below (Figure 11.1) gives some idea of the stubbornness and indeed of the success of the ECB stance given that its long-term goal of low inflation is concretely

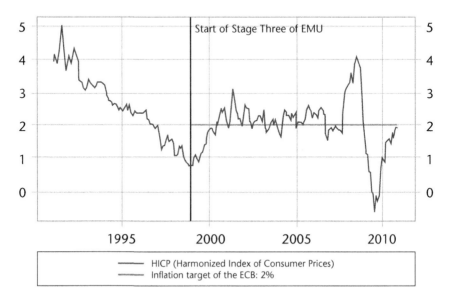

FIGURE 11.1 Inflation in the Euro area (annual percentage changes, non-seasonally adjusted).

Source: Eurostat (http://epp.eurostat.ec.europa.eu/portal/page/portal/statistics/search_database). Data prior to 1996 are estimated on the basis of non-harmonized national Consumer Price Indices (CPIs).

interpreted to be a 2 per cent inflation target. The Board still expects that, over the mid-term perspective adopted in monetary policy, price changes will remain moderate.

From the other side, the Executive Board is aware of the fact that the expansion of the money supply may eventually contribute to a significant increase in inflation once economies have taken up the slack that has resulted from the recession in the real economy, that is, once economies approach full employment again. These eventual effects on inflation from the expansionary monetary policies in many economies may or may not be economically undesirable but they are hardly a moral issue.

What does raise an acute moral issue of which people are only beginning to become aware is the net effect on the distribution of wealth and income in economies where large-scale injections of government funds to banks and other financial institutions have occurred. Let us be quite blunt about this. What we have witnessed in the past two years is a truly massive transfer of funds from the proceeds of general taxation to the financial sector as the government has made its bailouts. It may be countered that these bailouts are temporary and that most of the money lent will eventually come back to the government in future years or, in the cases where equity stakes have been taken, that the governments will be able to sell off the shares at a profit in years to come. That, almost by definition, is the purest wishful thinking for the most part. In the case of injections of loan funding this has gone to already crippled institutions and has in a number of cases taken the form of the government taking responsibility for 'bad banks' (read banks whose liabilities dwarf the real value of their assets, which consist of all manner of dodgy loans, and securities, i.e. institutions that are hopelessly insolvent). There is no hope of these institutions ever repaying in full the governments, and the government will simply act as a kind of liquidator, getting what it can from the dud loan and security portfolios and abandoning the rest. In the case of equity stakes taken by governments, the prospect of sale of the shares in the future at a profit back to the private sector is more plausible, at least for those institutions that can be turned around (could Lloyds TSB in the UK be an example?).

There has been a great deal of comment in political, media and academic circles regarding the equity of the large bonuses being paid to bankers, even as the system was clearly in a self-inflicted crisis brought on in large part by the blind greed and avarice of so many of the actors, if not the by downright ignorance and incompetence of those charged with managing funds. These criticisms are in our view fully justified (and they are already prompting a profound rethink of the whole remuneration and bonus system for bankers and financiers in the US and the EU). But what has not been remarked upon is a much more macro-level issue of equity/fairness. For, given that so much of the huge sums that have been transferred by government to the financial sector will probably never be recouped, we have witnessed in effect a huge transfer of wealth from the community at large; that is to say, from taxpaying individuals and businesses in general to the financial sector. In short, we have witnessed a huge redistribution from the community at large to what is broadly speaking the richest sector of the economy (and certainly has been the richest sector in recent times in the countries where the largest transfers occurred – the UK and the US). In the classic economic sense of progressivity/regressivity[13] of taxation, and bearing in mind that the progressivity/regressivity should be judged for the overall impact of both taxation *and* government spending, it would be hard to imagine a more *regressive* use of public funds on such a scale as we have in effect just witnessed. Margaret Thatcher's poll tax pales by comparison.[14] Since overall regressivity in the impact of government spending and taxation means that in the community as a whole, in effect, wealth is taken from the poor and/or middle-income individuals and businesses to give to the richest, it has rightly been regarded as profoundly inequitable and against any moral sense of justice or fairness. Hence, in this specific case, the bailouts mounted by the government sector and involving a huge transfer (unlikely ever to be paid back in full or in any significant amount) from the community at large to its richest business sector are inherently regressive and so profoundly unjust and unfair.

Some reflections on possible remedies

Our conclusion from this survey of the moral issues thrown up specifically by the financial crisis of 2008 and its aftermath has been that there is a colossal moral hazard inherent in the policy stance of the government and of the central banks, which is an invitation to recklessness on the part of financiers and bankers of all sorts. This by itself might not be regarded as immoral per se, as we saw (there is nothing inherently or in principle immoral about recklessness), but we did note that the financial system as a whole as currently set up is inherently prone to periodic large crises related to the consequences of the moral hazard and to this extent *as a system* it is not serving society at all effectively. In the case of the rating agencies we also found a serious moral hazard related to their incentive to overrate new securities and in this case the moral hazard is undeniably *immoral* because the temptation is to dishonesty in the ratings. Finally, we argued that there has been a huge inequity in the whole bailout operation that has been mounted insofar as it has involved a massive transfer from the taxpaying community at large to the financial sector, one of the richest sectors of any advanced modern economy.

A moment's reflection will reveal that these problems of moral hazard and inequity of distribution are not just a happenstance of this particular crisis: they are inherent problems of the way the whole financial system of capitalism is currently constituted. They have been seen in earlier crises – in 1929, in the Asian financial crisis of the late 1990s – and the contemporary crisis has just served to throw them up in relief. Moreover, the moral issues that are raised concern all three levels of critique as outlined in Chapter 2: Level 1 critique for example is involved in the actions of individuals in rating agencies; Level 2 is involved in the assessment of the service of central banks, governments and rating agencies to the community as a whole; and Level 3 critique is central to the assessment of the overall inequity of the bailouts since that critique goes right to the heart of the fundamental values that may be thought to underpin the functioning of the financial system of a capitalist free market economy.

With such a searching and often radically negative critique it is incumbent on us also to be constructive: to say in what ways we believe that the system could be improved to avoid some of the difficulties and moral issues uncovered. This is not the place and we would not in any case have the expertise to present in detail a blueprint for a transformed and well-functioning financial system in which moral hazard would be eliminated and financial crises would become a thing of the past. But we can offer some ideas on elements that in our view must be considered as part of any serious attempt at reform and improvement of the banking and financial system.

Taking the two major themes of our critique in turn, the first major theme has been that of moral hazard. The practical question becomes how we can reduce the moral hazards, in particular those that are a temptation to immorality. It is in fact quite difficult to see how the moral hazard inherent in the role of central banks as lenders of last resort to the financial system can be entirely eliminated. As long as there is fractional reserve banking there will be a need for some kind of guarantor to stand behind the system ready to inject liquidity if any one bank or institution faces a run on its reserves for whatever reason. This is the classic lender of last resort function of central banks. But it inevitably puts banks and other institutions in a position where they will be (tempted to be) more reckless than they might be if there were no such lender of last resort; the bigger they are the more likely they are to fall into this moral hazard (too big to fail . . .). One possible way to address this problem would be for the central banks and/or financial regulatory agencies to engage in a much more strict regulation of all aspects of the risk-taking activities of the banks and others and there has been much talk and even a little action on this. However, we must recognize that any such attempt at detailed regulation runs up against a fairly stiff ideological and in many countries political barrier to the extent that the financial sector is supposed to be the flower of laissez-faire free market capitalism; so any attempts to regulate the sector in detail are seen as a manifest ideological contradiction. In any case, in countries dominated by conservative or libertarian politics, to achieve such a degree of regulation will be difficult as the financial sector will strongly lobby its political friends against any real regulation and control. Hence, perhaps the only really effective way to eliminate the moral hazard involved in the lender of last resort function of central banks would be to eliminate fractional reserve banking altogether. That would be a radical step with huge short-term implications for the money supply and liquidity in general; but there is no inherent reason why it should not work on a long-term basis and it would certainly eliminate the moral hazards in banks' expansion of credit. It should be recalled that there were market economies long before there was fractional reserve banking so it cannot be argued that fractional reserve banking is somehow indispensable to a free market system! The issue has rather more to do with who has ultimate control of money supply, since in a 100 per cent reserve system banks would not in any sense create credit and the central banks would achieve perfect control of money supply.[15]

The second, and in moral terms, more serious moral hazard we identified concerned the rating agencies. Here, two remedies to eliminate the moral hazard of the temptation to dishonesty in the (over-)rating of securities suggest themselves: (i) most basically a reversion to the pre-1970 business model, whereby it would be investors who would pay the fees of rating agencies and not the issuers of the securities. Once again, since rating agencies survived perfectly well on this model from the early 1900s up to the early 1970s, we know that such a model can work fully effectively in practice. (ii) If rating agencies are to continue on their current model of issuers paying the fees, then it becomes imperative that the agencies are seen to be of the highest integrity and independence; in effect, like a strictly impartial referee or (as is common in the UK university system) external examiner. This at the very least points towards some sort of non-profit institution and one could be inclined to think of some sort of public sector ownership solution, except of course that among the securities rated are government bonds of various types! Hence, if the security-issuer fees model is to be retained for rating agencies it would need to be in the hands of some international politically independent not-for-profit agency whose operating costs would be funded by the world's central banks.

One particularly remarkable initiative in this context is that of the European Commission and the European Parliament, which favour establishment of the European Rating Agency in order to bring more competitive pressure to the market dominated by three large American agencies: Standard and Poor's, Moody's and Fitch. According to the Commission, financial instruments could also be rated by national central banks or by the European Central Bank. Pension funds, insurances and other institutional investors are encouraged not to follow the ratings of the three large agencies as closely as they had before. Michel Barnier, the European Commissioner for Internal Market and Services, believes that financial institutions and institutional investors excessively rely upon ratings provided by large rating agencies, while in fact they should assess credit risk on their own, if not entirely then at least to a much higher degree. Such an independent risk control should then be monitored by their supervising bodies. As an additional measure, along with internal risk assessment, banks should be obliged to consult two external ratings for each security from the financial market. Barnier also considers introduction of a flexibility clause enabling pension funds or insurances to keep securities in portfolios after their prices decrease. Moreover, the European Commission seems willing to launch new provisions concerning the rating of government bonds or even to ban rating of sovereign government debt by rating agencies. It is also possible that rating agencies will have to keep governments informed on a constant basis upon planned rating downgrade three days before actually doing it. At present this is just twelve hours.[16]

The third major moral issue we raised in relation to financial crises was in respect of the equity of the large-scale macro-level redistribution of wealth from taxpayers in general, that is, from the community as a whole to the financial sector, arguably one of the richest sectors of the economy; hence, in effect, a seriously regressive redistribution. To deal effectively with what is in effect an ever-present danger of large-scale regressive redistributions of wealth every time there is a financial crisis would involve not only a very much tighter regulation of the financial system and perhaps as we suggested above an end of fractional reserve banking, it would also involve dethroning the financial sector from the position of pre-eminence that it has arrogated to itself in most of the world's capitalist economies. This will certainly not be easy and most politicians even of socialist leaning do not even want to try it: just think of the manner in which British politicians are literally afraid of ever upsetting the City of London. But perhaps here we have reached the real nub of so much of contemporary political economy and business ethics: for who is to exercise ultimate control and guidance of the capitalist free market system – is it the financiers or is it governments? Or putting the same point in a slightly different way: is the capitalist system just one possible means among others to serve the broader ends and goals of human communities or is it an end in itself designed to serve the interests of high finance? We are not necessarily seeking to offer a definitive answer to these complex and fundamental questions, which go right to the heart of moral and political philosophy, but are saying that, in the aftermath of the contemporary financial crisis and what we know of so many others, they are questions that merit serious attention and ones on which every student of business ethics should be reflecting in detail to evolve an informed view.

A perspective: the views of Joseph Stiglitz

Another question worth asking is whether it had been possible to foresee the crisis that struck in 2008. Of course it had – answers Joseph Stiglitz, the Nobel Prize winner in economy, in his most recent book.[17]

'The only surprise about the economic crisis of 2008 was that it came as a surprise to so many' – this is how Chapter 1 of the book begins. The market with no regulation, bathed in liquidity and low interest rates, the global bubble in real estate market and galloping boom of subprime credits were a toxic combination. Adding the American fiscal and trade deficit combined with enormous US dollar reserves collected by China – an imbalance in global economy – it was obvious that things went terribly wrong – believes Stiglitz.

If it had been possible to foresee the crisis, then was it possible to avoid it? According to Stiglitz it certainly was, and the key word in that possibility was regulation, along with strong state involvement. Any successful economy – any successful society – comprises both elements: that of the government and that of the market. It is crucial to maintain proper balance between their roles, the problem being not only about 'how much', but also about 'how'. Had the American governments resisted the financial lobby, had they maintained the earlier regulation and developed it even further, then they would have succeeded in preventing the financial market faltering. This explicit statement, while debatable, should be given serious consideration, as the Nobel Prize winner encourages.

In his judgement, the so-called moral hazard is a phenomenon that stems from the lack of potential of market self-regulation. Deregulation of financial markets resulted in the emergence of businesses 'too large to fail'. Even more importantly, according to Stiglitz, those managing such businesses were well aware of the fact and deliberately took advantage of it. This way, we obviously have to deal here with an agency-like issue where those who make decisions are not those held responsible. And what is still more important, the costs of wrong decisions have burdened third persons who had not been involved in the problem (outside effects). It is American taxpayers and people in other countries affected by the crisis who paid and are still paying for bankers' mistaken decisions.

The crisis, according to Stiglitz, brought both new risks and new opportunities. He defines the new risks as follows:

1   Unless we devise a better financial and economic system, we shall experience still worse breakdowns in the future. This, in turn, may lead to general aversion towards globalization and to loss of openness of countries to one another.
2   The discussion and battle about economic ideas may be carried down from the level of scholarly debate to that of social conflict, which could get seriously out of control and lead to populist revolutions.

The opportunity is there to turn back to the 'old', traditional values – argues Stiglitz, emphasizing that what we really have to deal with is moral crisis. A pursuit of profit and of very narrowly interpreted short-term self-interest ruined social restraints and drove some people to attempt to make profit at the cost of other members of society. One of the most important issues in efforts to improve the world's economic condition is to restore broken trust and a sense of fairness. Unless there is trust and demonstrable fairness (justice) present upon each level of economic activity, no sustainable growth may be achieved.

CLASS QUESTIONS

1   It is really hard not to agree with the opinion of the American economist Stiglitz when he says, 'Unless there is trust and demonstrable fairness (justice) present upon each level of economic activity, no sustainable growth may be achieved.'
2   In the light of the most recent developments in the European Union in relation to sovereign government debt, what in your opinion are the most urgent reforms that need to be made in European financial markets and to what extent are these reforms necessary to address moral/ethical issues as opposed to purely technical economic issues?

Notes

1 One does not need to be a Marxist to recognize that the financial system associated with contemporary capitalism has been subject to recurrent crises, very often linked to speculative bubbles in various types of assets. From the tulips bubble of the seventeenth century through to the major crises of the twentieth and twenty-first century (1929, Asian financial crisis of 1997–8, contemporary crisis, to name but a few), the financial system that has accompanied market capitalism based on fractional reserve banking and on freely operating markets for all types of financial asset has proved to be inherently subject to producing a cyclical pattern of boom and slump in financial markets (often but not always paralleled by booms and slumps in the 'real' economy), which leads to recurrent crises. At least since the time of Keynes and Hayek in the 1930s, economists have been reflecting on this theme but without producing anything very clear cut by way of policy solutions to avoid such crises.

2 www.google.fr/search?hl=fr&rls=p,com.microsoft:fr:IE-SearchBox&rlz=1I7SKPB &defl=en&q=define:moral+hazard&sa=X&ei=QpdSTMH4GNq5jAfKzfzCBA&ved=0 CBgQkAE (accessed 30 July 2010).

3 Let us not forget that 'reckless' behaviour might simply be a case of risk-loving as opposed to risk-averse preferences by certain decision takers: c.f. the seminal treatment of this topic by M. Friedman and L. J. Savage (1948) 'Utility analysis of choices involving risk', *Journal of Political Economy*, 56(4): 279–304. However, the use of the term 'reckless' in this context is typically meant in the sense that the person who takes the risk does not bear (all) of the consequences if things go pear-shaped.

4 All of this is made very clear in the economic analysis of choices involving uncertainty as developed in the Friedman and Savage article (ibid.). The insurers take on the risks and so gamble; the insured are prepared to pay a premium to avoid the risks.

5 This can be concluded from the statement of Professor Janusz Czapiński given at a conference held in the Warsaw University School of Management in 2009, dedicated to the problems and nature of the crisis in Poland and worldwide.

6 With supreme irony in the country in Europe most associated with unbridled laissez-faire financial capitalism, Britain, two of the largest retail banks are now in effect nationalized with more than 50 per cent state ownership of shares: Halifax Bank of Scotland and Lloyds TSB.

7 'Light at the end of the bailout tunnel', *Wall Street Journal*, 12 April 2010.

8 That we refer to the financial system as in effect a huge casino should not be entirely surprising (and it is certainly not original). Keynes was in no doubt about this and we have already noted how all insurance involves deliberate calculated gambles taken by the insurer.

9 Bernard Madoff, a highly respected American Jewish financier/fund manager was exposed and convicted in 2008 for one of the biggest Ponzi schemes ever uncovered and which had been going on for some 20 years. For this fraud he was given a prison sentence that will in effect see him in prison until his death, given his age.

10 'Trustee in Bernard Madoff scandal files complaint against Stanley Chais', *Los Angeles Times* wire service, 2 May 2009.

11 The example of Greek government borrowing in 2010 is the clearest recent example of the impact of the rating agencies on the interest rate that must be paid on government debt instruments.

12 IMF (2010) 'Exiting from monetary crisis intervention measures: Background paper'. Washington DC: IMF, p. 8.

13 A tax system is said to be proportional if the percentage of total income/sales paid by all taxpayers is the same. A progressive system is one where taxpayers with higher income/sales pay a higher proportion of their total income/sales as tax. A regressive system is one where higher income/sales taxpayers pay a lower proportion of tax. It is usually held that for equity a tax system should at least be proportional if not progressive. However, it is important not to focus exclusively on any one tax but rather to consider

the overall impact of the whole array of taxes *and* government spending for an economy and to make an overall judgement thereby of the system.

14 The poll tax would have been a tax of a fixed lump sum amount to be paid by all households, irrespective of their incomes, for provision of local services. It would be blatantly regressive. It was never passed as such and in fact sowed the seeds of Margaret Thatcher's downfall in British politics.

15 Various types of liquid assets such as treasury bills or bonds might of course become a sort of 'near money' capable of boosting liquidity in such a system but at least there would be transparency; if I accept a bond in settlement of a debt at least the risk is patently obvious by comparison with accepting cash.

16 Regulation (EU) No. 1093/2010 of the European Parliament and of the Council, 24 November 2010, establishing a European Supervisory Authority (European Banking Authority), amending Decision No. 716/2009/EC and repealing Commission Decision 2009/78/EC.

17 Joseph Stiglitz (2010) *Freefall: Free markets and the sinking of the global economy.* London: Allen Lane.

PART IV

Organizational behaviour

12

ETHICS AND MANAGEMENT

The essential philosophical and psychological basis of ethical management driven by a progressive company

Loïck Roche

I did not say that for you to understand, I said it for you to use.

(J. Lacan)

Jean-Jacques Nillès explains that, as ethics defines principles and general laws, it represents a factor in taking the *right* decision in a given situation. What may be correct to do in one situation may not be right in another. Ethics allows for discussion, argument, paradox.

In other words, ethics states that not all ends justify the means.

Using ethics implies rejecting three illusions:

1   The first illusion is that it is not a statement of performance (as defined by John Langshaw Austin). *Saying is not doing.* A statement such as 'I pronounce you man and wife' may validate your marriage, but the issues are more complex.

2   The second illusion is that ethics in the fields of management and business does not refer to understanding the subject. As the philosopher Karl Popper said: 'Don't be duped by anything, not by fashion, not by intellectual terrorism, not by money, not by power. Learn to distinguish the True from the False everywhere, always!' We all agree but is this sufficient? No theory or class work has ever relieved a person of their stress (François Giroud) as no class in civic instruction has ever reduced delinquency; ethics, and particularly those in the business world, only makes sense if it is fully integrated (Spinoza said that nothing positive in a false idea is excluded by the presence of the truth as such). Ethics needs to be physically understood, not just emotionally or intellectually but also the difference between the spirit and the body.

3   The third illusion is that one can change. Man does not change. Hobbes taught us that man is a wolf and, to refer to Spinoza again – man can be controlled

by another man; each man and woman is restrained in their thoughts and in their body by the external influences to which they are submitted.

Even if we believe Lacan, who says that questions are only asked when answers are present, this does not necessarily mean that there is nothing to do. 'Never, never, never give up', said Churchill – never therefore give up looking for new answers. But to do this, one needs to think differently, sometimes confronting one's own convictions. To *'break our own toys'*, as Boris Vian suggested. It means accepting that one is no longer all-powerful, dominating everything including one's own suffering. Anna Karenin called these *'skeletons'*; Freud famously stated that *'man is not the master in his own house'*. For a company, the best is the enemy of its own good. Consider Popper's interpretation: 'Succeed [in business] by doing nothing that could become serious'! Find the right balance between excess and error – the balance that Aristotle called for in his thinking.

As authors, we do not seek to take responsibility away from others or to stigmatize the 'coward' so often found in organizations. We endeavour to show that, in order to react 'well', in the 'least bad way', it is necessary to react within a framework, within the rules. Rules, by defining 'organizational super-ego' territory, aim at avoiding excesses. Adopting these limits, such as the super ego that defines itself during childhood by accepting parental taboos and later those defined by school and society, offers the true opportunity to show what could be called ethical behaviour. Rules (wrote Spinoza) can threaten and irritate human pride by generating their reactions of humility, remorse, hope or fear.

> The crowd is terrible when it has no fear. [. . .] Letting each person judge what is good and what is bad is to take the risk of having many constructive or adverse disagreements, since it depends on the way in which each person feels, whether they are being helped or hindered.

This framework sets the limits within which people may act.

> Man has the power to be and to act in many ways, creating within himself and outside himself: from thereon, the challenge is to know how he can really be the author of these ways, and which ones he must create.
>
> (Pascal Sévérac's analysis of Spinoza's *Ethics*)

Ethics concerns every level of management

Let us now examine the philosophical (and to a lesser extent the psychological) grounding for our thesis that ethics must today be a primary driver for good management practice. In developing this thesis we are at Level 1 of the critique outlined in the methodology (Chapter 2) of this work. A good starting point would be to mention some of the major business scandals and failures of recent times, many of whose roots can be traced to ethical failures in management or by managers. Some leading examples include:

1   In the business world, and without condemning the financiers and auditors responsible for historic frauds and manipulation of stock exchanges, let us mention the Enron case (a bankruptcy showing a loss of US$68 billion with 5,600 layoffs), the false accounting at US telecoms operator WorldCom (the biggest bankruptcy in the United States), Vivendi Universal (share price manipulation), Parmalat – a company in the milk industry! (false invoicing and overvalued contracts to increase revenues and thus obtain further credit paid into their off-shore accounts from Lichtenstein to the Cayman Islands).

2   In the world of management, employees' stress and work-related illnesses (chronic tiredness, fibromyalgia, i.e. chronic pain that sleep cannot remedy); suicide at the workplace, the result of exposure to managers who, because they find themselves put into impossible situations, will use extremely violent management modes (as a defence mechanism). These and other managers who are unable to produce what Sartre called the 'practico-inert' – the inert, material condition that prevents them from shouting 'that they don't know what to do any more . . .' and are obliged to accept a role that they can no longer assume.

It is necessary to understand that ethics should not only be seen at the top of the company pyramid but also at all levels of management, 'from strategic reflection to professional acts'.[1]

The only management question is the question of decision

We owe this lesson to Helmut Schmidt, a former Chancellor of the Federal Republic of Germany who, when interviewed about his responsibilities at the end of his mandate (1974–1982), traced an interesting parallel between political and managerial functions. For Schmidt, the most tangible and pertinent expression of this parallel is that, in the end, the political question resembles the management question. And this single question, always in an uncertain, complex environment, is the question of decision – 'what do I decide?' Helmut Schmidt explains:

> when, as a politician or as a manager, I must make a decision, I am always alone. Because although initially I was able to rely on the notes given to me by my advisors, although I was able to discuss with my team . . . at the final moment, I am alone when I decide!

And, adding his true contribution to this subject, 'when I am alone [to decide], I run three risks: the risk of opportunism, the risk of charlatanism and the risk of error'. After excluding error which, by definition, is human and does not reflect on the honesty of the politician or the manager who acts in 'good faith' (Man, said Spinoza, can err through his imagination), one can easily understand that opportunism and charlatanism may lead to deviations that in turn could breed tomorrow's scandals.

The only question for man is the question of desire

The risk is even more obvious when one realizes that the only question for men and women is the question of . . . desire. Not only: 'What do I want?' that is, 'all the efforts', wrote Spinoza, 'impulses, appetite and man's volitions which vary according to that man's constitution', but also the effort that each individual exercises to preserve their being. 'This effort', wrote Sévérac (*L'Ethique de Spinoza*, p. 17), 'that every being employs to preserve itself, (and what Spinoza calls conatus) when applied to man, is known as Desire.'

Succeed in relying on someone 'bigger than oneself'

What then can one do when it is necessary to rely upon someone who is 'bigger' than oneself? This 'bigger than oneself' who is not there, because I am alone when I decide – this internal context in which I can decide, avoiding the three traps of opportunism, charlatanism and error – is the cultural reference. It is something that can be philosophical, psychological, literary, historical . . . in short, general culture. Something with which I am comfortable – which 'communicates with me' – and which, because it talks of things similar to those that I face, will help me to be more intelligent for the decision that I must take. Thus, Helmut Schmidt had the habit of relying on philosophy for his most important decisions. In fact, on three philosophers – Kant, Nietzsche and Popper.

Can ethics be taught?

Ethics is fashionable in all the leading business schools. It is only about 'social business' or 'sustainable development'. In class, 'responsible management' ethics fights with 'social responsibility' ethics. 'Is this sufficient?' ask Sophie Coignard and Marie-Sandrine Sgherri.[2] They maintain that, since the fall of Lehman Brothers, the leading business schools, 'breeding grounds for traders and leaders', have been numbered among the accused, teaching only technical skills for immediate use by companies and looking no further once students have graduated. Social myopia and lack of critical faculties could threaten the future managers of the economic world.

Without being too harsh – after all, Aristotle wrote his *Nicomachean Ethics* based on his high-school classes – we acknowledge that both schools and teachers are now concerned with ethics. But the teaching of ethics today is incoherent. As Nicolas Masson, Associate Director of the Pragma consultancy shows, and Sophie Coignard confirms, 'Classes in ethics only have an effect if they apply to real cases [or scenarii]. On the other hand, at the start of professional life [. . .] bad habits become quickly ingrained because it is difficult to turn back.'[3]

Following this logic, we find two tracks: having seen that one needs to rely on someone greater than oneself, the first track would put philosophy (and more broadly general culture) at the heart of teaching in business schools. To paraphrase General de Gaulle, it serves no purpose to jump up and down on a chair like a child repeating '*Ethics, ethics, ethics* . . .' if one does not start at the beginning, studying those philosophers who have devoted their thoughts specifically to ethics. Spinoza, of course, but also Aristotle (*Nicomachean Ethics, Eudemian Ethics,* and also *About Generation and Corruption, Virtues and Vices*) . . . A philosophy not to be accepted as such but, as for Kant and Voltaire, to be subjected to interpretation; understanding like Socrates that, through applying our reasoning in exchanges and dialogue with others, the rationality of our intelligence must be balanced by our reasonable behaviour, or risk its becoming a sectarian, immovable form of rationalism (a return to the practico-inert already referred to).

The second track, offered by Nicolas Masson, is that further classes incorporating the reconstruction of experiences based on ethics should be part of an 'after-sales service' offered by schools which may (we suppose) have a certain effectiveness. It is clear that classes taught in a theoretical context are bound to fail (other than giving those who organize or teach them a good conscience). There remains the method of teaching based on case studies – a more uncertain form of teaching that we view with benevolence and has the merit of existing.

Are ethics a professional skill?

This is the view developed by Jean-Jacques Nillès. After recalling that ethics are present in a positive manner in all aspects of management, he states that ethics can be approached by values and virtues (referential behaviours, e.g. intelligence of the situation, respect for the law . . .). The approach through virtues

> presents advantages in terms of method. Virtues being levers for action, they allow a declension of ethics in referential behaviours within a given business. It is thus possible to create a reference for the ethical dimension of that business. This was what was done, for example, for buyers at the CDAF (the Company of Buyers in France).[4]

However, this approach, even though rigorous, remains below our expectations when we speak of ethics in business or ethics in companies. Even if we understand that one can try to implement the tools (Chart of Ethics, the resulting forms of behaviour, methods for monitoring . . .), actions that will certainly allow the most obvious risks of abuse to be countered remain at the level of intellectual and not physical (totally integrated) understanding of this requirement for ethics. For example, preferring historical suppliers results in lack of competition. However, it is when and only when all aspects are completely integrated that they become a sort of second nature, a reflex. It is perhaps when the super-ego context has been put in place that people have some chance of respecting ethical rules in their daily actions.

Ethics generates progress

What could this super-ego context be, which weighs on companies and organizations and, in the end, leads to schizophrenic waves of destruction too often demonstrated in the field of management? Why does one feel that men balance themselves on narrow peaks and remain on the sunny side, not falling into the shadows? We need to be extremely vigilant, if not concerned, when we recall Lacan's remark that the most violent psychic wounds always arise within groups apparently subjected to total normality.[5]

The question: 'What will make a man in an organization behave in an ethical or unethical manner?' is the same that Leibniz asked himself: 'Will I go to the tavern or will I work?'. For Deleuze (1987),[6] in his analysis of Leibniz's work, the answer comes from the fabric of the soul: 'This should be seen as a welter of thousands of small inclinations (i.e. small perceptions, small tendencies), which twist the soul in every direction.'

'Why is it that the fabric of the soul leans more on one side than another? What is the action that, at a given moment, will fill the soul according to its importance?' asks Deleuze. This is what Leibniz calls deliberation. 'The fabric of the soul goes from the perceptive pole like the *tavern* [i.e. simplicity] to the perspective pole "*office*" [i.e. respecting the rules].' 'If the volume is small', continues Deleuze,

> if there really is no inclination, the individual will opt for simplicity. He is then led by necessity – he is no longer free. If his soul's capacity is large enough, he will opt for the difficulty [respecting the rules]. The individual is said to be free as soon as his action [here, respecting the rules] is an expression of his soul at its most voluminous.

According to Deleuze:

> The perfect or accomplished act is entelechy (*entelecheia*). With Aristotle, it is an act that has its own conclusion. The perfect or accomplished act is an act benefiting from permanence, as opposed to a successive act. It is not the act that has been accomplished, a past act, it is an act being performed.

This tendency towards the best, concludes Deleuze, this increase in the volume of the soul, is what Leibniz calls progress. 'I progress [this is also an act being accomplished]', continues Deleuze,

> if my soul increases its volume. To progress is to increase the area of enlightenment which belongs to every individual [and not that of another person]. Each of us [can progress], can become more enlightened by developing power and studying our own area of enlightenment. [And] this can only be achieved through knowledge [i.e. in part through education, as Aristotle had already understood].

Being able to increase the area of enlightenment of one's soul also allows one to shed light on the other areas in those with whom we work.

To create a super-egotistic envelope, the following elements need to be added as a third track, using examples:

1   Teaching philosophy – and more broadly teaching general culture – which must become the keystone of courses in management sciences . . .
2   The reproduction of professional experiences and activities based on ethics – the very role of management (the Director, the CEO and managers too) . . .

With these three tracks we may perhaps be able to create a company that we have called – *a driver for ethics*.

The force of example

Examples that are recalled and evaluated can become the footprint, the reference point in an organization. Examples can thus allow integrity to be shown when faced with an ethical dilemma – for instance, the extraordinary service, beyond client satisfaction, that defines the framework of the dominance of collective interest over personal interest.[7]

John Sadowsky, in his book *Les 7 règles du storytelling*[8] has collected several of these examples. It includes the now-famous story told by Tom Peters about a Federal Express employee and a helicopter, which illustrates the fulfilment of the company's promise to guarantee reliable delivery in whatever conditions, overcoming all obstacles. The telephone lines having been damaged by a blizzard, leaving the FedEx office out of touch with its clients, a young member of the staff decided to rent a helicopter using his personal credit card, to fly to the top of the mountain where the damaged equipment was located and restore the telephone lines, thus making FedEx operational again.[9]

At UPS, the main competitor to FedEx, long-serving staff speak of deliveries made on time in weather conditions so bad that they prevented their competitors from using the roads.[10]

A famous story at Nordstrom, says John Sadowsky, is about the customer who, about to travel, had left her air tickets in a Nordstrom shoe shop. The sales assistant tried to call the airline company to solve the problem but the company followed its rules and regulations. They replied that it was impossible to help the passenger. The sales assistant then herself paid for a 45-minute taxi ride to the airport to ensure that her customer could take her flight. Patrick McCarthy, a sales veteran at Nordstrom, analyses this story with admiration; the sales assistant's initiative is a model of ethics that everyone in the company should follow.[11]

Companies thus have many examples that, properly used, can describe what could create the *super-egoistic* framework.

Making the company a driver for ethics

This is a new vision of the company that we are calling for; a company that, without refuting its objectives, should also be seen as what Gianfranco Dioguardi called a driver for culture – better still, *a driver for ethics*.

A company that is a driver for ethics, because it is capable of creating an environment adapted to ethical behaviour and its implementation, would then be able to benefit from a language and a manner of thinking and reasoning. [Everyone], wrote Dioguardi,

> who has again become an authentic, rational being, will know how to interpret the role of an entrepreneur, operating within the context of his own action, applying a spirit of initiative and the essential creativity that, combined, will produce innovation and generate specific improvements.[12]

He continues:

> the company must again find its own 'intelligence', i.e. the ability and the capacity to make colleagues understand quickly not only what they do, what they should do and in what context. [They must absorb] the reality of which they are a part (i.e. the core of the company), the context in which they act and the external surroundings which condition them and stimulate them culturally, remembering the facts which occurred to create these same surroundings (i.e. history).[13]

This means that we must re-evaluate continuing education – we must work in parallel with the training for different professions, degree programmes and on an important part of continuing education for those who work in companies. Teachers should be dedicated to sharing, understanding and distributing what is commonly known as the basis of ethics, 'general culture' (whether through philosophy, psychoanalysis, literature, even – to cite other examples – the law, history, economics . . .). We will then be able to meet the demands that ethics imposes, understanding the present era and thus succeed in making the company what we have called a driver for ethics, i.e. (as Dioguardi encourages us to do), a true citizen's environment because it is capable of developing ethics, *ethically*.

The path to modern ethics

As there are many homes in the Father's house, as everyone has the right to be welcomed there if they respect the rules in force, so discussions about ethics in management are not yet over.

Philosophy and particularly Karl Popper have shown us the way. In companies, as in other walks of life, there is no truth. The question of truth was the Greeks' question – 'In what conditions is truth possible?' asked Socrates. We had to wait for Kant (at the end of the eighteenth century) to understand that this is far too ambitious a question. Kant substitutes another question: 'In what conditions is knowledge possible?' For Karl Popper, this same question is still too ambitious – he substitutes yet another question: 'In what conditions is progress possible?' But what is progress for Karl Popper? It starts with a problem he calls, P1 which firstly requires a number of people to solve it. We are no longer in the age of Diderot's and Alembert's Encyclopaedia, no longer at the time when knowledge could be compiled in a few books . . ., we no longer have the answer to everything. The more stupid ideas are discarded later – 'we make theories die in our place'. One or two ideas are then retained and tested. But above all, we do not find an answer. We get to what Karl Popper called the least bad solution (which is always but an approximation of the truth, an approximation for which he created the word *verisimilitude*). This expresses itself as a new problem that Popper calls P2. This new problem, he tells us, demonstrates progress. Why? Because it is even more complex and therefore more interesting than the initial problem. This illustrates progress in the company – moving from the P1 problem to a P2 problem is more interesting because it is more complex.[14]

How ethics may reward management

We look beyond the axes of progress that ethics in management illustrate, beyond the evidence for reflecting about the conditions for teaching, beyond a position that must be considered for the return of philosophy (to be taken in its strict etymological sense: *love of wisdom*). What we wish to demonstrate about management sciences and therefore company thinking is that ethics in the field of management is a gamble. A gamble like Pascal's bet. Not knowing whether God exists or not (that has little importance), but making the bet that if he exists, then I am more free – but paradoxically, liberty cannot be exercised within a framework, a territory.

So when we say that ethics in the field of management is a gamble, that is, if ethics are present, we believe that the people who make up the company will be able to live well, to live at peace with themselves. They accept the framework, the rules – what we have called the super-egoistic framework and Spinoza defined as Joy, Aristotle as Happiness. The alternative is Sadness, the continual 'murder of Hiram', the murder of the other, perceived as the ideal of my own self, the unbearable confusion between the company's possessions and my own. If there is ethics, man can progress. Progress demonstrated by growth in his performance, in that of the company and even further – progress in society, whose three inseparable elements are the basis of responsible management: the economy, social responsibility and the environment.

A reminder from Erasmus: 'Man is not born man, he becomes man'. What we propose here is the idea of introducing ethics into the workplace – ethics being understood as being a condition for Joy, Happiness in work wherever possible, relationships and confidence – this is modern courage!

Notes

1 J. J. Nilles (2008) 'Comment promouvoir et opérationnaliser l'éthique', *Journées d'étude éthique de l'entreprise: Réalité ou illusion?*, 13 juin 2008, Sciences Po.
2 S. Coignard and M. S. Sgherri (2010) 'Futurs managers, soyez gentil!', *Le Point*, 11 février 2010, p. 90.

3 Ibid., p. 94.
4 J. J. Nilles (2003) 'L'éthique est une compétence professionnelle'. Available online at www.journaldunet.com.
5 J. Lacan, in E. Kapnist and E. Roudinesco (2008) 'Jacques Lacan, la psychanalyse réinventée', *Arte*, France, INA.
6 Deleuze (1987) 'Cours Vincennes - St Denis La Taverne: 24/02/1987'. Available online at www.webdeleuze.com/php/liste_texte.php?groupe=Leibniz.
7 B. Birchard (2002) 'Once upon a time', *Strategy & Business*, 27. Available online at www.strategy-business.com/press/article/18637?pg=0.
8 John Sadowsky (2009), *Les 7 règles du storytelling*. Paris: Pearson.
9 A. Wylie (1998) 'Storytelling: A powerful form of communication', *Communication World*, 15: 30–32.
10 D. Cohen and L. Prusak (2001) *In Good Company: How social capital makes organizations work*. Boston, MA: Harvard Business School Press.
11 R. Spector and P. D. McCarthy (1995) *The Nordstrom Way: The inside story of America's customer service company*. New York: John Wiley & Sons.
12 G. Duigguardi (2003) *Dossier Diderot*, Castelnau-le-Lez, Climats, p. 277.
13 Ibid., p. 281.
14 K. R. Popper (1972) *Objective Knowledge: An evolutionary approach*. Oxford: Oxford University Press.

Further reading

Severac, P. (1997) *Ethique Spinoza*. Paris: Ellipses.
Spinoza, B. (1996 [1677]) *Ethica Ordine Geometrico Demonstrata* [*The Ethics*]. London: Penguin Classics.

13

MINDFULNESS AS A MEDIATOR BETWEEN THE EFFECTIVE AND THE ETHICAL MANAGER

Dominique Steiler and Raffi Duymedjian

The mindful manager: tuning ethics with efficiency

An expression that is frequently used by employees but is not, however, appropriate in times of crisis: to bury one's head in the sand. It indicates the inability by those with power to move their attention away from the flow of everyday activity. Above all, this expression accompanies overt frustration linked to the fact of being unable to 'take a step back' (another banal expression). Above all, it has undesirable consequences[1] from the ethical point of view. To accept the moral suffering that this state creates, the individual reduces the field of his moral conscience by, for example, hiding behind rules and procedures, generally giving priority to legal rather than moral considerations.

However, an ordinary individual might justify this state of hyper-concentration by holding that it would be a necessary condition for performance. Adopting a broader view, taking his head out of the sand, would risk reducing his productivity and losing his thoughts rather than focusing his energy on the task in hand.

We believe, on the contrary, that this drop in performance can be avoided without prejudice to the efficiency of the task in hand when the individual adopts a position of 'mindfulness', making him apt to simultaneously act, observe and understand the elements that make up the flow of activity as it really is. Ethics could then not be overridden by the strict requirements of economic efficiency; practical efficiency can be reconciled with the presence of an open field of moral conscience.

This proposition places us at Level 2 or sometimes even Level 3 of critique as defined in Chapter 2. In fact, a position of complete awareness suspends the judgement to observe things 'as they are' as far as possible, inside and outside the individual; 'things' being understood here in their plurality (people, statements, objects, spaces, but also standards, values, judgements, beliefs). This point of view will be the starting point for a reasoning, taking into account stress, contradictions that have been verified but are also apparent, leading to action that can be initiated with the full awareness of the facts and the consequences, without confusing morality with legality.

Origins and consequences of ethical efficiency: preparing the birth of the mindful manager

In this section, we will try to explain the causes and the consequences of the belief in an incompatibility between efficiency and reflectively maintaining one's distance – being reflectively 'mindful' in effect. We will then introduce full awareness as a form of relationship with oneself, the world and action – from this will emerge the profile of the mindful manager.

Causes and consequences of the apparent incompatibility of efficiency and reflective Mindfulness

There are numerous and varied reasons that establish and strengthen this belief in an incompatibility of efficiency and Mindfulness. Certain are invoked at times of crisis, others are more profoundly anchored in Judaeo-Christian culture, or to be more precise, in Judaism and the more puritanical versions of Protestant Christianity associated with Calvinism.

Thus, one hears that the acceleration of the economy justifies 'moving ahead' and that any slowdown would be detrimental to the smooth running of the organization. One must therefore ignore the past, always be productive, have no hesitation in ensuring permanent client satisfaction.[2] Projects are hardly finished when the next one begins, when indeed projects are started without any real objective or need. One thinks of concentrating on the present, but a present that is finally always conditioned by a future intention.

Time thus becomes more than ever one of the major factors for the creation of value that above all requires not being distracted from the action. An image is thus born of 'being occupied', a synonym of perseverance, effort, work. Emphasis is on 'doing', which is often reduced to proving that one is producing something with a commercial value. Political speeches inundate us with reforms, companies burst with strategies for change that validate this demand for production – visible in the infinitely positive connotation of 'pragmatism' to the detriment of thinking, often caricatured in the figure of the inert, contemplative philosopher.

Furthermore, this activity, even hyperactivity, expresses itself in a cultural context where effort, success, performance and suffering ('you will earn your bread by the sweat of your brow') have long been associated. This also justifies the means of access to an imaginary paradisiacal future (a job with prestige, higher salary, etc.). And one of the attitudes that demonstrates this race for efficiency is that which involves paying attention ('pay attention, remain concentrated!'). But this 'paying attention' is a focalization, therefore a reduction in the attention span, which fully corresponds to a mechanism of stress generation. Demand for performance is thus systematically associated with an intellectual and physical effort identical to that required in a dangerous situation: mobilization of energy, focusing the attention on a specific point. To this is added a moral value attributed to suffering that seems to give more worth to a performance obtained with distress than to success without suffering, seen as the sign of cheating or imposture. (Here the link to a puritanical Protestantism is patently obvious.)

Finally, the last cause could be said to arise from the prolongation of the Taylorian distinction, which separates conception from execution. Thus, the employee is not authorized to think about his actions – this is the responsibility of his hierarchy, the internal quality department or an external group of consultants. However, this disconnection no longer affects only the worker but now extends to management itself, ever more submitted to a need for the automation of the processes of decision in which the manager too becomes but a cog, like the worker in the machine system.[3]

Having looked at a certain number of causes, we now look at a few of the more serious consequences concerning morals and ethics.

The manager is more and more subjected to the technical dimension of his activity. This submission is twofold: submission to technical rhythm[4] notably through the restrictions of a system of computerized communication that imposes a tempo on social relations (the overflowing mailbox is one of the most violent symbols), and ideological submission to a set of managerial techniques that are seen as transparent and neutral through their appearance of conviviality and practicality, relieved of any presupposed morals or ethics because aiming for the imaginary performance objective.

Managerial activity is also more and more dispersed. The manager has buried his head in a number of different sandbanks without being able to invest fully in a specific activity. This fractioning of time – one is disturbed on average every 12 minutes in France[5] – implies a superior evaluation of so-called relational skills above and to the detriment of professional skills (Sennett 2007). However, at the same time that professions are disappearing, are dissolving into a range of common meetings and services, the system of standards, deontology or even the ethics of work properly done that are associated with them, are disappearing.

Finally, the obsession for doing something whatever the cost leads to setting aside of the self, which can lead to the chasm of despair and anxiety. It is shameful to be seen as feeble, to succumb to pressure, to show one's wounds. The external image is more important than what is felt. Feelings disappear in the heat of action. The manager is thus only assessing himself in relation to external references, losing the true meaning of his work.

We believe that these consequences converge, crystallize in the suspension of the critical mind, reducing the field of moral conscience and producing unthinking action (a mindless action). The manager develops an inability to judge either because the substance has been neutralized (made technical and thus subjected to the indisputable criteria of performance) or because it is not in his interest – better to protect oneself by applying the rules as the 'good' soldier obeys orders. In effect, the result is that the manager 'buries his head in the sand', staying with the action while the world moves on, concentrating on the tasks to be done while seriously narrowing his focus of attention as well as his capacity for moral judgement.

From Mindfulness to the mindful manager

'Burying one's head in the sand' defines a certain cognitive relationship with current activity and events, with what is now happening. Now this relationship is one that the whole productive organization maintains with its procedures and its staff. Ashforth and Fried (1988) described this attitude as Mindless, consisting of remaining focused on the crux of the action without any other form of reflection, leading to a loss of attention and an artificial commitment to the action.

It is notably as a result of and to counter observation that other forms of individual attitude were proposed, opening the field to a less narrow-minded form of action. Donald Schön (1984) developed his idea of reflection in and on action, establishing the profile of the reflective practitioner, for example.

More generally, this reflexiveness is the consequence of a more receptive, more open character that we may designate as Mindfulness. This defines an initially non-judgemental attitude, where the attention is concentrated on the present, in which each thought, each perception or event is seen and accepted. The attention is therefore voluntarily held by the present experience, which is viewed with curiosity. The attention does not seek to wander from the present in favour of abstract contemplation of the situation and its significance.

The conception of the notion of Mindfulness finds its origin in psychology based on research into decision-making processes, where it was seen (Langer 1989) that a closed attitude towards present action restricts the field of information handled and potential solutions. Then, the questioning changed form. The organization ceased to be seen exclusively as a system for handling information and making decisions, finding materiality in space, objects and matter. The very definition of cognition itself was transformed in postmodernist thought, going from the classic vision of an individual process, rational, abstract, detached and universal to a postmodern vision redefining it as social, embodied, located, engaged, specific (Smith 1999).

Henceforward, the mindful attitude allowed the reality of the present to be adopted without judgement and, above all, as an internal reality – one's own emotional reactions to stimuli felt, to ideas, values, beliefs that crossed our minds – and as an external reality – inanimate objects, bodies showing movement and emotions, physical spaces to be exploited, etc. Thus, the mental state of others being inaccessible, we can only live events and at best assume what they think, thereby rediscovering the formal indecisiveness of the others' intentions (Livet 1994). Much research was carried out based on this wider definition, using particularly the works of Jon Kabat-Zinn (1982), explaining Mindfulness for personnel development, showing its positive influence on health and well-being.

It is these twin features of the opening of the field of perception during action and the non-judgemental character of Mindfulness that concern us here.

Mindfulness authorizes what the 'head in the sand' forbids us, that is, to see a broader vision while refraining from judgement.

It is precisely here that Mindfulness questions even more brutally the mission, the place and the role of the manager. He has a more important role than the operators to create standards, rules, values, criteria and objectives that surround action and establish its relevance – and this underlines the urgency of defining what it means to be a mindful manager in the face of an ethical problem.

It would be simple, in a first analysis, to see a contradiction between mindful and being a manager. Mindfulness implies a non-judgemental attitude whereas one of the main skills of a manager lies in decision and judgement. The mindful manager would then become undecided, even irresolute.

But we can interpret Mindfulness for a manager as the ability to keep his system open to the perception of the information that he will need for reflection later, rather than have this area restricted through fear linked to the danger of the 'head in the sand' effect. Thus, guided by a prior perception limited by a group of thoughts, beliefs and emotions uniquely associated with the stress that is felt, he risks losing contact with himself as well as his moral and ethical senses. Being mindful will, on the contrary, allow him to fully capture in the same movement all the elements and, above all, each of the values that are involved in his action, both intrinsically and extrinsically. His and the society's ethical sense and values are after all an undeniable integral part of the social reality in which he moves and lives. He could thus take a decision as an ethical, mindful manager.

Ethical challenges and tensions of being a mindful manager

In this section, we will consider two major types of challenge that will face companies who wish to undertake an evolution of their traditional leadership culture towards an ethical Mindfulness culture. The first challenge will be to bring together what we believe, non-exhaustively, to represent the conditions for this change to succeed. The second challenge will then show the pitfalls and obstacles that could restrain this potential development.

Conditions for success

The initial challenge that will appear for companies who would like to develop mindful managers among their staff will be to promote and succeed in, first, the move from being a manager to being a mindful manager and second, the move from a mindful manager to an ethical, mindful manager. The capacity to act, to be aware – although increasing the field of perception and thus the manager's potential for decision and action – does not prevent the development of deviant behaviour that works against the interest of the staff and/or the company. On the contrary, it can increase the risk. Let us take a classic example to illustrate our point. It is customary to hear the term 'elite' mentioned in a national culture, or a company culture, to describe people who are more visible, who have more power. This notion of elite often goes together with a group and a level of skills that are distinctly above the average – one could therefore say a certain level of awareness that is above average. Unfortunately, economic and political events over recent years have demonstrated that elite does not always rhyme with ethics, far from it. The decline in the value of ethics is sometimes proportional to the hierarchical level of this elite. But, if the term elite means something, it is having responsibility and, for those who do not have the means or the ability, ensuring that the major human values are respected for the benefit of all and not for one's own benefit or the benefit of a single group. Thus the manager interested in a development of ethical Mindfulness, through a capacity for reflection about his decisions and undertakings, and with a clear orientation of the use of his personal qualities and skills for the benefit of all including himself, can become the source of an activity that is both ethical and economically efficient. Using this model, he will be able to generate sufficient motivation among his peers to follow this path. As Thomas *et al.* (2004) emphasize:

> the executive task we are describing is to lead with a commitment to ethics mindfulness, to model positive self-regulation that values *how* business goals are accomplished as much as the goals themselves. Such leadership helps build an internal culture rich in the activation of similar, positive self-regulation by others.

The ability of companies to promote these new ways of visualizing the role of manager or leader through a mindful approach will certainly create another challenge, which we see as having two stages. The first stage will be the ability by the leaders to accept that the business world is not inevitably guided and universally defined by conditions thought to be the only efficient option, that is, creating permanent stress for oneself and for others. It is true that present day working conditions are major causes of stress – short lead times, overload of work, taking decisions in complex and uncertain environments or the feeling that one has to put out one fire after another. It is, however, surprising to see how leaders can both complain about these conditions in trying to keep their heads above water (or even suffering ill-health) and, at the same time, only evaluating as efficient and successful behaviour the perpetual fight against others (clients, partners, colleagues, staff, management), against the elements (the market, competition, finance, raw materials, etc.) and, worse still, against themselves (culpability, negative self-judgement, personal constraints, perfectionism,[6] etc.). It has therefore become urgent for leaders to understand that their own stress, or stressing colleagues, is not productive. There is frequent confusion between short-term results achieved with much effort and considerable stress and long-term results that are often the consequence of cultures that care for organisms, relations and institutions.

The second stage follows on naturally from here. It concerns the low value that managers accord to, and indeed the difficulty that managers have, in accepting the value and necessity to learn new practices – bodily (breathing, dietary balance), behavioural (relaxed and open relations), mental (ability to meditate) and spiritual[7] (appreciating the right measure of things and values), not only to permit long-term performance but also to integrate an ethical dimension into their acts, including the responsibility to maintain their own health and well-being as well as that of the people under their responsibility. Mindfulness is a part of the skills that are difficult to integrate because they seem so distant from the culture and the contemporary social standards required for achieving performance. For example, it is a reduction in the focus of attention that systematically seems to be accepted and recognized as efficient in conditions for performance, whereas psychological research suggests that the ability to be mindful, by increasing the field of perception instead of diminishing it, actually improves the possibilities for performance (Csikszentmihalyi 1990). If one examines the language associated with an attitude towards performance we only find expressions of difficulty, reduction and rejection – not receptiveness: 'to focus one's attention on', 'to make an effort to concentrate on', 'to require careful attention', etc. All these everyday expressions seem to accompany the recognized qualities of leaders and also de facto the conditions required for a stressful answer whose accompanying efficiency, we repeat, is often only valid over the short term. The ability to be mindful, which we will simplify in three phrases (Levinthal and Rerup 2006), refers to what managers seem to spontaneously abhor in the interpretations of their own roles – winning attitudes, efficient teams and the competitive market – certainly through fear of non-performance, therefore rejection:

- Be completely in contact with and aware of the present moment: this may seem to exclude the ability for anticipation or strategic vision so dear to leaders.
- Be receptive to all experiences now being lived; see things as they are, not only from the outside, from inside oneself as well, whenever there is pressure to focus one's attention on the current problem only in its exterior dimension.
- Take a non-evaluative and non-judgemental approach to one's experience and decisions, even though eventually the basic knowledge and the position itself of the leader require taking decisions and therefore judging in advance (good or bad, right or wrong, true or false).

Let us now reconsider these three points to see how a mindful attitude can encourage the leader to adopt not only more ethical behaviour but also more efficient behaviour because it is less centred on what one could call the belief in 'the overwhelming power of stress'.

Developing the first point: in our experience with leaders during coaching sessions, the ability to be in and to face up to the present is frequently raised as a good way to face up to stress generated by an apprehensive projection of events to come. In answer to this affirmation, the response is very often immediate opposition: the manager needs to know how to anticipate. The idea therefore initially appears stupid because of the way in which it opposes one of the leader's key skills. However, once it has been explained that staying in contact with the present, here and now, does not exclude anticipation, but rather requires knowing how to anticipate without projecting a negative picture with its emotional consequences, many adhere to the concept.

The second point concerns the idea of paying attention instead of focusing on a single element (a danger?). In situations of stress, as is often the case when taking decisions, our system activates all its resources to concentrate on the problem in hand. One of our brain's rules for efficiency will be useful to illustrate this example. It concerns the management of our weakest resource, the ability to maintain attention. We have different strategies to improve this capacity to remain concentrated. Two of these interest us here. One is the automation of thought and behaviour patterns and the other is the reduction of uncertainty, both of which allow us to free up additional resources for attention. Thus, as Langer (2002) states: 'we learn, so that we will know what things are' and we could add – so that we think we control things. Unfortunately, we end up by confusing our automatic reflexes (a belief) and our knowledge (explanations) with the underlying reality of the phenomena (constantly changing). Thus, instead of seeking variants, it becomes more important to be able to exploit the weak signs of change and uncertainty. Expanding our attention facilitates this wider perception.

The last point refers to the position of non-judgement and non-evaluation of the experience in hand. Experience here mainly means the leader's interior experience. To imagine this, we could say that in a *mindless* approach, a thought may be taken as a truth. This is often the case in situations of stress because we do not have the time to think otherwise. Thus, if our past experiences led us to believe that this type of behaviour is not good, we will judge it as being bad as soon as this behaviour is present. In a *mindful* approach, a thought is considered as unique and other indicators will add to the pattern in order to take a decision. The key idea here is to succeed in seeing more clearly what the situation is, as it is. To be more specific, to succeed in remaining as close as possible to reality, untrammelled by our beliefs, our emotions, our experiences, etc., and above all our prejudices. Put yourself in a situation where an angry client comes to see you. In the mindless approach, you will certainly protect and defend yourself from what would be initially perceived and judged as an aggression. In the mindful approach, there will be an awareness of the ideas and emotions related to this client's anger that you will perceive as thoughts and emotions and not as a valid judgement of the person facing you. You can then tone down your emotional response, which is indeed quite natural, and listen to your client's remarks.

In these three points, we see a challenge for the leader to extend his skills and beliefs in efficiency in order to integrate new vigour but which could appear to be opposed to the conditions necessary for success. What is the link with the ethical challenges for the company? Simply that the company must be able to accept different behaviour in its method of functioning and its culture – new behaviour that is sometimes opposed to past models of performance – to allow people to be efficient while enjoying complete well-being, instead of keeping the destructive models or, worse, benefiting from these new skills to increase the workload (they manage stress better now, so they can work harder!).

Another condition for success is an ethical challenge for companies. Being mindful brings a person a certain freedom in the sense of becoming more conscious, of clarity of vision, an ability to discern more clearly the conditioning, the emotions – the stresses encountered when interpreting situations. The challenge is here: how can the company that is not a democratic space, how can the manager who is not representative of the worker's requirements, allow this new freedom to be introduced? We will speak of this later by evoking the possibility to express emotions, together with the obstacles. How can an employee express his feelings in front of what he sees as an aggression by his manager and, above all, how can the manager be both judge and jury, that is, know how to authorize what will be used against him?

The next challenge for companies will lie in their ability, not to find a balance at any cost, but to accept that management continues with imbalances. Faced with non-ethical behaviour, rather than looking systematically for the error, for the guilty person, and then eliminating the behaviour or the person, it could be important to understand that this research for perfection is futile. The mindful approach foresees the opposite path: learn to have a better awareness of this behaviour (detect it) and a better acceptance (I accept that this is part of the problem) in order to identify the subsequent needs and offer an appropriate solution.

Another challenge that presents itself is that of allowing the development of ethical and mindful behaviour – training. For today's managers, their main skills are learned during their (initial or subsequent) training and honed through real-life experience. Learning Mindfulness requires much more than just training. It requires being able to enjoy regular physical, emotional, intellectual and spiritual training for this skill. We have already mentioned that, for the manager, this calls for accepting regular training to achieve new forms of behaviour and, for the company, the need to accept offering its managers the time and space to undertake this training which requires . . . time; what the manager typically says he lacks most!

Now that we have looked at some of the conditions necessary for a company or a manager to act mindfully, it is also important to see the several pitfalls and obstacles that can appear during these efforts.

Obstacles

To start this section on the obstacles that can obstruct the ethics of mindful management, we will look at the problem of the spiritual dimension briefly referred to above in another context. The ethical dimension poses no problems because it fits easily into our Western culture based on Hellenic philosophy, and is therefore outside the field of spirituality – but the spiritual dimension is not a part of company culture because it is too often confused with religion. Mindfulness comes from oriental spiritualities, principally Buddhism and its practice of meditation.[8] Although Langer (1989) highlighted certain specific aspects between the Buddhist and scientific approaches, the holistic references to Mindfulness too often relegate it to the field of religion without understanding or integrating the fact that a lay spirit can be interested in the performance of the company (for example, generous behaviour and sharing within a team increase its efficiency). Very few studies have dealt with spirituality in management or in management training. Even if the relationship between spirituality and religion have been discussed elsewhere, we will refer here only to spirituality and its expression within the key values of humanity such as generosity, compassion, altruism, gratitude, equanimity, etc. Mindfulness, through its constitutive elements and a conscious, non-judgemental approach, leads by definition to the development of certain values. If I am open, aware and without judgement in the face of both myself and another, I can take a compassionate or altruistic position more easily and thus remain in better contact with the situation. The other person's anger, for example, will thus no longer instantly be seen as an aggression against me, but rather as the expression of a problem to be identified (using the example already given). By referring to our own experience, we see that we can express our spirituality very simply through our daily behaviour, and also therefore our behaviour in the workplace: by thanking a colleague, for example. Unfortunately, this dissension between religion and spirituality associated with beliefs about performance, or that the business world is an area of life in which this spirituality has no place, often prevents the full, unequivocal expression of the values mentioned above – absence of recognition by the company is thus often quoted as a recurrent problem.

The other obstacles are more directly linked to today's life in the company, and in the relationships between managers and employees.

It can be the same for the company's interference in a manager's personal life. Using the pretext (to which we also subscribe) that personal development is the best method for preventing stressful situations at work for managers and leaders, must one nevertheless arrive at a totalitarian attitude towards the staff – 'you must have personal development training if you are managers'? No, of course not – but it is here that ethical principles are sometimes confounded because the logic of freedom, which is constitutional in Western states, is de facto applicable as a reality in the workplace, thus coming into conflict with the fact that the company is not a democracy.

As we are speaking of training, let us continue by examining how it can become an ethical challenge for the company. There are few specialists who train in mindful approaches today. But, as was the case for the development and techniques of stress management, as soon as a new market appears, numerous so-called specialists appear in the marketplace. Thus several ethical problems arise. One concerns the trainer's competence and his selection by the company based on employees' expectations. It is important that the choice meets the combined interests of both company and staff. There is also the risk of the trainer becoming a guru who, for example, as a coach for the Board, can lead to subjective decisions being taken – if he does not take the decision himself! Finally, rarely but important to identify, we are in an area where many sectarian movements can have an interest and may seek to have a narrowly proselytising effect.

Furthermore, with respect to training, it is essential to set the example. As the staircase is swept from top to bottom, so the Board will be watched and judged very severely if any its members do not legitimize this action or commit themselves personally to it.

We will end this (non-exhaustive) tour of the obstacles to implementing mindful management ethics with the risk of the dictatorship of good ethical and mindful practices. As in all good practice, the risk lies in standardizing the activity to the extent that there is no place for imagination, and determining new behavioural limits that are even more ferocious than before, thereby stigmatizing any other form of behaviour.

Notes

1 www.scienceshumaines.com/index.php?lg=fr&id_article=324.
2 See the recent publicity for the UBS company 'We will have no respite'.
3 It should be noted that this separation of conception and execution reflects what Western culture defines as being between reflection and action, the philosopher and the man of action, a distinction unknown for example in classic Far-Eastern philosophy.
4 The technical alienation does not only concern the worker handling materials as during the industrial revolution, but also the knowledge worker (Drucker 1999).
5 http://eco.rue89.com/2010/09/26/au-bureau-vous-avez-12-minutes-de-temps-de-cerveau-disponible-167634.
6 Tal Ben-Shahar (2009) *The Pursuit of Perfect: How to stop chasing perfection and start living a richer, happier life.* New York: McGraw-Hill.
7 Spiritual is considered here in its lay and not at all its religious sense.
8 The term 'meditation' is taken here in its oriental sense, i.e. all the practices and exercises (physical, emotional, spiritual . . . the best known being meditation while sitting) which, used on a daily basis, lead to a more accurate awareness of reality. It has therefore a wider meaning than the Western sense often limited to the intellectual development of an idea.

References

Ashforth, B. E. and Fried, Y. (1988) 'The mindlessness of organizational behaviors', *Human Relations*, 41: 305–329.

Ben-Shahar, T. (2009) *The Pursuit of Perfect: How to stop chasing perfection and start living a richer, happier life.* New York: McGraw-Hill.

Csikszentmihalyi, M. (1990) *Flow: The psychology of optimal experience.* New York: Harper and Row.

Drucker P. F. (1999) *Management Challenges for the 21st Century.* Oxford: Butterworth-Heinemann.

Kabat-Zinn, J. (1982) 'An out-patient program in Behavioral Medicine for chronic pain patients based on the practice of mindfulness meditation: Theoretical considerations and preliminary results', *General Hospital Psychiatry* (4): 33–47.

Langer, E. J. (1989) *Mindfulness.* Cambridge, MA: Perseus Books Group.

Langer, H. (2002) 'Well-being: Mindfulness versus positive evaluation'. In C. R. Snyder and S. J. Lopez (eds), *Handbook of Positive Psychology.* Oxford: Oxford University Press, p. 215.

Levinthal, D. and Rerup, C. (2006) 'Crossing an apparent chasm: Bridging mindful and less-mindful perspectives on organizational learning', *Organization Science*, 17(4): 502–513.

Livet, P. (1994) *La communauté virtuelle – action et communication*. Paris: Ed de l'Eclat.

Schön, D. (1984) *The Reflective Practitioner: How professionals think in action*. New York: Basic Books.

Sennett, R. (2007) *The Culture of the New Capitalism*. Newhaven, CT: Yale University Press.

Smith, B. C. (1999) 'Situatedness/embeddedness'. In R. A. Wilson and F. Keil (eds), *The MIT Encyclopedia of the Cognitive Sciences*. Cambridge, MA: MIT Press, pp. 769–770.

Thomas, T., Schermerhorn Jr., J. R. and Dienhart, J. W. (2004) 'Strategic leadership of ethical behavior in business', *Academy of Management Executive*, 18(2): 61.

14

A CULTURAL APPRECIATION OF DIVERSITY OF ETHICAL STRATEGIES

Examples from European business

Taran Patel

Chapter overview

Past literature exploring the impact of culture on ethical decision making in businesses has mostly relied on the use of a somewhat 'stable' concept of national culture. National cultures have been related to ethical preferences and countries have been ranked as being high or low on the ethicality index as a function of their national cultures. In this chapter, we use a very different approach to culture. The Douglasian Cultural Theory (CT) treats culture as being dynamic and constantly evolving. We offer CT as an alternative approach to make sense of the diversity and dynamicity of ethical preferences. Using examples from the European business world, we demonstrate that every social system is made up of four dynamic cultures, each of which has different underlying value systems, different rationalities and hence different ethical preferences. Since these four cultural groups coexist in every social system, including nations and continents, we question the credibility of past research that categorizes entire nations on ethical rankings. Through the use of CT, we attempt to go beyond the *unity* versus *infinity* dilemma in the ethics discourse.

Introducing ethics and business ethics

'Ethics' is derived from an Ancient Greek word *ethikos* meaning 'the authority of custom and tradition' (Grace and Cohen 1998, p. 3). More recently, experts have provided other definitions of the term: 'a set of principles that guides business practices to reflect a concern for society as a whole while pursuing profits' (Nisberg 1988, p. 43), 'a systematic attempt to make sense of our individual, social and moral experience in such a way as to determine the rules that ought to govern human conduct, the values worth pursuing, and the character traits deserving development in life' (De George 1999, p. 20), 'the quest for and an understanding of the good life . . . putting every activity and goal in its place, knowing what is worth doing and what is not worth doing, knowing what is worth wanting and having and knowing what is not worth wanting and having' (Solomon 1994, p. 9) and finally, 'the activity of examining one's moral standards or the moral standards of a society, and asking how these standards apply to our lives and whether these standards are reasonable or unreasonable . . .' (Velasquez 1998, p. 11). Identifying a definition of ethics that is universally acceptable is a challenging if not impossible task. There are also diverse philosophical views that have influenced the ethics discourse in the past centuries: utilitarianism, deontology, teleology, egoism, virtue and the ethics of character (De George 1999). No philosophical approach is more acceptable than the others, but each contributes in its own way to the possible understanding of the many nuances of the concept of ethics (Svensson and Wood 2003).

Notwithstanding the different schools of thought that have emerged in past centuries, one might safely venture to say that a major chunk of past literature addresses the topic of business ethics at a normative level. Indeed in Chapter 2 of this book it is shown that this has been the major and in many ways the most interesting part of the subject and that it involves an inherently critical stance in relation to actual business practices. It is also shown in Chapter 2 how this normative critique can be carried out at a number of different levels. Many experts treat business ethics as a characteristic that corporations or its employees either have or do not have, thereby relying on Level 1 critique as discussed in Chapter 2 of this book. Also, past studies have tended to treat business ethics as an unchanging value system that guides or at least *should* guide the action of one and all in a corporation or in a nation. In this chapter we intend to question this latter, often implicit, assumption of an *unchanging* value system. We intend to demonstrate, through examples from European businesses, that individuals in all kinds of social entities (corporations, nations, continents, etc.) use ethical strategies that fit best with their social environment. This implies that ethical strategies might change with changes in social environments within the entity. Through our use of Douglasian Cultural Theory we wish to expose the diversity and dynamicity of ethical strategies of companies and show how ethical choices are influenced by the social context that decision makers find themselves in.

We clarify at the outset that although we question the static nature of ethics, we do not believe that there are infinite types of ethical value systems. As discussed in Chapter 2 of this book, many experts have argued in favour of either universalism or moral relativism in business ethics discourse. We wish to go beyond this *unity* versus *infinity* dilemma and propose a systematic tool to make sense of the diverse ethical strategies we observe in any social system. In that sense, we use the third level of critique as exposed in Chapter 2 of this book. There is evidence in current literature that people's ethical values can be explained by understanding their cultural backgrounds (e.g. Schepers 2006). Most of these studies use a static concept of culture, focused mostly at the national level (see Hofstede 1984). In contrast, we use a much more dynamic approach to culture as offered by CT. Although in this chapter we attempt to expose the diversity of ethical strategies found in European companies, our explanations would also be true for corporations in other parts of the world since our theoretical framework is not subject to geographic limitations or boundaries.

We begin this chapter by providing an overview of what extant literature has to say about the influence of culture on ethical decision making in companies. In subsequent sections we introduce CT as an alternative framework for ethical sense-making. We present the four cultural types of CT, their different values, rationalities and ethical preferences, while supporting, wherever possible, our arguments through illustrations of ethical/unethical practices in European companies.

National culture and ethics

National culture and/or the culture of the country of residence have been commonly evoked in extant literature to facilitate ethical sense-making. A recent study (Vitell and Hidalgo 2006) concludes that perceptions of the importance of ethics and social responsibility vary depending upon the country of residence, with US respondents having somewhat higher perceptions concerning the importance of ethics and social responsibility than their counterparts in Spain. Furthermore, the study claims that the US sample had significantly higher corporate ethical values, greater enforcement of ethical codes, less organizational commitment, lower idealism and lower relativism than the Spanish sample. Similarly, White and Rhodeback (1992) establish a significant relationship between non-US citizens and unethical practice. Jackson and Artola (1997) have compared French and German managers and find that their ethical attitudes and behaviours vary owing to their nationality. On the same lines, Armstrong and Sweeney (1994) and Chan and Armstrong (1999) have found that managers from Hong Kong and Canada have different ethical perspectives than Australian managers. Singhapakdi et al. (1994, 1995) compare US and Thai marketers and conclude that they are different in the way they view ethical problems and their professional and personal values. While most of these researchers have focused on identifying differences in ethical preferences based on nationality, others (e.g. Tsalikis and Nwachukwu 1991) focus on both similarities and differences between national samples. Tsalikis and Nwachukwu (1991) (as cited by Peppas and Peppas 2000) state that there are some similarities and significant differences between US and Nigerian students' views of bribery and extortion, with the latter group perceiving some scenarios less unethically than the former. We consider the findings of Tsalikis and Nwachukwu (1991) more convincing than the examples cited earlier in this section because they suggest similarities as well as differences across nations regarding ethical preferences. The categorization of one nation as more (or less) ethical than other nations is less convincing (see also Patel and Schaefer 2009). In creating ethical categories based on national origin or culture, researchers (see Armstrong and Sweeney 1994; Singhapakdi et al. 1994, etc.) have tried to simplify the complex exercise of ethical sense-making by resorting to excessive and sweeping generalizations characteristic of the universalistic approach.

Past literature also provides several examples of ethics-based comparisons between European and non-European nations and between the EU nations. For example, Whipple and Swords (1992) have compared ethical practices in the US and UK. They find that American business students were more critical with regard to confidentiality, research integrity and certain issues regarding marketing mix as compared to British students. Another study by Nill and Shultz (1997) compared European and US perspectives and proposed decision guidelines for use in cross-cultural contexts. Extant literature also reveals attempts to demonstrate that certain European nations are more ethical than others. Take for example, the comparative study across EU nations carried out by Jeurissen and van Luijk (1998). These authors conclude that northern European countries have a positive score on business ethical conduct, while southern countries have a negative score. Once again, by relying on a somewhat stable notion of national culture, these researchers have used the universalistic approach towards culture and ethics and have ended up categorizing entire nations as being more/less ethical than one another.

Unlike scholars who choose to rank nations on scales of ethicality based on their somewhat stable national cultures, there are others who argue that ethical preferences undergo changes as the country itself evolves with corresponding changes in its national culture. For example, Bucar et al. (2002) point out that the ethical practices in a country evolve with changing cultural and economic situations. Similar explanations have also been provided by Kilcullen and Kooistra (1999), who expose the changing role of business ethics and corporate social responsibility in the business environment over time. Following the same line of argument, Pava (1998) explains that periodic fading and re-emergence of religion might have an impact on ethical preferences of businesses in a country. We find the work of Svensson and Wood (2003) particularly illuminating in making sense of the dynamicity of ethical practices. They propose two principle parameters influencing the dynamics of ethics: time and culture. As time passes, cultures evolve and as a consequence ethical standards change. Actions and practices (e.g. slavery, child labour, environmental pollution, bribery, insider trading, corporal punishment, etc.) that were once acceptable have moved through the stages of being seen as questionable, then as not desirable and, finally as illegal. There are also practices that have gone from being unacceptable to being socially acceptable, and then legal: freedom of speech, freedom of association, freedom of religion, birth control, single parents, divorce, etc. (Svensson and Wood 2003). Therefore, as societies and their cultures evolve, perceptions of what is considered ethical or unethical also change. Increase in literacy in industrialized economies has led individuals to question what they see around them and to continually challenge society's moral precepts. The work of Svensson and Wood (2003) compels one to question the validity of studies that categorize nations as less or more ethical at a point in time based on the concept of stable national cultures. We believe that every nation passes through stages of economic, social and cultural development, which influence what it perceives as ethical and/or unethical. Countries that are new entrants into the European Union (e.g. Poland and Hungary) are currently going through similar periods of transition and are experiencing changes in their cultures and ethical preferences.

While we agree with this dynamic approach of ethical sense-making (see Bucar *et al.* 2002; Svensson and Wood 2003, etc.), we do not wish to endorse the viewpoint that there are as many ethical preferences as there are social contexts. In other words we support neither universalism nor moral relativism. What we wish to achieve is an instrument for ethical sense-making that goes beyond this universalism–relativism divide.

To summarize, a review of extant literature reveals two major streams:

1   literature that uses the universalistic approach for ethical sense-making and categorizes one nation as more/less ethical than another by relating ethical preferences to a somewhat static concept of national culture;
2   literature that treats nations and national cultures as evolving, thereby admitting the possibility of dynamic and diverse ethical preferences within the same nation. This stream of literature inadvertently promotes moral relativism.

Since our objective is to go beyond the universalistic–relativistic divide, we propose the use of the Douglasian Cultural Theory (CT) as a tool for ethical sense-making. Although CT supports the possibility of dynamic ethical preferences as seen in the second stream of literature above, it does not promote the idea of moral relativism or infinite ethical behaviours. CT proposes that there are four, and only four, cultural types. The four cultural types are the outcome of the different permutations and combinations of the two basic social dimensions (i.e. grid and group). Therefore, mathematically speaking, there can be only four cultural types and these are mutually exclusive and collectively exhaustive. Each of these four cultural types has its own values, rationalities and ethical preferences. However, the ethical strategies used by the four cultural types can evolve with changes in the social context. Thus, CT takes the ethical discourse away from the universalism versus relativism debate towards what cultural theorists have commonly referred to as *'constrained relativism'*. In the following section we discuss these four cultural types, their values, their rationalities and their ethical preferences. Rather than categorizing social entities (e.g. a company, a nation, a continent etc.) as more/less ethical than one another based on differences in their somewhat 'stable' cultures, CT focuses on broad similarities across, and differences within, social entities. Through our discussion of CT we hope to reveal the dynamicity and diversity in ethical practices among European companies.

The four dynamic cultural types, their rationalities and ethical preferences

Mary Douglas introduced CT in *Natural Symbols* (Douglas 1970) and expanded it in 'Cultural bias' (Douglas 1978). Since then, CT has been applied to study problems in a wide variety of fields such as workplace crimes (Mars 1982), ecology (Douglas and Wildavsky 1983), risk perceptions (Rayner 1986), learning and innovation (Patel and Patel 2009), ethical decision making (Patel and Schaefer 2009), etc. and to study organizations such as hospitals (Rayner 1986) and international strategic alliances (Patel 2007a; 2007b), etc. The basic premise of the theory is that people organize their ideas about the natural and social world in a way that is compatible with the social structure. The overall aim of CT is to provide a framework within which a cultural analyst may consistently relate differences in social structures to the strength of the values that sustain them (Gross and Rayner 1985).

In order to classify cultures, two social dimensions can be used: *group* and *grid* (Douglas 1970). The horizontal group axis represents the extent to which people are restricted in thought and action by their commitment to a social unit larger than the individual. High group strength results when people spend considerable time interacting with other group members, while the group strength is low when people lead their lives as individuals in a competitive and entrepreneurial way (Gross and Rayner 1985). As we move along the right of the group dimension, individual members are more deeply committed to a group, so choices are more standardized (Douglas 1996). A high group score implies that the group's boundaries are clearly defined and that the group is fairly exclusive (Gross and Rayner 1985). The vertical axis, that is, grid is a composite index of the extent to which people's behaviour is constrained by role differentiation (Gross and Rayner 1985). A high grid score occurs whenever members are differentiated based on sex, colour, position in the hierarchy, holding a bureaucratic office, descent in a senior clan, or point of progression through an age-grade system (Gross and Rayner 1985). Combining high and low strengths of grid and group gives rise to four cultural types, which are discussed in detail below. For each cultural type, we outline its values, its rationality and its ethical preferences.

Competitive culture (low grid–low group)

The competitive culture is characterized by individual spatial and social mobility and allows the maximum options for negotiating contracts or choosing allies (Gross and Rayner 1985). In this culture, ancestry or past is irrelevant and individuals are responsible for themselves, rather than for the larger group. Members give little importance to rules, regulations and procedures and prefer to focus on outputs and results. Members of the competitive culture do not apply pressure on themselves or on others for conformity to the group. In such a culture, all boundaries are provisional and subject to renegotiation (Coyle and Ellis 1994; Douglas 1996). Self-regulation, mutuality, and the respect for rights are the order of the day. The prototypical structure where the competitive culture is seen is the free market. The competitive culture's excessive focus on self-gain sometimes obscures the fine line between 'rights' and 'wrongs' (see Patel 2007a; 2007b). The preferred rationality of the competitive culture involves networking (Wynne and Otway 1982). In other words, members of this culture tend to shift the really vital discussions away from official channels of communication into informal discussions among those close to them.

At the outset it would seem logical to assume that the competitive culture would have a preference for the shareholder approach to business ethics owing to its individualistic tendency and focus on results. However, it would be erroneous to assume that the competitive culture focuses only on fulfilling self-interest. Many very competitive organizations are also the largest contributors to philanthropic causes, although the underlying motivation behind these actions could vary from a genuine desire to support the cause to improving the corporate image. Further, we reckon that methodological individualism would be a natural choice for members of the competitive culture since they have a natural inclination to hold themselves (or other individuals) responsible for their actions, rather than attribute responsibility to a larger group (e.g. the company, the country or the society), an approach that is in line with methodological individualism.

Parmalat, the famous Italian producer of dairy products, cheese, biscuits and beverages can be cited as an example of the competitive culture. Started as a small sausage and cheese shop in the Italian city of Parma, this family-run business expanded into an international giant under the leadership of Calisto Tanzi who took over the business from his father in 1961. The competitive strategies are visible in the spectacular growth of this firm, which is commonly attributed to the owner's relationships with government officials in Italy during the post-war period. This networking strategy is in line with the firm's competitive culture. Parmalat was recently under public scrutiny because of its unethical practices. Tanzi admitted siphoning over 500 million euros to family-owned subsidiaries. As mentioned earlier, the competitive culture has been known to prioritize self-gains over 'rights' and 'wrongs' (Patel 2007a; 2007b). The pressure to perform in a competitive environment could lead companies with a predominant competitive culture to focus excessively on profitability, thereby engaging in unethical practices. Press reports state that Parmalat's accounting firm Grant Thornton was aware of its unethical practices. However, pressures to compete exerted on both companies by global markets led them to collaborate in each other's unethical practices. This collusion reveals the underlying networking rationality of the firm and its partners. Their practices had major negative repercussions on other firms within their network such as Deloitte and Touche, Citicorp and Bank of America, where several thousand employees lost their jobs.

Hierarchical culture (high grid–high group)

This is the tradition-bound culture in which everyone knows his place, but in which that place might vary with time (Gross and Rayner 1985). This culture values security and obtains it by forsaking opportunities and social mobility. Hierarchy implies both compulsion and inequality. Coyle and Ellis (1994) have characterized hierarchies by unequal roles for unequal members and deference towards one's betters. Schwarz and Thompson (1990) contend that this culture is oriented towards processes, rules and regulations and is more concerned with the proprieties of who does what rather than the outcome. The preferred rationality of the hierarchical culture is paradigm protection. Therefore, this culture tries hard to protect the procedures, rules and paradigms on which the system rests (Thompson and Wildavsky 1986). Consider the Challenger disaster (Desjardins and McCall 2000) of 1986. The night before the launch, a senior official reiterated his earlier misgiving about launching the shuttle under less-than-ideal weather conditions. He was, however, compelled to prioritize the overall commercial interest of NASA over his professional judgement (Desjardins and McCall 2000). In this case, the hierarchical culture of NASA suppressed valuable information in favour of what it perceived as the common interest of the group.

Members of the hierarchical culture might prefer the stakeholder approach to business ethics. This is based on the understanding that this culture has a tendency to think in the interest of the entire group (high-group characteristics). However, it would also prioritize one stakeholder over the other, based on status, needs or other similar criteria (high-grid characteristics). The stakeholder approach serves the interest of a large group of people, not just the shareholders, while simultaneously allowing one to differentiate between primary and secondary stakeholders. Thus, the stakeholder approach would instinctively appeal to the hierarchical culture.

Zanussi is an example of the hierarchical culture. This company of Italian origin is now a wholly owned subsidiary of the Swedish conglomerate Electrolux and sells its products in sixty countries around the world. The company recently launched a tele-working scheme, allowing pregnant women and mothers to work from home. Zanussi also provides nursery facilities during working hours and the possibility of taking days off as a reward for overtime (Crane and Matten 2004). Thus, the company focuses heavily on improving working conditions of its female employees, who form a large proportion of its workforce. That the company treats its largest group of employees as a priority stakeholder reveals both its high-group and high-grid mindset. One of the objectives behind launching the tele-working scheme was also to reduce sick leave among women employees, a goal that the company has successfully achieved. One might argue that since the company's new scheme was geared towards serving its own interest (i.e. decreasing the number of sick leaves) rather than catering to the specific needs of its majority employee group, its ethical strategies are more competitive than hierarchical. Therefore, a more thorough investigation of its practices is required before we can draw conclusions.

We find more evidence of the company's high-group orientation in Crane and Matten's (2004) work. In the 1980s the company had to lay off a large number of its employees as a result of restructuring. Many employees who were laid off were unskilled and a large proportion of them were over 50 years of age. In response to this crisis, the company launched a programme targeted at improving the employees' situation: paid leave, reimbursement of travel expenses for interviews, training courses, help for employees who wanted to start up their own business, etc. As a result, most of the employees made redundant found new employment.

The efforts that the company put into the employability of its laid-off employees reveal its high-group behaviour. Since this company demonstrates both high-grid and high-group characteristics, this is an example of hierarchical ethical strategies.

Egalitarian culture (low grid–high group)

In this culture, the external group boundary is typically the dominant consideration (Gross and Rayner 1985). All other aspects of interpersonal relationship are ambiguous and open to negotiation. This culture is characterized by a small group, face-to-face interactions, participative decision making and a network of reciprocal exchanges (Douglas 1986). There are few constraints, group consciousness is high, and there is voluntary respect for others (Coyle 1997). The egalitarian culture takes an uncompromising and fundamentalist ethical stand. It concentrates all its defences at its boundary, protecting the vulnerable 'insiders' from the predatory 'outsiders'. It does this by totally rejecting any threatening information. This attitude often leads to schism in case of dissension. Thus 'expulsion' is the preferred rationality of the egalitarian.

We argue that the stakeholder approach would fit best with the egalitarian culture, which is characterized by equality among all the members and voluntary commitment to a common goal. Members of this culture would have a natural inclination to want to defend the interests of all the stakeholders, particularly those of its own members. The egalitarian culture would be uncompromising in its sanction against any action that jeopardizes the interest of its own members, and would tend to prioritize the interests of its members over other stakeholders. This culture might also have a preference for the corporate moral agency approach. Our suggestion is based on the premise that the corporate moral agency approach holds the corporation accountable to all stakeholders for its actions. In making the corporation accountable to the stakeholders, the power differential between the corporation and other stakeholders is being reduced (low-grid) and the interests of many stakeholders are being upheld (high-group).

A pertinent example of the egalitarian culture can be seen in the case of Huntington Life Sciences (HLS) (example taken from Crane and Matten 2004). HLS, the UK-based drug-testing company has faced considerable opposition from animal rights activists in past years. HLS became the target of animal rights activists in 1997 after a television documentary showed the staff mistreating animals (Crane and Matten 2004). In 1999, Stop Huntington Animal Cruelty (SHAC) was set up as a result of international collaboration between groups of animal rights activists from the UK, USA, Netherlands, Germany, Italy and many other countries. SHAC's objective was simple: to put LHS out of business in the UK. SHAC used 'ferocious' direct action methods (e.g. broken windows, rescued animals, paint-stripped cars, glued-up locks, office occupations, rooftop demos and blockades) to attack HLS and its supporters. Employees, investors, local residents and others connected to HLS have been verbally abused, issued with threats and even at times physically assaulted. Through such actions, SHAC forced HLS's investors to sell off their shares and move their financial listing out of the UK altogether.

A close inspection of SHAC's activities reveals all the characteristics of the egalitarian culture. Not only is it uncompromising in its stand against certain practices, it has also managed to bring together different bodies in the form of a coalition, united solely by a common ideal. This indicates high-group characteristics. Members of SHAC were unrelenting until they achieved their goal, which was to put HLS out of business in the UK. Many of their methods were perceived as 'harsh' by others. However, this did not lead them to change their methods. This indicates a deep conviction towards what they believed to be 'right'. Furthermore, their prime objective was to protect the rights of animals. All other aspects such as the methods used to achieve this goal were secondary. Hence, the ethical strategies pursued by SHAC in this case are those of the egalitarian culture and the rationality manifested in its actions is in favour of complete expulsion of the 'guilty' parties.

Fatalistic culture (high grid–low group)

In this culture, members' behaviours are strongly regulated according to their socially assigned classifications (Gross and Rayner 1985). Such situations emerge when people in strongly hierarchical structures have been excluded from decision making or where people in strongly competitive cultures have been thrown out owing to excessive competition. The fatalistic culture implies an element of coercion: people are not in this category by their own free will (Gross and Rayner 1985). Individuals in this culture have little choice how they spend time, whom they associate with, what they wear or eat, or where they live or work (Coyle and Ellis 1994). The fatalist endures social isolation similar to the competitive culture (both being low-group) without the latter's autonomy and the constraints of hierarchy (both being high-grid) but without the support of a loyal group that characterizes a hierarchy.

The ethical standpoint of the fatalistic culture can be best described as opportunistic and ad hoc. Fatalists might be quick to compromise on ethical viewpoints if this serves their interest and/or if they find themselves threatened. The fatalist would be non-committal and hence, unreliable. *Risk absorption* is the preferred rationality of the fatalistic mindset because the individual feels that (s)he does not control anything that happens to him/her. This culture is reactive rather than proactive. Consider the example of the Exxon Valdez case, which led to the destruction of a pristine environmental habitat in 1989 (Ferrell and Fraedrich 1991). The CEO of Exxon, Lawrence Rawl, was initially slow in responding to the disaster, but was forced to put corrective measures in place under mounting pressure from local communities, environmentalists and governing bodies. Since the company had no other options, it had to assume responsibility for its mistakes. However, its lack of proactivity in the matter reveals its underlying fatalistic tendencies.

The four cultural types of CT and their ethical preferences are summarized in Figure 14.1. Since the four cultures share some features on the basic grid and group dimensions, there are some similarities in their ethical preferences. Further, all four cultures are observed in every social system. This implies that every social system, be it a continent, a nation, a corporation, even an individual, is ethically plural or diverse. It is diverse because these four ethical strategies coexist in it, although one or more may dominate at a point in time (see Patel and Rayner 2008). Like the four cultures they are grounded in, these ethical strategies also compete for strength, thereby creating disequilibrium and dynamicity in the system.

The key question that we wish to address in this chapter is: Can CT successfully explain the diversity and dynamicity of ethical strategies of people? It is important that the four cultural types proposed by CT not be considered as static categories. Each culture applies pressure on members of other cultures in order to gain more adherents. Even tiny shifts that individuals undergo across cultural boundaries will result in a shift in their values and their behaviours (because they bring the person under the influence of a different culture). However, larger movements that take place within the same culture leave the individual's values and behaviours unaltered (Thompson 1996). This constant movement makes every social system a dynamic one in which the four cultures are constantly competing for dominance, with none ever achieving it (Thompson 1996). For example, if the culture at Zanussi

G
r
i
d

FATALIST CULTURAL GROUP:	HIERARCHICAL CULTURAL GROUP:
Understanding of ethics: changing set of principles depending on what suits them	Understanding of ethics: unchanging set of principles
Preference to ethical approach: opportunistic and ad hoc, non-committal and unreliable	Preference for ethical approach: stakeholder approach but with clear prioritization of stakeholders
Important values: protect self-interest, readily adapt to higher authority's stand on ethics, even if this is not the most ethical choice	Important values: Respecting procedures, rules and regulations is far more important that the results, 'who does what' is more important than the outcome
Reaction to change in ethics: reluctance to adapt, until they see self-interest	Reaction to change in ethics: find it difficult to adapt
Attitude to law: opportunistic, will not hesitate to bend the law if it serves self-interest.	Attitude to law: preference for legal formalism and legal realism.
COMPETITIVE CULTURAL GROUP:	EGALITARIAN CULTURAL GROUP:
Understanding of ethics: universal set of values	Understanding of ethics: universal set of values meant to protect in-group
Preference to ethical approach: shareholder approach, methodological individualism	Preference for ethical approach: stakeholder approach, corporate moral agency
Important values: equality, freedom, results more important than the process	Important values: equality, loyalty, consensual, participative, expect a relationship of reciprocal exchange
Reaction to change in ethics: flexible, quick to adapt	Reaction to change in ethics: adaptive if convinced of safeguarding interests of all members of the in-group, uncompromising if unconvinced otherwise
Attitude to law: preference for legal pragmatism.	Attitude to law: preference for natural law jurisprudence.

Group

FIGURE 14.1 Ethical strategies of the four cultures proposed by CT.

changed from a hierarchical to a competitive one, then the ethical strategies pursued by its employees would change as well. Similarly, if SHAC were dominated by the hierarchical culture rather than an egalitarian one, its members would tone down some of the methods used against HLS. The ethical strategies that organizations demonstrate are the result of the values of their dominant culture(s). A shift in their affiliations to another culture implies that the values underpinning their behaviours will also change, thereby leading to a shift in the ethical strategy used. Hence, we believe that it is important to treat ethical practices as a set of actions that are a function of the values sustaining different cultures. This helps to make sense of the dynamicity of ethical strategies that we see in the world around us without resorting to the categorization of nations, societies or other social entities as being more/less ethical than others. Further, as Thompson (1996) explains, if transactions fall into a number of distinct spheres, the same individual could be a member of different cultures in different contexts. Therefore, ethical behaviours of an individual could be different in different social contexts, that is, the same individual could exhibit a diversity of ethical behaviours in different situations. Thus, CT explains the dynamicity and diversity of ethical behaviours, without relying on universalism or moral relativism.

Lessons learned

While many philosophers (Aristotle and Kant for example) have attempted to minimize the distance between businesses and ethical values, many other past researchers have nonetheless continued to consider these as two mutually independent pursuits (Harting *et al.* 2006). In contrast, in this chapter we attempt to integrate ethics in the thought styles of social entities in such a way that ethical values become an integral part of business culture. One might suggest that in proposing the four cultural types, we have simply replaced existing categories of culture (see Hofstede 1984; Trompenaars and Hampden-Turner 1997, etc.) with new ones. However, the four cultures proposed by CT are not rigid categories. They are dynamic, fluid, ever changing and in constant disequilibrium with one another. Further, CT does not rely on categorizing nations based on their supposed ethicality or unethicality, nor does it treat every ethical preference as a function of the coming together of a set of unique situational variables. CT addresses the ethical diversity and dynamicity without relying on either universalism or moral relativism. Thus, CT serves as a good instrument for Level 3 critique of business ethics (see Chapter 2 of this book).

Extant literature on business ethics focuses on explaining different ethical approaches that individuals or corporations might adhere to, while failing to acknowledge the dynamic and pluralistic nature of business ethics. In contrast, we show how the four ethical preferences and strategies coexist in every social system by linking them to the four underlying cultures. Our examples show that one can find different kinds of ethical strategies in European companies or organizations at a point in time; for example, hierarchical in Zanussi, competitive in Parmalat and egalitarian in SHAC. Furthermore, CT is not limited by geographical boundaries in its application. Past researchers in the field have revealed the presence of the same four cultures in other kinds of social entities: a nation (see Patel and Schaefer 2009), a public-service organization (Rayner 1986), international strategic alliances (see Patel 2007a, 2007b), etc. Therefore, we assume that if examples of the diversity of four ethical preferences can be found in European companies, the same may also be true for other parts of the world. This raises critical questions regarding the crudeness of the use of ethicality indices, whose inherent simplicity have rendered them so popular today.

References

Armstrong, R. and Sweeney, J. (1994) 'Industry type, culture, mode of entry and perception of international marketing ethics problems: A cross-culture comparison', *Journal of Business Ethics*, 13(10): 775–785.

Bucar, B., Glas, M. and Hisrich, R. (2002) 'Ethics and entrepreneurs: An international comparative study', *Journal of Business Venturing*, 18: 261–281.

Chan, T. and Armstrong, R. (1999) 'Comparative ethical report card: A study of Australian and Canadian managers' perception of international marketing ethics problems', *Journal of Business Ethics*, 18(1): 3–15.

Coyle, D. (1997) 'A cultural theory of organizations'. In M. Thompson and R. J. Ellis (eds) (1997), *Culture Matters: Essays in honour of Aaron Wildavsky*. Boulder, CO: Westview, pp. 59–78.

Coyle, D. and Ellis, R. (eds) (1994) *Politics, Policy and Culture*. Boulder, CO: Westview.

Crane, A. and Matten, D. (2004) *Business Ethics: A European perspective*. Oxford: Oxford University Press.

De George, R. (1999) *Business Ethics*, 5th edn. Englewood Cliffs, NJ: Prentice Hall.

Desjardins, J. and McCall, J. (2000) *Contemporary Issues in Business Ethics*, 4th edn. Belmont, CA: Wadsworth.

Douglas, M. (1970) *Natural Symbols*. London: Barrie and Rockliffe.

Douglas, M. (1978) 'Cultural bias'. *Occasional Paper 35*. London: Royal Anthropological Institute.

Douglas, M. (1986) *How Institutions Think*. London: Routledge and Kegan Paul.

Douglas, M. (1996) *Thought Styles: Critical essays on good taste*. London: Sage.

Douglas, M. and Wildavsky, A. (1983) *Risk and Culture: An essay on the selection of technical and environmental dangers*. Berkeley, CA: University of California Press.

Ferrell, O. and Fraedrich, J. (1991) *Business Ethics*. Boston, MA: Houghton Mifflin.

Grace, D. and Cohen, S. (1998) *Business Ethics: Australian problems and cases*, 2nd edn. Melbourne: Oxford University Press.

Gross, J. and Rayner, S. (1985) *Measuring Culture: A paradigm for the analysis of social organization*. New York: Columbia Press.

Harting, T., Harmeling, S. and Venkataraman, S. (2006) 'Innovative stakeholder relations: "When ethics pays" (and when it doesn't)', *Business Ethics Quarterly*, 16(1): 43–68.

Hofstede, G. (1984) *Culture's Consequences: International differences in work-related values*. London: Sage.

Jackson, T. and Artola, M. (1997) 'Ethical beliefs and management behavior: A cross-cultural comparison', *Journal of Business Ethics*, 16(11): 1163–1173.

Jeurissen, R. and van Luijk, H. (1998) 'The ethical reputation of managers in nine EU countries: A cross referential survey', *Journal of Business Ethics*, 17: 995–1005.

Kilcullen, M. and Kooistra, J. (1999) 'At least do no harm: Sources and the changing role of business ethics and corporate social responsibility', *Reference Service Review*, 27(2): 158–178.

Mars, G. (1982) *Cheats at Work: An anthropology of workplace crime*. London: Allen and Unwin.

Nill, A. and Shultz, C. (1997) 'Marketing ethics across cultures: Decision-making guidelines and the emergence of dialogic idealism', *Journal of Macro-Marketing*, 17(2): 4–19.

Nisberg, J. (1988) *The Random House Handbook of Business Terms*. New York: Random House.

Patel, T. (2007a) 'The role of dynamic cultural theories in explaining the viability of international strategic alliances: A focus on Indo–French alliances', *Management Decisions*, 45(10): 1532–1559.

Patel, T. (2007b) *Stereotypes of intercultural management*. Delft, Holland: Eburon.

Patel, T. and Patel, C. (2009) 'Learning cultures for sustained innovation success', *Innovation: The European Journal of Social Science*, 21(3): 233–251.

Patel, T. and Rayner, S. (2008) 'A cultural analysis of corporate sustainability reporting practices: Examples from India'. Working paper series. Oxford: Saïd Business School.

Patel, T. and Schaefer, A. (2009) 'Making sense of diversity of ethical strategies in businesses: A focus on the Indian context', *Journal of Business Ethics*, 90(2): 171–187.

Pava, M. (1998) 'Religious business ethics and political liberation: An integrative approach', *Journal of Business Ethics*, 17(15): 1633–1652.

Peppas, S. and Peppas, G. (2000) 'Business ethics in the European Union: A study of Greek attitudes', *Management Decisions*, 38(6): 369–376.

Rayner, S. (1986) 'Management of radiation hazards in hospitals: Plural rationalities in a single institution', *Social Studies of Science*, 16: 573–591.

Schepers, D. (2006) 'Three proposed perspectives of attitude towards business's ethical responsibilities and their implications for cultural comparison', *Business and Society Review*, 111(1): 15–36.

Schwarz, M. and Thompson, M. (1990) *Divided We Stand: Redefining politics, technology and social choice*. London: Harvester Wheatsheaf.

Singhapakdi, A., Rallapalli, K., Rao, C. and Vitell, S. (1995) 'Personal and professional values underlying ethical decisions: A comparison of American and Thai marketers', *International Marketing Review*, 12(14): 65–76.

Singhapakdi, A., Vitell, S. and Leelakulthanit, O. (1994) 'A cross-cultural study of moral philosophies, ethical perceptions and judgments: A comparison of American and Thai marketers', *International Marketing Review*, 11(6): 65–78.

Solomon, R. (1994) *Above the Bottom Line*, 2nd edn. Fort Worth, TX: Harcourt Brace.

Svensson, G. and Wood, G. (2003) 'The dynamics of business ethics: A function of time and culture – cases and models', *Management Decision*, 41(4): 350–361.

Thompson, M. (1996) *Inherent Relationality*. Bergen: LOS Centre Publication.

Thompson, M. and Ellis, R. (eds) (1997) *Culture Matters: Essays in honour of Aaron Wildavsky*. Boulder, CO: Westview.

Thompson, M. and Wildavsky, A. (1986) 'A cultural theory of information bias in organizations', *Journal of Management Studies*, 23(3): 273–286.

Trompenaars, F. and Hampden-Turner, C. (1997) *Riding the Waves of Culture: Understanding diversity in global business*. London: McGraw-Hill.

Tsalikis, J. and Nwachukwu, O. (1991) 'A comparison of Nigerian to American views of bribery and extortion in international commerce', *Journal of Business Ethics*, 14(4): 249–264.

Velasquez, M. (1998) *Business Ethics: Concepts and cases*, 4th edn. Englewood Cliffs, NJ: Prentice Hall.

Vitell, S. and Hidalgo, E. (2006) 'The impact of corporate ethical values and enforcement of ethical codes on the perceived importance of ethics in business: A comparison of US and Spanish managers', *Journal of Business Ethics*, 64(1): 31–43.

Whipple, T. and Swords, D. (1992) 'Business ethics judgments: A cross-cultural comparison', *Journal of Business Ethics*, 11(9): 671–680.

White, L. and Rhodeback, M. (1992) 'Ethical dilemmas in organizational development: A cross-cultural analysis', *Journal of Business Ethics*, 11(9): 663–670.

Wynne, B. and Otway, H. (1982) 'Information technology: Power and managers'. In N. Bjorn-Anderson, M. Earl, O. Holst and E. Mumford (eds), *Information Society: For richer for poorer*. Amsterdam: North-Holland.

15

EMPLOYEE SURVEILLANCE AND THE MODERN WORKPLACE

Marko Pitesa

Chapter overview

Employee surveillance is rapidly becoming widespread in the modern workplace. The rise of information technologies is enabling the development of unprecedented methods of surveillance and employees as well as employers are now facing a need for a reassessment of the system of moral relations this phenomenon entails. This chapter provides an overview of the most widespread workplace surveillance methods and tries to identify the stakeholders and analyse the relations between them. Finally, the key findings of this ethical assessment are pointed out and guidelines for a morally responsible approach to workplace surveillance are proposed. The level of the analysis, in terms of the classification presented in Chapter 2, is primarily the relation between a single company and its stakeholders. However, many of these concerns relate to fundamental societal principles and as such can only be fully appreciated if one takes into account the rootedness of business in overall societal dynamics.

Modern employee surveillance

Jeremy Bentham once envisioned a method of controlling people by way of maintaining nothing more than a constant possibility of surveillance. The observing entity should not be visible to the observed subjects, which is to say that there is no telling when the surveillance is actually taking place. The very awareness of the fact that one *might* be watched at any given time brings the observed subject into compliance as the only definite way to avoid risk. In effect, this psychological game makes the observed subject internalize the intentions of the observing entity because any speculations as to the exact moment of observation are rendered no longer sensible. This model of surveillance thus ultimately provides the observer with an elegant and effective way of controlling the mind of the observed.

Although Bentham's system of control was designed to control prisoners and not employees, the psychological effects Bentham described and those at play in the modern workplace may at times seem surprisingly similar. Employee surveillance is becoming increasingly widespread and comprehensive. A recent survey found that 66 per cent of the companies surveyed monitor internet connections, 45 per cent track content, keystrokes and time spent at the keyboard and 43 per cent store and review computer files. Monitoring employee network activity even extended to the blogosphere and social networking sites. Furthermore, 45 per cent of the companies monitor time spent on the telephone and record numbers called, up from only 9 per cent in 2001, and 16 per cent actually tap and record phone conversations, a 66 per cent increase from 2001. Almost half of the companies now use video monitoring versus one-third in 2001. Employers have even been adopting the latest technologies such as Assisted Global Positioning and Global Positioning System to track employee vehicles, mobile phones and even ID/Smartcards.

Employee surveillance is greatly facilitated by the advancement of information technologies. The majority of the companies monitoring employees now rely on various IT solutions, making this once burdensome and expensive activity cheap and effective. In fact, most of the modern surveillance methods, and particularly those concerned with computer activity, do not include any human involvement. Disciplining resulting from network surveillance activities is virtually commonplace. More than 60 per cent of companies have disciplined employees for violations of network policies, 25 per cent have fired employees for inappropriate use of email and nearly one-third have fired employees for misusing the internet. The leading violations include access to pornography, online chat, gaming, investing, or shopping at work.[1, 2] Most of this was not even possible, let alone sanctioned, just twenty years ago.

Airline reservation agents, using telephonic headsets to perform their job, widely felt the impact of new surveillance technologies. The length and content of all their telephone calls is usually electronically monitored, and maximum time allowed between calls, sometimes set as low as 10 seconds, can be automatically regulated by computer. In addition, computers are even used to assess how polite agents are, using such criteria as the number of times they mention the customer's name. Evidently, the use of modern, technology-based surveillance is unprecedented in the history of the employer–employee relationship and, as such, challenges much of what has been established as appropriate, normal and expected in the domain of employer oversight. Technology is used to monitor personnel in ways never before imagined, urging us to rethink the moral concerns surrounding the phenomenon of employee surveillance.

To express it using the taxonomy presented in Chapter 2, the aim of any ethical analysis dealing with the issue of employee surveillance should be both positive as well as normative. It is important to adequately appreciate the drastic changes taking place in the domain of employee surveillance, to take stock of the concerns of the parties involved and to descriptively situate the moral challenges arising from the question of employee surveillance today within the existing body of ethics and legal regulation. However, one is also urged to go further and to try to offer a way to interpret these changes normatively, to offer a direction arising from the account of the situation and against the backdrop of moral concerns and established principles. Eschewing normative discussion lest one be exposed to academic criticism seems irresponsible when the issue in question impacts employees all around the world and when the lagging legal response is in need of an adequate account of moral complexity at play.

Analysis of key stakeholders

How is this tremendous growth in workplace surveillance justified? Employers are primarily concerned with competitiveness, job efficiency and profitability. Few would deny corporations the right to select the best possible employee for the job in a competitive economy, which at the very least includes some degree of insight into who a given candidate is and what he or she is capable of. Such insight is impossible without *background checks*, which often include extensive job application informational requirements, credit reports, and the like. On the other hand, the concerns in relation to efficiency, performance and productivity also form the basis of the need for *on-the-job employee surveillance*. Corporations have the right to manage the workplace toward profit and it is not unreasonable on their part to ask whether their employees are actually contributing to that goal. Being able to verify that an employee is doing the job he or she is paid for arguably constitutes a fundamental part of any employment contract. In addition, employees are increasingly becoming the most significant cost driver, as the increased complexity of their duties calls for ever higher levels of employee education, on-the-job training, and other factors that increase the necessary remuneration. Finally, employees are more and more becoming not just the dominant cost, but even more importantly the main source of profitability and innovation. In the knowledge economy, business success is less dependent on equipment or capital, both of which are becoming easily available, and employees make the decisive difference between winners and losers. How then could corporations be denied the right to do everything possible to influence and control this most important factor of modern business?

A number of other arguments can be put forward in defence of employee surveillance. First, surveillance could be necessary in order to make a fair differentiation between employees – hard-working employees should be compensated relatively more than their less effective co-workers. But if the employer is denied sufficient insight into employee activities, how is this differentiation to be made? Some degree of surveillance just might be necessary to counter misrepresentations regarding performance, hours and expenses, which morally harm the employees (by making a fair assessment of employee effectiveness harder) as much as they harm the employer. Another argument for surveillance is that companies are understandably cautious about their trade secrets, and in certain situations surveillance might be necessary to protect against leaks. The same logic applies to the protection of client data (from sensitive medical information to credit card details) that might be at risk if adequate protection measures, potentially including some surveillance, are not in place. Another justification for surveillance stems from legislation – employers are increasingly held responsible for the actions of their employees. It is therefore reasonable that employers should seek to gather as much information on their employees as possible in order to protect themselves from vicarious liability or negligent hiring charges. Finally, employee theft, sometimes speculated to be costing businesses billions of euros per year, is another potential justification for the implementation of employee surveillance.

Are these many arguments sufficient to justify workplace surveillance? This is the point at which one must look at how well these principles, rights and concerns apply to particular jobs. Many jobs are compensated upon specific performance, so what rationale could one give for surveillance in such instances? Evidently, the nature of the job makes an importance difference. In some cases, assessing actual performance of a certain activity might be almost impossible without surveillance. Aforementioned airline reservation is one such profession. If the agents weren't under surveillance, what would stop them from not taking any calls? But does this automatically entitle employers to subject these employees to permanent surveillance? Obviously, analysing the nature of the job does not tell us *how much* surveillance is appropriate. In order to find that balance, the moral stakes of both parties involved, employers and employees, have to be contrasted and appreciated in a broader context of societal dynamics and fundamental ethical principles. We thus proceed to outline the principal concerns of employees in relation to workplace surveillance.

The central concern for employees in the matter of surveillance is the right to privacy. There have been numerous attempts to lay firm foundations of the right to privacy philosophically. Privacy rights can be perceived as necessary to protect such values as self-determination, arguably essential to the individual's status as a person. This line of reasoning treats privacy as serving to establish a boundary between individuals, thus defining one's individuality. However, departing from such very general observations, there is little consensus in relation to the nature, extent and importance of privacy. Some countries do not recognize a legal right to privacy, while others consider it a fundamental human right. Legal regulation of workplace surveillance varies correspondingly, from the very poor protection of employee privacy in the US and many developing countries, to more ambitious regulation in the EU, New Zealand and Australia. Philosophical literature views the right to privacy primarily as the right to control information about oneself. But it is obvious that this right or privilege is considered subordinated to numerous other rights. For example, the state can issue an authorization for surveillance if more important interests, such as public safety, are at stake. In addition, most would argue that even in some everyday situations the right to privacy can be considered to be suspended or reduced. For example, public officials' right to privacy is sometimes argued to be reduced because of the public nature of their office and the public interests vested in them. It is also contended that employees renounce their right to privacy when they enter an employment contract to a degree to which the right to privacy might conflict with their contractual obligations. But this still does not help much in determining a just boundary of workplace surveillance. For example, inner feelings and desires of a candidate are certainly relevant to someone trying to assess a candidate's fitness for a position. The candidate may be secretly unenthusiastic about the job he or she is applying for, and the company could be considered to be justified in presuming this could affect the candidate's potential performance. But we are still not comfortable with the idea that Wal-Mart is somehow *entitled* to learn about our inner feelings and desires during a preliminary job interview.

Apart from the right to privacy, other concerns might go against the argument for an extensive surveillance in the workplace. It is easily imaginable how surveillance might create a suspicious and hostile environment, harming work morale and productivity. Employee health may be impacted as well – one study found that employees under surveillance suffer more often from depression and anxiety. In addition, they exhibit more often chronic fatigue, strain injuries and even neck problems.[3] Finally, the fact that workers are pressured to spend increased hours at work means that it may often be necessary to conduct some pressing personal business at the office. This fact must be respected and taken into account when designing surveillance mechanisms. There is a strong sense that intimate matters, such as medical reports or family issues, whether dealt with by employees from the workplace or not, should remain private.

Employee surveillance, thus, includes two principal stakeholders. On the one hand, employers have the right to verify that the employment contract is being respected by the employee, but they also face numerous other concerns that might call for some form of surveillance. On the other hand, employees are deeply person-ally affected by how their workplace is organized, and being under surveillance can be not only annoying but deeply frustrating, debilitating and unjust.

We continue with an overview of the most common modern workplace surveillance methods and an outline of how the conflict between the interests of employers and employees unfolds in these specific circumstances.

Specific instances and ethical concerns

Employee monitoring often begins even before the hiring decision. *Pre-employment testing* now routinely includes such techniques as background checks, tests designed to expose the candidate's personality, and inquiries into the nature of the candidate's off-work activities, for example the possible use of illegal substances. *Credit reports* are now widely used to learn about financial situation and past financial develop-ments of job candidates. An argument for obtaining a credit report may be that someone heavily indebted is more likely to have weak financial abilities or that that person may be more likely to embezzle money if tempted. But one might have a bad credit report because of circumstances outside that person's control, for example, exuberant medical expenses of a family member. Is it then fair to discriminate based on this criterion? In addition, even if someone actually is heavily in debt, is it really ever fair to even presume that this person is more likely to embezzle money? *Driving records* of prospective employees are also frequently checked. It is typical for companies to regularly check an employee's driving record if he or she is performing a job where driving is extensively required, for example delivery or courier services. Arguably, the employer bears the moral burden of insuring that the employee's driving ability is not exposing the public to risk. Similar argument can be put forward in relation to *criminal record checks*. The legal treatment of criminal record checks is usually such that the employer may deny employment to a candidate based on a previous conviction, as long as the felony in question is reasonably related to the job duties. Denying a bank job to a convicted bank robber seems defensible, whereas denying employment because of past arrests (in cases in which conviction did not ensue) or a past drug treatment is more likely to be considered unjust, and even illegal in some countries. The central argument for performing such checks is that of safety. Employers can be argued to bear a moral responsibility to scrutinize employees' criminal backgrounds so as to ensure the safety of the people this prospective employee will be in contact with, such as co-workers, customers, etc. Finally, the employer, at least in some countries, can reduce the risk of potential litigation by doing so, which arguably presents an incentive arising from legal practice.

But how far are we prepared to allow employers to go in selection based on such screening techniques? The judicial system is obligated to presume innocence regardless of previous misdeeds as a result of strong underpinning societal values. Not discriminating on the grounds of past deeds is an important part of the modern notion of fairness and, consequentially, our judicial system, not merely punitory but corrective. We deem second chances important and fair, and why should we not? Human beings are fallible but we still feel that we should not be made prisoners of our past wrongdoings as there is always hope for change. Are corporations not supposed to adhere to the same principles?

Drug testing, increasingly widespread among modern corporations, raises similar questions, but also adds some new dilemmas. Several major retail companies, including Home Depot, IKEA and Wal-Mart, have extensive drug-testing regimes for both prospective and present employees. Many stores even leverage their 'drug-free workplace' principles as a marketing tactic. The argument for this practice is simple – work efficiency is adversely affected by employees' substance abuse, and safety of the workplace can be affected as well. The problem with this argument, however, is that drug testing, as it is carried out today, might not be a proper way to test for on-the-job sobriety in the first place. An employee might be conscientious and always sober on the job, but experimenting with illegal substances in his or her own time. Modern drug-testing techniques are unable to make this difference. We are inclined to concede that whether employees are sober on the job is of employers' interest. But are we prepared to allow employers to discriminate against employees because of their off-the-job habits? In addition, the organizations could be argued to have a moral duty to help their employees experiencing a substance abuse problem (just as they usually have a responsibility to provide health insurance coverage in order to help their employees with other, medical, problems) instead of just firing them. Again, an important aspect of this dilemma is the nature of the particular employment. In Skinner vs Railway Labour Executives' Association, the Supreme Court of the United States held that the government's interest in ensuring the safety of the public justifies the rigorous testing regime employed by the defendant to monitor compliance with its sobriety politics. It is understandable how public interests attached to a particular profession might outweigh individual privacy concerns. But how can, for example, testing assembly line workers for marijuana be justified? First of all, there is no telling whether they engage in this activity exclusively in their own time, and, second, their job performance is usually effectively measured electronically and not projected by way of checking for sobriety. Arguably, employers would have no basis for testing in such cases, and yet, it is precisely low-level jobs such as these that seem to be at the centre of drug-testing efforts. One problem related to pre-employment testing, background checks and such procedures is their general unreliability and the related questions of whether the candidates in question are given an adequate opportunity to verify and, if necessary, challenge this themselves. Finally, background checks might unintentionally reveal information of a deeply private character that may bear no relevance whatsoever to one's work potential.

On-the-job monitoring is the second key area of the disparity of moral interests in relation to the informational content about employees available to employers.

Electronic performance monitoring is the key new element that amplified the concerns related to on-the-job surveillance. It makes all the traditional techniques easier, cheaper, faster and more comprehensive. It can make a difference between a traditional workplace and an equivalent of a panopticon prison. As such, it radically transforms the situation for which principles of conduct in relation to employee monitoring have been traditionally negotiated and established.

However, not only have surveillance techniques been transformed by the rise of information technologies, but also, in some cases, the original motivation for surveillance. Employees sometimes spend much of their working time sending and receiving personal emails or surfing sites unrelated to their work. Arguably, electronic performance monitoring is the only way to counter such computer-based inappropriate workplace behaviour. One might be tempted at this time to put forward the argument that as long as the work is done, which sites an employee visits is none of the employer's business. And, although this might make sense in many cases, selling such a line of reasoning when the employee in question spends half of his or her time at work surfing sex sites might still be difficult.

The most common methods of electronic performance monitoring are keystroke loggers, packet monitors for examining network traffic (including email and web activity monitoring) and electronic processing of video/audio data. *Email monitoring* has been particularly controversial because it has already led to a number of employees being fired. Separating private from business usage of email might be very difficult. Are we even sure what constitutes a private email? Just the fact of an email being sent from a private email portal would, arguably, still not be sufficient to qualify an email as private if the email is sent from a company's computer and through a company's network, particularly if these are clearly announced to be exclusively for business purposes. But then, one might be pressed to do some private business, for example, receiving the results of medical testing, using such a business-only network. Does that mean that the employer is entitled to this information? It is worth mentioning that the case law in the US has regularly supported this notion that any communication going through the system owned by a company is in turn itself automatically owned by that company. But are we comfortable with this reasoning? One counterargument often heard is that if two people are having a conversation in my house, a domain of my private property, we would still not consider that I am somehow entitled to the content of their conversation. Does the employment contract change that? As argued before, for many jobs it simply could not. If I am paid for my work and not for my not having private correspondence and private interests, then the economic interest of employers does not confer the right to monitor conversations, whether electronically or otherwise. One important factor, however, is an employer's interest in reducing liability exposure. Employers are expected to protect against sexual harassment and an otherwise hostile environment, and some degree of monitoring might be necessary to do that. In fact, more than 20 per cent of firms have been ordered by court to produce employee email records.[4] In addition, in order to ensure the respect for software licensing laws, proprietary information and trade secrets, employers might simply have to monitor some aspects of computer usage in the workplace. For example, even if we concede that employers are not entitled to monitoring employees' computer usage per se, the legal liability exposure for the possible pirated software installed on a company's computers would confer some rights of insight to the employer.

Audio surveillance is another controversial area of employment monitoring. Audio surveillance is legal if the employer maintains the system (which is almost always the case) or the employee's consent for monitoring has been obtained. Again, the ethical argument is obviously different for the employees whose phone communication constitutes an essential part of their working contracts (help-desk agents for example) and those who use phone communication only instrumentally, to perform a job the results of which are not confined to phone communication. *Video surveillance* is also increasing in popularity as a tool to monitor the workforce. The proponents argue that it discourages theft, physical confrontations and sexual harassment. Certainly, an organization can use video monitoring to reduce damaging actions by its employees and customers, thus potentially reducing its costs. However, video monitoring can rob employees of their privacy without a sufficient justification. Why should a company be allowed to video monitor employees if, for example, the potential loss due to theft is minimal? Most companies, however, are not required to produce such justifications. In addition to being potentially unnecessarily intrusive, video surveillance has been a tool of major misuses, such as zooming in on body parts of customers and co-workers.

Finally, the most modern, advanced and powerful surveillance techniques seem to require even less human power and money to implement and operate. For example, time and labour (TandL) systems are now widely used to locate employees by tracking their magnetic badges, GPS capabilities of employees' mobile phones are used to track employees' locations (particularly the locations of the travelling salespeople), etc., enabling major extensions to the traditional employee monitoring systems. These techniques of the future offer unprecedented surveillance possibilities and urge us to carefully weigh the interests of the parties involved.

Guidelines and conclusions

In relation to Level 3 of critique presented in Chapter 2, it is worth mentioning that the level of workplace surveillance differs around the world. However, these differences are primarily a result of the diversity in technological capabilities and not necessarily ethical outlook. This, however, remains to be seen. Namely, the question of surveillance has grown in importance only recently, and the legal response is in a nascent state, so the potential culturally based differences in reaction to this phenomenon cannot yet be observed. Western companies are performing the most far-reaching surveillance (which can be ascribed to technological differences) and European, Australian and New Zealand employees are enjoying the most privacy protection. However, the realistic situation worldwide is that employees can expect little legal protection for their privacy in the modern workplace.

Legislation has traditionally been slow to address ethical issues arising from rapid technological advances. This is an important reason why one has to think about the principles applicable to the moral relations arising from employee surveillance. By analysing the interests of the parties involved, one can discern some general patterns. Employee surveillance has to balance the employer's interest in managing the workplace and the employees' privacy interest. The employer's right to manage the workplace is grounded in their economic interests as well as a number of other concerns, from workplace safety to intellectual property protection. Employees, on the other hand, deserve to be respected and treated as free and rational persons, capable of choosing for themselves how they live their lives. In finding a compromise between these two concerns, several key guiding principles can be used.

First, do no (unnecessary) harm. It is often possible to choose among different ways to organize workplace monitoring, and a thorough analysis of the situation coupled with an active empathy for the concerns of the employees can go a long way in helping determine which methods would be the least intrusive while still accomplishing the desired result. For example, a considerate attitude would be to examine an employee's daily output only at the end of the day or at the end of the week instead of burdensome constant inspections. In fairness, many surveillance techniques, active personal oversight for one, serve only to provide employers with a sense of control, and not really to improve business performance. If an employee is slacking off, that will be just as evident at the end of a day (if it is not, because the job is somehow done, than what is the problem?), and just the absence of a constant oversight might add to the overall workplace productivity. Therefore, the first principle that employers should bear in mind is the relation between the effectiveness and intrusiveness of monitoring. In order for any method to be selected the employer should be able to demonstrate first that the goal of monitoring actually makes sense, as well as that the incursions into employee privacy and well-being are minimal and unavoidable.

Second, following the analysis of the interests of the parties involved, it can be inferred that this demonstration of ethical permissibility of an employee surveillance method can only be carried out along three main lines of reasoning. The employer can show that intrusions into employee privacy are justified by his or her reasonable economic interests, that it is justified by the interests of the employee while proving that this policy would not present a case of illegitimate paternalism, or that it is justified as a means to protect a third party's (e.g. public's) legitimate interests.

Third, an important requirement in all instances of employee surveillance must be a respect for the employee's privacy once the information is already gathered. Namely, many privacy incidents centred on the cases in which the information gathered for one of the three essential ethically permissible goals of employee surveillance was in fact used for different purposes. This rightfully creates a sense of betrayal on the part of the employee, and harms both the employee as well as the employer in the long run. In addition, a misuse of employee information is becoming increasingly dangerous. New technologies (e.g. genetic testing) now pose a serious threat to overall employee privacy and well-being if adequate measures to protect such information are not put in place.

Fourth, no surveillance whatsoever should take place without informed consent of the employee. In addition, some room for dialogue must be left open. Unilaterally presenting an employee with information that he or she is going to be subject to surveillance is not fair, considering the power relations between the employer and the employee. The employee must be given a chance to participate in the discussion on the measures impacting such personal issues as privacy and workplace well-being.

Fifth, employees must be given the opportunity to avoid being monitored in at least some situations. Employees often need to conduct some personal business at the office and this does not mean that they should be made to share their personal life with the employer. For example, even if broad surveillance measures are justified, the employer could still set up a phone or a computer that is totally unmonitored in order to give employees an outlet for personal matters.

Sixth, in order to ensure workplace fairness, hierarchical equity of surveillance should be aspired to. Surveillance often depends on the employee's status within the organization, which can create a rift between those who are subject to surveillance and those who are not. In turn, this unequal treatment in such basic aspects as privacy could make the monitored workers feel like second-order employees.

Finally, an important aspect in relation to employee surveillance to bear in mind is trust. Niccolo Machiavelli suggested that between being feared and being loved by one's subordinates, one should always choose to be feared, as fear is easier to produce and easier to control. But the modern workplace is not about control, it is about people, creativity and trust. At the end of the day, the selection of workplace surveillance methods sends a message about how one perceives employees as persons and what kind of relationship with them one wants to nurture. As hard as it might be for many employers, it is often necessary to choose between tight control on the one side and trust, motivation and creativity on the other.

CASE STUDY: HEWLETT-PACKARD SPYING SCANDAL

Hewlett-Packard (HP) is one of the largest computer companies in the world. It was founded in 1939 by Bill Hewlett and David Packard, then still students at Stanford. The first HP product, a precision audio oscillator, was to become one of the many innovative products upon which HP built its rapid success. HP's corporate culture was imagined as family friendly, stable and conservative, with emphasis on high ethical standards in conducting business activities. The fusion of radical innovation with high ethical standards eventually became known as 'the HP way'.

Indeed, HP earned the respect of the world as an institution with admirable business ethics policies. It gradually became perceived as a standard bearer of humanism and social responsibility in business. This unique reputation was consistently strengthened through responsible environmental policies, energy conservation and, most importantly, an unparalleled working environment that easily attracted the best and brightest. Arguably, the ability to recruit first-rate talent enabled HP to become a leader in the technology field. Top engineers, programmers and designers were readily joining HP, and key executives were easy to retain. HP's managerial ranks were extremely open, and employees at all levels and across functions shared the vision of a successful and morally upright HP. The reputation for fairness and open-mindedness at HP was furthered in 1999, when Carly Fiorina became the CEO. She was the first woman ever to serve as CEO of a company included in the Dow Jones Industrial Average. In February 2005, Fiorina was forced to resign and Patricia Dunn was promoted to chairwoman of the board. Having two women at the top of a Fortune 500 company was seen as a major victory in the fight against the career glass ceiling for women, and HP was again praised as a paradigm of an ethically admirable and socially proactive company.

However, shortly after the resignation of Fiorina, it became evident that confidential information in relation to HP's long-term plans was being leaked to CNET Networks, Inc., a San Francisco media company. This was a serious problem because it undermined the shareholder information-sharing process and in turn fostered an atmosphere of mistrust within the company. HP's need for information about the activities of its employees and the complexity of the related moral and legal issues were about to become the centre of a major controversy.

Patricia Dunn's response was to hire a private electronic security company to find the source of the leaks to the media. In turn, those security experts recruited private investigators who started spying on reporters responsible for publishing the leaks, as well as on a number of HP employees. The investigators used a method known as 'pretexting' to obtain call records of HP board members and nine journalists, including reporters for *The New York Times*, *The Wall Street Journal* and CNET. Pretexting involved the investigators misrepresenting themselves as the board members and journalists in the process of obtaining information.

On 11 September 2006, CNET News.com released a letter by the US House Committee on Energy and Commerce to Patricia Dunn in which she was informed of an investigation that discovered that 'lies, fraud and deception' were used to acquire personal information on behalf of HP. They stated that they are 'troubled' by this fact, 'particularly that it involves HP – one of America's corporate icons'. Dunn was summoned to testify before the Committee. She claimed she did not realize that pretexting involved identity misrepresentation and that she was absolutely sure that all the necessary information was obtainable legally.

Several other HP employees testified, including Kevin Hunsaker (former Senior Counsel and Director of Ethics and Standards of Business Conduct), Ann Baskins (former General Counsel) and Anthony Gentilucci (former Chief of Global Investigations). They all invoked the Fifth Amendment, in effect refusing to answer questions of the Committee. Dunn resigned as chairwoman of HP's board, and Mark Hurd, the CEO, succeeded Dunn as chairman.

Criminal charges were filed and arrest warrants issued against these key actors. Four felony violations were alleged: conspiracy to commit crime, fraudulent use of wire, radio or television transmissions, taking, copying and using computer data and using personal identifying information without authorization. The court decided that the charges would be dropped if the accused completed 96 hours of community service.

The case was quickly resolved and a lot of effort was put into restoring HP's reputation for ethical conduct. But, in order to appreciate the ethical dilemma Patricia Dunn faced, one must reflect on all the aspects of this situation. First, the leaks presented not just a major difficulty in relation to the shareholders, but also brought about a breakdown of trust within HP. The unknown employees leaking the information to the media were perceived as traitors of what has been established as a strong and proud HP corporate culture. Furthermore, the investigation, though unconventional, bore fruit. It was revealed that the actual sources of the leaks were board members George Keyworth and Thomas J. Perkins, both of whom were subsequently fired. In effect, Patricia Dunn succeeded in her quest to protect the information-sharing process. In addition, she did so without actually engaging in any illegal activity directly. The charges concentrated on the claim that she should have made an adequate effort to acquaint herself with the methods that were going to be used in the process of investigation. Was this element really under her control or were the investigators to respect the law regardless of HP's informational requirements?

No doubt that the wrong investigation company was hired, but questions linger as to whether any company at all should have been hired. Is it acceptable to spy on employees without their consent? What about when the stakes are as high as they were in the HP case? Which factors influence how we perceive this situation and does it merit a specific legal regulation?

CONCEPTUAL QUESTIONS

1   Who are the key ethical stakeholders in the matter of workplace surveillance?
2   What are their respective interests?
3   What is the role of employee consent in workplace monitoring?
4   What is hierarchical equity of surveillance and why does it matter?

CRITICAL QUESTIONS

1   Are there limits to the surveillance of employees? What are they?
2   Were there other, less ethically challenging options open to Patricia Dunn and HP when faced with the leaks?

Notes

1   AMA/ePolicy Institute Research (2008/2007) 'Electronic Monitoring & Surveillance Survey'. Available online at www.amanet.org/training/seminars/2007-Electronic-Monitoring-and-Surveillance-Survey-41.aspx (accessed 17 November 2009).
2   Similar figures are documented around the world, see: A. Schulman (2001) 'The extent of systematic monitoring of employee e-mail and Internet use'. Privacy Foundation. Available online at www.sonic.net/~undoc/extent.htm (accessed 17 November 2009).
3   R. W. Kolb (ed.) (2008) *Encyclopedia of Business Ethics and Society, Volume 5*. Thousand Oaks, CA: Sage Publications, p. 2325.
4   Ibid., p. 2263.

Further reading

Books and book chapters

Hartman, L. (2006) 'Technology and ethics: Privacy in the workplace'. In K. W. Krasemann and P. H. Werhane (eds), *Contemporary Issues in Business Ethics*. Lanham, MD: University Press of America.

Lane, F. S. (2003) *The Naked Employee: How technology is compromising workplace privacy*. New York: AMACOM.

Marcella, A. J. and Stucki, C. (2003) *Privacy Handbook: Guidelines, exposures, policy implementation, and international issues*. New York: Wiley.

Weckert, J. (ed.) (2004) *Electronic Monitoring in the Workplace: Controversies and solutions*. Hershey, PA: Idea Group.

Journal articles

Halpern, D., Reville, P. and Grunewald, D. (2008) 'Management and legal issues regarding electronic surveillance of employees in the workplace', *Journal of Business Ethics*, 80(2): 175–180.

Hoffman, W. M., Hartman, L. and Rowe, M. (2003) 'You've got mail and the boss knows', *Business and Society Review*, 108(3): 285–307.

Martin, K. and Freeman, R. (2003) 'Some problems with employee monitoring', *Journal of Business Ethics*, 43(4): 353–361.

Persson, A. and Hansson, S. (2003) 'Privacy at work: Ethical criteria', *Journal of Business Ethics*, 42(1): 59–70.

Whitman, J. Q. (2004) 'The two western cultures of privacy: dignity versus liberty', *The Yale Law Journal*, 113(6): 1151–1221.

Online sources

DeCew, J. (2006) 'Privacy'. In E. N. Zalta (ed.), *The Stanford Encyclopedia of Philosophy*. Available online at http://plato.stanford.edu/entries/privacy/.

PART V
Marketing and innovation

16

ETHICS AND MARKETING

David Bevan

Marketing is the art of getting people to change their minds.

(Jay Conrad Levinson)[1]

Marketing: How to create, win, and dominate markets

(Textbook title)[2]

The basic ethical problem marketing raises is how to design a system for producing, distributing, and monitoring products in an ethical manner when market relations play a central role in the process.

(George G. Brenkert)[3]

Chapter overview

In this chapter we turn our attention to the overwhelming reach of marketing: it is overwhelming in the sense that we are rarely free from its influences. While Human Resources Management (HRM) affects everyone in employment and trying to get a job, almost all of us have been involved in marketing as consumers, even if only indirectly through our parents, since before we were born. Think about the planning, the preparation and the resulting expenditure provoked by a new baby. We first suggest some key definitions of what marketing is and identify its ethical position first from its own perspective, and then from outside perspectives. We re-examine some indicative aspects of the traditional business ethics framework and bring these to focus on areas of specific relevance to marketing. We then take you through some specific areas of marketing practice that you may consider to be contentious, or at least worth an ethical discussion. Finally, and in the course of all this, we offer a range of readings on the conjunction of marketing and ethics for your further consideration.

In this chapter, while some of the critique will be at Level 1, most of the discussion will be at Level 2 (considering the wider impact of marketing practices on the wider society and stakeholders) and there will also be some brief excursions into Level 3 critique, when the intercultural aspects of globalized marketing are considered.

What is marketing?

Look away from this book, and look around you and almost everything you perceive will resonate with marketing. The book itself was marketed to someone, somehow. That is how it got from us to you. The room you are in at home or school, the transport you are in, will reflect a multitude of marketing choices that have been made – the furniture, the equipment, the windows and blinds, the fire or security alarm system, the lighting, what you are wearing and who else is in the room with you. So marketing is in an almost continuous relationship with consumers – it is almost impossible to avoid being engaged by it. Is marketing really concerned for the choices we make, for what we or others have bought? Or is marketing only interested in taking us to the *next* transaction?

To assist with identifying what we need (we use this word with a health warning, that it may be only a momentary, illusory need), everything is in some way 'branded', or not. 'Unbranded' is also a 'brand', unbranded has many marketing meanings – cheap, fake, carefree, cool; it will depend on context. 'Brands are for cattle!' might be a slogan on activists' or protesters' tee shirts. However we appreciate or perceive it, marketing is in the air. Even what is not there – anything you may perceive of as missing – has some resonance for marketing. In the globalized context of this book we may perceive commerce, or The Market, as a **dominant social paradigm**. Simply stated, we all see this market as something that operates through marketing.

Marketing is a continuous cycle of planning and executing, conceptualizing, targeting, pricing, promoting and delivering all manner of consumable ideas, goods and commodities, services and events to create and maintain the momentum of the market. As philosopher George Brenkert points out,[4] marketing envelopes us, permeating our lives through media (the internet, TV, movies, radio, newspapers, magazines, road, bus and subway adverts, screens in stores and on transport, labelling and branding, logos). The market provides the things we use every day (in the developed world); marketing in turn is influenced by how the market responds to it, reflecting back to us the image of what we have become as a result of our relationship with it.

The mainstream management view of marketing is exemplified in over four decades of successful textbooks from Professor Phillip Kotler. Kotler suggests that business should be driven by customers and markets. There is little room in the contemporary world for argument, this is certainly how things seem to be. Even if you have not studied marketing (yet), you may well be familiar with the technical language associated with marketing managers: market segmentation, targeting, brand positioning, campaigns and consumer orientation. The bland, generally held and uncritical view of marketing places it in a kind of miraculous or creative problem-solving role for hard-pressed business managers. Do you need to sell more, become more efficient, or make more money? Marketing can help: researching the market, targeting customers, developing cool products (even building in obsolescence), persuasively targeting, branding and packaging these vital goodies and helping you to retail them through multiple forms of advertising and promotion.

As with any attempt at a definition, your individual perspective will have some influence and you may take one of any number of perspectives. There is a benign, admittedly dated view that marketing is a somewhat idealized process by which consumers obtain what they need and want through exchanging products of value with others. There is a more **ideological** market-driven view that creating customer value and satisfaction is at the very heart of modern marketing thinking and practice. This pro-market approach typically suggests that needs and wants are natural and essential to the human condition.[5] So the need for food, water and shelter or security is just like the need for a new designer handbag or the latest mobile phone; these are just needs. If we (are unfortunate enough to) live in a rural society where such essential commodities are not available, then we may not be able to displace the need for food and water; but we can at least lead a less satisfied life without the latest handbag or mobile phone. Such a universal interpretation of needs leads easily to more critical interpretations of marketing: see Naomi Klein's book[6] in which she 'charges international companies – especially those enjoying high brand recognition – with exploitation, environmental pillage, human rights abuses, hypocrisy, kowtowing to repressive regimes, disowning their home-base workforces, driving down wages and much more besides',[7] or Professor Chris Hackley's recent volume from a more carefully deconstructive and academic perspective.[8]

Marketing puts us all right about many things – it has an essential role in informing consumer choice. Marketing claims to have liberated us from household drudgery with a range of labour-saving devices such as dishwashers, clothes washing and drying machines. Marketing tells us how to avoid disease, get an education, have a holiday and informs our political choices. It has also persuaded us that the way we naturally smell is seriously unattractive if not offensive (deodorant and toilet soap); and in selected markets it tells us both that it is better to be lighter skinned than dark (if you have darker skin, as in skin-lightening products sold in Asia and Africa), or better to be tan than light skinned (if you are pale, as in tanning products sold in Europe and North America). So on the basis of truthfulness or good taste, we can perhaps agree that there are aspects of marketing within business ethics about which we may be at least uncertain. Conventional wisdom reinforces the position that we rely on marketing to know what we need to buy. But we also know there is something slightly questionable going on.

How, you may ask, would respectable globalized firms such as L'Oreal, Unilever and Proctor and Gamble justify selling a skin whitening or lightning products ('Christian Dior Perfect Whitening Skin Repairing Essence' and 'Fair and Lovely')? Do such firms espouse some unpublicized sexist and racist agenda? Well, presumably they would say not. What is the ethical position of the global marketing agencies that develop and advertise these products, and the media that carry the advertisement, or the product placement? The response in such contexts from marketing is generally that there is a demand, or a need, from consumers, for these products and that further on the basis of the consumer being satisfied (that is, buys repeatedly and does not complain) then this is an entirely reasonable, even ethically defensible, situation. So, considering the principal of **universalism** for a moment, we might find that commerce/marketing will resort to claiming – we might suggest it does this somewhat spuriously – to be responding to the universal needs or wants of their consumers. This principle, neatly transferring any possible blame – by creating **moral distance** – to the consumer, is frequently employed as a means of explaining otherwise aberrant, irregular and clearly unethical practice.

From this general introduction you may perceive that at least a number of reasonable criticisms can be found to level against the ideological and generally held view of marketing. Let us consider and give examples of some of these in an overview suggested by Professor Hackley.

Marketing is perceived as lacking in genuine intellectual engagement with other disciplines. So, unlike accounting, organization studies, sociology and HRM, for example, where critical scholarship is widely embraced and taught to undergraduate and postgraduate students, marketing prefers 'even more of the same' as the antidote to any critique.

Marketing fails to respond coherently to criticisms that the practice of marketing does not deliver what it promises, or over delivers. We could ask why does marketing a drug cost so much more than the original scientific research and development, for which generally sick consumers or society/government has to pay? Or, how can marketing explain the success of YouTube which does not actually sell anything – it is just a virtual place to be.

Marketing places far too much emphasis on the narrow focus of commercial priorities and/or the self-interest or selfishness of consumers. It uses absurd and irresponsible terms such as 'retail therapy', as though shopping in itself is actually therapeutic, or explanations such as 'the consumers demand all this packaging on their luxury lipstick/plentiful cheap air flights'.

Marketing is complicit in environmental degradation and the overuse of resources – it only encourages more consumption. When did you last see an advert by a company recommending you buy fewer cosmetics/take fewer flights?

Marketing clings uncritically to outmoded concepts of limited value – new is best, faster is better, younger and thinner are far better than older and merely average and, of course, being single/alone is worse than death.

Marketing is dominated by commercial transactions and profit rather than relationships and value – endlessly buy me, buy me, buy me!

Marketing thus has no concept of moderation: it also inherently seeks to universalize Anglo-American, if not purely American, neoliberal economic market values – the freedom of the individual to make money and spend it as she wishes without recourse to societal impact, the domination of markets by globalized intellectual property rights and the uncritical promotion of the values of so-called democracy.

Finally, people actually have no say in whether or not they are marketed to. It is a fallacy that there is a free choice – or is it? Although as yet the general public has not worked out a means by which to charge marketing for the personal time and attention exploited in receiving its endless messages, perhaps such an innovation would change things.

All in all, this view of (potentially amoral) exploitation places marketing in the dominant position indicated in the textbook approach quoted above the introduction to this chapter. This in turn leads some, such as Professor Sid Lowe and others, to the opinion that marketing functions only as the means to a 'material enslavement of modern societies',[9] or to be the major propaganda engine of the entire political economy.[10]

Is this exaggerating? A salutary and somewhat neglected reading from marketing professional Victor Lebow, may assist you with crafting a response:

> Our enormously productive economy demands that we make consumption our way of life, that we convert the buying and use of goods into rituals, that we seek our spiritual satisfactions, our ego satisfactions, in consumption. The measure of social status, of social acceptance, of prestige, is now to be found in our consumption patterns. The very meaning and significance of our lives is today expressed in consumption terms. The greater the pressure upon the individual to conform to safe and accepted social standards, the more does he tend to express his aspirations and his individuality in terms of what he wears, drives, eats – his home, his car, his patterns of food serving, his hobbies.
>
> These commodities and services must be offered to the consumer with special urgency. We require not only 'forced shift' consumption but 'expensive' consumption as well. We need things consumed, burned up, worn out, replaced and discarded at an ever increasing rate. We need to have people eat, drink, dress, ride, live, with ever more complicated and therefore constantly more expensive consumption.[11]

Still unsure? The words of French TV station CEO Patrick LeLay may inform you further. M. LeLay claims[12] (author's translation) – 'let us be clear that the primary purpose of television is to sell to the public Coca Cola' (or other valuable branded products). For M. LeLay the mind of the consumer is an asset of the TV company. If you are watching his station he has (temporarily owns) your attention – and the TV company may sell access to your attention, moment by moment, according to the price of the market. But maybe you had worked that one out . . .

Ethics and marketing

This last, particular aspect of marketing practice directly confronts business ethics so far as we have discussed it. There is at least one irreconcilable breach here with one of the leading moral/ethical frameworks, Kantian duty or deontology, because this practice of marketing categorically seeks to treat humans as a means (here an asset or commodity to be sold) rather than as individuals. Let us recall the third formulation of Kant's Categorical Imperative: to treat other human beings always at the same time as ends-in-themselves and never merely as a means.

Following on further from this catalogue of ethical issues and in relation to indicative, traditional ethical theories, does marketing have any response? Indeed, as you might expect, it does: it claims that marketing has *prima facie* ethical legitimacy across all four dimensions of a framework suggested by traditional business ethics. It respects the autonomy of the individual (from Kant): the consumer is free to choose to buy or not. It provides a useful service to society (from utilitarianism); consumers need this information to hear about labour-saving devices and more economical products, and lead more enjoyable lives. It is legal (so compliant with the law, although of course ethics and law are not coincident (see Chapter 2 above). Finally, it is free to market because it wishes to do so (from liberalism). We shall discuss these possible moral philosophical perspectives in relation to marketing practice, along with a virtue ethics approach, further and invite you to consider these claims more fully.

Setting aside for a moment the overwhelming ethical condemnation of most marketing, implicit in the introductory sentence in this current section, for its instrumental exploitation of people as a means to a sale, let us reconsider Kant's other maxims. One aspect of a rule-based, **non-consequentialist** account of duty, or the **deontological** approach, would hold that marketing acts have the possibility of being good or otherwise in and of themselves, irrespective of outcome. So, and on this point alone, the ethics of marketing would be subject to judgement on **a priori** moral principles. What, a marketing professional might ask, is possibly wrong with the principle of providing information about the range of possible choices to consumers? This could even appear to be a good way of finding marketing as ethical when its outcomes – as we have discussed above – may appear as crude, exploitative, misleading, offensive, and even unfair. The problem in practice with moral principles is that they appear to be at least **culturally relative** if not entirely **subjective**. Remember that while we may all be content to agree that being happy in some broad sense is a generally good thing, everybody's precise arrangement of happiness is in fact different if not mutually exclusive. So, different cultural, ethnic and religious contexts tend to contribute to differing systems of value. This makes any system of universal principles at least problematic, if not impractical. Notwithstanding logic, **moral relativism** is rarely (that is to say never) adopted as a defence in orthodox ethical arguments because it is inherently **anarchic** – it defeats any system based on rules.

Chris Hackley (2009)[13] recalls some examples of infamous campaigns in association with *French Connection*, *Benetton* and *Calvin Klein*. At the time of writing this book there is an outcry against an 'all black' issue of Italian *Vogue* featuring only black models. Of course it simultaneously shows the beauty of black people, but there is an unintended consequence of cultural colonialism and elitism. Did the editors of *Vogue* envisage such criticism as this from sceptical fashion blogger 'Bella Straniera'?[14]

Given the number of global, particularly African, influences in fashion this season, it is not surprising that fashion editors would choose to set photo shoots in Africa. But the resulting photographs raise issues that were easily forgotten in the sanitized, rock-music-fuelled environs of an Oscar de la Renta show. Where are these prints from, how did Western designers end up appropriating them, and what does it all mean? Are Americans any better than the Europeans who became infatuated with Orientalism at the turn of the last century, or have we merely adapted the same attitudes to a different continent 100 years later?

Hackley points out one interesting aspect about such campaigns is that while they provoke offence from particular groups, and while they receive a lot of media attention, the actual number of formal complaints is small. Even notorious campaigns are not found to be offensive to all. Indeed, some (such as Benetton) are perceived as commercially successful campaigns, so is it the case that most people were in fact not offended? This shows some of the weaknesses or difficulties of claiming a priori principles as a reliable indicator of ethics.

A further complication for deontology arises in reference to the code of professional conduct by which national associations of marketing professionals operate. Let us briefly turn to the Advertising Standards Authority (ASA) based in the UK, which is a **quasi**-regulatory professional body that reassures us that it ensures all advertising, wherever it appears, meets the high standards laid down in the advertising codes. A code implies a regulatory framework that should perhaps look something like the ideal ethical framework that George Brenkert arrives at (see p. 234). The ASA has a range of codes across specialized industries (alcohol, banking, insurance), a variety of media (internet, broadcast and non-broadcast), and different groups of consumers (adults, children). The ASA works with other regulatory agencies in the UK – in health, food, safety and finance industries as well as with consumer protection – to reinforce its powers, and is there to protect the interests of consumers. The role of the ASA is to make sure all advertising, wherever it appears, is honest and decent. All very regular, and thus categorically on the face of it a profession driven by a deontological approach – a range of principles that govern its practice. Turning to the UK Chartered Institute of Marketing we can find the detail of such a code set out as a plausible list of a priori ethical principles. Members are required to adhere to a strict code of professional practice.

This code requires each individual to:

- demonstrate integrity, bringing credit to the profession of marketing;
- be fair and equitable towards other marketing professionals;
- be honest in dealing with customers, clients, employers and employees;
- avoid the dissemination of false or misleading information;

- demonstrate current knowledge of the latest developments and show competence in their application;
- avoid conflicts of interest and commitment to maintaining impartiality;
- treat sensitive information with complete confidence;
- negotiate business in a professional and ethical manner;
- demonstrate knowledge and observation of the requirements of other codes of practice;
- demonstrate due diligence in using third party endorsement which must have prior approval;
- comply with the governing laws of the relevant country concerned.[15]

It is difficult to take issue with any of these commendable principles of good conduct, but all the objections that we have identified previously to deontological principles apply equally here. What is the value of integrity if you are only integrated around making money? Why are only other marketing professionals selected for fair and equitable treatment? Who is to say what is misleading or false? And so on. The inadmissible *ethical relativist* is sneering at us from the door – there is nothing whatever here beyond marketing itself. In effect, this is at best Level 1 critique in the sense of Chapter 2.

Contrastingly, or conversely perhaps, starting with outcomes for a *teleological*, **consequentialist** or utilitarian ethical principle, we may consider the ethical status by reference to the consequences of marketing actions, rather than any ethical value in actions alone. In such an analysis, for example, we might consider the value of a public service advertisement designed to reduce car crashes from driving while intoxicated. Do the images of dead and seriously wounded people evoking a violent traffic accident cause public offence? And what about the case of sexual health from unwanted pregnancy and/or sexually transmitted infection? Is it acceptable to advertise to 13-year-old children the symptoms and risks associated with what are categorically illegal sexual relations for many jurisdictions? Or is it right – better for society – to have people aware of sexual protection from a young age? In these two cases, if the advertising resulted in less harm through more moderate drinking, a reduction in accidents from dangerous driving and less sexual infection, then on the grounds of a positive outcome for society such marketing would be considered ethically beneficial to society. Once again, highly vocal minorities intervene. One group asks if we balance our spending on informing the public of the dangers of drinking with our spending on informing the public of the delights of drinking – overwhelmingly we do not. Another group is against alcohol intake in any form irrespective of driving. A further group will see the sexual health campaign as attracting innocent children to sexual promiscuity. Another group will see this as licentiousness. Sexual minorities will have concerns for the representation or suppression of diversity. And, all of these groups represent at least one if not more groups of **stakeholder**. Once again cultural or moral relativism colours the perspective and a perfectly coherent ethical position for the utility of marketing is unattainable.

Similar problems arise with the **ethics of virtue**,[16] which proposes that moderation is virtue. Perhaps marketing would be ethical if it were able to sustain the claim that it seeks to strike a balance between excess and insufficiency, thus meeting the Aristotelian **Golden Mean**. Virtue ethics will encourage virtuous behaviour by an individual in any context rather classifying a range of actions as virtuous in themselves. Once again, the problem (as well as the strength) of this approach for a class of industry such as marketing is this intrinsic subjectivity. What may be considered virtue in the eyes of one individual may not be virtue in the eyes of another. Marketing managers may aspire to virtuous behaviour in their professional actions by for example not exaggerating the qualities of a product. Equally, they may be forced into doing exactly that by senior managers and or clients for whom maximizing sales is the only goal. In so doing, they serve the interests of shareholders in an enactment of Milton Friedman's vision of corporate social responsibility: Friedman is regarded as among the world's sharpest minds in marketing and strategy innovation.[17] This brings us back to George Brenkert's puzzle as expressed in one of the quotations at the heading of this chapter and one that is at the centre of business ethics: how can we value the market as an ethical realm? Brenkert suggests that no single moral principle is adequate to frame or develop an ideal ethics of marketing. While taking great care to repudiate moral relativism, he suggests the answer lies in another direction. This is to commend an *ethical pluralism* based on moral values and norms inherently crucial to marketing. The important, although not exhaustive, values he claims for marketing ethics are 'autonomy, freedom, justice, trust, truth and well-being'.[18] We agree that this seems to construct a reasonably comprehensive ideal ethical framework for marketing, nonetheless one which is far from evident in the practices we have sampled to date.

Rather, what we find at the moment is an evident marketing ethics that may be exclusively framed in the single principle of **individualism** or **egoism** as apparently derived from a perverse, or incomplete, view of liberalism. Mill's[19] vision of the freedom of an individual proposes that each individual is free to express him/herself and has absolute freedom to do as s/he wishes. Mill balances this freedom of personal, individual choice with the very clear provision that there may be no intention to harm others. Individualism simply abducts the freedom from the harm principle, resulting in a normative anti-morality or irresponsibility. This version of individualism, or egoism, is an effective reversion to a pre-social contract, Hobbesean state of nature.[20] Ethics is for man as a social animal and Hobbes had a last word to say on where egoism leads: outright conflict and war. Egoism is often paraded as a possible moral philosophy but, since it has no sense whatever of any possible duty to anybody other than oneself, it is in effect a cancellation of morality, a systematic immoralism or an anti-morality.

The practice of such individualism is realized and delivered through the project of the market. Free market ideologue Milton Friedman indeed speaks to specifically marketing points in *Capitalism and Freedom* (and elsewhere), a close reading of which will not occur here. Nonetheless, let us remind ourselves of the Chicago position on business:

The view has been gaining widespread acceptance that corporate officials and labour leaders have a 'social responsibility' that goes beyond serving the interest of their stockholders or their members. This view shows a fundamental misconception of the character and nature of a free economy. In such an economy, there is one and only one social responsibility of business, to use its resources and engage in activities designed to increase its profits so long as it stays within the rules of the game, which is to say, engages in open and free competition, without deception or fraud.[21]

Friedman's ideological free market would thus appear to be a comfortable place for marketing. Yes, it is OK to extend the truth because everybody does that in marketing, etc., it is the rule of the game . . . as long as you do not break the law . . . it is your right under the First Amendment. It would also be far better to legalize all drugs, treat them as alcohol and tobacco, because then the market could be controlled and people should be free to do as they wish with respect to what they put in their own body and take the responsibility for that. There should be no conscription, and jails should be emptied out and people put to work for the state, etc. But while no one mainstream business seriously challenges Friedman on his concept of CSR, it seems much of the rest of his project of ultraliberalism will have to wait for some time.

Finally, the law and ethics, as explained in Chapter 2, do not always coincide. Indeed, for one commentator, legitimacy appears as a scheme of the above outlined individualism: The law

does no more than symbolically consecrate – by recording it in a form which renders it both eternal and universal – the structure of the power relation between groups and classes which is produced and guaranteed practically by the functioning of these mechanisms. For example, it records and legitimates the distinction between the position and the person, the power and its holder, together with the relationship obtaining at a particular moment between qualifications and jobs . . . The law thus contributes to its own (specifically symbolic) force to the action of the various mechanisms which render it superfluous constantly to reassert power relations by overtly reverting to force.[22]

Nonetheless, marketing generally complies with the law to the extent that its project is not illegal. Far from it, indeed, the liberal individualist tendency that structures contemporary society positively reinforces the right of an individual to autonomous action within a framework of social norms. It perhaps unfortunately works out, unintentionally shall we say, that those with the most money have the loudest voice. In this way if we are all free to say what we like (to repeat an axiomatic fallacy of incomplete liberalism, and the perverse exaggeration of (un)enlightened self-interest), then the noisy overwhelm the silent, because one merchant's right to pollute one's senses with his message currently overwhelms any individual's right to privacy.

Having reviewed the main theoretical frameworks that have served as a basis for business ethics, we have proposed some illustrations based on the practice of marketing about how, or what, such ethics has to say to or about marketing. We have also suggested from both **normative** and descriptive positions what the state of play is and suggested that one compromise between ethics and marketing – one morally questionable means of understanding that marketing practice is ethical – may lie in the principle of egoism. You may not entirely agree with such an interpretation; you may think such a situation is more or less ethically OK, or maybe you just want to get back to market segmentation and consumer targeting and other marketing methods . . .

We are all stakeholders in marketing ethics whether or not we are in full accord, in diametrical disagreement, or sometimes one and sometimes the other. Let us now move on to consider a range of specific issues in relation to marketing and the host of ethical problems it faces as a means of suggesting ways in which each reader may be able to problematize or license the practices and ethics of marketing.

Beyond theory

Globalization itself suggests a further tier of ethical problems for marketing. Let us consider for a moment the concept put forward by Theodore Levitt[23] that the global firm 'operates with resolute constancy . . . as if the entire world (or major regions of it) were a single entity; it sells the same things in the same way everywhere', leading to, or based on, the idea that everyone wants the same thing in a homogeneous global market. This **absolutist** position is not entirely reliable because while all the world may like music, for example, or mobile phones, the use to which such items are put will vary from country to country or market to market. A bank currently marketing itself as global and at the same time right next to you, is in fact not everywhere – just everywhere that is a developed metropolitan market.

Then again, the way in which things are marketed is also different from market to market as we discussed in the previous section. Think of the effect of climate and culture on fashion, for example, or cars, cosmetics and food. The McDonalds burger and a Coke may be examples of a basic global product, but the detailed repertory of its outlet menus in each market will have regional variation compared to one with which we are familiar. So the global world is not absolutely homogeneous, but rather highly varied. Marketing, like ethics, may have to take some consideration of context.

For example, in the context of gifts: a gift can be entirely appropriate (under strict conditions) such as an agreed commission (which may not be a gift), or it can be wholly inappropriate. The same payment of €50,000 could be a gift or a commission. It could be a bribe or inducement, coercion, blackmail, graft or just plain corruption. How do you decide what to call it when one person thinks of it as one thing and another person calls it another? To what extent is an expected tip to a waiter a truthful reflection of how well he or she worked? If you always do it, does that make it right? Or are we all complicit in keeping waiting staff underpaid because we are expected to subsidize their pay? And what is the ethical principle of a tip based on percentage? Why does a waiter who serves you a bottle of champagne get a bigger tip than one who serves you a litre of mineral water – what actions has he performed in filling glasses to justify the proportionate difference in the tip?

What about political marketing – do politicians tell the truth? Or do we all know they are lying? To what extent is the marketing of political parties, and the presentation of the news a reflection of the interests of a few, or are they as truthful, factual and objective as they make out. And what about other media and marketing? Product placement in movies – the now implausibly old-fashioned slider phone in *The Matrix*, the (un)subtle use of places, cars, clothes and a whole range of commodities – is this truthful? Is it political?

And marketing to children across a range of media – thinking of the product range of Mattel as an example – what standards of honesty, decency and truthfulness do these reflect? Is it somehow plausible that McDonalds is the world's largest single distributor of toys? How will parents wean children off 'junk' food, if the 'junk' toy is not part of the Happy Meal™?

If we wish to find that marketing can plausibly confront this range of ethical problems then it is necessary to make an accommodation because it is mainly about business. George Brenkert tells it clearly: 'Satisfactory responses to these challenges will be possible only if we understand that marketing itself is a practical value-laden activity, which falls within the moral arena.'[24]

CHAPTER REVIEW QUESTIONS

1   Marketing is more than a necessary evil. Discuss and potentially justify this assertion by detailed reference to a range of examples of marketing practice that clearly align with ethics – you may not use any reference to the needs of the market.

2   'Children are people too, and they have a big influence on their parents and other adults. It would be irresponsible of me not to target them with some advertising. If I am not doing it my competitors will.' Respond to this position from the perspective first as a parent and then as a shareholder. For what industry could such a claim be ethically justifiable?

3   An enterprising IT consultant offers you, in confidence as an employer, a list of the websites visited by each of five potential employees for the post of HR Manager. Assuming there is nothing illegal about this, would you have a look through these lists?

4   Budget airlines employ a no-seat-allocation policy as a marketing advantage for cheaper seats: would it be ethically acceptable if this is done on the basis that

passengers board much faster if they are insecure and tense about whether they will get to sit with whom or just where they want?

5 Consider the following narrative. 'The supermarket is still open: it won't close till midnight. It is brilliantly bright. Its brightness offers sanctuary from loneliness and the dark. You could spend hours of your life here, in a state of suspended insecurity, meditating on the multiplicity of things to eat. Oh dear, there is so much! So many brands in shiny boxes, all of them promising you good appetite. Every article on the shelves cries out to you, take me, take me; and the mere competition of their appeals can make you imagine yourself wanted, even loved. But beware – when you get back to your empty room, you'll find that the false flattering elf of the advertisement has eluded you; what remains is only cardboard, cellophane and food. And you have lost the heart to be hungry.'[25] What does this say about the role of the consumer, and what is the contribution of the marketing professional to such a situation?

Acknowledgements

The author gratefully acknowledges the helpful comments of Laura Hartman, Patricia Werhane and Patrick O'Sullivan on earlier versions of this chapter.

Key terms

absolutist – an apparently unvarying principle (i.e. it is always wrong to lie)

anarchic – disruptive of the status quo

a priori – based on agreed first principles (it is always wrong to steal)

consequentialist – depending on outcome rather than principle

culturally relative – a perspective based on the norms of one culture as compared to any other

deontological – duty-based

dominant social paradigm – the principal framework of knowledge by which most people operate in the world

egoism – see **individualism**

ethics of virtue – based in Aristotle's notion that virtue comes from virtue, and the virtuous man always behaves virtuously

Golden Mean – an elaborate, careful, balanced approach based on Aristotle's ideas

ideological – any position based on an idealized view of reality (hence Friedman and the market; Marx and the worker)

individualism – the ideological belief that individuals know what is right for themselves

moral distance – using language to distance one class of people from another

moral relativism – variously defined: narrowly, as limited to ethics reliant on purely cultural difference; broadly, as ethics reliant on context or other transient, subjective values

non–consequentialist – depending on a principle or rule and not depending on outcome

normative – a view of ethics or reality based on how things should be in the world, invariable implying 'ought' or 'should'

quasi – in some way or other, so-called

stakeholder – a person or persons who affect or are affected by any action

subjective – a view of ethics or reality based on individual interpretation only

universalism – where a principle applies everywhere

Notes

1 *Guerilla Marketing International*. Available online at www.gmarketing.com/ (2007) (accessed 10 June 2008).
2 P. Kotler (1999) *Kotler on Marketing*. New York: Free Press.
3 G. G. Brenkert (2008) *Marketing Ethics*. Oxford: Blackwell Publishing, p. vi.
4 Ibid.
5 See for example P. Kotler, V. Wong, J. Saunders and G. Armstrong (2005) *Principles of Marketing*. Harlow: Pearson Education, pp. 8–9.
6 N. Klein (2001) *No Logo: No space, no choice, no jobs*. London: Flamingo.
7 *TIME* Magazine, 22 January 2000, 157(3). Available online at www.time.com/time/europe/magazine/2001/0122/nologo.html (accessed 20 July 2008).
8 C. Hackley (2009) *Marketing: A critical introduction*. London: Sage Publications.
9 S. Lowe, A. Carr, M. Thomas and L. Watkins-Mathys (2005) 'The fourth hermeneutic in marketing theory', *Marketing Theory*, 5(2): 185–203, 198.
10 E. S. Herman and N. Chomsky (1994) *Manufacturing Consent: The political economy of the mass media*. London: Vintage Original.
11 V. Lebow (1955) 'Price competition in 1955', *Journal of Retailing*, Spring: 8–9.
12 P. LeLay (2004) 'Ce que nous vendons a Coca Cola . . .', La Citation du Jour, *L'Expansion*, Paris. Available online at www.lexpansion.com/economie/actualite-entreprise/patrick-le-lay-reniant-sa-definition-du-metier-de-tf1-comme-la-vente-de-temps-de-cerveau-humain-disponible_105948.html (accessed 20 June 2008), originally in E. Demey (ed.) (2004) *Les Dirigeants face au changement: Barometre 2004*. Paris: les éditions du huitième jour.
13 See note 8 above.
14 http://gastrochic.blogspot.com/ (accessed 14 July 2008).
15 The Chartered Institute of Marketing, Moor Hall, Cookham, Maidenhead, Berkshire, UK. *Professional Marketing Standards: A guide for employers* (2005). Available online at www.cim.co.uk/MediaStore/ProfMarketingStandards/ProfessionalMarketingStandards05_web.pdf (accessed 15 July 2008).
16 Although we do not claim marketing aspires to virtue as one of its dimensions, it features in the framework.
17 J. Makower (2007) 'The marketing and strategy innovation blog'. Available online at http://blog.futurelab.net/2006/11/milton_friedman_and_the_social.html (accessed 14 July 2008).
18 Brenkert, *Marketing Ethics*, p. 32.
19 J. S. Mill (1963) 'On liberty'. In J. M. Robson (ed.) *Collected Works of John Stuart Mill*. Toronto: University of Toronto Press, pp. 213–310.
20 T. Hobbes (1968) *Leviathan*. London: Penguin Classics.
21 M. Friedman (2002) *Capitalism and Freedom*. London and Chicago: The University of Chicago Press, p. 112.
22 P. Bourdieu (2002) *Outline of a Theory of Practice*. Cambridge: Cambridge University Press, p. 188.

23 T. Levitt (1983) 'The globalization of markets', *Harvard Business Review*, 61(3): 92–103, 92.
24 Brenkert, *Marketing Ethics*, p. 39.
25 C. Isherwood (2010) *A Single Man*. London: Vintage, p. 89.

17

DEEPER INTO THE CONSUMER'S MIND

Market research and ethics

Caroline Cuny

Chapter overview

Marketing specialists usually arrive near the bottom of the list in studies about professional ethics. This negative image comes from the frequent reports made by the media on illegal or morally questionable marketing processes and also because of the visibility of marketing activities. Indeed, as consumers, we are all in direct contact with marketing campaigns and therefore more exposed to their excesses.

In any decisions, marketing professionals are faced with ethical issues. Indeed, their decisions may affect product safety, advertising message, price equity, or the behaviour of sales people. Thus, the marketing function, like any other business function in companies, raises issues according to the three levels of critical thinking (see Chapter 2). The first level includes all the individuals involved in marketing in businesses, that is, the ethics of individuals dealing with strategic or operational marketing, and their relationships with other people. The second level corresponds to companies' ethics related to their customers, suppliers, and the way their marketing actions impact people and societies. The third level is particularly applicable for multinational companies doing business around the world and the ethics principles they should follow to have, for example, fair relationships with different countries, customers, suppliers. Ethical issues may arise more frequently for marketing managers than other managers from other functions since they have to work across functions and stakeholders, often external to the company, that are likely to have conflicting interests and play a role at all levels.

An ethical approach to marketing

The Chartered Institute of Marketing (CIM) defines marketing as the 'management process that identifies, anticipates and satisfies customer requirements profitably'. Thus, inside the company, the functions of marketers are to identify the needs of the customers on whom the organization depends, but also to satisfy those needs (short-term) and to anticipate them in the future (long-term retention), taking into account the resources of the organization to create value for both. As such, marketing generates the strategy that underlies sales techniques, business communication and business developments, and the process through which companies build strong customer relationships in ways that benefit the organization and its stakeholders.

We must admit that this definition of value creation for companies and their stakeholders has sometimes led marketing executives not to give enough attention to their moral obligations – except when it is too late. The idea that companies do not have to worry about moral values when they are making decisions results from a very narrow vision of our economic activity, which would suggest that managers can and must only decide according to financial criteria such as profitability. In marketing practice, decisions are never neutral and values considerations are essential to the right functioning of an organization. Indeed, most business relationships require trust. However, trust could sometimes be lacking when consumers imagine that organizations make decisions based only on financial criteria and return on investment.

For these reasons marketers are required to follow a deontological approach that requires them to investigate whether each decision is fair in itself, regardless of its consequences. This analysis is based on duties and obligations that are shared by all marketers. Ethical codes and deontological rules exist around the world for marketing professionals wishing to undertake marketing activities: these codes of ethics allow the marketing function inside companies to question and criticize decisions and to finally decide in which way to act. Thus, these codes correspond to the national norms/ethical principles that ought to govern marketing activities in general or specific marketing activities – for example, market studies and direct marketing.

Actually, many ethical issues are raised because these deontological approaches are often violated. Although marketing professionals voluntarily chose to follow these ethical rules, or those from another country or professional organization, the existence of such rules is not sufficient to prevent unethical behaviour among marketing professionals. That is the reason why an 'ethical sensitivity', that is, an awareness of their moral obligations in their decision making and of potential ethical issues their decisions may generate, has to be developed, through education for example.

On the other hand, since marketers are also consumers, the notion that there is a barrier between professional and personal lives is even less true for them. As a consequence, it should be easier for them to follow an honest attitude both in their personal and their professional lives. Thus, most marketing managers avoid morally questionable actions; for example, lying about a price reduction to conclude a sale more easily or minimizing potential risks of the use of a product in an advertisement by reference to their own conception of good and evil.

Ethical issues in marketing studies

Ethical challenges are also present for market research and studies that represent an essential part of marketing activity inside an organization. Here the potential

BOX 17.1 EXAMPLES OF NATIONAL MARKETING DEONTOLOGICAL CODES

USA

The code of ethics of the American Marketing Association stipulates that marketing professionals are required to comply with three rules of ethics:

> As Marketers, we must:
>
> (1) **Do no harm**. This means consciously avoiding harmful actions or omissions by embodying high ethical standards and adhering to all applicable laws and regulations in the choices we make.
> (2) **Foster trust in the marketing system**. This means striving for good faith and fair dealing so as to contribute toward the efficacy of the exchange process as well as avoiding deception in product design, pricing, communication, and delivery of distribution.
> (3) **Embrace ethical values**. This means building relationships and enhancing consumer confidence in the integrity of marketing by affirming these core values: honesty, responsibility, fairness, respect, transparency and citizenship.
>
> Marketers are also expected to uphold the ethical values of honesty, responsibility, fairness, respect, transparency and citizenship.
>
> Source: AMA (2010)

France

In France there is a deontological code for direct marketing professionals concerning personal-related data protection. This states that:

> direct marketing operators consider that personal related data, respect for privacy and transparency of the treatment are the basis of fair commercial practices. They will ensure strict compliance with current French or European regulations in this area, particularly as regards the declaration of collected files and the implementation of the right of access. They accept, by the present Code, to comply with a number of uses and specific rules of professional ethics, in particular with regard to consumer information. These rules concern particularly three essential aspects:
>
> 1 Fair data collection.
> 2 Relationships with customers and prospects: Right to information and Right to refusal.
> 3 Relationships with other professionals: Purpose. Sensitive data. Updates; Dealings with third parties; Opposition lists.
>
> Source: CNIL (2010)

tensions between the actions of individuals within the firms and the actions of firms within society are illustrated (Level 2 of critique). Indeed in marketing studies, ethical issues could arise for the person involved in the collection of data, in their relationship with the participants in the study, and in their relationship with their customers; and in the end even corporate reputations may suffer some consequences.

The main ethical difficulties that arise for market researchers have to do with the integrity of their studies: for example, when their clients – consciously or not – put pressure on them to interpret data in a favourable way. However, the most delicate problems are those involving participants in studies. It is normally held that respondents have a number of moral rights, including the right to be informed about the study, the right to choose to participate, the right for anonymity, the right to feel safe and the right to be treated with respect. Again, ethical codes that recognize these rights exist around the world; for example the codes of the Marketing Research Society in Britain, of the Council of American Survey Research Organizations (CASRO) in the United States and ESOMAR in France. Despite the existence of these ethical codes, some market researchers may engage in morally questionable practices and, as a consequence, participation rates to market studies decrease. In America, CASRO believes that the refusal rate is today around 35–38 per cent and rising.

It is critical to ensure marketing remains ethical because the societal duty of marketers is to live in conformity with moral rules. This duty applies equally to both personal and professional lives. In addition, marketing professionals know that ethics is a condition of success in business. Concerning the market research sector in particular, treating participants with respect will encourage them to renew the experience later. This approach is therefore a way to retain a resource that is already limited. From a broader perspective, unethical actions or behaviours often have negative consequences: bad reputation, poor company image, bad employee mood, consumer boycotts and of course legal penalties. In contrast, ethical behaviour contributes to strengthening the company image, increasing staff morale and encouraging consumers to repeat purchases.

Deeper into the consumer's minds

A firm in the market economy survives by producing goods that people are willing and able to buy. Consequently, ascertaining consumer demand is vital for a firm's future viability and even existence as a going concern. Many companies today have a customer focus, or market orientation, and to understand their market and customers, market researchers seek to use the current scientific paradigms and technologies developed by other scientific disciplines: social sciences, psychology, sociology, mathematics, economics, anthropology and, recently, neuroscience.

Neuroscience aims to develop theories and paradigms to investigate and understand how our nervous system functions. The brain, which is part of this nervous system, is perhaps the most complex structure in the world, so any new paradigm and methodology aimed at a better understanding of its functioning is seen as a holy grail. As a consequence, sciences conducting investigations associated with brain functioning – that is, all the behavioural sciences (psychology, sociology) but also the marketing–consumer behaviour field – could also see the use of these paradigms as very important, even critical to progress in their theoretical frameworks.

However, new methods of investigating permitting a better understanding of consumers' motivations and needs can also be seen as unethical as a result of a certain misunderstanding of what they really are and how they can be used. This is the case of 'neuromarketing' studies, which have been developed recently thanks to the improvement of neuroscience techniques. Indeed, these new methods allow marketers to analyse the biological activity that is the basis of consumer behaviour while consumers are experiencing the marketing activity – product consumption, purchase decision making, viewing of an advertisement, etc.

Neuromarketing

The use of paradigms and tools originating in cognitive neuroscience for the study of consumer behaviour has been growing quickly for around ten years. The increase is such that the term 'neuromarketing' has been coined to describe the use of neuroscience methods. Actually, neuromarketing is not a new scientific field but simply 'the study of explicit and implicit mental processes, and consumers behaviours, in various marketing contexts such as evaluation, decision-making, memorization or consumption, based on neuroscientific paradigms and knowledge' (Droulers and Roullet 2007, p. 11). Neuromarketing should thus contribute, like cognitive neuropsychology or sociobiology, to improving and accumulating knowledge associated with mind/brain relationships, while maintaining, at the same time, a practical purpose in business life.

Neuromarketing is today used by some companies specializing in business consultancy (and some universities in the USA) as a sales argument likely to 'make a difference'. In Europe as well, new market research institutes have recently been created that have developed tests to improve advertising effectiveness through the use of cognitive science and neuroscience.

To better understand the great interest marketing professionals have towards these methodologies, we need first to remind ourselves that consumers' decision making can be influenced by content that they are not necessarily aware of. This has been abundantly demonstrated in various research findings (e.g. Fazio and Olson 2003; Lee 2002). In this area, one very famous (but already old) experiment by Nisbett and Wilson (1977) can help illustrate this important point. The participants were consumers in a supermarket, who were asked to choose 'the best pair of nylon tights' among a series. The respondents were unaware that the nylon tights were actually all identical, so most of them selected the last presented pair. However, the surprising results of this study did not come from the choices made by the participants but from the way they justified their choices: in fact, many of them gave a reasoned justification retrospectively, explaining that the chosen pair was softer, or appeared to be stronger. Nisbett and Wilson concluded that the reports provided by the subjects regarding their own decisions were therefore only a very rough measure of the real motivations underlying those decisions. We would not, from this perspective, necessarily have easy access to our own mental states; instead of such privileged access, we would act like any external observer trying to understand our motivations: by observing our own behaviour and by building the most rational explanation.

Thus, since participants in market studies do not always want to reveal or are not always aware of all of their thoughts, to access their mental states without having to ask them in an explicit and declarative way constitutes great progress. This reinforces the interest in neuromarketing where the use of measurements coming from cognitive psychology and neuroscience paradigms allows the researchers to collect data about consumers' behaviour without having to go through introspection.

Ethical issues in neuromarketing: knowing what is measured in neuromarketing studies

It is important to consider two linked questions when considering the ethical issues around neuromarketing. Why are neurological tools so critical to understanding human behaviour? Why do marketing professionals want to use such tools?

If man wants to know who he is, he needs to understand his brain. What was earlier studied by philosophers can nowadays be studied by neuroscientists. The study of the brain is replacing speculations and hypotheses made by philosophers on feelings, thinking, human actions or consciousness. This is why neuroscientific tools are seen as a great opportunity for marketing professionals to better understand our choices, preferences or evaluations as consumers. However, this is not because our minds and bodies are no longer seen as distinct; there remains nowhere in the brain that can be considered a separate and independent location that could be labelled the 'mind'. Rather, knowing the biological functioning of the brain, that is, the basis of behaviour, is a step towards knowing the meaning of behaviour. Indeed, behaviours and the meta-knowledge we have got about these behaviours (i.e. our knowledge of our mental processes) are produced by a great complexity of brain processes, but the personal meanings, the subjectivity we feel during these mental processes, cannot be captured by any of the neuroscientific tools. We do not know precisely why we feel a particular way about an action.

Nevertheless, in marketing, the use of these advances in new technology raises ethical issues at all three levels of the critical model developed in Chapter 2; these cannot be solved by a simple code defining right and wrong marketing behaviours (Level 1), or by a trustworthy attitude of the market researcher (Level 2), and in effect they raise questions of the universal values pertaining to the study of human beings and their rights (Level 3). Could advances in technology, such as those in neuroimagery, incite marketers to consider improving consumers as individuals, cultivating ethical behaviour or at least a certain vigilance as to moral values; or could they act as a catalyst for their shameful instincts?

Neurobiology is currently the only discipline to study in a strictly scientific, as opposed to speculative philosophical, way the basics of human behaviour, and this makes it more exciting and applicable than the findings of philosophy for marketers! - especially when it comes to helping the study of what consumers are not aware of, that is, what they do not know themselves. As we saw in the example of Nisbett and Wilson's (1977) study, our meta-cognition is actually very limited in the sense that we have restricted access to our knowledge. Consumer research has also demonstrated that fact, and new methodologies, called implicit tests, aiming to measure consumer behaviour without directly asking consumers have started to be developed (Rivière *et al.* n.d.).

What some consumer associations are afraid of could be called 'brain reading'. Actually, what is really feared is the potential for mental manipulation by marketing professionals thanks to neuroscientific tools, such as functional magnetic resonance imaging (fMRI). Although these fears could be legitimate for many uninformed consumers, one must say that these are probably unfounded fears: first, neuro-marketing typically needs to use functional imaging techniques and for these reasons it is using observations, interviewing, statistics or experiments. The goals of all these marketing studies thus remain the same. Second, the 'buy button' does not exist in the brain: a purchase decision involves a very complex process of cognitive and affective activations (still not elucidated), that is made up by certain personal and individual physiology, culture, history or experience. Third, neuromarketing devices do not allow manipulation of people's purchase decisions since it is a record-ing and not a stimulating technique. Finally, neuromarketing is becoming an academic scientific discipline per se and like any other behavioural science, it aims to advance our understanding of the underlying processes of human behaviour.

In addition to the ethical issues resulting from the use of neuromarketing tools for market research, ethical issues may also arise from the use in itself of these technological tools. Indeed, if, from a medical perspective, the balance of risks/benefits have to be monitored, the use of neuroscientific tools for marketing research purposes should tend to zero risk. In this context several potential risks have been in principle identified. Risks could be linked to the presence of a magnetic field or to certain radio frequencies, or even to the medical environment, for example submitting to an fMRI scan can reveal psychological pathologies, such as phobia. However, current data from the medical literature conclude that no such problems have yet been identified (Droulers and Roullet 2007). Moreover, in all countries where fMRI is available for research purposes, a detailed presentation of the study design and aims must go through an ethical committee whose objective is to check that the protocol is safe and that there is a real scientific, and not commercial, purpose.

Neuromarketing contributions to the marketing field

Given the potential negative perceptions of consumers and potential participants in marketing studies, it is worth asking what the differences are between neuro-marketing and classical marketing studies and whether neuromarketing is indeed useful.

Neuromarketing paradigms allow marketing research studies to be more rigorous and applied to topical research questions. Indeed, they bring new theoretical frameworks to marketing, namely, explicative and predictive models that are anchored in an evolutionist, empirical and refutable approach. Neuroscientific techniques partly solve the crucial problem of objective measurement found in the marketing discipline since its inception (Derbaix and Poncin 2005). In traditional marketing research a number of biases have been identified. These biases include declarative (explicit) measurement bias (the consumer must engage in introspection to express the content of his meta-knowledge), rationalization cognitive bias (some cognitions, because they cannot be accurately semantically translated, are distorted), social conformism bias (some individuals wish to feel a sense of social belonging and do not want to display some attitudes that differ from the standards of their community of reference), verbalization bias (some perceptual cognitions cannot be well described through language, the description of the percept is simplified), non-response bias (a consumer may refuse to answer a question or alter the truth of his answer), attribution bias (according to one's cognitive style, locus of control for example, the cause of events involving the individual will be attributed to endogenous or exogenous phenomena), bias associated with a very strong belief (patterns of causality guide the interpretation of an event), or contextual bias (some contextual element can affect the perceptual and cognitive processing of its central element).

Thus, the use of neuroscientific tools could improve the theoretical explanations framing our knowledge about human (thus consumer) behaviour and allow us to better monitor ethical issues coming from less scientific methodologies. As marketing is still evolving as a discipline, integrating new paradigms from other scientific disciplines could be seen as progress and perhaps should not be feared, provided the deontological approaches discussed above are followed by market researchers using such new paradigms.

Main neuromarketing tools

Neuromarketing tools use different methodologies that were developed in the field of cognitive neuroscience. Since the early 1990s their development both from the technical and the methodology sides has expanded, and one has to admit that they have literally revolutionized the 'quest' to understand the brain's functioning in real time, permitting researchers to 'see the brain think'. Two methodologies are usually distinguished: anatomical and functional methods. The first is designed to highlight brain structures and anything that might come and disrupt them (tumours, bleeding, blood clots or other deformities present at birth). Functional methods aim at measuring the activity of certain brain regions during certain tasks. Here we focus on the latter of these methods.

Whatever the tool used to investigate functional brain activity, they are all based on the principle that a behavioural activity may be associated with an activity of a group of neurons in a certain area (or region) of the central nervous system (for a deeper understanding of the neuroimaging techniques, see Cabeza and Kingstone 2006). Thus, based on this principle, the assumption is made that each human being has a set of common rules of functioning and behaving. However, the goal of neuroscientific protocols is not to ignore the individuality of each person, but to find the common rules corresponding to a particular context. For example, by investigating the different brain activations associated with the choice of a German versus a Japanese car, marketers aim at analysing what makes a French consumer prefer a German car. This study could be replicated in China among Chinese consumers, with the same aims, but different subjects: same protocols, but different processes or evaluations that lead to the same or different choices. As with any science, the way marketing solves the ethical issue of respecting the uniqueness of an individual participant while reporting the findings of a study is to use statistics, seeking to avoid generalizations when the main factors of explanations are not controlled.

However, apart from the statistics, to better understand the issues raised by neuromarketing it is important to consider the main tools used in market studies.

A Positron Emission Tomograph, also called a PET scan, was the first functional brain-imaging technique to be born and developed in the middle of the 1970s. The physiological phenomenon underlying PET (like fMRI) is based on the fact that cognitive functions are locally changing cerebral blood flows. Indeed, when a group of neurons becomes more active, local vasodilatation of cerebral blood capillaries occurs automatically, to bring more blood and therefore more oxygen to the most active regions.

During a PET scan, the participant must have a solution containing a radioactive element injected into the blood system – water or radioactive glucose for example. As a result of the vasodilatation and the presence of a radioactive element in the blood, a greater radioactivity will be therefore issued and recorded in the most active brain areas.

One should note that PET has been less and less used for two main reasons. First, because of the injection of a radioactive element into the participant – this is an intrusive method – and second, because of the rapid development of another technique – fMRI (see below). Indeed, images produced by PET do not compete with those of fMRI in terms of resolution, and to our knowledge, very few neuromarketing studies used PET in the investigation of consumer behaviour.

The alternative is fMRI, which also records the activity of different brain regions. This technique is based on the measuring of the quantity of certain elements present in the brain and is non-invasive. The method is commonly used in neuroscience to get a detailed picture of the brain.

In its simplest aspect, MRI allows us to observe the number of hydrogen atoms that make up the brain. When the hydrogen atom is affected by a magnetic field, its nucleus (composed of a single proton) may exhibit two forms: a high-energy form and a low-energy form. The fMRI aims to switch the protons from one form to the other.

To do so, protons must get some energy, which is realized by letting an electromagnetic wave go through the participant's head, situated between the two poles of a powerful magnet. When the magnetic signal is stopped, protons return to their low-energy form by emitting a typical radio signal. The signals emitted by the protons are collected by a radio receptor: the stronger the signal, the more numerous the hydrogen atoms in the brain region being studied. This procedure permits the observation of the amount of hydrogen atoms present at any time in a certain area of the brain. The same physical phenomenon underlying fMRI allows us to visualize brain activity while the scanned person performs a given task.

In fMRI studies, several methods can be used with the same principle but recording the radio signal of different molecules. In most cases (and neuromarketing follows this trend), fMRI records the radio signals emitted by the haemoglobin molecule. Haemoglobin has two slightly different magnetic signatures depending on whether it contains more or less oxygen (oxyhaemoglobin or deoxyhaemoglobin). The most commonly used method is intended to detect local changes in deoxyhaemoglobin concentration (method BOLD – Blood Oxygen Level Dependant). One should note that the increase in cerebral blood flow as a result of a greater activity in some areas of the brain is always greater than the oxygen demand in this area. Accordingly, it is the decrease in the concentration rate of deoxyhaemoglobin (diluted in a larger volume of oxygenated blood) in the brain area that fMRI will record as an increased activity in that area. Then, by subtracting the activation intensity shown in the fMRI image from another image recorded before the target test, the difference in activity across areas can be observed with the most irrigated, the most active areas, showing up.

The fMRI technique has been used very often in psychology to study human behaviour in general and more recently tested to investigate consumer behaviour in marketing research. Usually, when the media are reporting neuromarketing studies, they are referring to fMRI studies.

Another alternative is the electroencephalograph (EEG), a device able to record the electrical activity of the cerebral cortex. The collected data are called an electroencephalogram. Electroencephalography (EEG) permits the amplification of electrical activity generated by neurons. Indeed, several cognitive and motor functions produce characteristic neural activity patterns that cause a particular (meaningful) signature on electroencephalograms. EEG therefore records continuously global brain neural activity. The method is simple, painless and non-invasive. Cortical electrical activity is recorded using electrodes put on the respondent's scalp with a conductive gel for fixation and a lower electrical resistance. The electrodes are distributed regularly on the scalp of the individual and connected to amplifiers and recording consoles.

Essentially, EEG measures electrical emissions occurring during synaptic activation of the dendrites of many neurons from the cerebral cortex located right under the skull (approximately 80 per cent of the total mass of the brain [Bear *et al.* 2007]). The contribution to the final signal from each separate neuron is extremely low, but synchronization of neurons (i.e. simultaneous activity) occurring during the completion of a task allows the addition of weak signals from each neuron and generates a signal that is strong enough to be detected by electrodes on the surface of the skull. Computers then monitor brain activity captured by several dozens of electrodes at different locations on the scalp. As a result of its high temporal resolution, EEG is often used when it comes to understanding what series of processes are involved in the realization of a given behaviour. The EEG approach has the advantage of allowing a match between behaviour and a pattern of electrical activity (see cases below).

A better understanding of the detail of these neuromarketing techniques allows us to consider the ethical issues more closely. First, in using neuroscience tools, market researchers, like in any marketing study, are susceptible to undermining the consumer's right to privacy (Level 1), that is, the individual's right to control information about oneself. Neuroscientific tools may well lead to the collection of data that consumers may not know that researchers have in their possession (such as unconscious mental processes) or may not wish to share with a third person. However, these issues are also true for other methodologies employed by marketers that collect consumers' data through the use of information and technologies, for example the recording of navigation activities, number of mouse clicks, visited websites, etc. Informed consent for participation, assurance of data privacy and the original check by an ethical committee are all aimed at guaranteeing the participant's right to privacy (and are mandatory to conducting neuromarketing studies in academic settings).

Second, the use of the results coming from neuromarketing studies by marketers remain questionable (Level 2), even if an informed consent and the fundamental rights of individuals have been managed. How to be sure that there is a balance between the value creation for customers and the value creation for the organization and stakeholders? Should they be equivalent? Could neuromarketing be used to increase the memorization of an advertisement for unhealthy products?

Moreover, concerning the data collected by neuroscientific tools, debates exist in the scientific community about the interpretation of activation images (what exactly the BOLD signal means, or what are the best mathematical algorithms to compute the results). In relation to fMRI, most researchers recognize that the BOLD signal is well correlated to neuronal activity: an increase of signal corresponds to higher neuronal activity. However, a statistical mapping with a probability colour scale is not an end in itself. Just as a map is not equal to the land it represents, statistical mapping is neither equal to the activation of a neural network, nor to the underlying cognitive processes. The other issue is the one already discussed in an earlier section about the difference between knowledge functions performed by some brain structures and the purely phenomenological content, 'housed' by these functions. Detection of the activity of these areas gives us only partial information about what the participant has memorized, for example something visual because the results showed an activation of the visual brain areas, but the exact stimulus will not be known. This is also the case for higher cognitive processes – subjectivity or affective processes need to be inferred from a cerebral activity. The development of neuroscientific tools and their use in real life (or close to real life) phenomena, for example in business disciplines, may help to bring biological and behavioural phenomena closer. However, we still face a certain gap since our behaviours are the result of the contextualized expression of this neuronal activity, that is, behaviours result from the confrontation of the expression of the neurons and the impact of environmental factors.

Conclusion

Neuroscientific progress and advances could renew our understanding of the consumer mind and contribute to fruitful research, both for the verification of current marketing theoretical frameworks and for an extension of the discipline to other fields of study.

The concept of neuroethics has been conceptualized by Farah (2002) to frame three main domains of application: improvement in pharmaceutical treatments, use of imagery techniques in legal decisions and use of imagery techniques in marketing. According to us, the scientific practice of neuroscience in the marketing field should help to maintain and defend ethical and morally acceptable study frameworks and applications, respecting consumer rights, in particular consumer autonomy and freedom. The practice can also enrich the marketing professional's reflections, theoretical explanations and academic knowledge, and fertilize exchanges with other disciplines of the behavioural sciences.

CASES OF NEUROMARKETING RESEARCH AND THEIR ETHICAL CONSEQUENCES

Cognitive and social psychology research findings are not necessarily applicable to marketing (Shapiro and Krishnan 2001), particularly since relevant stimuli are often more complex (e.g. movies instead of static stimuli). Moreover, since the consumer, when purchasing or consuming a product, is rarely in direct contact with the advertisements suggesting the benefits of this product, there is no doubt that an important part of the total communication budget is at least partly used to improve consumers' memorization about product attributes and brands after having been exposed to an advertisement. Thus, one of the most researched areas in the field of advertising effectiveness remains memory measurement.

It is likely neuroimaging could help predict the long-term advertising memorization level. Rossiter and Silberstein (2001) conducted the first study to demonstrate the utility of neuroscientific paradigms and tools to predict the successful memorization of an advertisement. They used the method of evoked potentials (addition of EEG) and recorded the electrical activity of the right and left frontal lobes while participants were watching television programmes containing two advertising spots. The participants of the study were 35 right-handed women, chosen because they were mainly responsible for their home purchases. They undertook two sessions of tests separated by seven days and were informed that the second session was to answer questions about the first.

In the first phase of the study, participants watched an 18-minute television programme containing several advertising breaks (twelve ads in total). The first and the twelfth advertisements appeared respectively before the beginning and after the end of the programme; they were not analysed later on. Ads 2–6 and 7–11 were grouped in two advertising breaks of five spots each and were presented respectively 4 and 10 minutes after the start of the programme, at habitual times for advertising breaks. The television commercials were all new to the participants, although displaying brands that were known by them. Indeed, they were advertisements aired only on USA television channels, while the study took place in Australia with Australian consumers.

While the participants were watching the TV programme and advertisements, their electrical brain activity for both frontal hemispheres were recorded. A helmet with multiple electrodes was put on the scalp of the participants (EEG). This helmet also had a transparent slot allowing the eyes to receive a white flash in order to create and therefore collect an electrical brain activity reference (base level). The authors therefore compared this base response to the electrical activity during the TV ads: the measured electrical brain activity was the response latency of '*steady-state visual evoked potentials*' against the reference response following the white flash. The latency of these steady-state visual evoked potentials indicates the speed of reaction of the brain to other incoming stimuli.

In the second phase, the same participants were asked to perform a recognition task seven days later; 'recognition' meaning they had already been presented with the ad during the first phase, on ads from phase one or the new ads. A total of forty images were extracted from ten ads (advertisements 1 and 12 were not included). These images corresponded to the twenty fastest electrical responses and the twenty slowest responses obtained from the first phase by measuring the steady-state visual evoked potentials. Another additional constraint was chosen for the selection of images: they did not contain any information about the advertised brand, which would have made the recognition task too easy. Forty pictures from other USA ads, not known to the participants, were used as distractors. The eighty pictures were presented for five seconds each, with an inter-stimulus interval of one second.

The results showed a significant correlation between the maxima of electrical activity in the left frontal lobe associated with ads and the recognition score of these same ads. In other words, the pattern of electrical activity recorded during advertisement watching allowed the researchers to predict which images from the commercials were stored in long-term memory, in this case for seven days.

At a managerial marketing level, researchers stressed the fully operational character of this method, which permitted predictions about which advertising scenes would be retained best without having to explicitly ask participants. However, the link between this long-term memorization and purchasing behaviour, that is, the measurement of the influence of advertising on the final decision to purchase, remains unexplored.

A later study by Knutson *et al.* (2007) was the first to be undertaken involving a real purchase decision by the participants. The objective of the study was twofold: on the one hand, the aim was to identify the neural correlates of the preferences expressed by participants about products they could buy and of the processes involved in the assessment of the value of the product; on the other hand, the aim was to determine whether the activity in each of these two circuits is actually predictive for purchase behaviour. To explore these questions, Knutson *et al.* used the fMRI method to view participants' cerebral cortex activity while they performed a task called 'SHOP' ('Save Holdings or Purchase') in which they could buy products.

During each step of the 'SHOP' task, participants (1) were presented with a product by being showed either a picture of the product or its brand – attributes that are usually present in advertising, (2) were presented with the price of the product, (3) decide or not to purchase the product by clicking on 'yes' or 'no'. These two buttons representing the decision to purchase were located to the right or left of the computer screen and this location was randomized among participants in order not to create expectations.

Twenty-six persons participated in the study. They were paid $20 an hour and an additional $20 were granted them in order to buy the products presented during the two 'SHOP' sessions. The real prices of the products ranged from eight to $80, but the price displayed to the participants was lowered by 75 per cent. This price decrease achieved a 30 per cent purchase rate among the participants, allowing statistical analysis of the data collected in fMRI.

Participants were informed about the task to carry out before going into the fMRI scanner. To ensure a possible generalization of the results, subjects participated in two 'SHOP' sessions separated by less than two weeks. During each session, participants could choose to buy forty different products, allowing a check in the consistency of their choices. Eighty products were used in total. Half of the participants could choose to purchase products among a group of forty products during the first session, and then another group of forty products in the second; the other half of the participants did the opposite. The order of appearance of the products was pseudo-randomized (to avoid the effects of sequence) and repeated, so that each task lasted 9 minutes 20 seconds.

To motivate the participants, they could, at the end of the experiment, choose either to receive their purchased products or leave with the $20 that had been given to them at the beginning of the experiment.

The results indicated (1) that the activity of the accumbens nucleus, a region of the limbic system associated with the anticipation of pleasure feeling, correlated with the decision to purchase, (2) that the activity of the insula, associated with the anticipation of negative feelings such as pain, anger, fear and disgust, correlated with the presentation of excessive pricing for the product, (3) that the activity of the medial prefrontal cortex, involved in the integration of anticipated gains and losses, correlated with the presentation of reduced prices. In comparison with subjective data collected at the end of the experiment – verbal reports regarding the preferences of the participants and the price – the fMRI data were a better predictor of the real final purchase decision.

CLASS QUESTIONS

The two preceding illustrations of the use of neuroscientific tools to investigate consumer behaviour demonstrate that it seems possible to predict with some accuracy and efficiency the influence of advertising on memorization, and also to differentiate between effective and ineffective advertisements, and ultimately to predict purchase decision making associated with the advertised brand.

These two cases raise ethical issues and questions that could include the following:

1   How to address the issue of the consumer's right to privacy?
2   Is it fair for consumers to improve the impact of advertisements on their memory? Is it fair for organizations and stakeholders to have these data?
3   What are the issues raised by the interpretation of Knutson *et al.*'s findings? And by their use?
4   What could be the impact on our societies if advertising is more effective on sales? What are the ethical consequences of more effective marketing?

Further reading

Ioannides, A. A., Liu, L., Theofilou, D., Dammers, J., Burne, T., Ambler, T. and Rose, S. (2000) 'Real time processing of affective and cognitive stimuli in the human brain extracted from MEG signals', *Brain Topography*, (13) 1: 11–19.

References

AMA (2010) 'Statements of ethics'. Available online at www.marketingpower.com/AboutAMA/Pages/Statement%20of%20Ethics.aspx (accessed 28 August 2010).

Bear, M. F., Connors, B. W. and Paradiso, M. A. (2007) *Neuroscience: Exploring the brain*, 3rd edn. Philadelphia, PA: Lippincott Williams and Wilkins Publishers.

Cabeza, R. and Kingstone, A. (2006) *Handbook of Functional Neuroimaging of Cognition*. Boston, MA: MIT Press.

CNIL (2010) Commission Nationale Informatique et Liberté. Available online at www.cnil.fr/dossiers/conso-pub-spam/fiches-pratiques/article/codes-de-deontologie/ (accessed 28 August 2010).

Derbaix, C. and Poncin, I. (2005) 'Measuring affective reactions in marketing: An assessment of the main tools', *Recherche et Applications en Marketing*, (20)2: 55–75.

Droulers, O. and Roullet, B. (2007) 'Emergence of the neuromarketing', *Decisions Marketing*, 46: 9–22.

Farah, M. J. (2002) 'Emerging ethical issues in neuroscience', *Nature Neuroscience*, (5)11: 1123–1129.

Fazio, R. H. and Olson, M. A. (2003) 'Implicit measures in social cognition research: Their meaning and use', *Annual Review of Psychology*, (54): 297–327.

Knutson, B., Rick, S., Wimmer, G. E., Prelec, D. and Loewenstein, G. (2007) 'Neural predictors of purchases', *Neuron* (53): 147–156.

Lee, A. I. (2002) 'Effects of implicit memory on memory-based versus stimulus-based brand choice', *Journal of Marketing Research*, (39): 440–454.

Nisbett, R. E. and Wilson, T. D. (1977) 'Telling more than we can do: Verbal reports on mental processes', *Psychological Review*, (84): 231–259.

Rivière, P., Cuny, C., Allain, G. and Vereijkel, C. (n.d.) 'Digging deeper: Using implicit tests to define consumers' semantic network for the immunity concept', forthcoming.

Rossiter, J. R. and Silberstein, R. B. (2001) 'Brain-imaging detection of visual scene encoding in long-term memory for TV-commercials', *Journal of Advertising Research*, (41): 13–21.

Shapiro, S. and Krishnan, S. H. (2001) 'Memory-based measures for assessing advertising effects: A comparison of explicit and implicit memory effects', *Journal of Advertising*, (30): 1–14.

18

SOCIAL AND SOCIETAL MARKETING

Applications for public policy makers and companies

Carolina O. C. Werle

Chapter overview

The main assumption underlying this chapter is that marketing can give an important contribution to business ethics in general at all levels of critique. Marketers are often criticized in discussions about business ethics. Common critiques are that they manipulate consumers to buy things that they do not need, creating desire for frivolous products. The discussion about the dark side of traditional marketing techniques has been dealt with in other chapters; here we will focus, however, on how to use traditional marketing knowledge to promote social issues that may contribute to company social responsibility and to business ethics in general.

Societal marketing actions and social marketing campaigns are applications of marketing techniques in pursuit of a social objective. On one side, companies perform societal marketing actions to enhance their image in front of multiple stakeholders: employees, consumers and society as a whole. Communicating about corporate contributions to sustainable development or social causes characterizes the most basic level of critique in business ethics (Level 1) and it is considered, from a marketing perspective, as an efficient way to reinforce brand image and to enhance attitudes towards the cause and the brand among consumers. On the other side, public policy makers and associations develop social marketing campaigns aiming at changing consumers' negative behaviours such as smoking or drinking alcohol and/or promoting the adoption of positive behaviours, such as using seat belts or getting a mammography to prevent breast cancer. These campaigns include a moral appraisal of the role of some companies (i.e. tobacco and alcohol producers) in relation to the communities in which they operate, and illustrate therefore another level of critique in business ethics (Level 2).

In the context of business ethics, what is the role of marketing? Can we sell brotherhood in the same manner we sell soap? This question, raised by Wiebe in 1952, started the academic discussion at the basis of the definition of *social marketing* (Kotler and Zaltman 1971), or the application of marketing techniques to the promotion of social ideas. In the first part of this chapter we will define this concept and present some interesting applications in public policy. Another important social issue in marketing refers to the societal engagements that companies assume and communicate about. Corporate *societal marketing* is an important practice nowadays and benefits both the social causes and the image of the company. In the second part of this chapter societal marketing is defined, and a review of research in this field is presented and illustrated with practical examples.

Social marketing

Social marketing consists in 'the application of commercial marketing techniques to the analysis, planning, execution, and evaluation of programs designed to influence voluntary behaviour of target audiences in order to improve their personal welfare and that of their society' (Andreasen 1995, p. 7). The idea is to apply the marketing techniques normally used to sell a product or a service to the promotion of a social idea. This social idea could be to have people reduce their speed on the roads or campaigns to disseminate the use of contraceptive methods. While commercial marketing aims at influencing consumption behaviour with the ultimate objective of selling a product, social marketing deals with influencing behaviour towards increased welfare. It characterizes therefore an approach to business ethics that takes into consideration the moral responsibility of a company in relation to the wider community. The bottom line of social marketing is to change behaviour and not only attitudes or beliefs (Andreasen 1995). Therefore, social marketing enhances the 'potential for marketing to work positively for the good of society beyond merely "delivering a better standard of living"' (Andreasen 1994, p. 109).

Initial research in social marketing investigated the characteristics of effective prevention campaigns. The basis for the conception of prevention campaigns are models originally created in the health context, such as the Health Belief Model (Rosenstock 1974) or the Protection Motivation Theory (Rogers 1975; 1976). Research demonstrates that the determinants of the adoption of preventive behaviours depend on the target behaviour that is analysed and on the characteristics of the target population. For example, in the case of anti-smoking campaigns targeting adolescents in the United States, the most important feature to reduce smoking intentions is highlighting social risks associated with smoking (Pechmann *et al.* 2003). On the other hand, recent research on the effect of warnings inserted on cigarette packs on the smoking intentions of French consumers demonstrates that the most effective themes are health warnings and social messages (Gallopel-Morvan *et al.* 2009). In the case of obesity, prevention campaigns targeting low-income adolescents in France using social risks are also more effective but health risks framed in a negative way have positive effects too (Werle *et al.* 2010). These studies demonstrate that the kind of feature that needs to be highlighted in social marketing campaigns depends on the characteristics of the target population.

The main objective of social marketing efforts is to benefit target individuals and not the marketer. The aim of a social marketing campaign is to obtain behavioural change and promote welfare among the community in general. Promoting welfare is a major concern for public policy makers and non-profit organizations. But social welfare is not only a matter for public policy makers; today, companies also need to take into account the social and environmental impact of their activity. They are therefore interested in promoting social ideas to further justify their role in the society in a context of increasing unemployment, decreasing demand and financial crisis (Thierry 2005). However, the actions performed by companies with the objective of promoting a social idea are always directly or indirectly connected with an objective of profit. They characterize a basic level of business ethics that describes the ethical principles that companies follow (Level 1). Such actions influence the company's image and ultimately its consumers' perceptions. In such efforts social change is a secondary objective from the company's standpoint (Rangun and Karim 1991). Companies' efforts to promote social change characterize what is defined in the literature as societal marketing, cause-related marketing or socially responsible marketing.

Societal marketing, cause-related marketing and socially responsible marketing

In 1983 American Express launched a marketing action aimed at increasing the use of its cards and recruiting new consumers. During a three-month period, every time a consumer used his or her credit card, American Express donated one penny to the restoration of the Statue of Liberty. And every time a new consumer signed for a new card, one dollar was donated for the same cause. During the period, $1.7 million were donated to the Statue of Liberty because the card usage increased 27 per cent and new applications increased by 45 per cent (Cone study 2008). This is the first documented example of cause-related marketing. More recently, Yoplait, a French yogurt brand, launched the campaign 'save lids to save lives'. The brand encourages people to collect the lids of yogurts and send them back to the company. For each lid received, Yoplait donates 10 cents to a Breast Cancer Foundation. Thanks to this action, Yoplait donated $25 million to the foundation over the past 12 years (Yoplait.com) which represents 250 million products sold in this operation!

Societal marketing, cause-related marketing or socially responsible marketing are terms used to describe the integration of societal considerations in the development and application of marketing strategies (El-Ansary 1974). *Cause-related marketing* (CRM) was defined as 'the process of formulating and implementing marketing activities that are characterized by an offer from the firm to contribute a specified amount to a designated cause when customers engage in revenue-providing exchanges that satisfy organizational and individual objectives' (Varadarajan and Menon 1988, p. 60). Cause-related marketing is an increasingly popular activity that businesses are using to signal their corporate social responsibility (Brown and Dacin 1997). According to Drumwright and Murphy (2001, p. 164) *corporate societal marketing* 'encompasses marketing initiatives that have at least one non-economic objective related to social welfare and use the resources of the company and/or one of its partners'. The common point between these two terms is that the company integrates social concerns in its marketing strategy with the objective of achieving marketing objectives (e.g. brand sales) (Barone *et al.* 2000). The term *societal marketing* is broader than cause-related marketing: it includes actions that are not directly related to marketing objectives, such as philanthropy or charitable donations performed independently of the firm's marketing strategy, even though these actions contribute to the brand image and may indirectly impact direct measures of the achievement of marketing objectives. In this chapter we will use the term 'societal marketing' to refer to all the firm's actions that aim at increasing societal welfare. From a business ethics standpoint, societal marketing actions characterize the most basic level of critique in which companies simply describe and communicate about the ethical principles that guide their behaviour.

Societal marketing actions are developed by the marketing department of companies, sometimes in relationship with a non-profit organization, and they highlight the societal engagement of the company. There are basically two kinds of societal marketing actions: (1) the promotion of products or services using a social, humanitarian or ecological cause (Thiery 2005) and (2) the sponsorship of a cause independently of any product strategy. The former often involves tying the sale of a product to the promotion of a cause through the donation of a value linked to the purchase of the product. The latter is a more long-term strategic marketing action, also designed as advocacy advertising (Menon and Kahn 2003), where the benefit to the company is less concrete.

Companies can sell ecological products (produced in conditions that respect the environment and/or using ecological components), ethical products (produced in acceptable social conditions), fair-trade products (produced in developing countries, helping local populations to live in decent conditions), or products associated with a cause (a part of the revenues is donated to a humanitarian, social or ecological cause) (Thiery 2005, p. 63). The amount of money donated to the cause is associated with and sometimes contingent to the product sales. The ice cream brand 'Ben and Jerry's' is one symbol of this 'responsible marketing'. The firm devotes 7.5 per cent of its benefits to the support of societal causes through its foundation. The brand also makes its products with ingredients that come from fair trade and with recyclable materials, and it communicates about that. The firm claims that it does 'value-led business', which means that economic profit is not its exclusive consideration. They also defend causes and values through marketing, management and communication (benjerry.fr).

Another societal marketing strategy is the institutional sponsorship of a cause disconnected from any product strategy. To sponsor a cause, a firm can either make its contribution through a non-profit organization or directly, creating its own foundation or association. Normally, this kind of action is part of the institutional marketing strategy and the objectives are to express the company's values, reinforce employee engagement, and give a contribution to the society. The French automobile brand Renault is involved in a lot of programmes that concern for example the development of citizenship in South Africa ('Valued Citizens'), the education of women ('Women for Education') and humanitarian actions through the Renault Retail Group Foundation. In the same way, Danone developed 'Danone Communities' in order to establish humanitarian missions in poor countries. The company administration considers that these actions are not an expensive investment in brand image and can influence the sales indirectly by motivating employees and making them proud of working at Danone (Le Nouvel Observateur 2009).

Motivations to invest in societal marketing

Societal marketing actions aim at benefiting the social cause by raising awareness and/or funds, and increasing stakeholders' perceptions of the sponsor company (Brown and Dacin 1997). The objectives of firms when doing societal marketing can be diverse and vary from gaining national visibility, enhancing corporate image, thwarting negative publicity, pacifying customer groups, generating incremental sales, promoting repeat purchases, promoting multiple unit purchases, promoting more varied usage, increasing brand awareness, increasing brand recognition, enhancing brand image, reinforcing brand image, broadening customer base, reaching new market segments and geographic markets, and increasing the level of merchandising activity at the retail level for the brand (Varadarajan and Menon 1988, p. 60). There is empirical evidence both from consumer research and academia indicating the positive effects of societal marketing.

According to recent consumer research on consumers' reaction to CRM, 85 per cent of American consumers find it is acceptable for companies to involve a cause in their marketing, compared to 66 per cent in 1993 (Cone study 2008); 79 per cent would be likely to switch from one brand to another brand, if the other brand is associated with a good cause (compared to 66 per cent in 1993); and 38 per cent have bought a product associated with a cause in the last twelve months compared to 20 per cent in 1993. These results indicate that people are more socially conscious when seeking for products, but also that companies are communicating more about their societal engagements.

In France, 44 per cent of consumers take into account the societal actions of the companies (such as not using child labour, respecting employees' working conditions or not polluting the environment) when buying a product (Delpal and Hatchuel 2007). This percentage has increased six points in comparison to 2002. Moreover, 61 per cent of them would accept paying 5 per cent more for a product equal in quality when societal engagements are respected by the company; and 21 per cent have bought a product from a company that respects societal engagements in the last twelve months. Even if the concerns about societal actions is increasing,

French consumers are more cynical about company motives than Americans; 79 per cent of French consumers think that companies use ethical and citizenship arguments mainly for commercial reasons, which could constitute a brake for the evolution of societal consumption.

The general perception of societal marketing actions is positive, but there are potential negative consequences associated with this kind of practice. Vadarajan and Menon (1988, p. 69) highlight the risks of societal marketing, such as to incur 'negative publicity and charges of exploitation of causes'. Some consumers hold negative attitudes towards the firms engaging in societal marketing, such as scepticism about the implementation and cynicism about the motives (e.g. the main motivation being commercial reasons instead of altruistic reasons – Webb and Mohr 1998). The question about the motives behind these actions is important because it is directly linked with the potential negative consequences of this kind of strategy.

In some cases the company is perceived not to be legitimate in communicating about the cause: consider, for example, when Coca-Cola presents the company's efforts to prevent obesity or when Mars (the chocolate bar manufacturer) develops a campaign to promote exercising. Consumers may question the legitimacy of these actions, since neither Coca-Cola nor Mars seem to be truly concerned with the issue of obesity because of the products they sell. In this case a moral appraisal of the role of the company in relation to society reveals an ethical contradiction: these companies sell products that have negative outcomes for society and they try to reinforce their image by investing in societal marketing actions that counter these effects. In accordance with Level 2 critique in business ethics, societal marketing actions may negatively affect the company's image when consumers doubt the nature of the motives behind the company's CRM actions and their real overall impact on a society (Smith and Stodghill 1994).

Consequences of societal marketing actions

Societal marketing actions increase consumers' attitudes towards the brand in comparison with other more traditional marketing activities, such as sales promotion or sponsorship (Bloom et al. 2006; Westberg 2006). Companies obtain more positive results when sponsoring a social cause than when performing other affinity marketing strategies that are more commercial, such as sponsorship of sports or entertainment (Bloom et al. 2006).

Research indicates that consumers hold positive attitudes and purchase intentions towards companies that develop societal marketing actions or promote themselves as being socially responsible (Webb and Mohr 1998; Swaen and Vanhamme 2004). Hoeffler and Keller (2002) suggest that corporate societal marketing programmes help companies to build brand equity because they increase brand awareness, enhance brand image, establish brand credibility, evoke brand feelings, create a sense of brand community and elicit brand engagement.

Initial research on cause-related marketing indicated that consumers consider a cause-related magazine advertisement as a good way to raise money for social causes

(Ross *et al.* 1992), generating favourable attitudes towards the company and the cause. Thus, using advertising with a message related to a cause elicits positive attitudes towards the company (Nan and Heo 2007). In the same sense, Smith and Alcorn (1991) demonstrate that the intentions to buy a product are positively influenced by the company's societal activities. Yechiam *et al.* (2002) show that societal marketing increases the mean attractiveness of the promoted product, especially for inferior products, being a potential element of product differentiation for the company.

Societal marketing actions seem to be especially positive for firms that need to enhance their image. Dean (2003) investigated whether donating money to charity (conditioning it to corporate revenue or not) enhanced the image of firms that are described as irresponsible, average or scrupulous in terms of social responsibility. Results indicate that donations to charity (conditioned and unconditioned to revenue) positively influenced the image of irresponsible firms among consumers. For average firms, positive effects on image were only obtained when they performed a donation unconditioned to corporate revenue. In the same sense, Swaen and Vanhamme (2004) demonstrated that when a company that promotes itself as socially responsible is accused of behaving non-socially there is a bigger deterioration in consumers' trust in comparison with companies that are not using corporate social responsibility elements in their communication campaigns, owing to a contrast effect. However, companies perceived to be 'sin' industries, such as tobacco producers, may develop societal marketing actions associated with ethics that can lead to a positive evaluation from consumers (Szykman 2004).

Societal marketing actions are more effective in specific contexts: to promote hedonic products (Strahilevitz and Myers 1998) and for companies in mature markets (Barone *et al.* 2000). Strahilevitz and Myers (1998) show that charity incentives are more effective to promote hedonic products (e.g. hot fudge sundae), than in promoting practical products (e.g. laundry detergent). Charity incentives provide altruistic utility that is complementary with guilty feelings associated with hedonic consumption. Barone *et al.* (2000) investigated whether consumers are more likely to choose brands of companies engaged in cause-related marketing. Their results indicate that this influence depends on what is the company motivation that consumers perceive to be behind these social actions. Consumers' perceptions of why the company supports a social cause influence their perception of cause-related marketing efforts. The influence of these perceptions depends, however, on the competitive context of the company. If the company is in a mature market where offers are similar, any advantage in terms of societal marketing will influence consumers' choice. If, however, the company is in a very heterogeneous market with competitors having different characteristics, then only large societal marketing advantages will influence choice.

A large amount of research investigated the effects of the fit between the cause, the company and the consumer. The findings are mixed. Menon and Kahn (2003) demonstrated that high congruency between the brand and the cause is positive when the company promises a donation to a charitable cause when a product is purchased. However, when a company is sponsoring a cause through advocacy advertising (or more institutional societal actions), low-congruency between the cause and the brand elicits more favourable consumer perceptions. These effects are dependent on the level of elaboration: there is low elaboration for product-related societal actions and high elaboration for advocacy advertising. Higher fit between the company and the social issue is positive for product-related strategies if the elaboration of the sponsorship activity is facilitated. For advocacy advertising, lower congruence is better as long as it does not affect elaboration.

An important factor influencing the performance of societal marketing actions is the fit between the company's societal engagement and the consumers' values (Sen and Battacharya 2001). Consumers' reactions to societal actions depend on the perceived congruence between the company's character, as revealed by its societal efforts, and consumers' own values. This congruence is measured by the distance between the company's perceived personality profile and the consumers' values. The impact of societal marketing efforts on consumers' purchase intentions depends on the domain that is sponsored and also on the individual levels of societal-related beliefs. Consumers that are strong supporters of the societal domain sponsored by the company will have weaker purchase intentions for high-quality products of this company. Gupta and Pirsch (2006) demonstrated that company–cause fit improves attitudes towards the collaboration between the company and the cause and increases purchase intent. This effect is stronger when there is congruence between the company and the consumer, and also when the consumer values the cause.

Recent research on advertising effectiveness demonstrates that using advertising with a message linked to a cause elicits more positive attitudes towards the company (Nan and Heo 2007). For consumers high in brand consciousness, attitudes towards an advertisement with a societal message and the brand are more positive when there is high fit between the brand and the cause.

Basil and Herr (2003) studied the influence of societal marketing actions on the sponsored charity. An experiment demonstrated that the attitudes towards the charity are negatively influenced if the consumers hold negative attitudes towards the company or if there is negative fit between the company and the cause. Societal marketing enhances attitudes towards the charity only when the initial attitudes towards the company are positive or if there is positive fit between the organizations.

Conclusion

After this detailed discussion about the issues of social marketing and societal marketing, it is important to bear in mind the difference between these two concepts. The former characterizes Level 2 of critique in business ethics and questions the impact of a company's actions in the wider community in which it is located, while the latter illustrates Level 1 of critique in business ethics and simply describes the ethical principles and norms adopted and communicated by each company. The primary aim of social marketing is 'social welfare', while in 'commercial marketing' the aim is primarily 'financial'. This does not mean that commercial marketers cannot contribute to achievement of social good. The focus of social marketing is on the application of marketing techniques to the promotion of social ideas (e.g. a campaign to prevent skin cancer). Social marketing and societal marketing are similar terms, but the concepts are different. Societal marketing refers to the development of marketing actions that will consider what customers want, the company's needs and the interests of society as a whole. The company decides to promote a specific cause and communicates about it. It involves communicating about the importance of sustainable development, reducing waste to manufacture their products, or launching a foundation to support a specific cause. Societal marketing actions improve a company's image, both with clients and with other relevant publics.

CASE STUDY

Delta Air Lines was founded in 1928 in Monroe, Louisiana, USA. Delta serves more than 160 million customers each year with more than 5,600 daily flights. Its annual revenues in 2009 represented US$28.1 billion. With a global network, Delta and the Delta Connection carriers offer service to more than 350 destinations in nearly seventy countries (Delta Corporate Information 2010).

As many companies, Delta devotes a great deal of attention to the societal and environmental influences of its activity. For Richard Anderson, Delta CEO:

> Delta is firmly committed to our environment, safety and social responsibility. We have demonstrated this commitment in several ways throughout the world every day, as we partner with our employees, suppliers, customers, civic groups and non-profit organizations to make a difference in the communities where we live and work. Many of our programs are industry leaders and have won awards. We do not do these programs for the prizes: we execute them because they are the right thing to do.

For Scarlet Pressley-Brown, Director of Foreign Affairs and Community Relationship and Delta Force for the Global Good:

> The spirit of donation incorporated in volunteer staff of Delta symbolizes the heart and soul of the Delta people around the world. This is because our company is recognized as more than just an airline. We are leaders in corporate social responsibility.
>
> (Delta Air Lines 2010)

Delta is proud of its efforts on global diversity. The company promotes a culture of global inclusion and represents people of all languages, ethnicities and cultures. In support of this goal, Delta sponsors the United Negro College Fund, the Dr Joseph

Lowery scholarship at Morehouse University, the gay pride celebrations in New York, Atlanta and Minneapolis, as well as many other causes (Delta Air Lines 2010).

The company is also concerned about the environmental impact of its activity. Delta supports research on alternative fuels and involves employees and customers in initiatives such as recycling and carbon offsetting. In 2007, Delta became the first US airline to launch a programme of compensation for carbon. In addition, Delta has two recycling programmes: In-Flight Recycling and Aircraft Carpet Recycling. The In-Flight Recycling financed completely the construction of two 'Habitat is Humanity' homes, one in Atlanta (2008) and the other in Cincinnati (2009). Habitat for Humanity is an organization dedicated to the cause of eliminating poverty housing. Since its foundation in 1976, more than 350,000 houses worldwide have been built, providing simple, decent and affordable shelter for more than 1.75 million people (Habitat for Humanity 2010). Since 2007, Delta's recycling programme has recycled 221,000 pounds of used carpet, thus preventing them from going to landfills in the Alanta area. That is the equivalent of 70,000 square metres or about 15 acres of land. A partner in this issue is The Nature Conservancy organization. Delta Air Lines donated US$1,000,000 over three years to one of the first actions of native land acquisition, reforestation, rehabilitation and monitoring of carbon projects in the organization (Delta Air Lines 2010).

A third societal project Delta developed is related to the promotion of arts and culture. The company 'is an active partner in supporting community organizations, museums and exhibitions' (Delta Air Lines 2010). The company's current partners include the National Black Arts Festival, Atlanta Symphony Orchestra, Tribeca Film Festival, Minnesota Orchestra, High Museum of Art, Guthrie Theater, Fox Theater and many others.

Finally, Delta supports organizations of local communities working in health and welfare, with the improvement of research and education, in addition to the improvement of conditions of existence so that people can enjoy a healthier life. In support of global welfare, Delta sponsors the American Cancer Society, The Breast Cancer Research Foundation, St Jude Children's Hospital, Children's Miracle Network, Carter Centre and Habitat for Humanity, for example (Delta Air Lines 2010).

In 2010, Delta decided to highlight its support for breast cancer research. On 30 September, the company launched a campaign that enables customers to purchase pink lemonade (the colour used in campaigns to prevent breast cancer), encouraging them to share their stories on Facebook, as well as donating via iPhone and mobile devices (Campaign Delta Air Lines 2010).

This airline company is supporting:

> the Breast Cancer Research Foundation (BCRF) worldwide with the new Boeing 767–400 signature 'pink plane' and online with a virtual lemonade stand on Facebook and Sky Miles donations to BCRF when the customers download the Delta iPhone application or use the application to check in.
>
> (Campaign Delta Air Lines 2010)

Richard Anderson, Delta CEO, said:

> The personal impact breast cancer has had on me and so many of our customers, employees and families has motivated Delta to always give more in our support of the Breast Cancer Research Foundation. I've launched the first pink lemonade stand on Delta's Facebook page in honour of my mother who died from this horrible disease many years ago. The combined efforts of more than 75,000 Delta employees and millions more of our customers are making a difference in raising funds necessary to find a cure. All proceeds from the sale of the pink lemonade and US$1 from the sale of each package of Jelly Belly Sports Beans benefit BCRF.
>
> (Campaign Delta Air Lines 2010)

QUESTIONS

1   At what level of critique in business ethics do you situate Delta's societal actions?
2   Discuss Delta's new strategy of selling pink lemonade to raise money for the Breast Cancer Research Foundation.

References

Andreasen, A. R. (1994) 'Social marketing: Its definition and domain', *Journal of Public Policy and Marketing*, 13(1): 108–114.

Andreasen, A. R. (1995) *Marketing Social Change: Changing behavior to promote health, social development and the environment*, San Francisco, CA: Jossey-Bass.

Barone, M. K., Miyazaki, A. D. and Taylor, K. A. (2000) 'The influence of cause-related marketing on consumer choice: Does one good turn deserve another?' *Journal of the Academy of Marketing Science*, 28(2): 248–262.

Basil, D. Z. and Herr, P. M. (2003) 'Dangerous donations? The effect of cause-related marketing on charity attitudes', *Journal of Nonprofit and Public Sector Marketing*, 11(1): 59–77.

Bloom, P. N., Hoeffler, S., Keller, K. L. and Meza, C. E. B. (2006) 'How social-cause marketing affects consumer perceptions', *MITSloan Management Review*, 47(2): 49–55.

Brown, T. J. and Dacin, P. A. (1997) 'The company and the product: Corporate associations and consumer product responses', *Journal of Marketing*, 61(1): 68–84.

Campaign Delta Air Lines (2010) 'Delta takes support of The Breast Cancer Research Foundation online and overseas'. Available online at http://blog.delta.com/2010/10/01/delta-turns-pink—it-must-be-october/ (accessed 3 May 2012).

Cone (2008) 'Past. Present. Future. The 25th anniversary of cause marketing', Cone/Duke University Behavioral Cause Study. Available online at http://cdn.volunteermatch.org/www/corporations/resources/cone_research.pdf (accessed 3 May 2012).

Dean, D. H. (2003) 'Consumer perception of corporate donations', *Journal of Advertising*, 32(4): 91–102.

Delpal, F. and Hatchuel, G. (2007) 'La consommation engage s'affirme comme une tendance durable', *Consommation et modes de vie*, 201: 1–4.

Delta Air Lines (2010). Available online at www.delta.com/about_delta/global_good/ (accessed 3 May 2012).

Delta Corporate Information (2010) 'Stats and facts'. Available online at www.delta.com/about_delta/corporate_information/index.jsp (accessed 3 May 2012).

Drumwright, M. and Murphy P. E. (2001) 'Corporate societal marketing', in *Handbook of Marketing and Society*. Thousand Oaks, CA: Sage Publications, pp. 162–183.

El-Ansary, A. I. (1974) 'Toward a definition of social and societal marketing', *Journal of the Academy of Marketing Science*, 2(2): 316–321.

Gallopel-Morvan, K., Gabriel, P., Le Gall-Ely, M., Rieunier, S. and Urien, B. (2009) 'The use of visual warnings in social marketing: The case of tobacco', *Journal of Business Research*, 64(1): 7–11.

Gupta, S. and Pirsch, J. (2006) 'The company–cause–consumer fit decision in cause-related marketing', *Journal of Consumer Marketing*, 23(6): 314–326.

Habitat for Humanity (2010). Available online at www.habitat.org/eurasia/learn_about_habitat/who_we_are.aspx (accessed 14 October 2010).

Hoeffler, S. and Keller, K. L. (2002) 'Building brand equity through corporate societal marketing', *Journal of Public Policy and Marketing*, 21(1): 78–89.

Kotler, P. and Zaltman, G. (1971) 'Social marketing: An approach to planned social change', *Journal of Marketing*, 35(3): 3–12.

Le Nouvel Observateur (2009) 'Le profit ne peut être le seul objectif'. Available online at http://hebdo.nouvelobs.com/sommaire/economie/084287/le-profit-ne-peut-etre-le-seul-objectif.html

Menon, S. and Kahn, B. E. (2003) 'Corporate sponsorships of philanthropic activities: When do they impact perception of sponsor brand?' *Journal of Consumer Psychology*, 13(3): 316–327.

Nan, X. and Heo, K. (2007) 'Consumer responses to corporate social responsibility (CSR) initiatives', *Journal of Advertising*, 36(2): 63–74.

Paperblog.fr (2010) 'BenandJerry's plus de 30 ans d'engagement malgré une independance perdue'. Available online at www.paperblog.fr/2761159/ben-jerry-s-plus-de-30-ans-d-engagement-malgre-une-independance-perdue/ (accessed 15 October 2010).

Pechmann, C., Zhao, G., Goldberg, M. E. and Reibling, E. T. (2003) 'What to convey in antismoking advertisements for adolescents: The use of protection motivation theory to identify effective message themes', *Journal of Marketing*, 67(2): 1–18.

Rangun, V. K. and Karim, S. (1991) *Teaching Note: Focusing the concept of social marketing*. Cambidge, MA: Harvard Business School.

Rogers, E. M. (1976) *Communication and Development: Critical perspectives*. Beverly Hills, CA: Sage.

Rogers, R. W. (1975) 'A protection motivation theory of fear appeals and attitude change', *The Journal of Psychology*, 91: 93–114.

Rosenstock, I. M. (1974) 'The health belied model and preventive health behavior', *Health Education Monographs*, 2(4): 354–368.

Ross, J. K., Patterson, L. T. and Stutts, M. A. (1992) 'Consumer perceptions of organizations that use cause-related marketing', *Journal of the Academy of Marketing Science*, 20(1): 93–97.

Sen, S. and Bhattacharya, C. B. (2001) 'Does doing good always lead to doing better? Consumer reactions to corporate social responsibility', *Journal of Marketing Research*, 38(2): 225–243.

Smith, G. and Stodghill, R. (1994) 'Are good causes good marketing?', *Business Week*, 21: 64–66.

Smith, S. M. and Alcorn, D. S. (1991) 'Cause marketing: A new direction in the marketing of corporate responsibility', *Journal of Consumer Marketing*, 8(3): 19–35.

Strahilevitz, M. and Myers, J. G. (1998) 'Donations to charity as purchase incentives: How well they work may depend on what you are trying to sell', *Journal of Consumer Research*, 24(4): 434–446.

Swaen, V. and Vanhamme, J. (2004) 'See how "good" we are: The dangers of using corporate social activities in communication campaigns', *Advances in Consumer Research*, 31(1): 302–315.

Szykman, L. R. (2004) 'Who are you and why are you being nice? Investigating the industry effect on consumer reaction to corporate societal marketing efforts', *Advances in Consumer Research*, 31: 306–315.

Thierry, P. (2005) 'Marketing et responsabilité sociétale de l'entreprise: Entre civisme et cynisme', *Décisions Marketing*, 38: 59–69.

Varadarajan, R. and Menon, A. (1988) 'Cause-related marketing: A coalignment of marketing strategy and corporate philanthropy', *Journal of Marketing*, 52(3): 58–74.

Webb, D. J. and Mohr, L. A. (1998) 'A typology of consumer responses to cause-related marketing: From sceptics to socially concerned', *Journal of Public Policy and Marketing*, 17(2): 226–238.

Werle, C. O. C., Boesen-Mariani, S., Gavard-Perret, M. L. and Berthaud, S. (2010) 'Social risk efficacy in preventing youth obesity', in D. W. Dahl, G. V. Johar and S. M. J. van Osselaer (eds), *Advances in Consumer Research*, Duluth, MN: Association for Consumer Research.

Westberg, K. (2006) 'The effect of corporate societal marketing on consumer attitudes: A comparison of strategies', *Australian New Zealand Marketing Academy Conference (ANZMAC) Proceedings*, Queensland University of Technology, Brisbane, December 4–6.

Yechiam, E., Barron, G., Erev, I. and Erez, M. (2002) 'On the robustness and the direction of the effect of cause-related marketing', *Journal of Consumer Behaviour*, 2(4): 320–332.

19

DESIGNING FOR A BETTER WORLD

Josiena Gotzsch

> The design profession can no longer claim excellence in design unless we have considered the concept of responsibility as a central part of the design problem.
> (Clive Roux, CEO of the Industrial Designers Society of America)

> Remember, the great and good companies will be remembered in the future as those considering posterity, sustainability, quality of life and a better future for humanity. The choice is yours.
> (Stefano Marzano, CEO and Chief Creative Director of Philips Design, 2009)

For some of us design is the end result of a creative process resulting in a product, such as a 'designer' chair or a stylish car. Others may look at design as a creative process going further than product appearance, delivering products with improved ergonomics, functionality and integrated brand identity. Aesthetic quality is at the artistic roots of the design profession and is undeniably a very important characteristic of many successful products, but it is not the only aspect that design has to offer. Where designers traditionally have used their expertise for the creation of products, awareness is developing that these same skills could be useful within less familiar territories, such as the development of services or as a problem-solving activity in business.

Next to this possible enlargement of applying design expertise, there is an increasing ethical dilemma for the design community. On an individual level, designers are participating in the development of products for users in developed countries. However, is it fair to utilize a large part of the planet's scarce resources for the wealthier part of the world population only? To make it worse, the development of these new products is contributing to polluting our planet with production processes, increased use of energy and waste of discarded products.

As a consequence, awareness is growing within the design community that designers could and possibly should do better by offering new solutions to a wide range of societal needs; ethical, humanitarian and environmental issues (Amatullo and Breitenberg 2006; Manzini 2006). Isn't there a better way of using design knowledge and drive, in a fairer way that makes more sense, instead of developing mass-produced products only, placing creative energy in designing a better world?

This chapter positions design at Level 2 of critique among the three levels proposed in this book. It illustrates the role designers can or even should play in proposing greener and more human, more ethical solutions; and so in effect it is examining in a critical manner the broader social responsibility of the company in relation to the wider community in which it is located, as value for many quality projects designing greener and fairer products starts at the very beginning of the development process.

In the last century design as a discipline significantly evolved. The perception of what design is and can do is therefore far from clear to everyone. The design process is fundamentally a pragmatic, user-centred problem-solving activity with creative, artistic roots. Its user-centred process is vital for the creation of innovative solutions. Design is a service-providing function within business and it is the designer's job to propose delightful, appropriate solutions that shape the future. Designers are rarely in a decision-making role, but the strength of a great proposition is difficult to ignore.

When user needs and society change, design will aim to respond to these changes. In the last century, society and the way we lived changed considerably. As a consequence, the design discipline has adapted to these changes in society and the output of the design process has changed. Once, great aesthetics were enough to distinguish a product. With demanding consumers this traditional notion of design, based purely on styling, is no longer valued. A mix of aesthetics, technology, ergonomics, price, brand identity and green and social issues may be needed to create a truly appealing offer.

As a consequence, design activity has become more complex. And in a competitive environment, multiple professions – designers, engineers, marketers, sociologists – need to team up to create an appropriate answer to user needs. With this development, design has become an activity involved in multidisciplinary cooperation.

More recently, new boundaries have been crossed by applying design skills or so-called 'design thinking' to a wider spectrum of business issues, that go further than the traditional design domain: product or graphic design. The award-winning design agency IDEO promotes the use of design methodology to improve a variety of business issues varying from designing products to rethinking services and processes and solving social problems (Brown 2008). Broadening the application of the design process is an important step, not free from criticism within the design community itself. Applying design thinking in a broader sense is an expansion of the established territory of design.

New challenges such as the latest financial crisis and environmental concerns have placed ethical and green issues on the agenda of designers. Environmental or 'green design' still has more attention from the business community and hence from designers than 'social design', but a designers' association such as the Industrial Designers Society of America (IDSA) (Tischler 2010) has attributed the theme 'designing for a better world' as one of the criteria for their Industrial Design Excellence Award (IDEA). Designers' conscience also plays its role: awareness that products once designed with passion are piling up at landfills and polluting the planet is not a comfortable feeling for a profession that specifically enjoys creating and not destroying. Why waste creative talent working on issues that are not worth it from an ethical viewpoint?

To conclude this historical development of the design discipline in a nutshell, design has enlarged its area of attention from product development to the development of services and processes. Design has also evolved by integrating far more aspects than only aesthetics. Nowadays, functionality, ergonomics and at least some environmental considerations are likely to be incorporated into the design brief at the start of the development process. Pushing this further with a true integration of ethical aspects is a simple and quite logical step to take, in line with the potential development of society in developed wealthy countries. In the future, companies are likely to pay additional attention to environmental and ethical constraints, especially if these are combined with economic benefits. After all, embracing environmental and ethical and humanitarian issues is appealing. It is important for our planet and society, an exciting challenge for innovators and may even be a new opportunity for business.

After this introduction, the chapter analyses the historical and most recent development of the design discipline in further detail. It then opens up to the wider context of sustainable development with changes in ethical considerations in the business and design community. After these first two sections, ethics and design truly meet with a description of two short case studies that both contribute to designing for a better world.

The first case study concerns Conserve India, an Indian non-governmental organization. Conserve India started its activity of reducing India's waste by focusing on collecting non-biodegradable plastic shopping bags that no one wants. Contacts with the rag pickers, who are among the poorest people in India, made the organization change its objective. It motivated the founders of Conserve India to find a way to improve the lives of the rag pickers and their families. The organization expanded its activity to create designer bags and other fashionable products out of recycled plastic waste. Their handbags, belts and home decoration products are now commercialized outside India – in America, Europe and Australia. The sales results are used to improve the work and the living conditions of the workers in this organization, to educate workers, to finance a medical van and to support schools for children in the slums. Conserve India calls this 'fighting poverty through fashion'.

The second case study is a 'Philanthropy by Design' project by the multinational company, Royal Philips Electronics. The 'Chulha' project from Philips Design is a cooking stove for healthy indoor cooking. The stove reduces smoke inside the living environment by approximately 90 per cent in comparison with indoor open-fire cooking. With this project Philips Design used its design expertise to confront a stunning social problem. A total of 1,619, 000 people of which many are women and children die each year of illnesses related to in-house open fires and smoke. Philips won the INDEX Design to Improve Life award in 2009 for this project. Both cases are simply exceptional stories of innovation for the environment and society.

Design origins and recent developments

From 'form follows function' to green and social design

During the last century, design's focal point evolved with the changing needs of society. Designing is in its essence a human-oriented creative activity. So when the needs of society change, design is very likely to respond to these changes by trying to bring the best possible solution within the new context.

At the start of the industrial revolution, machines and products needed to be tailored to people and technical progress had to be adapted to human requirements. While engineers and technicians developed machines and products with technical constraints in mind, the first industrial designers concentrated on making products easier and safer to use, and giving products a better look.

One early design movement was based on the 'form follows function' principle. This implies that the product's form almost logically follows the product's function. In 1896, the American architect Louis Sullivan published an essay describing this principle. He stated that in nature shapes are dictated by their function; for example, the shape of a tree is 'designed' to receive a certain amount of sunlight and to resist storms. Even colours and aesthetics have a function in the natural world, used to catch attention. Concerning form and function Sullivan (1896) states:

> Whether it be the sweeping eagle in his flight, or the open apple-blossom, . . ., the branching oak, the winding stream at its base, . . ., form ever follows function, and this is the law. Where function does not change, form does not change. The granite rocks, the ever-brooding hills, remain for ages; the lightning lives, comes into shape, and dies in a twinkling.

Sullivan (1896) suggested that form also follows function in the man-made world. As an example he discussed the shape of a, then modern, sixteen-floor tower block as a result of its function as an office building. The '*form follows function*' design philosophy became an important principle in product design and architecture.

From 1919 to 1933 the influential 'Bauhaus' design school created buildings and products matching this functionalism principle. The Bauhaus designers wished to valorize the new technological possibilities of industry at the same time. A product was said to look modern because a machine made it, the so-called '*machine aesthetics*'. As a result product styling became minimalist, using geometrical shapes and few decorations. The appreciation of machines and technical process combined with a drive for functionality and form pureness appeared to be a particularly strong combination in the hands of artistic designers and architects. Remarkably, some of the Bauhaus products are still in production more than eight decades after their creation. They became true design classics and the durability of their aesthetics underlines the strength of the 'form follows function' principle. After the Second World War multiple design schools in Europe and the United States were inspired by this principle and the Bauhaus educational system.

With progress in technology came mass production, automobiles and planes. In addition to the fascination and the liberty that automobiles and planes brought, they carried a dream for a modern, new society specifically after the Second World War. Aerodynamic shapes make automobiles and planes more efficient products, so aerodynamic shapes in the designs of cars and planes are functional and make sense.

Surprisingly, aerodynamic styling soon achieved symbolic value in addition to its functional value. Associated with the cars and planes, aerodynamic styling signified modernism and technical progress in society. The curved initially pure shapes are pleasing, referring to organic shapes in nature, as if in contrast with the underlying man-made technology. As a result, aerodynamic product styling or streamlining became very fashionable for all kinds of mass-produced products in the United States, also for products that did not move at all: bread toasters, refrigerators, vacuum cleaners and even pencil sharpeners.

Raymond Loewy was one of the industrial design pioneers adding multiple streamlined features to his products. The title of one of his books *La laideur se vends mal* (Loewy 1952), meaning 'ugly products are difficult to sell', explains the role of the design discipline in the 1950s – making products fashionable and appealing with the objective to raise sales and profits. The flamboyant American streamlining relates with consumerism and a material world in a period where our natural resources still seemed unlimited. Like the designers before him in the Bauhaus period, Raymond Loewy wanted his product designs to be 'modern'. With his slogan MAYA, meaning 'Most Advanced Yet Acceptable', he proposed product designs for his corporate clients that would make a positive difference in the market by being advanced, but still acceptable.

In the European market after the Second World War, styling based on streamlining features was combined with more sober styling elements of the Bauhaus period. Scarcity of resources and Europe's reconstruction phase in the 1950s resulted in a more modest, calmed-down version of streamlining in Europe, using less chrome and expressive shapes. It brought some great classical designs of which the Citroen DS is a brilliant example. Both in architecture and product design the 'form follows function' principles also proved to be useful in this period. However, applying these functionality principles too much can lead to too sober, severe designs.

In the 1980s, after almost three decades, newness was needed. With the expression '*less is a bore*', a breakthrough for intentional provocative designs came from the Italian design group Memphis. With references to neoclassical shapes and flashy contrasting colours, which some called bad taste, the Memphis movement broke away from the European previously rational and functional approach in product design. From the early 1980s Memphis created cheerful, often not overly functional furniture and decorative products such as lamps and vases. The intense and rapidly spreading global interest in the Memphis designs highlighted the need for surprise, novelty and an interest in meaningful joyful product aesthetics. Companies in the consumer goods industry, such as Philips and Sony, effectively recognized the power of these new more emotional designs and started creating products with aesthetics and meaning appealing to specific user groups. The 'my first Sony' product line was one result of this movement. Communicative and more emotional product characteristics came to the forefront.

The history of design has known more movements than Bauhaus, Streamlining and Memphis (Sparke *et al.* 1997; Bürdek 2005; Vogel 2009), but the selected movements are specifically interesting as they demonstrate how designers have responded to changing needs in society in a growing competitive context. The focus on functionality at the start of the last century corresponds with the initial period of industrial production, having few rival firms and with consumers having limited choice. Then, to improve functionality, ergonomics became important. When mass production seriously took off in the United States, companies added streamlining aesthetics to their products to enhance product appeal. Subsequently, this fashion aspect lost attraction and a wider variety of communicative and emotional product aspects became important, leading to personal and meaningful designs targeted towards specific user groups. At present, green design issues and social design are gradually surfacing. How does design progress from the previous Bauhaus, Streamlining or Memphis movements to the integration of green design and social design, taking these ethical values on board? To explain, a comparison between this development and Maslow's theory of human motivation appears interesting.

In his theory of human motivation, Maslow (1943) described five stages of growth in individuals and represents these in a pyramid of needs. The pyramid contains five consecutive levels: basic physiological needs followed by a second level, representing security and comfort, then a third, representing belonging, friendship and love, a fourth level related to the need for esteem, and ultimately, at the top of the pyramid, self-actualization. According to Maslow, an individual needs to fulfil a lower level of needs first before moving to a higher level. This strict order of the different levels has been contested by other scholars.

If we suppose for the sake of developing our argument, that society, which is a collection of individuals, can grow through phases, as proposed by Maslow, then it may be that a part of Western society is climbing the Maslow (1943) hierarchy of needs, moving from basic needs (corresponding with functionality in products) towards needs for comfort (corresponding with ergonomics), and then needs for love and belonging (which relate to interest in more meaningful and emotional product designs). The level for self-esteem and esteem by others links with status elements in products and the wish for individualized products. At present, the fifth and highest level of this hierarchy concerning 'self-actualization' or the development of a person's full potential is specifically attention grabbing for the future direction of design. At the level of design, even if not in other respects, morality can be seen as part of the fifth, self-actualization level of the Maslow pyramid. The growing importance of 'green design' and 'social design' corresponds neatly to this need for morality. Ecological design is in itself an ethical issue. After all, it is not particularly ethical to leave a polluted planet for future generations.

In times of crisis, society might fall back to the lower levels for a while, being more concerned with basics such as product price and function than with fashion, status, ecological impact or social consequences. Yet, when the economy recovers, green and social values are likely to reappear on the wish list.

From designing products to designing services and processes

The previous section described the historical development of industrial product design and suggests a possible explanation for the growing relevance of green issues and social issues as part of 'good' design quality. A more recent evolution of the design discipline concerns using the design process as a creative problem-solving tool in other domains than traditional product design (Brown and Wyatt 2010). This new application might involve using design expertise to develop services, solve social problems and imagine strategic directions for companies. Tim Brown, CEO and currently president of IDEO, states: 'Thinking like a designer can transform the way you develop products, services and processes – and even strategy' (Brown 2008).

Our society is changing from a production to a service society. Companies need a creative approach to respond to these transformations. This requires adaptations and stimulates the search for innovative responses. The design process is not a cure for all problems, but its creative approach can play a part in the search for solutions. Critical thinking, identifying the real problem spots, and asking both fundamental and naïve questions, lead to understanding what is really needed. If this is combined with creativity, flexibility and the objective to create solutions in sometimes unexpected ways, this may become a core competitive asset for a company.

An example of incorporating design thinking in other fields than research and development is taking place in some business schools. Roger Martin, Dean of the University of Toronto, believes that design thinking – approaching management problems as designers approach design problems – may have important implications for management education (Dunne and Martin 2006). David Kelley, founder of the design firm IDEO, was the main force behind the Hasso Plattner Institute of Design, or D-school at Stanford University, where business students take elective classes in 'design thinking' (Wallance 2010).

Empathy for users: the one thing that has not changed

Altogether, design has developed from its early roots in functionality and aesthetics towards a discipline integrating a diversity of issues, such as green and social design. Furthermore, the design process is now applied to more areas than purely product and graphic design. In this flexible spectrum of applying design skills, one crucial aspect has not changed: its focus on users. Design is, in its essence, a user-centred problem-solving activity. An understanding of people and the context of usage are the starting points for new ideas and propositions. Placing the customer in a central position, creative insight into motivations, values, preferences and priorities, and analysing weak spots in existing solutions give the foundation for the design of desirable solutions. In the past, such a user-centred 'design research' process might have led to an aerodynamic product styling or improved ergonomics, because that appealed to customers at that very moment. Today, the answer might be the integration of technology in an even smaller product, or an ecologically friendly solution.

High consumer expectations and severe competition have made it even more important to understand what might surprise or delight a potential consumer. New specialists from human sciences, such as anthropologists and sociologists, are there-fore integrated in development teams. Their specialized skills not only aim to understand existing user habits, but also to uncover unarticulated user needs. Stefano Marzano (2007), CEO and Chief Creative Director of Philips Design, clearly expresses the importance of a user-centred design approach: 'The high design process focuses on people. We look at people as the centre, the core and the drive of what we are doing. And if we do it right, we are going to be rewarded . . .'.

It is the company's task to imagine a solution that better corresponds to users' needs, for example by using a new technology that allows improvements for its users. Sometimes this user focus combined with new technology leads to a radical innovation. Bill Ford, the Executive Chairman of the Ford Motor Company, illustrated this concept in a speech during a company meeting in 2006:

> My great-grandfather once said of the first car he ever built: 'If I'd asked my customers what they wanted, they would have said a faster horse.' . . . At Ford, we're going to figure out what people want before they even know it – and then we're going to give it to them. It's where we began and it's where we must go.
>
> (Ford 2006)

Ernesto Gismondi, Chairman of the north Italian lighting company Artimide made a similar statement. His company commercializes lighting systems that the company's development team has imaged as a meaningful offer to their users. When requested how his company does market research, Ernesto Gismondi annoyingly reacted: 'Market? What market! We do not look at market needs. We make proposals to people' (Verganti 2008). Artimide and some other design-driven companies, such as Alessi and Kartell in the north of Italy, aim for radical design innovations, designing meaningful breakthrough products, earning sufficient high margins on the successful products to cover for the failures that they learn about from their users.

When business, design and ethics meet

The ethical perspective in the business community

Embracing sustainability and ethics seems appealing. It is important for our natural environment and society, a challenge and an opportunity for innovators, and potentially positive for the brand identity. However, companies following a dominant theme in the literature of economics and later of strategic management (a theme that in Chapter 2 has been suggested to be purely ideological at root – see Chapter 2 above, p. 26) have tended to take as their sole or at least overriding goal the maximization of profits (for shareholders). As Friedman stated in 1970:

> There is one and only one social responsibility of business – to use its resources and engage in activities designed to increase its profits so long as it stays within the rules of the game, which is to say, engages in open and free competition without deception or fraud.

Naturally, companies need to be profitable to survive in the first place. However, profitability does not justify all actions. The recent 2008 financial crisis has demonstrated that some companies or individuals have placed so much focus on profitability that the rules of the game were not respected at all and that rules of common sense were broken by greediness. As a reaction to this economic destabilization, Bill Clinton, former president of the United States, claims that the company's responsibility is not only to investors and shareholders but also means being accountable to society and the environment. He qualifies the belief that companies must choose between doing good and being profitable as outdated (Clinton 2009). Aiming to be profitable and to act in a morally good manner at the same time sounds ideal, but is not going to work automatically; at times some profits may have to be sacrificed for the social good, even in the long term.

Environmental constraints are interesting because they oblige R&D to look at existing solutions differently, hence giving opportunities for innovation (Gotzsch 2007). Green technology is expected to be a major growth sector, promising to generate profits and employment. Some scholars describe sustainability as an emerging business trend that managers cannot ignore. Environmental innovations are likely to bring financial advantages in the production process as a first step. Lubin and Esty (2010) predict the trend in environmental development to follow a certain roadmap. Companies might first start using clean technology to improve existing processes, followed by redesigning products using ecological constraints, and then transforming business models.

Ethical questions to the design community

Now the search for environmental and ethical solutions is prudently surfacing, what will be the role of the design discipline? Until recently, design was adding value to the economic pillar of business only by making products better and more attractive in order to raise commercial results. Responding to corporate clients, design has focused on profitability, the other two pillars of the so-called 'triple bottom line' – people, planet, profit – were quite ignored. In other words, if all goes well, 'good design is good business'. With good intentions and an overestimation of the availability of natural resources, the design community has, as creative solution seekers, contributed in creating goods for a small part of the world population only.

Unfortunately, our planet's ecosystem has difficulties in keeping up with the actual pollution and usage caused by human activities. Moreover, if we do not change our industrial model, this will get worse. Inspired by the lifestyle of citizens in the developed countries with values based on material well-being, the emerging countries have also started consuming more products, placing a further burden on the planet's capacity. We should all have the right, but how can this pattern of consumption be extended on a global scale? What will happen when people both in India and China, instead of using bicycles start using small cars while dreaming of their next bigger automobile? And this pattern of consumption has not developed in Africa yet. The question is simple. What happens if the emerging countries adopt our lifestyle? Can our one and only planet cope with this and remain mankind's safe haven?

The need to solve ecological problems together with awareness of our limited natural resources make clear that the present 'rules of the game' have changed. The model that started with the industrial revolution is not sustainable when applied on a global scale. Ezio Manzini (2006), professor at the Politecnico di Milano, states that unwittingly the design community has acted as 'active agents in oiling the wheels of a catastrophic machine'. Although this sounds depressing, the important message is that things need to change. The society, companies and the design community, need to act more intelligently by greening manufacturing processes, developing essentially waste-free ecological designs, possibly using the 'cradle to cradle' concept (Braungart and McDonough 2002), changing consumption models and values. And also by asking the questions: Do we need all these products?; How can we extend their lifespan? Probably it means introducing new products whose industrial materials return directly to 'their' company after the product's life, hence making the company reuse these materials in the most efficient way. It is challenging, and creativity will be needed to solve these issues. As a part of the solution, the design community can contribute by finding the tools and alternatives to support all pillars of the 'triple bottom line', moving from 'good design is good business' towards 'good design is responsible design'.

A part of the design community is making changes into the direction of responsible design. The Designers Accord was founded in June 2007 by Valery Casey. This association of designers, educators and business leaders has the objective to make sustainability a mainstream idea in all aspects of design practice and production. The Designers Accord adapted a kind of 'Kyoto Treaty of design' and aims to collectively build good practice around environmental and humanitarian issues (designersaccord.org). The association wants to accelerate awareness and know-how throughout the design community, inspire design education and influence policy through design thinking.

Design awards are also drawing attention to ecological and societal issues. The non-profit Danish organization INDEX, established in 2002, appoints design awards for solutions responding to the theme 'Design to Improve Life'. This international design contest takes place every two years (www.indexaward.dk). The team that designed the Philips Chulha stove (one of the cases described at the end of this chapter) obtained the Design to Improve Life award.

The International Council of Societies of Industrial Design (ICSID), founded in 1957 and serving as an international association in over 50 countries, stimulates and honours exceptional industrial design projects that make a positive impact on our social, cultural and environmental quality of life. In January 2011, ICSID announced the biennial World Design Impact prize (www.icsid.org).

The Industrial Designers Society of America (IDSA), the largest organization of professional industrial designers in America, has the objective to inspire design quality and responsibility. Every year IDSA organizes the International Design Excellence Awards (IDEA). This design award is co-sponsored by *Business Week* magazine. In 2010, the IDSA committee decided that for their future design contests, products would be evaluated on their social, ecological, cultural as well as economic responsibility (IDSA.org). According to Clive Roux, CEO of the Industrial Designers Society of America: 'The design profession can no longer claim excellence in design unless we have considered the concept of responsibility as a central part of the design problem' (Tischler 2010).

Where, in the past, design has focused on finding solutions related to functionality, aesthetics, ergonomics or product attachment with the objective to create products that sell well today and tomorrow, the same creativity and pragmatic design approach is useful to also deal with environmental and societal topics. To illustrate this, the chapter ends with two exceptional case studies, demonstrating where design and ethics successfully meet.

THE BEAUTY OF CONNECTING DESIGN AND ETHICS

Conserve India: fighting poverty with fashion bags

Anita and Shalabh Ahuja founded Conserve India as a non-governmental organization (NGO) in 1998. Conserve India's initial activity involved recycling waste in their neighbourhood in Delhi, India – specifically plastic waste bags that were not yet locally recycled. Their city cleaning/waste recycling activity confronted the couple with the 'poorest of the poorest' people; inhabitants of Delhi's slums – collecting the trash in hideous working conditions (Naaman 2007). Confronted with these deprived circumstances, the mission of Conserve India evolved into aiming to combine both recycling waste and improving the lives and working conditions of the least advantaged citizens.

For the first years the couple looked for the best possible ways to valorize the collected plastic bags. They experimented with the plastics in a small workshop at their home, trying to create a new thicker material out of numerous thin plastic bags and also by pasting the plastic on canvas. Direct new applications of the plastic bags were also tried: creating a shelter for homeless people by weaving bags together, for example.

The breakthrough of their ideas came in 2003, with the help of a volunteer internship student from Britain. After all this trial and error, Conserve India then succeeded in finding a procedure to compress the plastic bags into flexible and resistant sheets (Prakash 2005). The thin plastic bags could be 'up-cycled' into thicker plastic sheets that were going to be the basic material for fashion accessories. Conserve India calls this material Handmade Recycled Plastic (HRP).

Volunteers and interns have been crucial for the development of the organization and have 'donated' their ideas and energy. Their contributions have varied from the invention of HRP to product designs and website development. Conserve India has also established relationships with international design schools. Many of the products of Conserve India – handbags, belts, necklaces, shoes, purses, wallets, home

FIGURE 19.1 The plastic bags are selected on colour, cut open, washed and dried.

Source: Conserve India.

FIGURE 19.2 In a next step the plastic bags are compressed in a thicker, flexible material.

Source: Conserve India.

decoration, cushions, lamps and other products – are designed by volunteer young international and Indian designers, often during an internship period. On their website, Conserve India continues to put out a request for volunteers to support their activity.

To obtain the HRP, the plastic bags need to be collected, selected by colour, cut open, washed, dried and compressed (see Figures 19.1 and 19.2). The existing colours of the plastic bags are mingled to achieve a resulting colour. This avoids the usage of additional colorants. The rubbish pickers select the colour nuances of the different plastic bags. Many of them speak different dialects, and do not have the same words for 'pink' or 'light green'. Names of Indian film stars and movies are, therefore, attributed to the different colours (Bahree 2007). Selection, opening, washing, drying and compressing of the plastic bags takes place at the workers' home and is all done by hand.

Conserve India products are exported to multiple countries – Canada, North America, Australia, Israel, Japan and many countries in Europe and are sold in fair-trade shops such as Alter Mundi, Article 23, Oxfam stores and in multiple privately owned shops (see Figure 19.3). The organization started exporting its products before trying to sell in India, because products made from rubbish lacked appeal in their home market a few years ago.

The revenue created from export allows better remuneration for those work-ing for Conserve India. The organization tries to offer training and educational

FIGURE 19.3 Conserve India handbags.

Source: Conserve India.

opportunities to the often self-employed workers, potentially creating better job opportunities within the organization or elsewhere. Profits are also used to support the education of children whose parents work for Conserve India. A mobile medical health clinic and loans allowing some of the organization's workers to develop their own businesses are also financed by the generated profits. Additionally, Conserve India proposes to help others to expand the concept and support them to set up the Conserve India concept elsewhere (conserveindia.org).

At present, Conserve India provides jobs to some of the poorest people in Delhi, contributes to improving life conditions and cleaning the local environment. Creating fashionable items out of rubbish has resulted in innovation against poverty.

Philips Chulha stove: 'Philanthropy by Design' project

Philips Design is part of the multinational group Royal Philips Electronics and started the 'Philanthropy by Design' programme in 2005. The intent of this programme is to donate design expertise and creativity to help solving important social concerns. This approach is driven by commitment to social responsibility. The projects should deliver a real contribution and at the same time enhance brand image, trust and customer loyalty. Additional offshoots are gaining insight into future growth regions, stimulating different innovative ways of working and possible reinforcement of employee commitment.

In 2007, the 'Philanthropy by Design' project focused on air pollution caused by indoor cooking on an open fire. Looking at the figures communicated by the World Health Organization (WHO), indoor pollution is an extremely important social problem. The WHO estimates that every year 1.6 million people die from diseases caused by low air quality and carbon monoxide toxins inside their homes. Specifically India is affected, with approximately 25 per cent of the victims often women and children. The major cause of the low air quality is indoor cooking on an open fire using wood or other biomass materials inefficiently. The problem is specified as 'the killer in the kitchen'.

Philips' designers tried to search for a solution to this vital problem, aiming to make cooking in rural areas healthy within the constraints of minimal local resources. The design brief also specified that a solution should respect local culinary habits, be easy to access – hence local production and distribution – and should be low cost. In the 2007 workshop NGOs shared their insights concerning the 'killer in the kitchen' problem with the Philips designers. As a first result of this workshop, a stove design proposal was created by a small team of Philips designers based in the Netherlands and India.

After initial ideas, further insight into the needs of users and other stakeholders was gained in India. Multiple issues, such as cooking behaviour, local production methods and distribution channels were investigated by a team from Philips Design in collaboration with local organizations, entrepreneurs, self-help groups and families in India. The exploration into culinary habits included observations of and informal in-depth interviews with families. Existing production facilities and distribution of stoves were also examined. The design research was directed towards a solution allowing the use of different biomass fuels, enabling baking, steaming and boiling, suitable for the usage of non-standard cooking vessels and also adaptable to local logistics.

In a workshop session various stakeholders were asked to imagine and visualize the ideal stove. Further improvements by the Philips design team led to a modular design of the stove and chimney facilitating distribution, installation and repair. Propositions also included an indoor trap to clean the chimney without climbing onto the roof, and filtering the air before being projected into the open air.

The prototypes were tested in rural and semi-rural houses, allowing a few more changes for the better on the designs. Eco-efficiency, emissions and the product's technical performance were tested in a laboratory. The stoves appear significantly faster, using less energy consumption and are suitable for the various culinary habits. The products are relatively cheap and are specifically cleaner and healthier than existing indoor open cooking fires, because indoor air pollution is reduced by more than 90 per cent.

For further development, approximately 250 families in India are using the stove and giving feedback on its usage (Capell and Lakshman 2008).

The stove and chimneys are made out of concrete and covered by clay (see Figure 19.4). The components are simple to produce in roadside factories using low-cost fibre reinforced plastic moulds.

An information package has been created to facilitate product diffusion. It explains production, distribution, installation and maintenance of the stoves. Self-help groups and citizens are allowed to use the design specifications of the Chulha stove for free. The hope is that this product will create better living conditions, and at the same time stimulate local entrepreneurs to take care of production and distribution, hence turning this project into a self-sustaining local business activity. In other countries,

FIGURE 19.4 The Chulha stove (by kind permission of Philips).

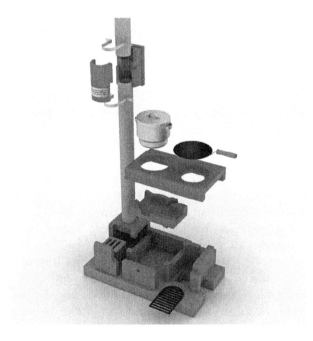

FIGURE 19.5 Modular structure of the Chulha stove (by kind permission of Philips).

such as in Pakistan and Bangladesh, the Chulha stoves could also provide healthier solutions to similar culinary needs.

With the Chulha project Philips Design has donated design expertise beyond the daily 'routine' of product design. The design team worked with various non-traditional partners by acting as coordinators in a co-creation process in the context of a developing country.

The product might not be hi-tech, but appears to be a pragmatic solution, responding to the reality of the cultural and economic situation. It responds to a key design brief objective: making indoor cooking healthier by trapping the smoke in the chimney and significantly reducing indoor pollution (see Figure 19.5).

The Chulha project gives the Philips designers insight into an important developing region and creates a better understanding of new consumers. It also gives experience in new ways of co-creation through cooperation with NGOs and local entrepreneurs in developing countries. The product increases local credibility in the Philips brand (Capell and Lakshman 2008).

The project won multiple design prizes: an IDEA award and also a Red-Dot award in 2008, INDEX: Design to Improve Life award in 2009, and continues to gain attention with a nomination for the ICSED World Design Impact prize in 2011.

Conclusion

Design as a discipline has evolved and its area of application significantly enlarged. In the past, design has focused on finding solutions related to functionality, aesthetics, semantics and ergonomics in order to sell products better. It has been the argument of this chapter that the same creativity and pragmatic design approach can and should be used to tackle bigger issues related to environmental topics and societal injustice.

Designers have always concentrated on finding solutions requested by companies and aimed to propose novel and different solutions for society. Awareness of the fact that we have to take better care of our planet's ecosystem and resources, the wrong caused by the recent financial crisis, and social inequality and poverty in large parts of the world create the insight that somewhere we need to do things differently and better. Design innovation has a role to play in confronting these issues. Very likely the future roadmap for design leads to this combination of ethics and design.

References

Amatullo, M. and Breitenberg, M. (2006) 'Design advocacy and global engagement: Design matters at Art Center College of Design', Cumulus Conference 'Ethics: Design, Ethics and Humanism', *Cumulus Working Papers*, Nantes, June.

Bahree, M. (2007) 'Bag Lady'. Available at Forbes.com, 26 November.

Braungart, M. and McDonough, W. (2002) *Cradle to Cradle: Remaking the way we make things*. New York: North Point Press.

Brown, T. (2008) 'Design thinking', *Harvard Business Review*, 86(6): 84–92.

Brown, T. and Wyatt, J. (2010) 'Design thinking for social innovation', *Stanford Social Innovation Review*, 8(1): 30–35.

Bürdek, B. (2005) *Design, History, Theory and Practice of Product Design*. Basel: Birkhäuser.

Capell, K. and Lakshman, N. (2008) 'Philips: Philanthropy by Design', *Business Week*, 11 September, p. 66.

Clinton, B. (2009) 'Creating value in an economic crisis', *Harvard Business Review*, 87(9): 70–71.

Dunne, D. and Martin, R. (2006) 'Design thinking and how it will change management education: An interview and discussion, *Academy of Management Learning and Education*, 5(4): 512–533.

Ford, B. (2006) Published speech at the Ford Motor Company Business Review, 23 January.

Friedman, M. (1970) 'The social responsibility of business is to increase its profits', *The New York Times Magazine*, 13 September, pp. 122–126.

Gotzsch, J. (2007) 'Les perspectives du développement écologique des produits', *Technology Review*, édition française MIT, 4: 80–83.

Loewy, R. (1952) *La laideur se vends mal*, republished in 1990 by Gallimard: Paris.

Lubin D. and Esty, D. (2010) 'The sustainable imperative', *Harvard Business Review*, 88(5): 42–50.

Manzini, E. (2006) 'Design, ethics and sustainability: Guidelines for a transition phase', Cumulus Conference 'Ethics: Design, Ethics and Humanism', *Cumulus Working Papers*, Nantes, June.

Marzano, S. (2007) CEO of Philips Design. Available online at www.youtube.com, Innoday – Stefano Marzano.

Marzano, S. (2009) 'Driving innovation in corporate culture: How design supports the CEO into turning this challenge into an opportunity'. Published speech, *Design Management Institute DMI*, April. Available online at www.dmi.org/dmi/html/conference/europe06/sp_marzano.htm (accessed 4 May 2012).

Maslow, A. (1943) 'A theory of human motivation', *Psychological Review*, 50(4): 370–396.

Naaman, R. (2007) 'Inde: une ONG lie le recyclage au commerce équitable'. New Value by Design. Available online at www.novethic.fr.

Prakash, P. (2005) 'La deuxième vie chic des sacs plastic de New Delhi'. Available online at www.eco-citoyen.org.

Sparke, P., Hodges, F., Coad, E., Stone, A. and Aldersey-Williams, H. (1997) *The New Design Source Book*. New York: Quarto Inc.

Sullivan, L. (1896) 'The tall building artistically considered', *Lippincott's Magazine*, 57: 403–409.

Tischler, L. (2010) '2010's Best Designed Products', *Fast Company*, 1 July. Available online at www.fastcompany.com/magazine/165/july-2010 (accessed 4 May 2012).

Verganti, R. (2008) 'Design meanings and radical innovation: A meta model and a research agenda', *The Journal of Product Innovation Management*, 25: 436–456.

Vogel, C. (2009) Notes on the evolution of design thinking: A work in progress', *Design Management Review*, 20(2):17–27.

Wallance, L. (2010) 'Multicultural Critical Theory. At B-School?', *The New York Times*, January 10.

PART VI

HRM and employee relations

20

'YOU TAKE THE HIGH ROAD . . .'

Analysing the ethical dimensions of high performance work systems

Keith Whitfield, Rachel Williams and Sukanya Sengupta

Introduction

The last twenty-five years have witnessed remarkable interest by employing organizations in the development of so-called high performance work systems (HPWS) aimed at leveraging increased competitive advantage from the more strategic deployment, development and utilization of workers.[1] These initiatives have in common the notion that workers can be the source of substantial and inimitable competitive advantages that yield significant and long-term gains for their organizations.

Considerable research has examined the nature and effectiveness of such strategies. It has occasioned a heated debate on the methodologies deployed, and the robustness of the results generated. There has emerged a fundamental difference of opinion between those who see such strategies as heralding a more enlightened approach to people management, centred around increased involvement by workers in decision-making processes and a higher level of commitment to the organization (the 'high-roaders'), and those (most notably in the critical management studies (CMS) research tradition) who see it as a sophisticated means through which employers can gain greater control over their workers' activities and intensify their work effort. The former school view the HPWS process as potentially yielding mutual gains for employers and employees, whereas the latter school view it more as a zero-sum game in which employers aim to extract greater surplus value from the labour process.

This chapter aims to examine this literature from an ethical standpoint, and particularly to contrast the high-road/mutual gains position to that focusing on its less positive aspects. Case studies are used to illustrate key points, and to suggest how one might form an opinion on the ethicality of an HPWS.

Due recognition is made of significant differences between those examining a given performance-oriented work system in terms of what they deem to be evidence of ethical or unethical behaviour. In this sense, the analysis is distinctly normative. By the very nature of the subject and its underlying debate, the focus is on the organization rather than individuals within it, though the detailed analysis required to address its key questions does involve examining the actions of individuals within it. Essentially, our concern is with the ethicality of the actions of the organization towards its employees (which would locate the discussion at Level 1 of the framework presented in Chapter 2). However, the reflections of the critical management studies approach are also and perhaps largely at Level 2 of critique in line with the tradition of Critical Social Theory of the Frankfurt school (as discussed in Chapter 2 above). Finally, it is our definite view that there are ethical standards that are widely agreed and can form the datum for an analysis of the ethical properties of the high performance work system.

High performance work systems

It has long been recognized that the management of workers represents a key aspect of organizational strategy. However, it is only in the last quarter-century that this has become a topic of intense scrutiny. The beginnings of this change are typically rooted in late twentieth-century work by various US-based business school academics, especially those located at Harvard and Michigan universities, although it is also evident that many of the themes within this literature have a much longer lineage. Of particular note is the work of the human relations school highlighting the importance of the human factor in performance and the limits of the scientific management approach associated with the work of Frederick Winslow Taylor and put into practice most fully by the Ford Motor Company.

A key element in this change of approach is the need to develop a more holistic perspective of the management of workers. Rather than seeing human resource practices as autonomous, the new approach views them as part of a bigger package, not just among themselves but also with other parts of the organizational structure, particularly the operations and financial systems. Whether there are, in reality, strong systemic effects is, however, a matter of some conjecture.[2]

High performance work systems are seen to have two main elements.[3] The first is *production systems*, which focus on how work is organized, involving inter alia the flexible assignment of workers to jobs, capturing the benefits of teamworking and devolving decision making towards the point of production. The second is *employment systems*, which provide the environment within which production systems operate, such as job security guarantees, encouraging information flows throughout the organization, integrated payment mechanisms and structures for skills formation.

These systems can be operated in a wide variety of ways and the main divide is deemed to be whether the underlying logic of the production system is centred around *lean production* or *team-based production*.[4] A further key divide suggested is between those involving an increase in *employee involvement in decision making* and those aimed at *intensifying the work process*.[5]

The concept of lean production developed out of research on the world automotive industry.[6] Its key concepts are just-in-time product and inventory control and continuous improvement (*kaizen*), and its main rationale is to take the production process away from so-called Taylorist/Fordist modes of production.[7] Teamworking is seen to involve the development of teams that are truly autonomous with responsibility for key parts of the production process residing within the group itself rather than external bodies.[8] These approaches evolved out of different traditions and focus attention on distinct mechanisms for leveraging competitive advantage, though it is possible in principle for them to coexist.

Employee-involvement processes are seen to be aimed at yielding production improvements via increasing the commitment of the workforce, their engagement with the work process and discretionary effort. By contrast, intensification processes are seen to achieve performance improvements via cost reduction and intensifying the work process.

On the basis of these distinctions, Godard has divided HPWS into four main types (see Table 20.1). These are: (1) lean involvement; (2) lean intensification; (3) team intensification; (4) Team involvement.[9] Godard further notes that it is team involvement that is most advocated by proponents of the high performance paradigm and those who see HPWS as the source of mutual gains for firms and employees. By contrast, the two intensification categories, and especially lean intensification, are seen as the archetype of the zero-sum or even negative-sum type of HPWS that has called the mutual gains perspective into question.[10]

The stated aim of many organizations introducing HPWS is to move to quadrant 1. However, Godard concludes that there is a tendency for organizations to gravitate towards an intensification approach owing to the substantial costs associated with an involvement approach, and from the fact that workers in team involvement systems are subject to major performance pressures and they are thereby difficult to sustain. This conclusion suggests that it is more likely that organizations move to quadrant 3 or 4. Some of those adopting a more sceptical approach[11] suggest that the rhetoric implies that they are moving to quadrant 1,

TABLE 20.1 Godard's classification of high performance work systems

		Work practices	
		Team system	*Lean system*
High-commitment employment practices	Yes	1 Team involvement system	2 Lean involvement system
	No	3 Team intensification system	4 Lean intensification system

Source: Godard (2004).

TABLE 20.2 Boxall and Macky's classification of high performance work systems

		Intensification	
		Low	*High*
Involvement	High	1 Ideal HIWS model: higher involvement without increased stress	2 Highly empowered but highly pressured HR model
	Low	3 Unrationalized low-skill work	4 Traditional Taylorism and possibly fake attempts at involvement

Source: Boxall and Macky (2009).

but the reality is that they go towards quadrant 4, 'enjoying' traditional Taylorism/Fordism and 'fake' involvement.

Boxall and Macky have suggested, however, that the relationship between involvement and intensification is more complex than Godard suggests.[12] Rather than being opposites, they may be independent factors that coexist. A move to greater employee involvement might result in a higher level of work intensification; indeed, this may be the norm. They therefore suggest that the high commitment practices dimension in Table 20.1 should be further subdivided into high/low involvement and high/low intensification forms of such practices, as shown in Table 20.2. In this depiction, quadrant 1 is the HPWS ideal of high involvement without stress, quadrant 2 is the pressure-cooker organization, quadrant 3 is archetypal low-achieving organization, and quadrant 4 is the traditional Taylorist/Fordist organization.

In short, work intensification might not be the antithesis of a high performance strategy but might be a natural consequence of attempting to introduce many forms of HPWS, severely questioning whether such a process inherently generates mutual gains for organizations and their workers. Indeed, it is possible that the advent of HPWS has intensified intra-organizational interest conflict, thereby reducing or eliminating any mutual gains that might otherwise have been obtainable.

The impact of HPWS

The potential for HPWS to be implemented in different ways with different implications for workers and their well-being raises a question as to whether their development is a 'good' thing for workers and whether their introduction can be regarded as ethically sound. There is profound disagreement within the literature. Whereas many studies show positive benefits for workers,[13] others show quite the reverse.[14] Most notable among the latter is a study of the introduction of autonomous teams in a manufacturing plant in the USA that has shown it has introduced a form of 'concertive control' into the production process.[15]

The bulk of the research on HPWS has focused on their impact on organizational performance. It has raised many questions about methodology, the nature of a high performance work system and the causal chain linking work practices to performance.

A key finding is that the introduction of an HPWS generally yields performance improvements for the organization concerned. A further finding is that there are extensive complementarities between practices, such that 'bundles' of practices interact to increase their joint impacts beyond what would occur if introduced singly. However, others like Godard point out that the number of cases on which the claim is made is small and that there may well be diminishing returns. Furthermore, there is a lack of consensus about the exact configuration of the bundle of practices, and a debate as to whether the practices can be put together into a package applicable anywhere ('best practice') or whether the practices have to be consistent with each other ('best internal fit') and/or with the wider operation of the organization ('best external fit').[16]

Many commentators have noted that there is a lack of consistency between the measures that have been used to proxy high performance work systems. The range of practices examined varies substantially between studies,[17] and some are seen as 'new' in some studies and 'traditional' in others.[18] The use of statistical techniques to define these rather than strong theoretical frameworks might also be seen as problematic.

A major critique of the HPWS literature is that it is too focused on count-ing practices and needs to move beyond this to study the processes that link intended practices to outcomes.[19] In this view, the true difference is not in terms of which practices are put in place or how many thereof, but how they are imple-mented. For example, practices such as performance appraisal and merit pay are implemented in very different ways that have varying impacts on trust, satisfac-tion, commitment and performance. The suggestion is therefore that HPWS research must go beyond simply counting practices and identify the processes through which such practices operate – or 'open the black box', as some researchers say.

Less extensive than the HPWS/performance literature is research on the impact on employees. The nature of these analyses varies massively from large-scale survey research to participant observation and so comparison is difficult. Moreover, as in the HPWS/performance literature, the definition used for HPWS varies substantially and care needs to be taken to ensure that like-for-like comparison is being undertaken.

The picture is decidedly mixed. Some studies show a strong positive relationship and others a negative one. Many show no significant relationship between HPWS variables and key measures of worker well-being. There is also no strong pattern that can readily explain the direction and/or strength of these results. Examples of positive and negative employee outcomes can be found in quantitative studies based on large surveys and in qualitatively oriented case studies. They can be found in studies of organizations in manufacturing and in the service sector. They can be found in North American- and European-based studies.

There is a suggestion that the relationship is more likely to be negative at high levels of practice adoption, and that team responsibility for a good or service is associated with negative worker outcomes such as work overload, role stress and fatigue.[20] A key issue would seem to be the degree to which workers have strong options to working in their current organizations. Thus Godard suggests that the outcome seems to be decidedly worse for workers where they can be coerced to cooperate, either because employers are readily able to relocate production or where the workers face harsh labour market conditions. Where either or both of these are possible, the introduction of an HPWS would seem to be more likely to worsen the situation for the workers concerned.

Are HPWS ethical?

The potential for limited mutual gains or worse and/or 'fake' involvement from the introduction of HPWS raises the question whether their advent has been ethical. Moreover, the further suggestion is that such negative outcomes and broken promises are an inherent feature of the way in which such systems are organized. Thompson has suggested that there is insufficient cohesiveness across different parts of the organizational structure to allow local managers to keep their part of the HPWS bargain with their employees. Specifically, 'there is a massive tension between the degree of stability necessary for HRM and HPWS to operate effectively and the insecurity inherent in current forms of corporate governance . . .'.[21] There is also evidence that job-related stress has increased contemporaneously with the advent of HPWS.[22] Whether this has occurred because of this development or from other, unrelated, factors is unproven. But the critical management studies literature certainly points in the HPWS direction. The evidence, indeed, suggests that the key factors underpinning this increase in work stress are changes in work organization that have closed gaps in the working day and increases in household working hours that have increased the conflict between working time and other commitments.[23]

Recent years have seen a huge increase in interest in corporate social responsibility. Part of this responsibility is a duty of care towards employees. A key question is whether organizations introducing HPWS have shown due care towards their workers. Clearly, those intensifying the work process behind a veil of 'fake' involvement are breaching this requirement and are acting unethically. Those introducing new systems without due regard for the impact on sections of their workforces are similarly breaching their duty of care. On the other hand, others might simply be making assumptions that their innovations are simply reorganizing their workers' productive activities without any negative impact on their well-being. In short, evidence that employers are behaving unethically in relation to the introduction of HPWS requires detailed information in relation not only to their consequences but also to the attitudes of employers to them and such consequences. Such information is not widely available and is difficult to acquire.

Moreover, even if such information was available, it is likely to be interpreted in very different ways. For instance, while for some a closing of the gaps in the working day is seen as a legitimate attempt by employers to use the labour power available to them to better effect, for others it is viewed as a policy of sweating the workers beyond the reasonable.

Drawing a strong conclusion from the extant literature is therefore fraught with difficulties. Nonetheless, some broad conclusions can be made. First, there is still only limited evidence supporting a strong version of the intensification hypothesis, especially that relating to 'fake' involvement. To a large extent, such evidence requires detailed analysis, using qualitative research methods that are sophisticated in their design. To date, these have been notable by their absence.

Second, it is by no means certain that increases in work effort are always and everywhere seen as negative by the workers concerned. Indeed, the job-demands/employee-control/job stress (JDCS) literature has suggested that an increase in job demands can yield a positive outcome in terms of worker well-being if accompanied by increased autonomy and social support.

Third, it is not clear that a decline in worker well-being following the introduction of new work practices is necessarily a 'bad' thing. Workers are only one of a number of stakeholders in any organization and any change is likely to have a negative impact on one or more of these. Unless a very constraining notion, such as Pareto-optimality (where change is only seen as positive where no stakeholder is made worse off as a result and at least one better is off), is imposed on the situation, it is likely that interpretations of whether a change is positive will depend on the perspective from which it is viewed.

Fourth, there is growing evidence that organizations are becoming increasingly aware of the business case for investing in employee well-being, which is viewing its improvement as of benefit to its own performance. The classic position on this was presented in the Black Review of work, health and well-being undertaken in the UK. The Review Committee commissioned Price Waterhouse Coopers (PwC) to examine existing case evidence on the impact of employer well-being initiatives. The conclusion reached was that there is a substantial return to such initiatives for the organization itself in terms of improved performance, and that this is a definite area where mutual gains were possible. While there are abundant grounds for questioning the validity of these conclusions on the basis of sample selection, research design and interpretation, they do suggest that improving employee well-being is not always and everywhere a zero-sum game between firms and employees.

Finally, even if the evidence was clear and unambiguous as to whether HPWS had a positive impact on employee welfare, it is by no means clear that they would be regarded by all as ethical. For some, such employee outcomes might be seen as less favourable to them than would be potentially possible, and possibly merely the bare minimum required to forestall changes that would yield a more favourable employee outcome. For others, this might be seen as reflecting collusion between employers and employees that was detrimental to others, such as consumers or taxpayers.

Overall, the evidence on the ethical nature of high performance work systems is far from conclusive, and is likely to stay that way given the contested nature of the terrain and the complexity of the subject area. Nonetheless, further progress can be made towards answering the question. This requires, among other things, intensive analysis of existing case material that permits the derivation of more precise conclusions as to the causal chain linking high performance practices and employee outcomes.

Competing views of high performance work practices

Many case studies have been written that provide examples of the practical effects of implementing HPWS in organizations. Most are exemplars and aim to show this approach as a best practice way of increasing performance and commitment among employees. They tend to be linked to studies produced by professional bodies or government departments and are contained in reports that encourage organizations to adopt these processes.

Academic articles are, by their very nature, typically more critical of HPWS and those in the critical management tradition suggest that these processes often do not deliver the promised results. While fewer examples are available of companies where HPWS have been introduced and have resulted in a reduction in positive working conditions than the reverse, the extant research evidence makes it clear that many organizations exist where workers have experienced this much less positive result.

Supporters of HPWS often use case studies to provide evidence on how these practices can be successfully implemented. They describe the positive outcomes and frequently include quotations from managers and workers describing the benefits they have gained. These case studies are published to provide evidence for organizations that are interested in introducing some of these practices and the authors therefore select processes that have been successfully introduced, while failing to mention any not resulting in the expected benefits. The result is that it is often difficult to interpret the reports, and it is easy to be overwhelmed by the conflicting views.

One difficulty in interpreting case studies is that they are written from the author's personal viewpoint. We all have our own ethical standpoints against which we evaluate information, and yours might be different from that of the author (see Chapter 2). For example, if an employer requires workers to be available to work five hours overtime a week, this may be viewed as a positive policy by some; it provides the employer with flexibility and offers the employees the opportunity to earn additional pay that is paid at a premium rate. However, for some, this is seen as a negative policy encouraging workers to remain at work for extended periods, which has a negative impact on work/life balance and may cause additional stress owing to childcare difficulties. It is therefore important to be aware of the author's standpoint when interpreting their conclusions. It is not necessarily unethical behaviour to intensify work if the employer has done all that can be expected in terms of minimizing the negative impact of it, but the interpretation of 'what can reasonably be expected' will vary between individuals.

Another consideration to determine is the reason why the new working methods were introduced. If the motives for the changes are understood it will be easier to decide whether the results are those that the organization hoped to achieve and therefore to assess what impact was intended. For example, have the changes been implemented to increase profitability and meet the demands of shareholders or have they been introduced to improve the working life of employees so that they experience increased enjoyment in their jobs, manage work/life conflict better and work in a more efficient manner? If the first scenario is true, it is possible that short-term gains will be required and less concern will be placed on employee views; if the second is the motivation for changes, then it is more likely that the changes will be beneficial for the employees. This is not to say either approach is correct as some people will believe that one is legitimate and others will have a different view. However, the writer's ethical viewpoint will determine whether or not they consider that an approach is reasonable and this will influence how they approach the case study.

On the basis of the existing evidence on the ethicality vis-à-vis employees of attempts by employers to implement high performance work systems, it is hard to come to any other conclusion than 'not proven'. Much of the information is not sufficiently rich to allow a judgement to be made either way, and that which is points in different directions. Moreover, it is extremely difficult to make strong general statements in this area. Knowledge must be examined on a case-by-case basis from which general statements can only be made with a great deal of caution. Nonetheless, what can certainly be said on the basis of the wide set of literature we have reviewed is that there are potentially some very clear ethical issues surrounding HPWS; and this is hardly surprising since we are after all looking at people and not at mere machines.

To finish we present reviews of two published case studies to indicate the type of questions that need to be asked to judge whether the introduction of new work systems can be deemed ethical or not. The first, Metaswitch, gives a positive view of the impact and was written to extol other organizations to consider such a change. The second, Coberg, offers a much more negative view and is highly critical of the way the organization introduced its changes. Key differences can be observed in how the cases are written and the information used to build the case analysis. Most notable is the depth of information that is needed to assess the ethicality of any given change.

COMPETING VIEWS OF HIGH PERFORMANCE WORK PRACTICES

High performance work practices at Metaswitch[24]

This case is described in a report that was produced for the Chartered Institute for Personnel and Development and the UK government's Department for Trade and Industry. It describes the benefits of introducing high performance work practices and is published as an exemplar of the way they can benefit both the organization and employees.

Metaswitch designs and manufactures telecommunications hardware and software. Its directors place emphasis on recruitment and recruit almost entirely for entry-level positions as they believe that it is important for their future success to identify young, talented individuals and train them in the company's culture. There are over 3,000 applications for the 20–25 vacancies available each year and there are a number of hurdles for potential candidates. First, candidates attend a preliminary interview lasting a day that includes solving a selection of technical problems. It is used to identify appropriate aptitudes in software engineering. Candidates invited back for a second interview face further tests, presentations and interviews. They also attend a social gathering with staff and a meal with the selectors.

Once a new recruit takes up employment they receive comprehensive training and a formal individual development plan. The development process covers both technical and personal skills. Annually, throughout their employment, everyone has at least one full review and three or four development plans. Considerable investment is made into developing the 250 staff, with £3 million spent each year on training.

In addition to training reviews, a performance review is carried out every nine months by the employee's manager. This review doubles up as an appraisal and provides the employee with an assessment and some advice about how performance can be improved. This overall assessment is then linked to development goals. The review and development plan are very important in growing the business and most senior managers have been with the company since they joined as graduates.

Metaswitch is owned by the employees through the employees' benefit trust. Individual employees' profit shares are based on contributions that are assessed and measured every six months. Each manager makes an assessment of the staff for whom they are responsible, that then builds up into the unit's contribution which, in turn, builds up into a company list. In the final analysis, Metaswitch has an overall list where every member of staff is ranked; the profit share is based on that ranking.

The HR director emphasized:

> There is a lot of loyalty among our employees. One of the things that we always try to achieve is the position where people should not have to worry about their remuneration package. This leaves them free to concentrate on what they're doing.

Generous remuneration has contributed to low staff turnover but this is only part of Metaswitch's HR strategy. According to the *Sunday Times'* '100 Best Companies to Work For 2010' survey, staff felt cared for by management and felt that they were always supported when they needed to learn new skills.

This case is published in a booklet that promotes the use of high performance practices to business. It has been written in a very positive light, almost as an advert, and therefore requires critical reading. It fits into the team involvement category and suggests that by selecting carefully and rewarding and developing employees well they will be committed to the organization and more productive.

The difficulty with any case is that it only provides a snapshot of the company. In the case of Metaswitch, it is likely that all policies are implemented fairly and consistently across the organization but the only way of knowing this would be to investigate further. Additional evidence could be obtained by contacting the company and asking questions or seeking further references to the company in other publications. What we know, though, is that a brief case study on its own is not going to tell us the whole story.

Nevertheless, even with a case like this, it is still possible to question some of the processes and ask whether they are introduced for the best motives. In the case of Metaswitch, the recruitment practices and reward practices both provoke questions.

Metaswitch's structured recruitment practices outline social events that help the selectors to 'get to know the candidates socially'. It is assumed that this is to identify which candidates will fit into the organization, but do the social events lead to managers recruiting the candidates they like, perhaps those in their own image? What information would you need from the company to determine whether this was a fair and reasonable part of the selection process? Is it fair in any circumstances to judge candidates during social events? Is it ethical to only recruit candidates because they fit into the organization and perhaps have similar backgrounds to the senior managers? Is it ethical to recruit candidates because you believe they will work hard without complaining; is this accurate selection or exploitation?

The case discusses the reward process and describes how managers rate employees and, 'Metaswitch has an overall list where every member of staff is ranked and the profit share is allocated based on that ranking' (Sung and Ashton 2005, p. 37). If the organization has selected the employees carefully to ensure that they are likely to be committed and work hard and has then trained them so that they have the skills needed to perform their jobs, is it reasonable to ensure that a large number are at the bottom end of the ranking and will be less well rewarded than their colleagues? A ranking system will ensure that, regardless of the final performance of all employees, some will end up at the bottom of the lists. Therefore, employees may be committed, hard working, carefully balancing home and work pressures and still obtain a low ranking – is this ethical? What will be the impact on the employees at the bottom of the list? If all employees are adequately rewarded for their efforts, then does it matter where they appear on a ranking chart? Does the ranking system extract extra effort from those at the bottom; does this intensify the work?

High performance work practices at Coberg[25]

This case describes a company called Coberg, a light engineering firm based in north-east England. The company implemented a significant change programme including a single status structure, monthly meetings between individual workers and their team leaders to mark their performance against a set of competencies and replacing the traditional skilled apprenticeship training scheme with firm-specific on-the-job training. It also attempted to instil a new corporate culture that sought to denigrate old ways of doing things. Managers labelled the older skilled workers 'Jurassics' and this led to the social production of inter-generational subcultures. In an attempt to reduce any outward resistance to the changes, management opened up a 'window of opportunity' to workers and allowed those who were unable to accept the changes in the company to retire. In Coberg, management saw it as legitimate to redesign not only the labour process but also attitudes and beliefs.

Some older workers chose not to accept early retirement, but to remain and 'contest the effect of the changes'. The company was implementing new manufacturing practices such as total quality management, just-in-time inventory control and teamworking, and these led to workers being removed from familiar working patterns and social groups and placed into new working arrangements, often with different colleagues. Some workers objected to established arrangements being broken down and to the new culture that emphasized the positive aspects of the new situation and was critical of the past.

Any attempt to empower the workers and encourage commitment was finally lost when further redundancies were necessary. There was no formal consultation with the workers – instead, the names of those who were to lose their jobs were called out via a tannoy; they were sent to the HR department and escorted off the premises.

A worker tried to understand the approach taken by management:

> I know at the end of the day they are bosses and it's their factory, but I think the workforce deserves more than a moment's notice . . . I'll trust them no more. It gets everybody's backs up and so, what they have been working towards the past few years, they've destroyed it all straight away.

This case describes a lean production system and suggests that the changes have resulted in intensification. High performance working practices are discussed in relation to communication, training and teamwork, but the effectiveness of these is not clear. The case is approached from the employees' point of view and describes how a difficult change process impacts on the workforce. When considering the ethics of this it is important to consider 'what is the other side of the picture?' We are told that new working methods are being introduced and that 'management' are trying to change working practices and attitudes, but we have no information about what they are trying to achieve, what specific practices they are changing or whether or not they have tried to implement any more positive processes to assist these changes. The case refers to the workers resisting the new practices, and the impact of any such resistance on the outcome of the change process.

If considering this case from an ethical viewpoint, two key areas to examine are the employers' motives and methods of consultation. We need to consider whether the organization considered the impact the changes would have on the employees before they implemented them. The workers complain that their social work patterns are disrupted and their familiar working practices are removed. Change is difficult for all organizations and can lead to an uncomfortable and stressful time for everyone, but were the employers reasonable? The answer to this question will vary depending on the reader's ethical stance. Some will consider that, if new working practices can be seen to be beneficial to the organization, then it is reasonable to implement changes to working practices even if this is difficult for some long-serving employees. Furthermore, responses to any change will be mixed and often the people who are unhappy tend to voice their concerns even if they may be in the minority. Therefore, the representativeness of the negative reaction may be questioned. Others will question whether these changes could have been introduced more gently, embracing the concerns of the workers, and making a real attempt to gain their support for the new processes. Another viewpoint may be that the organization was wrong to even try to implement these new working practices as they aim to increase productivity with no benefit to the employees. Yet others may argue that the well-being of the workers is inextricably linked to the longevity and productivity of the organization. After all, most employees will be made redundant if the organization shuts down or suffers losses. What information would be needed to assess whether the employers acted reasonably? To what extent were the changes legitimate and implemented in a fair and reasonable way?

We are told in the case that no consultation took place regarding the second round of redundancies, but it is not clear whether any consultation happened when the initial changes were discussed. Older workers were offered early retirement, but it would be useful to know whether this was on an individual or collective basis, and whether the terms were attractive. We are told that older workers were referred to as 'Jurassic', which is obviously a derogatory term, but it is unclear whether this term was used officially and by all managers, or if it was just overheard being used in a private conversation. If developing recommendations for this company, this information would be important as it would determine whether the behaviour of a few individual managers needed to be addressed or whether this was an attitude condoned by senior managers. If managers believe that significant changes are necessary to ensure an organization's survival then is it acceptable that workers who are not supportive should be encouraged to leave? Why would managers wish to implement changes without consulting with workers?

Notes

1 E. Appelbaum and R. Batt (1994). *The New American Workplace.* Ithaca, NY: ILR Press.
2 P. Boxall and K. Macky (2009) 'Research and theory on high-performance work systems: Progressing the high involvement stream', *Human Resource Management Journal*, 19(1): 3–23.
3 K. Whitfield and M. Poole (1997) 'Organizing employment for high performance: Theories, evidence and policies', *Organization Studies*, 18(5): 745–764.
4 E. Appelbaum and R. Batt (1994) *The New American Workplace*; C. Berggren (1992) *Alternatives to Lean Production: Work organisation in the Swedish auto industry*. Ithaca, NY: ILR Press.
5 J. Godard (2004) 'A critical assessment of the high-performance paradigm', *British Journal of Industrial Relations*, 42(2): 349–378.

6 J. P. Womack, D. T. Jones and D. Roos (1990) *The Machine that Changed the World*. New York: Macmillan.

7 Boxall and Macky 'Research and theory on high-performance work systems'.

8 Berggren, *Alternatives to Lean Production*.

9 Godard, 'A critical assessment of the high-performance paradigm'.

10 R. Delbridge (2007) 'HRM in contemporary manufacturing'. In P. Boxall, J. Purcell and P. Wright (eds), *The Oxford University Press Handbook of Human Resource Management*. Oxford: Oxford University Press, p. 22.

11 Ibid.

12 Boxall and Macky, 'Research and theory on high-performance work systems'.

13 E. Appelbaum, T. Bailey, P. Berg and A. Kalleberg (2000) *Manufacturing Advantage: Why high-performance work systems pay off*. Ithaca, NY: ILR Press; R. Batt (2002) 'Managing customer services: Human resource practices, quit rates, and sales growth', *Academy of Management Journal*, 45: 587–597; S. Hutchinson, J. Purcell and N. Kinnie (2000) 'Evolving high commitment management and the experience of the RAC call centre', *Human Resource Management Journal*, 10(1): 63–78.

14 A. Danford, M. Richardson, P. Stewart, S. Tailby and M. Upchurch (2004) 'HPWS and workplace partnership: A case study of aerospace workers', *New Technology, Work and Employment*, 19(1): 14–29; Danford *et al.* (2008) 'Partnership, HPWS and quality of working life', *New Technology, Work and Employment*, 23(3): 151–166; R. Delbridge (1998) *Life on the Line in Contemporary Manufacturing*. Oxford: Oxford University Press.

15 J. R. Barker (1993) 'Tightening the iron cage: Concertive control in self-managing teams', *Administrative Science Quarterly*, 38: 408–437.

16 P. Edwards and S. Sengupta (2010) 'Industrial relations and economic performance'. In T. Collins (ed.), *Industrial Relations: Theory and practice*. Oxford: Blackwell Publishing.

17 S. J. Wood (1999) 'Getting the measure of the transformed high-performance organization', *British Journal of Industrial Relations*, 37(3): 391–418.

18 Godard, 'A critical assessment of the high-performance paradigm'.

19 Boxall and Macky, 'Research and theory on high-performance work systems; K. Macky and P. Boxall (2008) 'High-involvement work processes, work intensification and employee well-being: A study of New Zealand worker experiences', *Asia Pacific Journal of Human Resources*, 46(1): 38–55.

20 Godard, 'A critical assessment of the high-performance paradigm'.

21 J. D. Thompson (2003) *Organizations in Action. Social science bases of administrative theory*. New Brunswick, NJ: Transaction Publishers, p. 365.

22 F. Green, K. Huxley and K. Whitfield (2010) 'The employee experience of work', in A. Wilkinson *et al.* (eds), *The Sage Handbook of Human Resource Management*. London: Sage.

23 F. Green (2006). *Demanding Work: The paradox of job quality in the affluent economy*. Princeton, NJ: Princeton University Press.

24 J. Sung and D. Ashton (2005) *High Performance Work Practices: Linking strategy and skills to performance outcomes*. Department of Trade and Industry, in association with Chartered Institute of Personnel and Development.

25 Strangleman and Roberts (1999), reproduced in S. Jenkins and R. Delbridge (2007) 'Disconnected Workplaces: Interests and identities in the "high performance" factory'. In M. Houlihan and S. Bolton (eds), *Searching for the Human in HRM*. Basingstoke: Palgrave Macmillan.

References

Appelbaum, E. and Batt, R. (1994). *The New American Workplace*. Ithaca, NY: ILR Press.

Batt, R. (2002) 'Managing customer services: Human resource practices, quit rates, and sales growth', *Academy of Management Journal*, 45: 587–597.

Bélanger, J., Edwards, P. K. and Wright, M. (2003) 'Commitment at work and independence from management: A study of advanced teamwork', *Work and Occupations*, 30: 234.

Boxall, P. and Macky, K. (2009) 'Research and theory on high-performance work systems: Progressing the high involvement stream', *Human Resource Management Journal*, 19(1): 3–23.

Danford, A., Richardson, M., Stewart, P., Tailby, S. and Upchurch, M. (2008) 'Partnership, HPWS and quality of working life', *New Technology, Work and Employment*, 23(3): 151–166.

Godard, J. (2001) 'High performance and the transformation of work? The implications of alternative work practices for the experience and outcomes of work', *Industrial and Labor Relations Review*, 54(4): 776–805.

Godard, J. (2004) 'A critical assessment of the high-performance paradigm', *British Journal of Industrial Relations*, 42(2): 349–378.

Handel, M. J. and Levine, D. I. (2004) 'Editors' introduction: The effects of new work practices on workers', *Industrial Relations*, 43(1): 1–43.

Hughes, J. (2008) 'The high-performance paradigm: A review and evaluation', *Learning as Work Research Paper*, no. 16.

Hutchinson, S., Purcell, J. and Kinnie, N. (2000) 'Evolving high commitment management and the experience of the RAC call centre', *Human Resource Management Journal*, 10(1): 63–78.

Ichniowski, C., Shaw, K. and Prennushi, G. (1997) 'The effects of human resource management practices on productivity: A study of steel finishing lines', *American Economic Review*, 87(3): 291–313.

Jenkins, S. and Delbridge, R. (2007) 'Disconnected workplaces: Interests and identities in the "high performance" factory'. In M. Houlihan and S. Bolton (eds), *Searching for the Human in HRM*. Basingstoke: Palgrave Macmillan.

MacDuffie, J. P. (1995) 'Human resource bundles and manufacturing performance: Organizational logic and flexible production systems in the world auto industry', *Industrial and Labor Relations Review*, 48(2): 197–221.

Newell, H. and Scarbrough, H. (2002) *HRM in Context: A case study approach*. Basingstoke: Palgrave.

Ramsay, H., Scholarios, D. and Harley, B. (2000) 'Employees and high-performance work systems: Testing inside the black box', *British Journal of Industrial Relations*, 38(4): 501–531.

Sung, J. and Ashton, D. (2005) *High Performance Work Practices: Linking strategy and skills to performance outcomes*. Department of Trade and Industry, in association with Chartered Institute of Personnel and Development.

Whitfield, K. and Poole, M. (1997) 'Organizing employment for high performance: Theories, evidence and policies', *Organization Studies*, 18(5): 745–764.

21

ETHICAL CHALLENGES IN BUSINESS COACHING

Pauline Fatien Diochon

Chapter overview

Since the late 1980s, business coaching has generated an increasing interest, mostly in Western organizations, where new skills seem to be required to face uncertain and changing environments. Therefore, coaching appears as a support to managers looking for new landmarks or ways to achieve increased performance, as well as to HRM managers who have adopted it as a new business tool to develop their employees. However, there are risks in adopting this 'solution' too rapidly and its implementation requires great care. Since many different stakeholders are involved, a full range of expectations are raised, either explicitly or implicitly, consciously or unconsciously, making coaching a rather ambiguous practice. Thus coaching raises a number of underlying ethical issues relating to the use of coaching made by the three main stakeholders: the coach, the coachee and the sponsor. Who really benefits from coaching in organizations? What interests does the coach serve? Under which conditions should coaching be implemented as a successful HRM practice?

The potentially contradictory pressures raised by the use of coaching are heavily focused at Level 1 of the three levels of analysis developed in this volume. The realm of coaching illustrates how the treatment of employees by the organization itself raises a number of ethical issues as managers disguise the rationale for adopting such practices, coached employees and coaches themselves hold different expectations of what the purpose of the activity is and the coaching process can be seen as both support for high-flying managers and assistance for weak performers. These tensions create risks for all three stakeholders involved in the coaching process.

Business coaching: past and present

Business coaching is a practice that has gained increasing attention across the world: according to a recent survey on the development of coaching worldwide, coaches are active in almost half of the 162 countries studied (FBCA 2009). In the case of thirty-three countries, coaching is in a growth phase while in another fifty it is a recently introduced activity. There are a minimum of 43,000 business coaches operating today, 80 per cent of them based in Europe, North America and Australia where only 20 per cent of the worldwide population live. The seven countries with the highest numbers of coaches are the United States of America, the United Kingdom, Germany, Australia, Japan, Canada and South Africa. Coaching is said to be accepted and used as a business tool in twenty-eight countries with fourteen of these in Europe.

Although business coaching appears to be a new business tool, it has deep roots in older practices of help for individuals in certain professions. Indeed its heritage in sport and in the philosophical and political arenas gives coaching all the more prestige in its practice in business.

The sport model is very popular as competition, yet collaboration and passion are highly valued in firms today. The philosophical reference is also prominent as most coaches refer to Socrates' maieutics to describe their non-directive approach; they do not push their own preconceived solution but try to help clients deliver their own 'truth'. Some feel closer to shadow political counsellors, like Richelieu used to be for the French King Louis XIII in the seventeenth century. This political connotation reminds us that initially coaches (as vehicles) were constructed to transport the Hungarian King Matthias Corvinus during his reign from 1458 to 1490, at a time where means of transport were slow and uncomfortable (Stec 2010). Coaching is thus fundamentally associated with an innovative and prestigious support for physical movement, an aspect we may connect with the use of coaching to foster individual or organizational change processes in business today.

Business coaching can be broadly defined as an individualized counselling service that has become a resource for various professional situations including 'career transition', 'job dissatisfaction', 'poor performance' or 'specific professional challenge'. Its recipients fall typically into two main categories (Feldman and Lankau 2005): (1) executives who have performed highly in the past but whose current behaviours or performance interfere with, or are not sufficient for, current job requirements; (2) managers who have been targeted for advancement to the executive level but are lacking some specific skills. Thus two coaching goals seem to be in tension, between remedial and developmental purposes. As we will see below, a wide variety of issues may be addressed, from interpersonal issues for 'external development' (e.g. assertiveness, understanding difference, work/life balance) to intrapersonal ones for 'internal development' (e.g. self-awareness and confidence) (Kampa-Kokesch and Anderson 2001).

Between 2003 and 2007, six French Vice Presidents (VPs) of one of the world's largest strategic consulting firms chose to benefit from external individual coaching on a voluntary basis (Fatien and Muller 2008). Interviewed on their reasons for resorting to coaching and on the benefits they thought to have gained, all mentioned the need to develop very specific skills required by their new position. If the traditional training arrangements were efficient to develop the hard skills they had had to master up until that point, they proved inadequate in developing an array of soft skills – collective work, teamwork and client service – required in their new commercial, managerial and strategic functions. Notably, through the 360° feedback, they were now evaluated on their command of these skills. Thus, the final goal was not so much improving relationships but rather to acquire the expected behaviours that could help them climb the hierarchical ladder of this 'up or out' system. In such a competitive context, coaches may also appear as partners that offer a safe area, a break away from organizational life, troubles and urgency. With coaches on their side, the VPs could find a reassuring presence to work with increased confidence on the development of their resources (ibid.). They even sometimes took the opportunity to put the organizational system at a distance to understand the rules of the game . . . and decide with increased awareness how (and even if) they wanted to play it! For some, business coaching was also used to explore broader personal issues, such as the balance between professional and personal engagements.

The fact that coaching is often introduced as a new professional resource, commonly used today to develop a broad scope of needs, and in the above example associated with the development of skills that the traditional training system could not address, facilitated the recourse of the VPs to coaching. Coaching thus reduces what could be called the 'psychological access cost' associated with the need for already successful managers to acknowledge that some help could prove useful. Also the fact that coaches were pre-selected and came to the VPs' offices reduced the 'logical access cost'.

From the HR side, coaching can be perceived as a way to answer the psychological contract that implicitly ties employees and organizations together. Indeed, coaching may provide ways to increase employees' employability and guarantee their 'market value'. Besides, coaching can be a signal for the coached employees that the firm demonstrates an interest and invests in them. Coaching can also become a tool for organizational recognition. As a conclusion, coaching tends to be perceived as a 'win–win' situation that fosters organizational performance and individual value.

Through these situations, we see that the reasons for promoting or accepting coaching are broad and we can organize them along two continua. The first describes the origin of help brought by coaching, linked to the arrangement itself or to the content of the work with the coach. The second continuum describes the nature of the work, functional, aligned with the job requirements, or existential needs. We can thus position, as illustrated in Figure 21.1, the main reasons for resorting to coaching, as expressed by the recipients in this consulting firm.

The practice of coaching

Business coaching is a wide umbrella composed of many different practices (Cox *et al.* 2010). The practice often tends to focus exclusively on the figure of the external individual coach, from outside the organization, in the framework of a three-party

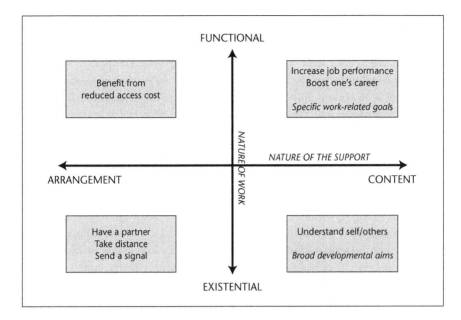

FUNCTIONAL

Benefit from
reduced access cost

Increase job performance
Boost one's career

Specific work-related goals

NATURE OF WORK

NATURE OF THE SUPPORT

ARRANGEMENT

CONTENT

Have a partner
Take distance
Send a signal

Understand self/others

Broad developmental aims

EXISTENTIAL

FIGURE 21.1 Typology of clients' reasons for resorting to business coaching.

contract. However, there are others. Coaches can belong to the companies in which they intervene – known as internal coaches. They can also be colleagues that provide mutual help through peer coaching. Each of these situations is in face-to-face interaction, but teams can also be coached through collective or team coaching processes.

It is important to ask why the coach figure has come to be relied upon by managers in organizations today. It may be because of its 'professed' specificity that differentiates it from traditional actors offering assistance, such as trainers, mentors and consultants, and even therapists. But how exactly is coaching different?

One aspect of coaching that is clearly different from conventional interventions is the personal, private interaction, at least for non-group situations. Within organizations that require increasing levels of subjective involvement, one may need to discuss personal issues face to face. Classic collective seminars offered by trainers may be too generic and inappropriate to allow self-expression or even intimate self-disclosure (Amado 2004). As one-shot interventions, such seminars may not foster transformations that require long-term processes.

As regards the mentoring relationship, mentors are often senior and experienced managers appointed to act as references during a certain period of development; they may help newcomers get acquainted with a new job and understand the organizational culture, for example. For their part, coaches, considered as professionals in helping, deal with broader issues. They are often perceived to be on the same level as the client, like a friend or a brother, more akin to partners than idealized models – even though some coaches like to exert an ambiguous influence. In fact a good balance between similarity and difference must be found.

As alternative figures of help, consultants deal with business issues more at the organizational level. They appear to be either technical experts, delivering performance solutions on strategic or operational issues, or analysts using a socio-psychological or systems approach likely to challenge the organizational context and lines of responsibility. On the other hand, compared to therapists, coaches are more results- and action-oriented, which may reassure clients who would rather be compared to healthy champions than to patients suffering from a psychological condition.

Finally, the growing popularity of coaching may have to do with its 'attractive offer', when it appears to represent mediation between what have been considered as inevitable long-term lasting antagonisms: the social and economic dimensions of the organizational project and the possibility to reach, at the same time, increased efficiency and personal well-being. The role of the social dimension in today's organizations may be linked to the 'leadership' that firms endorse more and more to cope with the decline of traditional collective references that used to provide landmarks: religion, family and school. The reduced weight of these institutions, and of 'destiny', force people to rely on their own resources and to build or create their own life. Working on the self becomes both an injunction and a necessity in a social and organizational environment driven by the double imperative of autonomy and performance. The ability to use emotional intelligence and soft skills appears to be one of the key requirements. However, this may appear difficult for people facing urgent and complex situations and who as a consequence lack distance with regard to themselves and their organization. Perhaps for these reasons the help of an external third party appears to be all the more welcome.

These different contexts require the coach to master a broad range of skills and knowledge. This may explain the composite profiles and backgrounds of the coaches: psychotherapists, former executives, athletes, lawyers, business academics and management consultants. According to the coaching settings, they will have to demonstrate abilities in a variety of disciplines including psychology, or psycho-sociology, sociology or strategy, etc. This kaleidoscope of situations explains that today coaching remains a heterogeneous field, difficult to precisely define and regulate because of its chaotic frontiers (Fatien Diochon and Nizet 2012); some people even compare it to 'the wild west of yesterday' (Sherman and Freas 2004).

Coaching as a three-party contract

Most of the time, coaches intervene in organizations because they have been carefully selected to help a specific client or team. As firms become more and more familiar with coaching, they professionalize their coach selection process while developing a better understanding of the main issues at stake. They often rely on a group of coaches to get a pool from which they can choose one or two coaches that they can introduce to the employee designated to receive coaching – the coachee. Then, once there has been an agreement on the choice of the coach, an engagement contract will normally be signed between the three parties: the coach, the coachee and the sponsor. The question of who is the final client raises itself here. If International Coach Federation (ICF) defines the client as 'the person(s) being coached' and the sponsor as 'the entity (including its representatives) paying for and/or arranging for coaching services to be provided', it is not as clear for all coaches. Thus a first ethical issue concerns the interests served by the business coach: who does the coach serve? In the case of conflicting demands between the sponsor and the coachee, whose interests should prevail?

According to the traditional professional standards, the contract should establish the objectives of the coaching sessions, the roles and responsibilities for each party. This stage is quite important since it sets the guidelines and the expectations of the future intervention. In most coaching contracts, the objectives will be clearly stated; some coaches may even offer to quantify them (for example a consultant working on improvement of social skills might arrange to have two team lunches every week), while others will remain voluntarily vague because they know from experience that different levels of expectations may coexist under a single demand and evolve through time. Such agendas may be numerous, sometimes well-grounded but sometimes detrimental. For this reason codes of ethics are established to identify how the coach should behave. For example, ICF codes of ethics outline standards of ethical conduct that address professional conduct at large (for example 'accurately identify one's coaching qualifications, expertise, experience, certifications'), the potential conflicts of interests, the professional conduct with the client, the confidentiality/privacy issue (notably, be clear about the feedback process). So, we see that another ethical challenge arises in this three-party contract: failing to appropriately define a contract.

Ethical issues with the three parties

As we see above, most of the time coaching involves a three-party contract, meaning that the stakeholders may share similar but also contradictory interests. We will now explore the underlying ethical issues associated with how individuals in organizations treat each other and how organizations treat their employees: the potentially conflicting perspectives of the stakeholders around the three-party coaching contract.

Ethical issues for the coach: professionalism is not all!

Business coaching has become a popular activity as organizations have sought new ways to support their employees and in particular senior management. Being mostly in its introductory or growth phase, coaching remains an unregulated field that can rapidly become a 'souk', or catch-all term, where it represents a convenient and fashionable umbrella to address any activity where someone brings help or advice to another. Indeed, we may find various domains covered by coaching such as business, school, family, couples, beauty, phone and home decoration. The term 'coaching' could rapidly suffer from overuse, meaning 'everything but nothing'. Thus, this attractive activity may be seen as a rescue path for professionals who need to inject new blood into their activity. Business coaching may thus attract 'food coaches' looking for more business contracts. For them, having access to a company is very important as it allows them to increase the scope of potential clients. They may be seduced by the lure of high rates; a one-hour coaching session's price ranges from €100 to €500, but very few live from this demanding and energy-costly activity. Thus the motivations for offering coaching may range from the most professional to the most self-centred to the therapeutic. How many coaches face the 'rescuer syndrome' by caring for others as a way to curve their own problems? That is why, during their selection process, an HR manager should inquire about the background of coaches, their qualifications, their training, their supervision by more experienced peer coaches. They should also be sure that they have a wide portfolio of activities that allow them not to rely exclusively on coaching to survive. This financial self-sufficiency constitutes some guarantee that coaches will refuse a mission if they do not feel competent. Thus a critical ethical challenge faced by the coach is having an adequate training, background or expertise to address the situation at stake. Ethical concerns especially arise when working with clients with issues traditionally seen as best suited to therapy, mentally unwell clients or those with 'deep-rooted' issues.

If the professionalism of coaches may prevent the worst excesses, we may question what makes this professionalism fully suitable. The respect of deontological charters does not appear to be enough as there is often a gap between what people say they do and what they actually perform. In the case of 'food coaches' for instance, who tend to consider their own interest first in the coaching process, what traditionally appears as a firewall proves unreliable. Supervision may be light or mild, coaches may accept a non-voluntary client that in many situations a 'good' coach, following a deontological charter, would not accept.

We could summarize the don'ts for coaches through what could be called 'the seven deadly sins for coaches':

- to rush to coaching without appropriate training (greed);
- to make the minimum effort required (sloth);
- to be attracted by what appears to some as a lucrative market (gluttony);
- to be jealous of clients or colleagues (envy);
- to consider oneself as a new guru (pride);
- to seduce by wrong arguments/to lie (lust);
- to show too much emotion and overpass the boundaries of the role (wrath).

(Adapted from Denis Cristol, organizer of a workshop on coaching, AFREFF, Negocia, Paris, January 2010.)

Ethical issues for the client: I want more!

If clients have to be careful, they may not necessarily be innocent figures themselves. Their relationship with their coach may also be subject to ambiguity. Clients may try to influence their coach, because they want to use them and manipulate them (by professing wrong information, exerting pressure on them, etc.). An ethical issue for the client is to avoid falling into dependence with the coach or the coaching, and being able to find the right distance.

Indeed, because the coach–coachee relationship may go far beyond their paying contract, they may want to get the coach's attention through a deeper implicit relational contract. As Fustier describes, the helping relationship ranges from the pure economic commercial contract, strictly restricted to the obedience of the written contract, but may go beyond the commercial frontiers and be interpreted in terms of personal 'gift'. Then coaches are expected to give a bit of themselves: expand the length of the coaching session, talk about non-professional issues, become friends, etc. This 'relational time' spent with the coach corresponds to the 'non sterilized social work' that Fustier (2000) contrasts to the 'purified social work' subject to direct productivity for an efficient solution. Thus, sometimes, clients look for such 'non sterilized social work' and expect the coach to provide relational time. In the most extreme cases, clients try to have coaches' exclusivity, becoming jealous of other colleagues that could work with their coach, and at the end become dangerously dependent on them.

Needless to say developing 'inappropriate' (whatever that may mean) personal relationships with clients, such as becoming sexually intimate with the client, is ranked as the most delicate and potentially the most serious ethical challenge by coaches (Coaching at Work 2010).

Ethical issues with the sponsor and the organization: coaching as a 'blinding help' and a 'poisonous gift'?

Let us now consider the issue of the relevance of coaching towards the organizational setting in which it is introduced. The sponsor, embodied typically in the organization by the supervisor or the HR manager, has a great influence on the coaching setting. If most of the time the intervention of a coach follows a diagnosis by the organization that there is a need for coaching, sometimes such upfront analysis is lacking and coaching can easily appear as a 'magic tool', as a way to fix a problem rapidly without getting the full picture (Berglas 2002). When diagnoses are defined as a 'person problem', they are often problematic insofar as behaviours may be caused by the systems in which various actors operate. Then coaching may need to subject the organization to an in-depth analysis and that is why it appears essential to consider the whole system of command: 'relevant others may not only be potentially part of the solution, but they are usually directly or indirectly part of the problem' (Tobias 1996, p. 89). If they do not consider the system that can potentially produce (and support) the 'person problem', coaches may inadvertently contribute to unethical situations: for example, the psychologization of problems leading to the scapegoating of an individual, the externalization of the coach who becomes a 'loudspeaker', or even worse the reinforcement of the initial difficulties. Thus one of the first ethical issues at the sponsor level deals with the degree to which the 'wider system' should be called into question.

The case of 'psychologization' occurs when a situation that should be considered on different levels, such as social, historical and political levels, is reduced to a psychological issue. If so, coaches participate in the overinvestment in behaviours leading to the de-socialization of causal explanations and the exclusion of organizational responsibility (Amado 2004). As a result, the intervention of the coach may be counterproductive in the long run; by allowing managers to close their eyes to the roots of the dysfunction, it only treats the symptoms for a short period of time with an 'artificial bandage'. At best, coaches delay the need for real management of the situation; at worst, they stigmatize people and reinforce their feeling of guilt.

When coaches intervene in favour of the 'bad' person or for 'bad' reasons, they also sometimes endorse a role that others do not want to play in the organizations. Executives that do not want to face a certain reality can rely on the coach to do what they do not want to do themselves. They contribute to the externalization of the traditional role of operational managers or of HR managers. They can also appear as a substitute to the managerial dimension of a job or a tool for managers lacking courage who prefer to avoid face-to-face disagreements or confrontations.

In addition, coaching can maintain or reinforce the failures that it is expected to address. Hence, when coaches are sent for by isolated executives, to help them find individual answers to their problems because new technologies, organizational structure and overwork hinder face-to-face relations, we could wonder whether they do not confirm and accelerate the 'defeat of the collective' (Amado 2004, p. 45). This individualized support contributes to making people think that they have to develop a personalized relationship to their work and organization without any reference to the group. In a vicious circle, colleagues appear to be required less and less in the realization of work. Because they are expected to answer people's request for increased performance and for finding happiness at work, coaches may contribute to supporting the 'cult of performance' raising 'the cost of excellence' (Aubert and Gaulejac 1991).

When coaches comply with these ambitious requests, they give birth to extraordinary expectations that seldom materialize. Coaching may thus appear as a 'poisonous gift' when it confronts people with an imperative for success. Failures are all the less understandable when support was provided to help reach a target. Thus accepting coaching can appear 'risky' as it places people in a context of expected success. Furthermore, one could ask, should the workplace provide happiness? Some psycho-sociologists, for example, express doubts; they question the type of happiness reached in this case (Amado 2004). By inducing new criteria of a 'proficient happiness', does not coaching contribute to instrumentalizing and thus trivializing morals in order to allow them to conform to the 'socially correct'?

Indeed, the type of development that coaching offers may be 'instrumental' (Brunel 2004). This means that human development is formatted according to criteria favouring organizational utility, and often not in keeping with the best interests of the person. This instrumental shift in the development of the person inside an organization questions the actual possibility of the real development of people in organizations (Amado *et al.* 1991). Amado *et al.* are not sure that individual and organizational developments are alike or even compatible. Such an association appears possible with the rise of an 'instrumental rationality' that leads people to wonder 'how' they can achieve results but not why; in such cases, people focus on the means to achieve goals but not on their meaning. Indeed, most behavioural coaching practices aimed at the adaptation of individuals to organizations may be affected in this way (Orenstein 2002); and this clearly raises some very basic moral issues or rather moral omissions.

Conclusion

As a conclusion, we can say that the three-party contract involved in most business coaching arrangements impacts upon all the stakeholders with ethical challenges that require each stakeholder to both recognize and deal with appropriately. Here are the main 'ethical traps' to be aware of:

Regarding the triangular contract:

- failing to appropriately contract (too lose or too rigid contracting);
- failing to serve different – sometimes conflicting – interests.

For the coach specifically:

- having inadequate training, background, expertise;
- working with clients with issues traditionally seen as best suited to therapy or other practices of help (consultancy, for example).

For the client:

- getting dependent on the coach or on coaching;
- finding the appropriate distance with the coach – avoiding developing inappropriately personal relationships.

For the sponsor:

- not taking into account the 'wider system';
- asking the coach to do one's own job, because of lack of courage to face difficulties;
- using the coach as an 'artificial bandage' to hide real roots of problems.

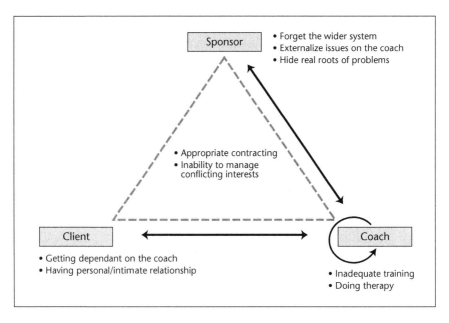

FIGURE 21.2 Main 'ethical traps' in the three-party business coaching contracts.

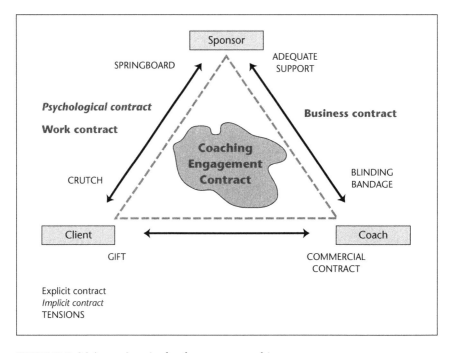

FIGURE 21.3 Main tensions in the three-party coaching contracts.

Since business coaching involves multiple stakeholders, it thus gives rise to various expectations that may be explicit or implicit, conscious or unconscious and creating a situation that contains multiple tensions and thus moral issues (between the coach and the coachee, between the coach and the sponsor, between the coachee and the prescriber). The main tensions are synthesized below.

- Between the coach and the sponsor – adequate support/blinding bandage: when coaching is appropriately implemented, for example following an individual and organizational diagnosis of the situation, it may be a sign of responsible organizations providing adequate support to its members. However, when coaching is adopted rapidly as a magic tool, it may conceal organizational dysfunctions and prevent systemic diagnosis of the underlying problems. Then coaching, by just treating the symptoms, allows the roots of the problem to persist and even spread – in this sense it is simply a blinding bandage.
- Between the coach and the client – contract/gift: clients may expect their coach to stay in the strict commercial boundaries of their contract or, alternatively, to 'give' more of themselves. Most difficulties arise when the two parties do not share the same understanding of their relationship.
- Between the client and the sponsor – springboard/crutch: coaching is sometimes perceived as a 'springboard' offered to the more successful employees, and represents a way to improve performance. However, for some, coaching can become a 'crutch' designed to support the weakest in the organization.

The case of Thierry's career in the following case illustrates some of these tensions and challenges that face both organization and coachee when the parameters for the use of coaching and perceptions of stakeholders are not clearly defined.

MINI-CASE – 'THIERRY WAS SENT TO COACHING TWICE'

Thierry, 50, is pursuing a brilliant career in an international company that develops, produces and supports world-leading airliners. He had just been appointed Head of the Marketing and Sales department when he was interviewed about the reasons and contexts that explain why he had 'been through' two coaching experiences during the past four years.

'When I first went to coaching four years ago, it was really not my choice, I was sent there. The Executive Committee had heard about coaching and thought, "Why not coach our top managers? We have to take care of them!" It was as if they did so because coaching was fashionable . . . Today, four years later, I do not hear so much about coaching . . . But at the time I started my coaching sessions, I had real trouble understanding why I had "sent to coaching", although I had a hunch. During a board meeting a few months earlier, I had reacted rather emotionally to an absurd and unethical financial package proposed by a very twisted guy. The ethical issue is crucial in our activity because we are leaders in collaboration with countries where corruption is widespread. But the committee seemed to overlook this point. Be that as it may, my boss considered that I had shown too much emotion and not behaved as expected from a top manager who is supposed to bring solutions, not problems. But emotional reactions, I believe, as potential signals of problems, should not be deadened. As an illustration, we just have to remember what happened to the Challenger Space Shuttle . . . So I ended up doing coaching, and it went pretty well, even if at the beginning it was difficult.

'The HR manager had introduced me to Francesca, a coach who used to be a maths teacher. Being an engineer myself, I could not grasp what a person that reduces any situation to an equation to be solved could have brought to me. I would have preferred somebody with a stronger background in psychology. I guess such a coach would have more to bring to me. In the end it was not so easy to refuse to work with Francesca. She knew the HR manager well, who wanted to provide her with business contracts since she was quite new on the market. But I did not want to sacrifice myself just to ensure that my company would provide her with business. So, I was firm: I said that I would agree to do coaching on the condition that I would select my coach. That is what happened; I chose a coach following the advice of one of my acquaintances, and she was accepted by the HR manager. Over the course of one year, we met twice a month, for about three hours each time. Based on the emotional incident in the meeting, I worked with my coach on what had been taken for my non-conformist behaviour: I discovered that in fact I have a "hyper sensitivity" that drives me to feel in advance exactly what's going on. Thus, with my coach, I progressively learned to be less passionate about my job and put some distance between myself and it. For example, when faced with intellectual dishonesty like in that meeting, I used to react "badly", which proved to be detrimental to me. Now I have learned to behave more adequately: I don't react anymore! In organizations, the one who gets nervous is wrong . . . which may explain why everyone hides their feelings.

'Two years later, business coaching suddenly reappeared when I took charge of a new marketing team. The situation was not very favourable since my predecessor had been a real harasser. Was this the reason why my teammates were proving rather odd? One was on sick leave for depression, the other had genuine communication difficulties, paradoxically blaming people for not talking to her. So the HR manager thought that coaching would be very useful for me in this situation. I find this idea rather counterintuitive. If I had been the HR manager, I would rather have first conducted an organizational diagnosis of the situation to investigate the reasons that allowed this situation to persist over time. Another solution could have been to move or even fire the troublesome employees! Why was I designated as the one who needed help? On top of that, I rapidly got the feeling that business coaching was a way to spy on what was going on in my department. This coach was a former HR manager of the company, who had switched to consulting and coaching. Of course, she tried to act as independently as possible. But first I had difficulties in trusting her since I always saw my colleague in her. Second, she suffered from a great deal of pressure from above and had difficulties in resisting this. Rather than asking me face to face, my boss introduced a third party to develop a report on me. That is where organizational breakdown starts!

'Actually, I think that common sense in management has been lost because most managers lack courage and take refuge in what is most easily at hand; they keep the noble part and externalize what is difficult and bothering: the human side. Even this second coach with whom I finally worked did not understand why she had been sent to me. "You don't need this", she said, "the top managers would probably better benefit from coaching than you". We decided to stop the face-to-face meetings. But since she was also a consultant, I offered her the chance to do some team building with my staff. We ended up going jogging in the countryside and it was fun! In the end, everybody was happy: the board had introduced a new HR practice with the luring promise of solving people problems, the coach had business, and as for me, I showed that I was a good soldier . . . Apart from this implicit subjective appreciation, no official feedback was ever conducted on the coaching.'

This case has been adapted from Amado and Fatien, 'Value of ambiguity. The case of business coaching', Paper presented at the 25th EGOS Colloquium, July 2009.

CLASS QUESTIONS

1   What are the different practices of business coaching in firms today? Have you ever experienced any of them?
2   Based on the 'professed' specificities of business coaching compared to other helping practices, how would you define a typical situation for offering coaching to employees in an organization?
3   What are the different reasons that may explain the rise of business coaching in the world today? Would you say that business coaching is a new practice?
4   Why can coaching be perceived as an ambiguous practice?
5   Identify the ethical issues raised in the mini-case for each of the parties involved (the coach, the coachee and the sponsor).
6   What advice would you give to an HR manager who wants to offer coaching to their employees and avoid ethical traps?
7   Based on the typology of recourse to coaching by top managers in their consulting firm (Figure 21.1), what would be a similar typology to express the reasons HR managers would provide coaching to their employees?

Suggested further reading

Brunning, H. (ed.) (2006) *Business Coaching from Systems-Psychodynamic Perspective*. London: Karnac Books.
Kilburg, R. R. and Diedrich, R. C. (eds) (2007) *The Wisdom of Coaching: Essential papers in consulting psychology for a world of change*. Washington DC: American Psychological Association.

References

Amado, G. (2004) 'Le coaching ou le retour de Narcisse?' *Connexions*, 81: 43–52.

Amado, G., Faucheux, C. and Laurent, A. (1991) 'Organizational change and cultural realities: Franco-American contrasts', *International Studies of Management and Organization*, 21: 62.

Aubert, N. and Gaulejac, V. D. (1991) *Le coût de l'excellence*, Paris: Editions du Seuil.

Berglas, S. (2002) 'The very real dangers of executive coaching', *Harvard Business Review*, 80(6): 87–92.

Brunel, V. (2004) *Les managers de l'âme*, Paris: La Découverte.

Coaching at Work (2010) 'Poor Practice 2010 Survey', 5/4: 14–18.

Cox, E., Bachkirova, T. and Clutterbuck, D. (2010) *The Complete Handbook of Coaching*. London, New Delhi, Singapore, Washington DC, Los Angeles: Sage.

Fatien, P. and Muller, M. (2008) 'Is there anybody to question executive coaching? The role of coaches as a third party', Academy of Management Paper Presentation, Div. MC, August 7–12, Anaheim, CA, USA.

Fatien Diochon, P. and Nizet, J. (2012) *Le coaching dans les organisations*, Paris: La Découverte.

FBCA (Frank Bresser Consulting and Associates) (2009) 'Global Coaching Survey – The state of coaching across the globe: The results of the Global Coaching Survey 2008/2009'. Available online at www.frank-bresser-consulting.com/globalcoachingsurvey.html.

Feldman, D. C. and Lankau, M. J. (2005) 'Business coaching: A review and agenda for future research', *Journal of Management*, 31: 829–848.

Fustier, P. (2000) *Le lien d'accompagnement*. Paris: Dunod.

Kampa-Kokesch, S. and Anderson, M. Z. (2001) 'Business coaching: A comprehensive review of the literature', *Consulting Psychology Journal: Practice and Research*, 53: 205–228.

Orenstein, R. L. (2002) 'Business coaching: It is not just about the executive', *Journal of Applied Behavioral Science*, 38: 355–374.

Sherman, S. and Freas, A. (2004) 'The wild west of business coaching', *Harvard Business Review*, 82: 82–90.

Stec, D. (2010) 'Passion's first profession: The personification of an object and emergence of coaching', in *Journal of Management History*, 18 (3).

Tobias, L. L. (1996) 'Coaching executives', *Consulting Psychology Journal: Practice and Research*, 48: 87–95.

22

ETHICAL ISSUES FOR INTERNATIONAL HUMAN RESOURCE MANAGEMENT

The case of recruiting the family?

Mark Smith and Christelle Tornikoski

Chapter overview

Human resource management (HRM) is a rich environment for the consideration of ethical issues with a multiplicity of human interactions in the management of people, their expectations and their needs, alongside the corporate goals of the organization. At face value, the claim that HRM places people at the heart of organizations and as a key element of business strategy would seem to create a high ethical standpoint for the management of people. However, as critics have argued, the rhetorical nature of much HRM discourse as well as the 'hard' side to many HRM policies means ethical issues are widespread (Legge 1995; Guest 1999). Indeed the ambiguous nature of HRM, even within one national setting, opens up one of the serious ethical challenges leading to misinterpretation and bad faith and in an international context – the scope for ethical challenges and multiple interpretations becomes manifold (Vadera and Aguilera 2009).

Employment ethics has tended to deal with both personal ethical issues in the working environment and wider social responsibility of business to their employees. Personal ethical issues around the management of people extend from cases of personal integrity of individual employees to the management dilemmas created by employee misdemeanours (readily identifiable as Level 1 critique as outlined in terms of Chapter 2 of this book). Meanwhile, the wider social responsibility of business in employment terms is significant when we consider the lives, careers and livelihood of employees or groups of employees (this corresponding to Level 2 critique in terms of Chapter 2). This chapter addresses an area that has received less attention, that of recruitment in an international environment and particularly in relation to the recruitment of expatriates. This brings together both themes of personal ethical issues of recruiters and the wider social responsibility of HR policies towards their employees; hence, Levels 1 and 2 of critique, but also by virtue of the potential for clashes between different ethics of recruitment and employment in different countries it may also raise some issues of what was described in Chapter 2 as Level 3 critique. International experience has increasingly become a key requirement to managerial career progression in most top multinational companies. Yet the selection of candidates often involves vague notions of suitability, and brings both family and spouse into the decision process. Henceforth, key notions of individual fairness and equality are often raised and/or challenged. In this sense we bring together these two areas of ethics – the personal ethical and the wider social responsibility – relating to HRM in considering the ethics around recruitment and selection of employees for particular posts – along gender and ethnic differences for example – and the wider implications for social justice and inequalities among employees and the population at large.

Ethics and HRM

HRM and line managers

In Storey's (2001, p. 6) well-used definition of human resource management it is described as 'a distinctive approach to employee management which seeks to achieve competitive advantage through the strategic deployment of a highly committed and capable workforce using an integrated array of cultural, structural and personal techniques'.

For some, the distinction from the bureaucratic approach of personnel management is an important step and the emphasis on the workforce's willing contribution to business strategy and success a sign of the Human Relations School origins of HRM (Guest 1999). For others there is little new in human resource policies and little to support the case that there is a more employee-centred approach (Legge 1995). Johnsen and Gudmand-Høyer (2010, p. 331) capture these critiques when they say: 'HRM has been accused of shaping the dreams, desires, hopes and aspirations of human subjects when cynically aligning the individual with the organization, thus producing manageable resource units that are optimally mobilized and configured.'

Indeed for Greenwood (2002, p. 261) HRM, in all its forms, falls well short of being ethical and she wonders whether it can indeed be ethical at all: from her perspective the 'management' in HRM is a euphemism for 'use'.

One of the challenges of considering the ethical dimension of HRM is that it captures a multitude of different policies and practices. Early pioneers in the subject proposed universal models of HRM that now receive less support as firms have adopted a variety of approaches linked more closely to specific internal resources, and comparative studies have demonstrated many ways to manage human resources. As Clark and Mallory (1996) demonstrate, the conceptualization of HRM cannot be isolated from the institutional and cultural environment in which a firm is located, so no one single model of HRM can be considered applicable across contexts. Even within a single national setting, authors have pointed out the stark differences between so-called hard – focused on headcounts and costs – and soft approaches – focused on human development and commitment (Legge 1995; Guest 1999).

Furthermore, even where HR policies may appear to adopt a high ethical standpoint, the reliance on line managers as the main conduit for HR policies means that actual HR practice may fall short of these ethical standards. As Macklin (2007, p. 266) points out, even where HR managers may try to uphold ethical decision making, they may witness or be forced into unethical decisions, for example sanctioning discrimination against certain groups, lying about job prospects or supporting inappropriate line management decisions. For Ackers (2009) it is a fallacy that HRM can bring the interests of employees and managers into line without adequate representation from the employee side. This pluralist approach to HRM means some kind of 'voice' is needed for internal stakeholders of the organization in their interactions around the employment relationship. Finally, as has already been outlined by Gazi Islam in Chapter 6 of this book, the tradition of Critical Social Theory of the Frankfurt school has been deeply critical of the reification of employees, which they see as inescapably present in all HRM precisely insofar as employees are thought of as resources in the economic sense, as mere pawns to be moved around, as any other resource. (Reification means reduction to the status of mere object as opposed to recognizing the subjectivity of human beings as persons.)

Recruitment and selection

Recruitment and selection have often been considered as one process with recruitment being the generation of an applicant pool for subsequent selection or promotion. However, increasingly organizations, faced with challenges of skills shortages, changing employee expectations and demographic shifts, can be seen as developing distinct recruitment strategies to develop a pool of applicants (Orlitzky 2007), while the selection is the process by which the choice of a candidate(s) is made that meets organizational goals within legal requirements. Selection often has a technical focus on 'objective' tools but there is also a strong influence of subjective opinions and norms in the decision process.

In many countries such recruitment and selection decisions are subject to a legal framework that outlaws discrimination and aims to promote the selection of future employees based on individual merits. Indeed, demographic and social change means that relying on old stereotypes and norms limits the pool of potential applicants. There are, however, many other factors that come into play and managers seeking employees that 'fit' into the existing organization may adopt a range of more subjective criteria. Macklin (2007, p. 266) highlights a case where a manager only wants to employ men for production jobs and knowing full well that such a criterion is illegal he tells his HR partner 'you will nevertheless find a way to only employ men'. So while practices in recruitment and selection should be valid, reliable and legally defensible this might not always be the case (Catano *et al.* 2009). However, if ever legal transgression is observed and publicly denounced, organizations might face not only expensive legal penalties but also a serious blow to their corporate image.

In many countries HR professionals have ethical codes of conduct that may complement organizational codes. For example, in Canada members of the Certified Human Resources Professionals (CHRP) are required to meet certain professional standards in the practice of recruitment and selection. Similarly, members of the Chartered Institute for Personnel and Development (CIPD) in the UK have a professional code of ethics that requires them to 'advance employment practices that promote equality, diversity and inclusion'. However, the business pressure on HR managers may challenge ethical codes and the very fact of dealing with the interests of different stakeholders or managers and employees creates tensions (Perkins and Daste 2007). For example, Catano *et al.* (2009) point to personal ethical challenges created by selection tools that are effective at measuring job performance but also discriminatory against certain ethnic groups or the design of selection tools to undermine union membership by eliminating pro-union attitudes.

Discussion around selection often focuses heavily on psychometric testing as a way to select the best candidates for the job and the greater efficacy of such methods when compared to the standard job interview. In practice, a range of practices are used to select candidates and the relevance of these to job requirements may vary. Using methods such as sample work, simulations, alongside interviews and personality testing allows a selection based on performance facets of the job. However, managers' perceptions of the requirements for the job and suitable candidates are often coloured by more subtle perceptions of what makes a person good for the particular role. Notions of what makes a 'good firefighter ' or a 'good police officer' help reinforce particular selection decisions that may, on the one hand, help maintain organizational cultures (people who fit) but, on the other hand, limit entrance of 'atypical' groups and reinforce inequalities. Even in assessment centres where 'objective' tests are in place, and selectors have received training, justification for decisions based on similarity with existing management, accents and appearance may be made.

The ethical challenges created by norms and subjective criteria also extend to recruitment in the international context. Despite the discourse on the benefits of diversity for both domestic and international organizations, the relative informality of some expatriate recruitment decisions provides the opportunity for a reinforcement of models of what makes a 'good expatriate' and a suitable candidate for a particular destination. In the context of global careers and multinational organizations, where experience of international assignments has become increasingly important for top jobs, this subjective selection in decision making can both limit the supply of candidates meeting the criteria for top management jobs and undermine access for some groups. The next section considers the key elements of expatriate assignments and recruitment decisions for international assignments.

Recruiting for international assignments

The function of international assignments depends on the global strategy defined by the company and its translation in terms of human resource management. The reasons to send employees abroad might be either for specific staffing needs such as filling positions due to a lack of local talent or for organization development purposes such as control and coordination, diffusing knowledge and know-how, and instilling corporate culture, or alternatively for management development purposes (e.g. Bonache and Cervino 1997; Stahl and Cerdin 2004) such as the development of cross-cultural managerial competences. As such expatriates have often been considered as strategic resources. Henceforth the more strategic the use of international assignments the more functions they play in terms of developing a cadre of internationally experienced managers and organizational development.

The combination of global mobility, strategic responsibilities and high levels of interactions with a variety of cultures and nationalities means that recruiting and selecting suitable expatriates is an important function in the multinational environment. Jordan and Cartwright (1998) review the vast literature on expatriate selection and suggest that selection of expatriates should be based upon three key attributes – openness to experience, a medium level of extroversion and a low level of anxiety and neuroticism, plus four competences – relational abilities, cultural sensitivity, linguistic ability and stress handling. These competences and attributes permit expatriates to cope with adjustment to a new environment and deal with interactions in uncertain and novel situations. However, expatriation is not only demanding personally on the individual assigned to a new environment but also on their families (Starr and Currie 2009).

Indeed, a key characteristic of a long-term international assignment is the relocation of the expatriate and often his/her family. As such the organization might take on responsibility for more aspects of the employee's life than in the home country, including security, education, tax advice and many other aspects of non-work life (Bonache 2006). In this way the organization becomes inextricably involved in the family life of the international assignee, even where an expatriate 'commutes' and leaves their family at home. These family, dual career and work–life issues are important in influencing an offer to relocate and/or decisions to take up alternative mobility arrangements such as frequent flying and commuting (Meyskens et al. 2009).

However, this relationship between family and multinationals has often been implicit rather than explicit with consideration of family adjustment and support in the host country often given relatively little attention. Research has nevertheless shown how the influence and the involvement of the expatriate family play an important role at every stage of an international assignment (Starr and Currie 2009). For instance, this family influence has been found from the willingness of the expatriate to accept an assignment (Konopaske et al. 2005) to the effectiveness of the repatriation management (Suutari et al. 2012).

The family dimension to the expatriation process also means that non-work elements implicitly become part of the recruitment and selection decision (Tornikoski 2011). We recognize that these considerations may influence recruitment decisions for non-international positions too: in the domestic setting employers may be reluctant to employ women of childbearing age for fear of having to cope with employees with care commitments or maternity leave, while marriage and parenthood may be viewed as positive stabilizing factors for men. What is different about the recruitment decision for international assignments is the greater integration of firm and family, since the organization may eventually take on some responsibilities for aspects of the employee's family life. Furthermore, for dual earning couples, mobility requires both expatriate and spouse to change their professional lives.

While the strategic role of expatriates has become increasingly important in the control and coordination of multinational companies, the approach to recruitment and selection has not always been so strategic. Harris and Brewster (1999) describe the *coffee machine system* whereby decisions about who might be a suitable candidate are made through chance encounters among a small network of managers reinforcing models based on the characteristics of previous expatriates and group norms. This ad hoc process is perhaps not surprising when we find that some assignments often need to be filled at short notice: the important control function of an international posting means that employees may be required in place in a relatively urgent time frame. The limited lead times is often a factor constraining the preparation of expatriates for adjustment to their new lives and we can extend the impact of this to rushed recruitment decisions.

For others the process can be more ordered but notions of what makes a 'good expatriate' may still come into play. For instance Adler's (1994) classic studies on the barriers women face in gaining access to international assignments illustrates another way in which assumptions about what makes a good expatriate can reinforce certain norms around who is recruited and thus limit the supply of expatriates. Adler's studies were premised on the hypothesis that recruiting managers worked on a number of assumptions. First, that women do not want to take up international assignments and there is therefore no need to include them in the recruitment process for such positions. Adler subsequently found that male and female MBA graduates expressed an equal desire to take up international posts. Second, recruiting managers and MNCs were reluctant themselves to select women for such positions as they were regarded as high risk. Adler, and others since, found support for this exclusion mechanism blocking access to international assignments. Third, that host country nationals would resist a female expatriate since gender equality was not recognized in the same way across countries. Adler and others subsequently identified the so-called 'gajin effect' whereby women are foreigners first and women second and that there may in fact be benefits of having women in expatriate positions.

The work on the lack of female expatriates suggests that multinationals are often guilty of making challengeable assumptions about what women and men will do and want to do. These assumptions extend to women as employees and also to their male spouses who would also be required to follow their partners. The norms around men and women's roles in expatriation come from women's traditional role as a trailing spouse, supporting the family and the (male) expatriate in the adjustment to non-working life. Having had no job to relinquish in the home country, or at least a position that was expendable for the sake of the husband's, women were in a position to follow. By looking at more recent studies on 'trailing spouses', we can see how these norms are changing and are culturally determined. For example, we find quite different expectations among Finnish and Japanese women relocating for the partner's work (Riusala and Suutari 2000; Simeon and Fujiu 2000). Similarly, other studies on dual earning couples demonstrate that organizations are not well placed to support recruitment decisions involving an impact upon two careers (Mäkelä *et al.* 2011). Furthermore, when the trailing spouse is male conventional norms and support networks can be challenged.

Harris and Brewster (1999) describe a model of selection for international assignments that illustrates how recruiting managers' assumptions of what is a suitable expatriate narrow the potential pool of recruits. They describe the process by which managers selected expatriates based on a 'fit' with previous models and that this fit was strongly founded on gendered norms. Harris and Brewster describe two broad methods of recruitment. In an open system positions are advertised to all eligible employees while in a closed system nominations are made from within recruiting managers' networks. In the latter case there is a strong influence for gendered norms as identified by Adler and others. Similarly Harris and Brewster also outline two types of selection: one formal and one informal (see Table 22.1). In the formal selection procedure criteria and measures are clearly defined and selectors receive training. By contrast, in the informal approach selectors do not work with predefined criteria or measures and receive no training. Using this 2x2 matrix they find that the proportion of female expatriate managers was higher in systems where there are formal selection procedures and open methods of recruitment.

Both the level of openness in the recruitment process – providing information for a small 'suitable' group or a wide pool of potential applicants – and the level

TABLE 22.1 A typology of recruitment and selection for international assignments

	Formal	*Informal*
Open	Clearly defined criteria Clearly defined measures Training for selectors Open advertisement (internal and external) Panel discussions for selection	Less defined criteria Less defined measures Limited training for selectors No panel discussions Open advertisement Recommendations
Closed	Clearly defined criteria Clearly defined measures Training for selectors Panel discussions Nominations only (networking and reputation)	Selectors' individual preferences determine criteria and measures No panel discussions Nominations only (networking and reputation)

Source: Harris and Brewster (1999).

of formality of the selection decision – based on previous assumptions or careful specification of job characteristics – are likely to influence the process by which expatriates are assigned to posts overseas. We can extend Harris and Brewster's model to formal and informal consideration and assumptions around the family since the same notions of 'fit' can be seen to apply.

At one level these recruitment decisions for international assignments may fall between jurisdictions and thus conventional legal pressures to avoid discrimination and promote diversity and open recruitment may not apply or at least be blurred. Wilkinson *et al.* (2010) point out how multinationals' ability to transfer activities between institutions and environments may allow them to avoid their domestic legal responsibilities by shifting work outside their organization or outside their country in order to bypass regulations. Indeed, inter-organizational networks across national borders create greater scope for a breakdown in the relationship between an employee and a single employer. However, at the same time multinationals are subject to the same pressures, leading domestic organizations to be more open and seek the benefits of a varied and diverse workforce – competition for the best talent, demographic changes and an imperative to manage corporate image.

Nevertheless, ethical issues in international human resource management have tended to focus on the treatment of employees in the host country context, particularly in relation to corporate social responsibility. The media spotlight has highlighted employment conditions of often very young employees making sportswear or assembling high technology devices in Asia (Asgary and Mitschow 2002). Studies on ethical behaviour in relation to expatriates have tended to focus on how expatriates behave when faced with ethical challenges vis-à-vis host or parent countries' nationals with which they work. For example, Bailey and Spicer (2007) found that where parent country nationals were well-integrated into the host country they expressed ethical considerations similar to those of the host country nationals. On the other hand, issues of perceived injustice among host country nationals in relation to the differentials between local and expatriate compensation packages (Chen *et al.* 2002) raise wider ethical issues for how employers should treat international and culturally diverse groups of employees (Levels 2 *and* 3 of critique as discussed in Chapter 2 above).

What both of these approaches miss is the ethical conduct of the multinational towards its more senior (internal) employees and their families – in particular the recruitment for international assignments. International assignments involve working across jurisdictions and under the influence of norms and expectations from the host and home country. Ethical programmes implemented within organizations have tended to focus on written standards, training, advice mechanisms, misconduct reporting, disciplining violations and the integration of ethical conduct into performance appraisal (Vadera and Aguilera 2009). In the context of multinational companies, an additional dimension comes into play since organizations, and their ethical codes, need to take into account cultural and national differences that are not necessarily present in the national setting (see Chapter 2, Level 3 critique). However, by considering or even second guessing the expectations of one group of stakeholders, parent country employees and clients or employees in the host country, multinationals may find themselves undermining the position of another group of stakeholders, the pool of recruits for international assignments from home and other host country environments.

These decisions will also be influenced by the home country environment. Managers in multinationals originating from countries with a strong equality ethos may be more likely to adopt a broader notion of what is a suitable expatriate. Langlois and Schlegelmilch (1999) find different approaches to corporate codes of ethics among multinationals with different national origins relating to employee conduct, supplier relations and political interests. Singh *et al.* (2005) find quite different content of ethical programmes between organizations originating from Anglo-Saxon countries and those coming from Sweden. However, the organizations too can make a difference. Weaver *et al.* (1999) find that, in addition to contextual factors, management commitment was important in determining the approach adopted. The commitment of top management is also a key consideration when we consider the integration of systematic HR processes, such as equality in recruitment. Ethical codes can sometimes be more about external window dressing than real factors for changing and improving conduct. Integrating an ethical dimension to HR processes is more challenging but perhaps offers a means to an enhanced ethical approach of multinationals towards more of their stakeholders.

Conclusions

The debate about whether human resource management is or can be ethical has occupied researchers for more than two decades with no clear resolution in sight. However, while the ethics of human resource management as an approach to managing people may be debatable, creating ethical standards for different HR processes is perhaps conceivable. We have seen that in both the domestic and international arenas, the assumptions, implicit and explicit, used in recruitment and selection of employees have the potential to deny individuals access to posts and deny organizations access to the full range of talent, reinforcing inequalities and out-of-date norms. By giving a 'voice' to such stakeholders, assumptions may be challenged since a managerial voice alone may simply perpetuate outdated norms and approaches inappropriate for twenty-first century societies. This would challenge the 'unitarist' bias of some HRM proponents and would allow managers to become aware of and take into account alternative perspectives.

Vadera and Aguilera (2009) stress that for ethical programmes to be effective in organizations, and particularly in multinational organizations, these programmes need to be fully integrated into the strategy for managing human resources. This means recruitment of employees from both host and parent countries that are capable of formulating and communicating ethical programmes, integration of ethical programmes into a broad training and development strategy and evaluating and rewarding employees on the basis of their conduct and communication of ethical programmes. However, since human resource management in subsidiaries is often multidimensional in character – reflecting the diverse institutional and social environment in which it is embedded – linking ethical codes to strategic HRM may imply a greater control of what may be ultimately local practices. Kolka and van Tulder (2004) argue that this trade-off may lead organizations to adopt a more relativist approach since an 'open attitude towards stakeholders in different countries and settings . . . [means] a universal, standardized approach does not really fit' (ibid., p. 58). Consideration of stakeholders could also extend to the families of employees on expatriate assignments since the hidden role they tend to hold means that they are represented by norms and expectations of managers within employing organizations rather than having a voice themselves.

Asgary and Mitschow (2002) argue that any universal set of ethical rules for a single multinational must be based on a complete review of the social, political and cultural situation in the countries affected: no small task and difficult to reconcile, and inevitably involving issues of metaethics, that is Level 3 critique as outlined in Chapter 2. However, as multinationals seek to develop a common approach across country settings – for example through the management of a common organizational culture separate from home or parent culture – consideration of a common set of ethical norms regarding the management of its internal human resources becomes more of an imperative. This includes the families of employees as stakeholders since, although they might be considered a complication in recruitment decisions, ignoring the family has long proved a short circuit to failure in expatriate appointments.

ETHICAL CASE OF INTERNATIONAL RECRUITMENT AND SELECTION

The pharmaceutical industrial sector includes some big names – GlaxoSmithKline, Sanofi-Aventis, Novartis, Roche, Bayer, AstraZeneca for Europe, and Pfizer, Johnson and Johnson, Merck and Bristol-Myers Squibb from the US – as well as a multitude of smaller players. Innovation and Research and Development (R&D) have always been key factors of competitiveness for most of the companies in this sector.

Paul leads an HR team in a large European pharmaceutical multinational company (MNC). He has HR responsibility in one of the big research centres located in Belgium, named ACE, where Mr Phil Dunord has been working as the managing director for more than eight years. The largest share of the company's new products is invented in the company's laboratories and licensed by its R&D centres. However, two-thirds of the rest of the company's products are manufactured under licence from foreign pharmaceutical developers, though a significant percentage of their products are off-patent drugs manufactured and distributed without licensing from the original manufacturer (since the patents on such drugs have expired).

The European MNC acquired an Indian pharmaceutical company called SPECINDI located in Agra and which had been their partner for more than 20 years.

SPECINDI was acquired with the aim of merging with ACE since they had complementary knowledge and know-how. SPECINDI has four teams of researchers experienced in dealing with protocols and tests of new medicine on animals and humans. This acquisition signalled the beginning of an important and long-expected restructuring of ACE. The research teams needed to find new ways of collaborating and working complementarily. The objective of their collaboration was to obtain an uninterrupted process from the creation of new chemical molecules through to the approval, or not, by regulatory authorities and the start of medical trials on humans.

As the managing director of ACE, Mr Dunord had been involved at the heart of this strategic thinking, planning and reorganization process for more than three years prior to the actual merger. Most of the ACE and SPECINDI staff's fears of the restructuring and of their potential layoff had been allayed. The initial integration of the new distant employees in the daily research collaboration had been well planned and was going relatively smoothly. Cross-cultural training had been provided to both units for two years prior to the merger and diversity management had been one of the top human resource management priorities since the beginning of the integration process. This process was handled with a clear and monthly communication of the challenges, the goals and the progress to the employees of both Belgian and Indian units as well as working with the trade unions, especially at ACE.

The former CEO of SPECINDI, Mr Naman Sahni had been extremely helpful in this acquisition/merger preparation. Prior to the acquisition, an internal survey (designed by ACE, translated and adapted by SPECINDI) had shown that his employees had a high regard for him and were therefore ready to make extra efforts in the long run to adapt to the expected stressful organizational change. They understood what was individually and collectively required from them to attain the strategic objectives *he* had set up for *his people* for the future. His leadership aura, representativeness and charisma had been recognized within the multinational executive board and HR team, and long discussed before the acquisition. One outcome of the negotiation between ACE and SPECINDI had been that Mr Naman Sahni would stay in the merged organization, ACE–SPECINDI, for a minimum of three years after the acquisition to render this organizational transition possible. This explains part of the rather smooth progress Paul and his HR team had been witnessing.

However, Mr Sahni announced one month ago that he would have to retire in the coming eight months for medical reasons. This destabilizing news has been kept confidential at the top executive level for the moment but will be released in the next month. Since this announcement, Dunord, together with Sahni and the HR team, have been scanning the human resources of the company for a potential successor at the head of ACE–SPECINDI in India. Three possible candidates have been identified within the European MNC and one external candidate. The four potential candidates are described below.

Franck (43 years old, Belgian) has been working in an Italian research unit for seven years in Turin. He has held different positions from lab assistant, researcher, research team manager, to the unit managing position for the last year. His research centre has been collaborating for five years with another Indian partner of the company. In addition, his international managerial competencies have been overwhelmingly approved at a number of executive meetings in recent years. He is married to Jenny (40 years old, Swedish), a manager in a medium-sized editing company. She loves her job in this company where she has been working for five years after two years of 'painful' job searching and taking care of their children. Their son, Erik (15 years), who initially had some difficulties coping with his new Italian environment, now studies in a very good Italian high school. He speaks Swedish, Flemish, French, and Italian fluently. He has been a member of a very active football team that has competed at the national level for four years. He also plays the piano at the conservatoire of music. His sister, Mathilda (12 years) goes to the nearby college. Even though she has faced fewer difficulties in terms of cultural adaptation after their move to Turin, her allergies have required a lot of care and attention for the last five years. She seems to have overcome the most troubling ones now.

Phil Dunord contacted Franck two weeks ago regarding the job opportunity in India. He was very surprised and interested by this job offer. He took this as a great professional opportunity for his career since he loves challenges and working in an international environment.

Anna (38 years old, English) is a very fast-rising female manager in an English research unit of the MNC. She is a well-known chemist researcher who has already played a key role in the development of two major molecules. One molecule is already in pre-clinical tests and is very promising as a possible preventive remedy against Factor V Leiden thrombophilia, a rare blood-clotting disorder caused by a mutation of the gene of the same name. The research team she has been managing for three years is made up mainly of Indian native researchers. She has been noticed for her capacities in 'smoothly' and effectively handling diverse cultural issues while avoiding an impact upon the research processes. In addition, she speaks Hindi and had already mentioned she might be willing to go to India to her superiors if the opportunity arose in the future. She has been living with Pierre, a French researcher in biology, for four years in a south-west London suburb.

She was delighted to hear of the job opportunity that Dunord told her about two weeks ago.

Adhip (42 years old, Indian) is a very promising senior manager. He has already become known as 'The Chosen One' since Naman Sahni has officially made clear that Adhip would succeed him in two or three years. He has already been working with the executive board of SPECINDI for four years and has had two previous international expatriation experiences: one in Australia and the other in Belgium. He has shown excellent diplomatic competencies during the acquisition negotiations with ACE and the representatives of the multinational. He is single, although he has elderly and sick parents, for whom he organizes care, who regularly remind him that he has to find a wife quickly. This still does not seem to be his priority despite the importance given to marrying young in Indian culture.

Adhip was the first one to be informed by Mr Sahni about his decision to step down and leave the company. He was really affected by this unexpected and sad news. Both took time to carefully discuss the different options offered to Adhip for his future both within and outside SPECINDI before Mr Sahni informed Dunord and his HR team. Nevertheless, Naman Sahni really emphasized how much he expected of him for the sake of *his people* in SPECINDI. Therefore, Adhip was well prepared when Mr Dunord contacted him one week ago.

Pawel (41 years old, Polish) is the head of a competitor pharmaceutical unit in Delhi. He is also a friend of several directors of the multinational's executive board. He has been living in India for ten years. He is married and has three children (12, 10 and 6 years old). His wife, Norma, does not work and takes care of the children. She is also involved in numerous charities and NGOs for child protection and education. She speaks Polish, English and Hindi, while Pawel still does not speak Hindi. Their children have lived most of their life in Delhi and therefore behave more like Indian than Polish citizens even though they regularly visit their grandparents in Poland.

Pawel was pleasantly surprised when he got a phone call from Mr Phil Dunord a few days ago. The news of Mr Naman Sahni's health condition saddened him because the former CEO of SPECINDI is a well-respected man who had really worked hard to offer excellent working conditions to his employees. He hoped that he would overcome this difficult time of his life and recover in the coming years. He told Phil Dunord that he was honoured and grateful for this offer and that he was considering it very seriously and with enthusiasm. He nevertheless had to check the non-competition clause of his working contract and would quickly come back to him.

You are a member of Paul's HR team. What would you do? Who would you select?

CLASS QUESTIONS

1   Identify the key strengths and weaknesses between the candidates and the arguments to defend the application of each one of them.
2   Indicate thoroughly what ethical issues you would face as an HR professional in this selection process.
3   Consider how you would balance the competing interests of the stakeholders in this case.

Further reading

Pinnington, A. H., Macklin, R. and Campbell, T. (eds) (2007) *Human Resource Management: Ethics and employment.* Oxford: Oxford University Press.

References

Ackers, P. (2009) 'Employment ethics'. In T. Redman and A. Wilkinson (eds), *Contemporary Human Resource Management: Text and cases.* Harlow: Financial Times, Prentice Hall.

Adler, N. (1994) 'Competitive frontiers: Women managing across borders', *Journal of Management Development*, 13(2): 24–41.

Asgary, N. and Mitschow, M. C. (2002) 'Toward a model for international business ethics', *Journal of Business Ethics*, 36: 239–246.

Bailey, W. and Spicer, A. (2007) 'When does national identity matter? Convergence and divergence in international business ethics', *Academy of Management Journal*, 50(6): 1462–1480.

Bonache, J. (2006) 'The compensation of expatriates: A review and a future research agenda'. In I. Bjorkman and G. Stahl (eds), *Handbook of Research in International Human Resource Management*. Cheltenham: Edward Elgar, pp. 158–175.

Bonache, J. and Cervino, J. (1997) 'Global integration without expatriates', *Human Resource Management Journal*, 7(3): 89–100.

Catano, V. M., Wiesner, W. H., Hackett, R. D. and Methot, L. L. (2009) *Recruitment and Selection in Canada*, 4th edn. Toronto: Nelson Education Ltd.

Chen, C. C., Choi, J. and Chi, S-C. (2002) 'Making justice sense of local–expatriate compensation disparity: Mitigation by local referents, ideological explanations, and interpersonal sensitivity in China–Foreign joint ventures', *Academy of Management Journal* 45(4): 807–817.

Clark, T. and Mallory, G. (1996) 'The cultural relativity of human resource management: Is there a universal model?' In T. A. R. Clark (ed.), *European Human Resource Management: An introduction to comparative theory and practice*. Oxford: Blackwell, pp. 1–33.

Greenwood, M. R. (2002) 'Ethics and HRM: A review and conceptual analysis', *Journal of Business Ethics*, 36(3): 261–278.

Guest, D. E. (1999) 'Human resource management – the worker's verdict'. *Human Resource Management Journal*, 9(3): 5–25.

Harris, H. and Brewster, C. (1999) 'The coffee-machine system: How international selection really works', *The International Journal of Human Resource Management*, 10: 488–500.

Johnsen, R. and Gudmand-Høyer, M. (2010) 'Lacan and the lack of humanity in HRM', *Organization*, 17(3): 331–344.

Jordan, J. and Cartwright, S. (1998) 'Selecting expatriate managers: Key traits and competencies', *Leadership and Organizational Development Journal*, 19(2): 89–96.

Kolka, A. and van Tulder, R. (2004) 'Ethics in international business: Multinational approaches to child labor', *Journal of World Business*, 39: 49–60.

Konopaske, R., Robie, C. and Ivancevich, J. M. (2005) 'A preliminary model of spouse influence on managerial global assignment willingness', *The International Journal of Human Resource Management*, 16(3): 405–426.

Langlois, C. C. and Schlegelmilch, B. B. (1999) 'Do corporate codes of ethics reflect national character? Evidence from Europe and the United States', *Journal of International Business Studies*, 21(4): 519–539.

Legge, K. (1995) *Human Resource Management: Rhetorics and realities*. Chippenham: Macmillan Business.

Macklin, R. (2007) 'The morally decent HR manager', in A. H. Pinnington, R. Macklin and T. Campbell (eds), *Human Resource Management: Ethics and employment*. New York: Oxford University Press.

Mäkelä, L., Känsälä, M. and Suutari, V. (2011) 'The roles of expatriates' spouses among dual career couples', *Cross Cultural Management: An International Journal*, 18(2): 185–197.

Meyskens, M., von Glinow, M. A., Werther, W. B. and Clarke, L. (2009) 'The paradox of international talent: Alternative forms of international assignments', *The International Journal of Human Resource Management*, 20(6): 1439–1450.

Orlitzky, M. (2007) 'Recruitment strategy'. In P. Boxall, J. Purcell and P. Wright (2007) *The Oxford Handbook of Human Resource Management*. New York: Oxford University Press, Chapter 14.

Perkins, S. J. and Daste, R. (2007) 'Pluralistic tensions in expatriating managers', *Journal of European Industrial Training*, 31(7): 550–569.

Riusala, K. and Suutari V. (2000) 'Expatriation and careers: Perspectives of expatriates and spouses', *Career Development International*, 5(2): 81–90.

Simeon, R. and Fujiu, K. (2000) 'Cross cultural adjustment strategies of spouses in Silicon Valley', *Employee Relations*, 22(6): 594–611.

Singh, J., Carasco, E., Svensson, G., Wood, G. and Callaghan, M. (2005) 'A comparative study of the contents of corporate codes of ethics in Australia, Canada and Sweden', *Journal of World Business*, 40: 91–109.

Stahl, G. K. and Cerdin, J-L. (2004) 'Global careers in French and German multinational corporations', *Journal of Management Development*, 23(9): 885–902.

Starr, T. L. and Currie, G. (2009) '"Out of sight but still in the picture": Short-term international assignments and the influential role of family', *The International Journal of Human Resource Management*, 20(6): 1421–1438.

Storey, J. (2001) 'Introduction: From personnel management to human resource management'. In J. Storey (ed.) *Human Resource Management: A critical text*. London: IT.

Suutari, V., Tornikoski, C. and Mäkelä, L. (2012) 'Career decision making of global careerists', *International Journal of Human Resource Management*. Available online at www.tandfonline.com/doi/abs/10.1080/09585192.2011.639026.

Tornikoski, C. (2011) 'Total reward bundle: A theoretical approach – the case of expatriate package'. In C. H. Antoni, X. Baeten, R. Lucas, S. Perkins and M. Vartiainen (eds), *Pay and Reward Systems in Organizations – Theoretical approaches and empirical outcomes*. Lengerich: Pabst Science Publishers.

Vadera, A. and Aguilera, R. (2009) 'The role of IHRM in the formulation of ethical programs in multinational enterprises'. In P. Sparrow (ed.), *Handbook of International Human Resource Management: Integrating people, process and context*. Oxford: Blackwell.

Weaver, G. R., Trevino, L. R. and Cochran, P. L. (1999) 'Corporate ethics programs as a control system: Influences of executive commitment and environmental factors', *Academy of Management Journal*, 42(5): 539–552.

Wilkinson, A., Gollan, P. J., Marchington, M. and Lewin, D. (2010) *The Oxford Handbook of Participation in Organizations*. Oxford: Oxford University Press.

23

COMPETENCY MANAGEMENT

Between managerial development and ethical questioning

Pierre-Yves Sanséau

Introduction

Major changes in managerial approaches are at the core of business ethics considerations. What are the opportunities and the limits for companies in terms of managerial orientations in order to adapt to new fast-moving contexts? Can employees be forced to adopt new managerial principles as the only way to adapt? What are the impacts of managerial tools and actions on the community of workers?

In this chapter, our aim is first to introduce the competency management approach and then to analyse its strengths and limits in terms of ethical considerations. The concept of competences has developed since the 1980s and has the power to put the individual back at the centre of the organization in a place where they are finally recognized as a key actor and contributor in the performance of the company. While moving from a traditional vision of management, which, for a long time, has considered the individual more like a substitute for the company, more passive than active, and having to observe and comply with operating rules dictated by direction and managers, competency management has deeply modified the stakes of the contemporary organization. The question of a new type of recognition in a competency-based organization is raised and has to be analysed. New approaches have to be considered while putting ethics at the core. This chapter shows how a renewed managerial approach, with a great potential to move away from traditional approaches of management also introduces tensions and questioning in the company for the different stakeholders.

The chapter considers the ethical issues raised by competency management within the three levels of critique developed in Chapter 2. At Level 1 of critique we can consider competency management in relation to the discourse of how individuals ought to be treated and how managers ought to behave within organizations. At Level 2 we can consider the relationship between the management and valuation of competences inside the organization and the role that a company plays in relation to the wider labour market. Finally, the cross-national dimension of the Level 3 critique is considered in relation to how competences are constructed and valued in different national settings and the impact of this on the management of individuals by competence.

The concept of competence: multiplicity of scientific fields and diversified approaches

The concept of competence, since it became a major concern in the scientific field of management in the 1980s, has concerned several disciplines linked with education and work. A difference in the approaches and in the positioning has appeared, reproducing the segmentation of theoretical postures based on different or even opposing origins.

Ergonomists have developed the concept of competence through major evolutions of the nature of work, moving from a material dimension to a dimension increasingly more directed towards an immaterial one with the evolution of economies around services and towards a mode of production oriented around knowledge. Ergonomics tends to define competences as knowledge, skills, ways of reasoning, and abilities mobilized for a specific task (de Montmollin 1986). Competences are thus considered as different in ergonomics from capacities, which are not sufficient to explain the success or the failure of an operator facing a specific task. They are indeed very close to 'expertise' on both difficult and easy tasks (Wickens and Hollands 2000; Vicente 2004).

On the other hand, for psychologists, the term 'competence' would seem to have made its appearance around the 1990s, building on the development and the measurement of competences, in line with the assessments of competences. However, at the end of the nineteenth century, the notion of 'test' appeared with the idea to measure inter-individual differences in elementary processes such as sensation, perception and reaction time. The first tests were used, for example, to select tramway drivers in the USA and train conductors and drivers in France at the beginning of the twentieth century. Around this time also appeared the IQ (intelligence quotient) notion in order to allocate individuals according to their memory, mental imaging and other faculties (Weiner 2003). In the sciences of education, a third field, which is rather close to the framework of the psychology of work in its approach, defines competence as knowledge in use, corresponding to a moving and complex but structured unity, operational and adjusted for the action.

The sociology of work, a fourth field that has invested in the concept of competence, has been based for a long time on the concept of qualification. This concept, central in the sociology of work but subject to debate, is based on hierarchical classifications, diplomas validating knowledge and collective agreements. In a context of transformation of the models of production and work organization and the crisis of the Taylorist model, the concept of qualification reveals its limits because of its rigidity, difficulties in adapting to services and weak adaptation to the knowledge acquired in a work context. Thus 'competence' can be translated as an individualization of the wage relation, owing to a weakening of the collective dimension in the companies (decline of trade unionism, social conflict and collective bargaining) and chronic instability for the workers (lifelong learning, professional mobility, multiplication of professional and work situations) (Friedmann 1955).

Finally the field of the management sciences underlines that the concept of competence has always been at the heart of management and specifically of human resources management (HRM). A major change has, however, occurred; it deals with the evolution of the traditional concept of required competences to that of held competences. The change resulting from technology and perpetual mobility has made an approach based on the work station and employment obsolete. For the company, its human resource or human capital remains but the key is now located around the competences held by the individuals in the organizations, the basis of the 'model of competence'. Having the right competences, at the right time and in the required situations should constitute a factor of success for many companies (McClelland 1973; Lawler III 1994).

Competences in management sciences: three major approaches

Developing the concept of competence within management sciences generally allows us to identify three levels: individual competences, collective competences and strategic competences. These levels are useful in identifying the applications of competency-based management and also in drawing out the potential ethical tensions for employees, organizations and stakeholders. The concept of competence often refers to the traditional segmentation of knowledge, know-how, knowing 'how to be'. This definition has been specified and refined around a concept of capacity of implementation in a given context, of potential success in a situation of work. This approach is no longer 'static' but is directed towards a concept of dynamism, continuous training and 'operationality'. Developed in the United States in the 1990s, this approach suggests competences are based on a 'successful action' and performance. Later in Europe, the concepts of initiative and responsibility in professional situations and of practical intelligence of the situations were developed (Klein 1996; Bouteiller and Gilbert 2005).

First of the three levels, individual competences, refer, for a person, to this contextual and validated operational know-how. We focus here on a person as a unit in a professional context (Boyatzis 1982; Spencer and Spencer 1993; Sanséau 2011). The second level incorporates collective competences. They refer to the interaction of people in work situations, including a combination of individual competences, knowledge and tacit know-how or informal exchanges supported by solidarity. Collective competence would be the advantageous way to face complexity. The individual initiative would be obsolete if all the actors did not engage in the same way with a synergy between the individuals in the organization, the key to effectiveness and risk minimization (Sanséau 2011).

The third level is one of strategic competences. Originating from the 'resource-based view' of the firm in the field of strategic management, this concept appeared in the 1990s. In contrast to the concept of individual competence, where the practices preceded the theoretical approaches, the concept of strategic competence first appeared in the theoretical field to give place thereafter to more concrete applications. If this concept seems close to the competence approach in management, it also has differences. Hamel and Prahalad (1990) define strategic competence as a set of several knowledge-specific technologies in a company, know-how controlled by all or some of the employees, which confers to the company a durable competitive advantage on the market. The authors characterize strategic competence around three indicators: the value attributed by the customer, a differentiation from the competitors, the elasticity which is defined as the capacity to create bridges towards the markets of the future (Wright *et al.* 1994).

Between the dimension of individual competences that would be the prerogative of the field of HRM and the approach by strategic competences that concerns strategic management, it is possible to differentiate two approaches or visions. The first approach, developed in the HRM field, is centred on a desire to go beyond the rigid design of knowledge and know-how of the individuals in companies, based on a Taylorist vision of work. The competences held exceed those that are strategically required, which gives the company new breath to adapt to a fast-moving and competitive context. The HRM approach tends to go beyond a positive or descriptive study of work, trying to highlight what the workers could bring to the company, while mobilizing their own competences. The second approach, based on the concept of strategic competence, deals with the implementation of the strategy of the company to ensure its development and survival.

However, some authors argue that this proximity between the concepts of competences in HRM and in the field of strategy is only superficial. Indeed, strategy and HRM do not define the term 'competence' in the same way. In the field of strategy, competence is a collective concept that indicates organizational routine; it refers to a competitive advantage and especially underlines what competences do rather than what they are. Thus, in the strategic approach, their effects are emphasized more than their nature. By contrast, in HRM, the concept of competence refers to an individual-level notion, specified and detailed, and encapsulates a set of qualities and knowledge held by a person.

International approaches in terms of competency management

These various fields underline the diversity of the origins, approaches and objectives of 'competence', as well as the management of competences. Consequently, is it necessary to adopt a single approach or cross-approaches? Moreover, which definitions of management of competences should be adopted in management sciences where there is a multiplicity: definitions based on the contents, definitions focusing on the training and acquisition of employees, definitions related to the implementation of the management of competences? The perimeter is extremely broad and, taking into consideration the positions and the objectives of the scholars, the approaches are multiple but also rich in terms of complementarities.

Through a comparison of the approaches in North America and France by Bouteiller and Gilbert (2005), a comparative reflection on management of competences makes it possible to contextualize a number of concepts and of objectives. Two currents with different sources, objectives and conceptualizations, can be distinguished, but are finally relatively close in terms of action.

The North-American approach finds its origins in the work of McClelland, who aimed to identify the attitudes and characteristics of the most powerful individuals in situations of work, qualified 'high achievers'. For McClelland (1973), the key competences mobilized by workers could constitute an indicator of their performance. This competence approach concerned mostly 'white collar' workers in an economical logic, detached from an instrumental or strategic point of view. The idea of competence is based on the concept of competitive advantage of the firm, in reaction to an increasing competing context of the mobility of the employees. It was clearly defined in terms of the performance required for the success of the task. McClelland (1973) proposed a definition of competence in which one finds the spirit of the Anglo-Saxon approach. Competence is a unit that integrates an individual perspective (knowledge and personal traits), a cognitive dimension (behaviours or designs of oneself – attitudes, values and images of oneself) and a social dimension (skills – know-how or skills – and motives – interior forces generating the behaviours with work). The management of competences in North America is illustrated by an instrumentation targeted at the executives and managerial key competences of a generic type described as 'soft skills'.

The French approach of management of competences that dominates Latin countries in Europe and many countries in Africa seems much less targeted and sometimes rather broad. Initially initiated by large companies in the 1980s with the aim of training, careers guidance and management of careers, it was characterized in the 1990s by work reorganization, control of the productive organizations, management of the workforce and an orientation around poorly qualified workers. This French approach distinguishes in a recurring way three components of competences: (1) knowledge, '*savoir*' (theoretical competences); (2) know-how, '*savoir-faire*' (practical competences); (3) knowledge of being, '*savoir-être*' (social and behavioural competences). Adopting a Level 1 critique, we can see how the normative approach of how workers ought to be – *savoir être* – could include an ethical tension. This triptych retained in many countries remains the reference, but the definitions are many and different according to the fields and approaches developed in companies. In terms of instrumentation, each company develops its own frame of competences or adapts existing frames and the emphasis is clearly put on know-how. Once again, these tools could hide managerial ways of doing and acting and one can question this approach from an ethical standpoint.

Thus, we can at last identify two relatively distinct models in the management of competences. The idea of a 'universal' model falls away, which sometimes brings problems to the HR professional in search of clear perspectives and universal and recognized tools. However, this difference actually introduces a double advantage: first, to widen the spectrum of tools of analysis in a field not yet stabilized; second, to offer possibilities for a better understanding of the hidden logics behind the managerial HR policies of companies in a more and more globalized context. Recognizing the heterogeneity of principles of the various actors involved is fundamental to Level 3 of our analysis (see Chapter 2). Thus, although the concept of competence is dense, and without precise frontiers, it is enriched by the variety of meanings adopted by those using the term. In order to lessen the impact of confusion from these debates, one can adopt the following posture: considering the concept of competence in terms of utility rather than meaning. So we move from 'what are we talking about?' to 'what do we need as a concept?'

Management of competences at the crossroads of ethical considerations

If the goal of managing by competences is to go beyond hierarchical and traditional principles of management while offering more opportunities for employees in terms of responsibilities and empowerment, leading to a more efficient organization, it is also subject to multiple tensions linked with the content and the context. Thus, management of competences integrates a strong ethical dimension, mostly related to the Level 1 critique outlined in Chapter 2. We present below three fields of tensions in the management of competences that underline that, beyond a purely positive or descriptive study of this approach to management, we must also examine the rules governing business behaviour and the decisions and actions of managers and employees.

A gap between the positivist and the practical approach?

Beyond the concept of competency management, we have to consider the practices. The study of these practices helps us to develop a better understanding of the gap illustrating the descriptive side of a management approach and its implementation. We are here at the core of the Level 1 critique of how the management of competences ought to be and how they are experienced by employees and managers. We introduce the tensions here with five examples: the assessment of competences, the reinforcement of individualism and the managerial control, the collective dimension and the reality of the awaited roles for managers.

One of the most visible managerial activities of the management of competences is illustrated by the annual appraisal. As the reviewer is usually the manager, the two concerned actors have usually known each other for a while. So, the valuation of the manager is generally conditioned by the perception of the employee developed over time. The manager will have a predetermined image of the reviewed person, resulting from prior events and specific behaviours of the employee. The usual tendency for the reviewer will be to classify the employee in terms of positive versus negative aspects: good/bad, efficient/not efficient. Considering these aspects, some authors underline these biases related to the annual assessment, arguing that managers may take the opportunity to punish some employees.

As we already indicated, management of competences is mostly presented as an alternative to classical management, based on individual work and performance. If, in the 1970s and 1980s, management was revisited with the idea of developing workers' involvement and collective dimensions in order to lessen the impact of the division of labour, management of competences would pretend to go further. The idea is to mobilize all the competences of the company with the objective of offering the best for the client and the company. But, it appears that management of competences is in its implementation, and also an individualist model of HRM. Each employee is asked to develop their competences with individual objectives for a common objective but the review of competences is usually not collective but individual. So, this could reinforce individualism at work and have a negative impact on collective dimensions at work – dissent, rivalry – and in the organization.

One of the leading ideas of management of competences is to offer the employee more autonomy at work in terms of initiative, creativity and responsibilities. It also includes the idea that each employee can manage his present and future competences by influencing his training, career development and employability. Each employee has the right to suggest improvements on their tasks and professional activities but also concerning their personal and professional development. However, when competences are at the heart of management, we also discover that control is the other tendency. If a company tends to adopt a new approach of management, it is usually to get better results. And the effect is also more control on the actors of the company: more reporting, increasing financial and economic pressure on people and groups, more control on individual behaviours. When management of competences is mobilized by a company, middle management is usually at the centre of the processes. These managers are asked to be both implementers and reviewers. As a result, employees can perceive a contradictory situation in which they would have to share with their managers, to contribute to improving work and results by diffusing information to the managers, information that could be used to evaluate and perhaps to punish.

In organizations, the collective and group dimensions are crucial for collective performance and objectives: group results provide results greater than the sum of the individual competences. So there is a tendency to implement processes based on collective dimensions across companies as project groups integrate activities and tasks. However, in order to support this collective dimension, collective acts of management are also required; yet the reality seems to be mostly in the opposite direction: most management activities are developed around the individual. Management of competences is designed to give individual answers to individuals. In recruitment, remuneration, training, annual appraisal and management of careers, the approach is also mostly individual without taking into account the collective dimensions. If processes are collective, this also needs to be considered in elements of training or reviewing. In most companies, remuneration seems to be the only domain where this collective dimension has become a reality. In sales teams, for example, team pay has been practised for years, yet the annual appraisal remains individual in most companies.

Management of competences attributes new roles to managers: development of the competences of their employees, guidance, management of careers, counselling and sometimes internal coaching. This is a new posture considering the classical roles of the 'classic' manager – organizing, directing, controlling. In order to develop these expected new roles, middle managers must be equipped with the competences themselves and offered the time and space to do so. The reality is mostly quite different. If new roles are allocated in order to manage by competences, managers do not have the opportunities to develop them. In fact, these new tasks are more or and less added to what was expected before. So many managers express difficulty in assuming this double task: everyday management plus the management of competences of their employees.

The reaction is sometimes brutal: some managers refuse to assume these new tasks because of the workload. They pretend to do it but, in fact, little is done. The only visible task they undertake is the annual appraisal, but this may be done mechanically without developing the sense and potential of the management of competences. So, once again, the management of the activity does not make it possible for the manager to go beyond the traditional tasks, and developing competences is sacrificed to the realities of day-to-day management.

Management of competences at the crossroads of the interests of stakeholders

Despite these individual tensions, for stakeholders of the company, the management of competences offers opportunities for development and progress. Since the objective of competency management is to restructure management on a new basis (the competences), it is a new vision of management to be implemented. However, within the company, stakeholders are numerous and do not always share the same views and objectives, creating ethical tensions between the role business plays within the wider community and the actions of individuals towards stakeholders, including the workforce, trade unions and even shareholders.

For the company's shareholders, management of competences usually appears as a great opportunity. Thinking and acting 'competences' is a kind of new managerial paradigm. If the traditional company is based on qualifications, the competences-based company has the power to mobilize the present, potential, hidden competences in order to present a new face to the internal and external client: a new face based on a combination of individual competences – mobile, dynamic, adaptable – offering the company the power to be flexible, to develop processes, to save time in management of the interfaces, to reduce hierarchical levels, to better define work organization, to enhance client satisfaction and general performance, and to improve adaptability of the internal work force. Moreover, management based on competences gives the opportunity to go beyond situations illustrated by a management according to qualifications. Qualifications often mean collective management with no possibility of addressing the single worker. In terms of work organization, task design, remuneration and bargaining with the workers' representative, traditional management appears to be less flexible. This situation is usually owing to the fact that qualification principles are based on collective frames of remuneration and career development. Thus, shareholders may expect a better return on investment in a company with a management based on competences.

For the employees, management based on their competences offers new frontiers on various dimensions. The first one offers the opportunity to move to new jobs and positions in the company. If the annual appraisal highlights effective or potential competences for a worker, it opens doors to move around in terms of activity. Some employees can also develop other skills (by training or education) to add to held competences and redesign their career or start a new professional life. In fact, management of competences is an act very close to the concept of employability. Employability means the worker developing, enhancing their competences and skills in order to be able to move around in the company but also outside the company. Both the manager and the worker are involved in a process of keeping the competences at a level to protect employability, a level determined by the internal and external labour market.

In addition, for employees, management by competences may also mean the opportunity to increase their salaries and wages. If the company recognizes and puts the emphasis on the mobilized competences of the staff, it opens up the way for pay to recognize competences – mobilized competences are those required by the market or client. This aspect frequently occurs in sectors in which the job market is tight or in hi-tech industries. However, while it may be a path to permanent improvement, this method of reward may be unequal for the workers with obsolete competences. The approach has, of course, advantages, but also disadvantages: it can be a factor both of motivation and of poor motivation. The annual appraisal is becoming a ritual in most companies but we have to look forwards. It is also an opportunity for the worker to articulate their expectations for the future and, in many cases, it is the only such moment in the year. From this official face-to-face meeting between the manager and the employee, records will remain that may be used by the worker, the manager or the HR service to work on employability and career evolution. This evaluation is also strategic for the worker to position him/herself among co-workers and among other employees in the company. It may be a way to better understand the company from the inside and to discover the opportunities offered in terms of evolution.

All of these considerations should not hide the fact that, for workers, competency management is sometimes more complex than it seems because it also changes the terms of the relationship between the employer and the employee. If the employee has more resources and the right to move around, the employer always expects more from him in terms of results and performance. This effort is not always understood or accepted by all and can create difficult situations in which workers refuse to adapt to new rhythms, tasks and missions.

Competency is always the result of a combination of resources issued from the person and from the context. In a company, it means the employer has a moral responsibility to offer all the resources to the employees in order to develop their competencies. In too many observed cases, the opposite situation occurs: management asks employees to mobilize their own resources but do not offer much to facilitate and develop these. If the employee can develop their resources with training, various experiences and education, the employer has the duty and power to propose the right resources on his part: good working conditions (adapted fees and resources), appropriate management (communication, adapted objectives, feedback, follow up, plans for the future, etc.). Finally, we should not forget a point that regularly disappoints workers: the subjectivity that takes place in the annual performance review. Bad relations or poor considerations during the year between the employee and their manager can influence the appraisal result and impact on opportunities, desire to progress or salary improvements.

For unions, management of competences has two faces. The first one is illustrated by the fact that this style of management helps to move away from the recurrent dimensions of traditional management: dependency in the relationship between the employer and the employee, poor opportunities for the employees to express themselves or to be creative, and limited impact on work, the destiny of the company and the employees themselves. The idea of valorizing the (human) resources and the potential of the worker is a positive signal, liberating the worker from the constraints of narrowly defined tasks. However, on the other hand, unions quickly understood that both they and the workers could be threatened by this managerial approach – we have already seen the limits of the approach from a worker's perspective. For unions, there is a real risk of losing power and influence. Individualization of the work relationship also means weaker collective dimensions in the company and a potential loss of union influence. The unions also have to adapt their own approach and tools. Moreover, the process of the annual appraisal meeting offers a way to bypass the classic role of unions to communicate, represent and defend workers with management. So, in a context of management of competences, unions may lose some of their classic and preferred resources and have to rethink their role and *raison d'être* in the company.

It is important not to forget the client as central to the activity of the company. For the client, the mobilization of employee competences might be full of benefits: better products, better services, timely delivery, customer-oriented service, etc. But, and we will see this in the following case, some companies may intend to use the competencies of the employees for a single goal – organizational performance. If, as we have already underlined in this chapter, competency management is also designed to improve performance, it is not the only objective. Focusing on performance alone could be risky for a company and deter clients. The case illustrates deep managerial change in a company through the introduction of management of competences and highlights how a business ethics frame can be useful in analysing a case and questioning the behaviour of present and future managers.

CASE: FRANCE TELECOM MOVE FROM A PUBLIC TO A COMPETITIVE STATUS

A story at the core of business ethics

France Telecom is known as a major player in the telecommunication sector (third-largest telecommunication company in Europe, 192.7 million customers worldwide in 2010). Up to 1988, France Telecom was known as the Direction Générale des Télécommunications, a division of the French Ministry of Post and Telecommunications. France Telecom officially became a company in 1990, first with public status. Then, it moved gradually to a competitive context in 1998 and became a private company in 2004. As a result, it has had to significantly adapt its organization and managerial practices in the last decade.

In terms of organization and management, in the 1990s France Telecom was a very centralized and traditional company. Decades of public status with a non-competitive context deeply influenced the organization and management style. Until 1997, all employees had civil servant status with guaranteed work and job security. Working conditions were good with high wages and many internal benefits. France Telecom was at that time making healthy profits as telecommunication prices in France were high with no rivals.

In order to adapt France Telecom to a competitive context, the general board decided to transform the company in three major directions: a new CEO coming from the private sector, a total reorganization of the company divisions and units with fewer hierarchical levels and a new approach to management.

The management style was at that time very conservative, directly issued from a military model that one can qualify as bureaucratic, following Max Weber's approach of organizations: a pyramidal vision of the company, centralized decision making and power, numerous categories of civil servants, poor communication. Top management originated from French public engineering schools and the staff was composed of civil servants who usually entered the company aged 18 via a national competition. The model was that of qualification and the way to progress from one category to another was to pass internal examinations or 'concourses'. The client had no space at all in this organization. Indeed the client was known as the '*usager*' or user and could wait for a telephone connection for months without any power to pressurize or transfer to other telephone providers.

Changing the system was a big challenge for all: workers, unions, managers and even the owner of the company at this time, the French state. Moving from a managerial approach to another was for some specialists a question of time (company and people will adapt, they've got no choice . . .), a question of major change to a new managerial paradigm for others. When the second option was proffered, few understood what it was about. The decision was to introduce management based on the competences of civil servants in order to cope with competition. A drastic change had to come and a number of ethical tensions quickly appeared.

The first change was in the classification system. In the existing system, the employees, as civil servants, were positioned in a grading frame of qualifications based on their qualification level and their seniority within the company. With this system, an employee could calculate at which level they would be within ten years. With the competence-driven approach, the frame was totally revisited, mixing qualifications and competences. After months of difficult negotiations with the unions, a new frame was designed. It was a first step, and perhaps the easiest, since the next was to position employees on this new frame. The task was attributed to managers. It was a huge challenge for them to present the reform, the meaning and even the notion of competence and then to determine the position of everyone on the frame. Each manager had first to determine with the employee their level of competence with different tools and, after hours of exchanges, to decide their position. Many workers and employees did not recognize themselves in this new framework, arguing that their seniority and experience should be the first consideration.

The second major change was the creation of an annual appraisal for each employee. It did not exist before, simply because it was not seen as necessary. Civil servants were qualified to do their job and that was most important. However, as soon as the client approach emerged, the question of performance and then of improving competences became crucial for a company moving to a competitive context. For some employees, and some managers, the change has been difficult. Some employees did not see, or did not want to see, the meaning of the change. They refused to meet their manager, jointly positioning themselves on the new frame of competences and refused their annual performance review, claiming that it was a subjective exercise and that they knew themselves their level of performance. Some managers did not easily adopt the spirit of the managerial change and expressed their frustration at the difficulties. The ethical tension of forcing people to adopt new principles of management highlights how employees' expectations of how things ought to be can be undermined. Furthermore shifting any employee, any civil servant, to a competence-based model when they have been hired under a totally different regime undermines their expectations of how their career should be.

The third big change was the demand for new types of competences to support the company in a new competitive context. While dealing with a management based on its competences, France Telecom quickly discovered that it had to develop new kinds of competences, from a situation of competences dominated by the technical to one where the crucial competences in a competitive context were business competences. To do so, two orientations were developed in the mid 1990s: a general move for technical employees to business activities with a strong emphasis on the development of a new kind of competence and the hiring of new competences through the massive arrival of young commercially minded employees under private employment status. If the client was getting for the first time strong consideration from the company, many workers did not appreciate this new orientation and apparent rejection of what had been their core competences for decades.

Following this major managerial reform, the period following the turn of the century was illustrated by another step: the introduction of strongly performance-oriented management. The company, with a private status, owned by shareholders, had to make profits and to compete in a global market. Newly hired managers, hired from the private sector, implemented a result and performance-oriented management for workers and employees still attached to their previous company model. This management style apparently reached its limits between the beginning of January 2008 and the end of January 2010 when, over that period, a shocking number of France Telecom employees committed suicide at their work place in thirty-four individual incidents. Certainly, therefore, ethical issues should be central within HRM, since at France Telecom the introduction of competency management became for some employees at any rate a matter of life or death.

CLASS QUESTIONS

1   How do competences differ from traditional notions of skills and qualifications?
2   What are the main differences between the two main streams in competency management?
3   How might managers use competences in management at different levels of the organization?
4   How do the ethical implications generated by competency management differ from those of more conventional management of human resources?
5   How and why does competency management give us the opportunity to revisit the stakeholders' interests in the company?

About the France Telecom case:

6   Can one manager or worker/employee or even client, considering their professional background or personal values, refuse to adapt to managerial changes linked with the evolution of the competitive environment?
7   What limits should there be when a company asks to its employees to change their core competences?
8   If you were a manager facing a situation of widespread professional and personal disillusionment illustrated by employee suicides, and considering the pressure of all stakeholders on company results, how would you react?

Further reading

Coff, R-W. (1997) 'Human assets and management dilemmas: Coping with hazards on the road to resource-based theory', *Academy of Management Review*, 22(2): 374–402.
Galunic, D. C. and Rodan, S. (1998) 'Resource recombinations in the firm: Knowledge structures and the potential for Schumpeterian innovation', *Strategic Management Journal*, 19: 1193–1201.

Huselid, M-A., Jackson, S-E. and Schuler, R. S. (1997) 'Technical and strategic human resource management effectiveness as determinants of firm performance', *Academy of Management Journal*, 40(1): 171–188.

Lucia, A. D. and Lepsinger, R. (1999) *The Art and Sciences of Competency Models. Pinpointing critical success factors in organizations*. San Francisco, CA: Jossey-Bass/Pfeiffer.

Mascarenhas, B., Baveja, A. and Jamil, M. (1998) 'Dynamics of core competencies in leading multinational companies', *California Management Review*, 40(4): 117–132.

References

Bouteiller, D. and Gilbert, P. (2005) 'Intersecting reflections on competency management in France and in North America', *Industrial Relations*, 60(1): 3–28.

Boyatzis, R. E. (1982) *The Competent Manager: A model for effective performance*. New York/Toronto: John Wiley & Sons.

de Montmollin, M. (1986) *L'intelligence de la tâche. Eléments d'ergonomie cognitive*. Berne: Peter Lang.

Friedmann, G. (1955) *Industrial Society: The emergence of the human problems of automation*. Glencoe, IL: Free Press.

Hamel, G. and Prahalad, C. K. (1990) 'The core competence of the corporation', *Harvard Business Review*, 68(3): 79–91.

Klein, A. L. (1996) 'Validity and reliability for competency-based systems: Reducing litigation risks', *Compensation and Benefits Review*, 28(4): 31–37.

Lawler III, E. E. (1994) 'From job-based to competency-based organizations', *Journal of Organizational Behavior*, 15: 3–15.

McClelland, D. C. (1973) 'Testing for competence rather than for intelligence', *American Psychologist*, 28: 1–14.

Sanséau, P-Y. (2011) 'Competencies for the technological Europe of tomorrow', in D. G. Assimakopoulos, E. G. Carayannis and R. Dossani (eds), *Knowledge Perspectives in New Product Development*, Heidelberg: Springer.

Spencer, L. L. and Spencer, S. M. (1993) *Competence at Work. Models for superior performance*. New York: John Wiley & Sons.

Vicente, K. (2004) *The Human Factor*. London: Routledge.

Weiner, I. B. (2003) *Handbook of Psychology*. New York: John Wiley & Sons.

Wickens, C. D. and Hollands, J. G. (2000) *Engineering Psychology and Human Performance*. Upper Saddle River, NJ: Prentice Hall.

Wright, P. M., McMahan, G. C. and McWilliams, A. (1994) 'Human resources and sustained competitive advantage: A resource-based perspective', *International Journal of Human Resource Management*, 5(2): 301–326.

PART VII

The ethical future?

24

EPILOGUE

Towards an ethical future for business?

*Patrick O'Sullivan, Mark Smith
and Mark Esposito*

At the end of this book with its very diverse range of contributions in which we have delved into the implications of an ethical approach across a very wide range of business and management studies disciplines, it will be useful to draw some of the very diverse strands and lines of thinking together in some sort of synthesis. The purpose of this epilogue chapter is therefore threefold: first, through a quick summary of the applications of an ethical approach across most of the business disciplines, to show that business ethics, far from being a merely peripheral concern or afterthought, deserves to be given a central place across all of the various business specialisms, not only in theory but perhaps above all in practice. We will show how this represents a very fundamental challenge to the discipline of strategic management, at least as it has been taught in a wide range of business schools over the past 30 years.

Second, we will show how this integration of an ethical approach into all of the disciplines implies the systematic adoption of a critical attitude, both by the theoretician of management behaviour and by business practitioners. We will emphasize again how this critical attitude can be seen methodologically as having three different levels, each probing ever further into the ethical foundations and presuppositions of business activity.

Finally, the chapter will reflect on the deterioration of the reputation of business as it was practised in the heyday of what can now without embarrassment or exaggeration be described as the era of cowboy capitalism between 1990 and 2008. This disenchantment can be dated from the financial crisis high point of autumn 2008, and the continuing weakening of the macroeconomic performance since then of the developed world's economies at least is only heightening the disenchantment. As the stream of scandals gets longer, even if now predictable, and faced with cynical resignation by many, the case for a more ethical approach to business is becoming stronger than ever. But perhaps, we shall suggest, this is only a return to ancient more ethical roots for business. Meanwhile, at the political level, even some right-of-centre politicians facing the current patent irrational 'animal spirits'[1] of the financial markets have begun to wonder very loudly about who is and ought to be in charge of the economy: markets or politicians.

Ethics across the board

The first achievement of this book has hopefully been to show how significant ethical issues arise across the whole range of business disciplines and to have suggested the lines of a more morally and socially responsible approach to these issues. To quote but a few brief examples from some of the previous chapters, a whole array of ethical issues of honesty and the encouragement of socially responsible consumption have been raised in respect of marketing. In the area of finance, the perils of moral hazard in central banking have been examined in detail and a critical look has been taken at the role and typical behaviour of contemporary bankers. In the field of human resource management, ethical issues with discrimination and diversity have been raised and the whole set of implicit presumptions of the discipline, some of them pregnant with moral import, have been subjected to a searching critique. The role of leadership at various levels of management in inculcating a more morally upright approach has also been examined, as also has the very topical issue of the rights to privacy of individuals and of what is to be considered as acceptable surveillance. The list is not exhaustive but it gives some idea of how ethical issues, far from being a specialist peripheral matter, can and indeed should be integrated across a very wide array of business disciplines and practices.

Normative business ethics and the spirit of critique

What is common to all of these different applications of ethical reflections across the various disciplines is the adoption of a critical attitude in relation to the current practices and modes of theorizing in these disciplines. In various guises this approach has in effect been highly critical of the approach to business ethical questions that derives from the standpoint of Milton Friedman and others (as described in Chapter 2 above) and which sees the ultimate goal of all business activity as the maximization of profits in the interest of the firm's owners, the shareholders. Repeatedly, the failure of this narrow approach to take into account morally significant impacts (often not covered in the legal framework within which business operates and so completely outside the range of the Friedmanite radar) has been exposed, and instead an approach to business based on the interests of all its stakeholders (and not solely the shareholders) has been taken. Putting the same point in a slightly different way, most of the contributions have taken the view that the social responsibility of business is not entirely exhausted in the pursuit of profits as upholders of the Friedmanite view or unreconstructed followers of Adam Smith might argue, but would hold instead that, in view of its location within a community and to the extent that a business benefits from being situated in a well-organized law-abiding stable community, it may be said to have a social contract with that community from which will flow various social responsibilities to the community.

The challenge to conventional strategic management

To those who are familiar with the debates about the scope of business ethics (the Crane and Matten oxymoron argument[2]), the above will be familiar. What is less obvious perhaps is the challenge that the adoption of a thoroughgoing stakeholder or social contract approach poses to a great deal of the literature and models of strategic management. Often American in origin and implicitly if not always explicitly drawing on Friedman, it has almost invariably been presumed that the ultimate goal of business strategy is to 'make money', to 'maximize shareholder wealth', etc. This mantra has been trotted out by generations of students of the subject as though it were an indubitable axiom. But of course when we adopt the approach of a stakeholder capitalism or of a social contract theory in which the social responsibility of a business may be conceived in a much wider sense, the axiom of traditional strategic management theory is exposed for what it really is: a statement of one possible view about the socio-economic organization of human society and so a statement of a political ideology. It is none other than the basic article of faith of a ruggedly individualistic ultraliberal political philosophy that has been definitive of the American dream and whose roots may be traced back to the Calvinist puritanism brought to the US in the eighteenth century by the Pilgrim Fathers.[3]

A convergence with Critical Social Theory of the Frankfurt school

Since throughout the volume there has been a sustained critical attitude in relation to management theory and practices and since in the end we unmask the ultimate presuppositions and axioms of strategic management as politically ideological in nature, there is an interesting convergence between the broad drift of the very diverse contributions of the volume with the so-called Critical Social Theory of the Frankfurt school of social theory. In the works of the early exponents of this school such as Horkheimer, Adorno and Marcuse they arrive at their systematically critical attitude from a starting point in Marx's critiques of the role of ideology as a source of false consciousness in capitalist societies and the resulting emancipatory role for Critical Social Theory. The contributors to this volume, however, come from a wide variety of backgrounds and political persuasions; and so while there is at the end a remarkable convergence with the tradition of Critical Social Theory in the Frankfurt school it would be a serious mistake to dismiss this convergence as simply a neo-Marxist rejoinder to ultraliberalism. The spirit of critique must ultimately always in the end lead us to create, unless our criticisms are to remain purely negative and destructive; or, put in terms of the Hegelian dialectic, the antithesis must ultimately pass over into a new synthesis. Hence, while our critiques in this volume are in their spirit (their willingness to call into question certain practices of capitalism as we know it today) very close to the spirit of critique of the Frankfurt school, that does not mean that the ultimate conclusions for change need to converge with those of neo-Marxism. Rather, since past political experiments with Marxism are today as tarnished in reputation as those of extreme ultraliberalism, what we face is a real challenge to be creative in the way we define the appropriate role of a socially responsible business within some optimal form of overall socio-economic organization.[4]

Levels of critique

The spirit of critique that is inherent in any normative business ethics thus converges with the tradition of Critical Social Theory; but this work has also made a novel contribution to the methodology of criticism by distinguishing three different levels at which the critiques of business ethics may be carried out. For the want of better labels these have been termed as Level 1, Level 2 and Level 3 critique; and throughout the volume we have endeavoured to identify at which level or levels each chapter is operating. Level 1 critique in business ethics confines itself to the moral appraisal of the activities of people within companies and in relation to the company. In this work, the dominant level of critique is exemplified for example in Chapters 3, 12, 15 and 21. Level 2 critique looks at the moral responsibilities of the company as a whole or of certain of its managers/employees in relation to the wider community in which the company operates (where in some cases of international business this could be the whole of humanity). This level of critique is predominant in for example Chapters 4, 9, 11 and 19 of the book. Level 3 critique is particularly relevant to contemporary international business since it comes into play when a business is operating in a number of different communities with possibly different moral codes: its task is to conduct a critical morality of moralities that compares these with a view to trying to establish an overarching moral code that can fit multiple communities if not the whole of humanity. Level 3 critique can be found in Chapters 2, 10 and 16 above.[5] Each of these levels of critique has its validity and contribution to make to a comprehensive business ethics. What is important in the view of this volume is that we should not confine ourselves to any one level of critique. In particular, a business ethics that remains at Level 1 of critique will probably never touch on questions of wider social responsibility of companies or of the 'social contract' of business with the communities within which it is doing business. And of course in an international business context if we are to reach definitive normative recommendations rather than falling back into an impotently indecisive moral relativism we cannot avoid developing a Level 3 critique when moral codes differ significantly as between societies.

The future of business is more ethical business

Our final word in this epilogue chapter is that, whether one may like it or not, the future of business is inevitably going to have to be more ethical; hence, the analyses of the chapters of this book, which seek to show how to integrate moral considerations into all of the key functional areas of business activity, will be of increasing relevance. Dating from the early 1980s, the Reagan and Thatcher years in the US and UK respectively, and gaining great momentum with the domino fall of the old Marxist régimes in the USSR and Eastern Europe, the 1990s and early 2000s can fairly be described as the heyday of what has come to be known as 'ultraliberal capitalism'[6] or slightly more pejoratively as 'cowboy capitalism'. Ultraliberalism was marked by a systematic deregulation of various sectors of the economy, in particular of the financial sector, by what Margaret Thatcher described as 'rolling back the frontiers of the state', and at least in the Anglo-American world, by an almost blind faith in markets and in the superiority of the private over the public sector. After decades of growing abuse of state power and of growing corruption (especially in the old communist block) it was easy to see how the message of deregulated free market capitalism and wholesale privatization developed such an appeal. However, as the years passed, ultraliberal capitalism began to show its true colours in the form of a rapid widening of the gap between the poorest and richest in society, a growing tendency to monopolistic concentration and abuse of dominant positions (Microsoft, mergers and acquisitions in telecoms, etc.) and a stark realization beginning from around the year 2000 that in fact private sector capitalism is in the end just as prone to corruption as state communism; all that changes is the beneficiaries, who are on the take! The faith in ultraliberalism took a severe hit in 2002 with the Enron scandal, which saw the ignominious and shameful collapse of a company that had been hailed as the icon of aggressive red-blooded capitalism but that was revealed to be rotten at the core, its chief executives consumed by personal greed and devoid of any sense of responsibility even to their fellow employees, let alone to the wider society.[7] And then there came the financial crisis of autumn 2008 whose ripples spread out to generate arguably the worst and most sustained economic downturn since the Great Depression of 1929 and thereafter. As we write today, the Western world in particular is still feeling acutely the effects of this downturn, mired in a sovereign debt crisis fuelled by the hysteria of an unregulated and out-of-control bear market and with stubbornly high unemployment and low business prospects. What is particularly interesting about each of these two key episodes from the point of view of this book is not just that they cast a big question mark over the ideology of ultraliberal capitalism and its promise of beneficence for all if only businesses are left free to maximize their self-interest (profits); each of the episodes had at its core some serious moral failings on the part of many of the key actors involved. At Enron, for example, the personal greed of Messrs Lay, Skilling and Fastow knew no limits and, moreover, the whole edifice to camouflage seriously bad performance of the sprawling company was nothing but a deception, an act of dishonesty of gigantic proportions. As for the financial crisis of 2008, we have seen in Chapter 11 above how problems of moral hazard were endemic in the regulatory system; and once again questions of untrammelled personal greed arose in respect of the bonuses that senior executives were being paid, even as their institutions were having to be saved from failure by massive injections of state money. And the scandals arising from a narrow profit-maximizing, cost-cutting approach to business continue: 2010 saw the huge oil spill in the Gulf of Mexico generated at least in part by lack of suitable precautions taken by the oil major BP when drilling in very deep oceanic waters, all the more shocking since BP has tried to portray itself as a green company that respects the environment scrupulously. In 2011 we witnessed the tragic consequences of the tsunami in Japan which caused once again a nuclear accident of a scale that will ultimately rival that of the Chernobyl nuclear disaster in Ukraine; and where Tepco, the private sector power company was accused both of cover-up and of laxity in respect of safety.

The days of a blind faith in ultraliberalism and the beneficence of a ruthless pursuit of self-interest by all are therefore past, and being replaced by a new era where a more ethically aware and sophisticated approach to business is being taken. To a significant extent this is being led by governments who are introducing tighter regulations for accounting (the US Sarbanes–Oxley Act for example as a direct reaction to Enron), for the financial sector (today the EU and the US are considering much more stringent regulation of the whole financial sector and of retail banking in particular and detailed legislation is imminent as we write) and of course respect for the environment by business is at the heart of the Kyoto Protocol of the UNFCCC.[8] Businesses too, aware of the serious blemish to their reputation from the unending stream of scandals, are to a significant extent taking the initiative themselves to be more socially responsible. Some of this newfound zeal for CSR may of course be little more than cynical greenwashing but many businesses too are genuinely making an effort to be responsible corporate citizens and in fact it is increasingly difficult for businesses to rely just on superficial greenwashing; today it may even do more harm than good to a company's reputation among consumers who are all too aware of the cynicism of certain companies, especially of banks and financial institutions.[9]

Moreover, business schools around the world, stung by the criticism that they have been turning out monsters to captain industry (Lay, Skilling and Fastow all had good MBA degrees), have begun to treat business ethics not just as an exotic optional course for socially minded students but as a course that needs to form part of the core curriculum of any respectable business school. Initially, these courses tended to be bolted on to existing core curricula and they perhaps sat uneasily with the existing cores, dominated as they were by an approach to strategic management and to corporate governance that emphasized shareholder wealth maximization (i.e. profit maximization) as the overriding goal of every private company. Today, however, the realization is growing that business ethics is not just a bolt-on but rather a new frame of mind that needs to imbue the thinking of all of the business disciplines with a wider sense of social responsibility; and we have noted above frankly the challenge that this more socially responsible approach represents to traditional strategic management theorizing. This book, by seeking to integrate a critical ethical approach across all of the business disciplines, has sought to make a modest contribution to these developments.

We may not share the apocalyptic vision of Marx of a capitalist system that is hurtling inevitably towards its own self-annihilation, but one thing is for sure: the days of cowboy capitalism are numbered; for a sustainable free market system *the future of business is ethical business.*[10]

Notes

1 The phrase is of course from John Maynard Keynes.
2 See A. Crane and D. Matten (2010) *Business Ethics*, 3rd edn. Oxford: Oxford University Press, Chapter 2.
3 The Calvinist roots of American-style capitalism have been well expounded by, for example, Max Weber in his classic work: M. Weber (2002) *The Protestant Ethic and the Spirit of Capitalism*. London: Penguin Books. The German original text dates from 1905.
4 This latter question about optimal socio-economic organization is an essentially politico-economic question about which we perhaps also need to think creatively . . . but that is not the concern of *this* volume, whose concern has been business ethics.
5 This latter would in effect be a set of universal moral values such as the UN Declaration of Human Rights, Kant's Categorical Imperative, etc.
6 For a more detailed outline see Chapter 2, page 27, of this volume, the discussion of Friedman's position.
7 ENRON has by today become a byword for greed and corruption, and most people are familiar with the basic details of the scandal that made news headlines around the world in 2001 and 2002. Numerous cases studies and films have been made about it: see, for example, www.caseforest.com/case-study-Enron-The-Terrible-Scandal.aspx.
8 The Kyoto Protocol (signed 1997, implemented from 2005) is the instrument that set in place detailed quantitative targets for emissions of greenhouse gases and for emissions trading for the world's economies. It derives ultimately from the United Nations Foundation Convention on Climate Change (UNFCCC) signed at the Rio Earth summit of 1992. For further details see http://unfccc.int/kyoto_protocol/items/2830.php.
9 One has only to think of the recent revelations of systematic overcharging by banks, and in particular the revelation that in the UK banks were systematically selling insurance policies that were totally unnecessary and indeed useless. For further details see www.ppirefundsuk.co.uk/ppi-claims.
10 There is perhaps a certain historical circularity in this closing injunction since, as theorists such as Max Weber (see note 3) have argued, in its early days capitalism relied heavily on Calvinist puritanism with its strict moral injunctions for its success; and many of the early 'captains of industry' had a profound moral sense. One thinks of the Cadbury family who in the midst of nineteenth-century English capitalism believed that it was their duty to provide a decent level of social housing for their workforce at Bournville, just outside Birmingham.

INDEX

a priori 228–9
Abrahamson, E. 86, 93
absolutism 31, 233
Acharya, V. 111
Ackerman, R.W. 50
Ackers, P. 319
acquisitions 106, 108, 327
Adler, N. 322–3
Adorno, T. 351
adverse behaviour 106–13
advertising 229–30, 249–51, 261
Advertising Standards Authority (ASA) 229
aesthetics 270–2
affirmation 75–6, 81
Africa 14, 16–17, 69, 138, 229, 336
Agarwal, A.S. 104
Aguilera, R. 325
Ahuja, A. and S. 277
AIG 102, 153
air quality 280–1
airlines 262–3; reservations 207, 209
alcohol 230, 232
Alcorn, D.S. 260
Alessi 275
alienation 77–8
alignment 60, 62–3, 66–8
Alter Mundi 279
Amado, G. 311
American Express 256
American Marketing Association 240
American Society for Training and
    Development 69

Amministrazione Autonomia dei
    Monopoli di Stato (AAMS) 91–3, 95–6
Anderson, R. 262, 264
animal rights 199
Ansart, S. 118–33
Antwerp 15–16
Applbaum, A.I. 38
appraisal 337, 339–41
architecture 270–1
Aristotle 68, 103, 113, 170, 172–4, 177,
    202, 231
Armstrong, R. 193
Artemide 274
Artola, M. 193
Asgary, N. 326
Ashforth, B.E. 181
Asia 62, 143, 324; East 144; South 145;
    Southeast 134
Asian financial crisis 158, 160
Assisted Global Positioning 207
Atlanta 263
Atlantic Ocean 13–14, 16, 20
attention 180–2, 185–6
audio surveillance 213
Austin, J.L. 169
Australia 193, 209, 214, 250, 303
avoidance 53

background checks 208, 212
bailouts 101–2, 147–8, 156–60
Baily, W. 324
Baltic 16, 151
Bangladesh 283

Bank of America 197
bankruptcy 127, 135, 151
banks 3, 101–4, 107, 109–13, 118–20,
    131–2, 150–4, 159, 161, 354; core
    business 120–5; Islamic 134–46; societal
    role 125–31
Barley, S.R. 86, 94
Barnier, M. 162
Barone, M.K. 260
Basel agreements 112, 128
Bashar, O.K.M.R. 134–46
Basil, D.Z. 261
Baskins, A. 217
Battilana, J. 88
Bauhaus 271–2
Bear Stearns 101, 107–8, 112
Bebchuk, L. 108
Belgium 15, 326–8
Belize 104
Ben and Jerry's 257
Benetton 228–9
Bentham, J. 30, 206–7
betting 91–2, 94
Bevan, D. 223–37
biases 245
bills of exchange 121
bingo 91–2, 94
Black Review 293
Blinder, A. 106
Boeing 263
Bogle, J.C. 102
Bolivia 104
bonuses 3, 43, 102, 104–8, 110–12, 118,
    159
Booth, L. 110
Bouteiller, D. 336
Boxall, P. 290
Boxembaum, E. 93
BP 354
brain 68, 241–50
brand image 53, 224, 254, 257–61
Brazil 49–50, 55
breast cancer 256, 263–4
Brenkert, G. 224, 229, 231, 234
Brewster, C. 322–4
BRICSA 49, 55
Britain *see* United Kingdom
Brown, B. 54
Brown, T. 273
Buddhism 187
Burke, R.J. 67
Bush, G.W. 153
Business Decision, Human Choices
    65–6
Business Process Paradigm 66

Business Week 277
Butler, J. 81

Calvin Klein 228
Calvinism 180, 351
Canada 109–10, 112–13, 193, 303, 320
capacities 71
capital requirements 112
capitalism 3–4, 9, 25–8, 349, 351, 353,
    355; finance/economics 141, 155, 161,
    163; organizational strategy 74, 81
Capitalism and Freedom 231
carbon monoxide 280
Carroll, A.B. 50, 54
cars 276
Cartwright, S. 321
Casey, V. 276
Castro, F. 69
Catano, V.M. 320
cause-related marketing (CRM) 256–61
central banking 150–3, 157, 160–1
central planning 25–6
CEOs 104–8
Certified Human Resources Professionals
    (CHRP) 320
Challenger 198
Chan, T. 193
charity 260–1
Chartered Institute of Marketing (CIM)
    229, 238
Chartered Institute for Personnel and
    Development (CIPD) 295, 320
Chase Manhattan 154
chemical waste 13–17
Chen, C.R. 107
Chernobyl 354
Chicago 231
child labour 29
China 49, 55, 158, 163, 276
Christianity 180
Chulha 270, 277, 280–3
Churchill, W. 170
cigarettes 255
Cincinnati 263
Citicorp 197
Citigroup 153
Citroen DS 271
civil servants 342–3
Clark, T. 318
class 8–9
Clinton, B. 275
CNET Networks 216–17
coaching 302–6, 311–15; as three-party
    contract 306–12
Coburg 295, 297–9

Coca-Cola 227, 233, 259
codes of ethics 7, 29, 37–40, 43, 239–41,
   307
coercion 200
coffee machine system 322
Coignard, S. 172
collateralized debt obligations (CDOs)
   110–11, 127–9
collateralized debt swaps (CDSs) 127–9
collective competences 334, 338–9
communism 10, 25, 69, 353
commuting 321
company social responsibility 6–7
competences 332–44
competition 54, 126; competitive culture
   196–7, 201–2; competitiveness 84, 208
congruence 54, 60–73, 260–1
connectivity 65–6
consequentialism 71, 230
conservatism 69; in finance 109–10
Conserve India 269, 277–80
constants 70–1
consumers 140, 227–8, 241–4, 247, 249,
   254, 256, 258–61
Continental Europe 87, 104
control 37, 71, 338
Convention Against Corruption 5
Copoeru, I. 34–46
corporate culture 40–1, 53, 110
Corporate Financial Performance (CFP)
   51–5
Corporate Social Performance (CSP) 51–5
corporate social responsibility (CSR) 27–8,
   37, 354; finance/economics 119–20,
   131, 141; HRM 292, 324;
   marketing/innovation 231–2, 254, 257,
   260; organizational strategy 49–59
corruption 5, 19, 28, 140, 314, 353
Council of American Survey Research
   Organizations (CASRO) 241
cowboy capitalism 349, 353, 355
Coyle, D. 197
Crane, A. 22, 198
Creating the Congruent Workplace 60
credit 119, 121–3, 126–9, 131, 135, 152,
   158
credit cards 256
Crédit Coopératif 131
Credit Lyonnais 123
credit reports 210
critical management studies (CMS) 287–8,
   292
critical methodology 22–3
Critical Social Theory 7–10, 74, 288, 319,
   351–2

Cuba 69
Cultural Bias 195
culture 71, 191–5, 202–3; four dynamic
   types 195–202
Culture Theory (CT) 191–3, 195–6,
   200–3
Cuny, C. 238–53

Daiwa Asset Management 144
Danone 258
data 66–7, 248; protection 240–1
D'Aunno, T. 88
Davis, K. 50
De Gaulle, C. 172
De Groot, H. 86
De La Renta, O. 229
De Laroisière, J. 130
Dean, D.H. 260
debt 3, 104, 107, 135, 210–11, 353
decision making 171–2, 186, 289
default 128–9
Deleuze, G. 174
Delhi 277, 280
Deloitte and Touche 197
Delta Air Lines 262–4
Denhardt, R.B. 35–6
Denmark 89, 92, 95
deontology 75, 228–30, 239–40, 245,
   308
Department for Trade and Industry 295
deposits 109, 127, 136–7
deregulation 164
derivatives 110, 121, 130, 150, 156
Descartes, R. 30
design 267–77, 283; Conserve India
   277–80; Philips Design 280–3
Designers Accord 276–7
desire 172
dignity 75–6, 79
DiMaggio, P. 88, 93
Dioguardi, G. 175–6
direct action 199
discrimination 141, 324
diversity 80, 324
division of labour 65
dollar 163
donations 256–7, 260
Douglas, M. 191–2, 195
Dow Jones Industrial Average 216
drug testing 211–12
Drumwright, M. 257
Dunn, P. 216–17
Dupuy, C. 128
Durkheim, E. 65
Duymedjian, R. 179–90

Eastern Europe 151, 353
ecology 24, 29, 257, 275–7
economics 120, 125
efficiency 37–9, 82, 179–80, 186, 208
egalitarian culture 199–203
egoism 231, 233
Egypt 137
elaboration 261
electroencephalography (EEG) 247–8, 250
Electrolux 198
elites 183–4
Ellis, R. 197
email monitoring 212–13
emerging economies 49–50
emotion 68, 186, 314
Emotional Intelligence 67
empathy 274
employability 340
employees 208–10, 214–16, 296–7, 338,
    340–4; approach 39–41; involvement
    289; surveillance 206–8; *see also* workers
Enlightenment 30, 76
Enron 54, 171, 353
entrepreneurship 123–4
environment 5, 24, 29, 140, 354;
    marketing/innovation 262–3, 268–9,
    275–7, 283; organizational strategy 49,
    61
equity (financial) 107, 128, 143
equity (socioeconomic) 147, 156–60
Erasmus 177
ergonomists 333
ESOMAR 241
Esposito, M. 3–21, 49–73, 349–55
Estonia 15
Esty, D. 275
Ethics Everywhere 43
ethikos 191
Ethisphere Institute 42–3
Europe 22, 24; finance/economics 120,
    158; HRM 303, 326–7, 334, 336;
    marketing/innovation 242, 271–2;
    organizational behaviour 191–4, 203,
    214; organizational strategy 62, 64, 89,
    91, 94–5
European Central Bank (ECB) 158, 162
European Commission (EC) 90, 162
European Parliament 162
European Union (EU) 14–15, 94, 104,
    150, 158, 164, 209
exchange traded funds (ETFs) 144
executive compensation 69, 101–13
expatriation 317, 320–4, 326
exploitation 75, 81–2
Exxon 200

Facebook 263–4
fair trade 257
Fairchild, G. 93
fairness 106, 158–60, 211
fake involvement 290, 292–3
false consciousness 8–10, 351
family 321–4, 326
Farah, M.J. 249
fashion 229, 233, 269, 277–80
fatalistic culture 200–2
Fatien Diochon, P. 302–16
Federal Reserve 109, 150, 158
FedEx 175
Fifth Amendment 217
Fiji 104
finance 27, 350, 354
financial crises *see* Asian financial crisis;
    global financial crisis
Financial Services Authority (FSA) 101,
    105
Finland 323
Fiorina, C. 216
Fitch 155, 162
flexibilization 82–3
Fombrun, C.J. 53
football 91, 93, 104–5
Ford Motor Company 274, 288–90
form follows function 270–2
formal structure 40–1
Fortune 500 companies 216
Foss, N.J. 77
Foster, D.P. 111
four-dimensional model 54–5
fractional reserve banking 155, 161, 163
France: finance/economics 119–20, 131,
    151; HRM 303, 333, 336;
    marketing/innovation 240–1, 255,
    258–9; organizational behaviour 181,
    193; organizational strategy 89, 91–2, 95
France Telecom 342–4
Frankfurt school 288, 319, 351–2
frauds 119, 171, 217
free markets 3–4, 155, 161, 196, 231–2,
    353
free trade agreements 145
Freetown 13, 16–17, 19–20
French Connection 228
Freud, S. 170
Fried, J.M. 108, 111
Fried, Y. 181
Friedman, M. 26–9, 31, 52, 105, 231–2,
    275, 350–1
Fuld, D. 106
functional magnetic resonance imaging
    (fMRI) 244, 246–7, 251–2

functionality 270–2
funding structure 109
Fustier, P. 309

G20 101
gajin effect 322
gambling 87, 89–96, 154
Gaming Tax 90
Gdansk 13, 20
Gentilucci, A. 217
Germany 95, 105, 171, 193, 199, 303
gifts 233
Gilbert, P. 336
Gismondi, E. 274
Glass-Steagall Act 126
Global Compact 4–5, 10, 134, 141
global financial crisis (GFC) 3, 275, 349,
    353–4; banking ethics 118–19, 125–7;
    executive compensation 101–5, 107–10,
    112; Islamic finance 134, 137–8, 145;
    policy response 150–1, 160
Global Positioning System 207, 214
globalization 233
goals 37–9
Godard, J. 289–92
Golden Mean 231
Goldman Sachs 119, 153
Goleman, D. 67–8
goodwill 49
Google 147
Gotzsch, J. 267–84
Great Depression 353
Greece 95
green design 269, 272–3
Greenwood, M.R. 318
Groom, B. 102
Gudmand-Høyer, M. 318
Gulf Cooperation Council (GCC) 145
Gulf of Mexico 354
Gupta, S. 261
gurus 188

Habermas, J. 76, 88
Habitat for Humanity 263
Hackley, C. 225–6, 228–9
Hadith 138–9, 144
halal 139–40, 144
Halifax Bank of Scotland (HBOS) 101
Hamel, G. 335
Handmade Recycled Plastic (HRP) 278–9
Happiness 177, 310
haram 134–5, 139, 141
Harris, H. 322–4
Harvard 288
Harvard Business Review 86

head in the sand 179–83
health 182, 184–5, 210
Health Belief Model 255
hedonic consumption 260
Hegel, G.W.F. 30, 352
Hegendorff, J. 106
Hellenism 187
hermeneutic data 67
Herr, P.M. 261
Hewlett-Packard 216–18
hierarchy 200; hierarchical culture 197–9,
    201–2; hierarchy of needs 272–3
High Banks 121
high performance work systems (HPWS)
    82–3, 287–95; Coburg 297–9;
    Metaswitch 295–7
Hinkley 83
hoarding 139–40
Hobbes, J. 169, 231
Home Depot 211
Hong Kong 193
Honneth, A. 74–9, 81
Hoover, H. 126
Horkheimer, M. 351
House Committee on Oversight and
    Reform 106
HSBC Amanah 137
Huang, R. 109, 112
human capital 74, 77, 83
Human Process Paradigm 66
human relations 80, 318
Human Resources Management (HRM)
    208, 223, 350; coaching 302, 304, 310,
    314–15; competences 334–5, 337–8,
    340, 344; high performance work
    systems 296, 298; international 317–20,
    325–7, 329; organizational strategy
    74–5, 77
human rights 5, 209
Hungary 89
Hunsaker, K. 217
Huntington Life Sciences (HLS) 199–200,
    202
Hurd, M. 217

IDEO 268, 273
ideology 8–10, 25–7, 69, 74, 161, 225,
    232, 351
ijarah 136
IKEA 211
Imam, P. 137
immobilism 51
immorality 148–9, 153–4, 160–1
incentives 78, 80, 101–8, 111–12, 148–9
inclusion 80

India 49, 55, 158, 269, 276–83, 326–8
individual 24–5, 34–6, 39–40, 42, 209;
    competences 334–5, 338; individualism
    231–2, 338; individuation 70
Industrial Designers Society of America
    (IDSA) 269, 277
industry 121, 270–2
inflation 158
information technology (IT) 92, 95,
    206–7, 212
inside-out perspective 62
institutional investors 128, 162
institutions 86–9; institutional orientation
    53; institutionalization 93–4
instrumentality 38, 76–7, 79, 82–3, 311
insurance 127–9, 137, 143, 147–9, 154
integrity 229–30
intensification 289–90, 298
interdependence 82
interest 29, 121, 135–6, 140, 144
international assignments 320–9
International Coach Federation (ICF) 307
International Council of Societies of
    Industrial Design (ICSID) 277
International Design Excellence Awards
    (IDEA) 269, 277, 283
International Financial Services London
    (IFSL) 137
International Labour Organization 5
international law 14
International Monetary Fund (IMF) 138
Internet 207
interviews 296
investment banking 121–2, 126
Investment Securities LLC 154
invisible hand 25
involvement 289–90, 292–3, 297
iPhone 263
IQ 333
Iran 137–8
Ireland 3, 150
Islam, G. 74–85, 319
Islamic Bank of Asia 143
Islamic finance 110, 134–46, 154
Islamic Finance Consultation Unit (UKKI)
    144
Islamic Financial Services Board (IFSB)
    143–4
Istithna' 136
Italy 87, 89–96, 197–9, 274–5, 327

Jackson, T. 193
Japan 144, 151, 303, 323, 354
Jennings, M. 67
job security 83, 288, 342

Johnsen, R. 318
Jones Lang Lasalle 42–3
Jordan, J. 321
Judaism 180
just-in-time 289, 298

Kabat-Zinn, J. 182
Kahn, B.E. 260
Kant, I. 30, 172–3, 176, 202, 228
Kaplan, S.N. 104
Karenin, A. 170
Kartell 275
Keller, C. 104
Kelley, D. 273
Kerviel, J. 119
Keyworth, G. 217
Khan, H. 134–46
Klein, N. 225
knowledge economy 208
Knutson, B. 251
Kohlberg, L. 40
Kolka, A. 326
Kotler, P. 224
Kpodar, K. 137
Kramer, R.M. 27 8
Krugman, P. 109
Kunda, G. 86, 94
Kuwait 137
Kyoto Protocol 354

labour 5, 82, 214, 287 *see also* work
Lacan, J. 169–70, 174
Langer, E.J. 187
Langer, H. 186
Langlois, C.C. 325
language games 30
Latin America 91
Lawrence, T.B. 88–9
laws 29, 54, 232
layoffs 198–9
leadership 55, 183–4, 306, 327
leaks 216–17
lean production 288, 298
Lebanon 110
Lebow, V. 227
legitimacy 54, 87, 89, 93–5
Lehman Brothers 3, 101, 106–8, 128, 152,
    172
Leibniz, G. 30, 174
LeLay, P. 227
lenders of last resort 161
less developed states 28–9
levels of critique 4, 6–9, 11, 22–33, 352
leverage 107, 112
Levitt, T. 233

liberalism 9, 231–2
liquidity 151, 153, 157, 159, 161
lived experiences 66–7
Locke, J. 30
Loewy, R. 271
long-termism 111–12
L'Oreal 226
lotteries 91
Lowe, S. 227
Lowery, J. 263
Lubin, D. 275
Lukacs, G. 74, 80
Lychenko, A. 13–21
Lyon 123

Maak, T. 80
McCarthy, P. 175
McClelland, D.C. 336
McDonalds 233–4
McFadden Act 126
Machiavelli, N. 216
machine aesthetics 271
Macklin, R. 319
Macky, K. 290
Madoff, B. 119, 154
Maier, M. 67
maieutics 303
makruh 139
Malaysia 137–8, 143, 145
Mallinger, M. 67
Mallory, G. 318
management 12, 34–9, 42–6, 169–78, 319;
    coaching 310, 314–15; competences
    332–44; control systems 39–42; high
    performance work systems 296, 298–9;
    mindfulness 180–9
Manzini, E. 276
Marcuse, H. 351
market research 238–42; neuromarketing
    242–52
marketing 223–35, 350; social/societal
    254–66
Marketing Research Society 241
markets 25–6, 125–6, 155, 224
Mars 259
Martin, R. 273
Marx, K. 8–10, 27, 65, 351, 355
Marxism 74, 80, 352–3
Marzano, S. 274
Maslow, A. 272–3
mass production 271–2
Masson, N. 172–3
Matrix, The 234
Mattel 234
Matten, D. 22, 198

Maybank 143
Mazza, C. 86–98
MBAs 322, 354
measurement 51–3, 55, 78, 111–12, 243,
    245
Mediterranean 14–15
Melmendier, U. 108
memorization 250–2
Memphis 272
Menon, S. 259–60
mentoring 305
mergers 327
Merrill Lynch 102, 153
metaethics 7, 29, 31
Metaswitch 295–7
methodology 4, 6–7, 12, 22–3, 245
Michigan University 288
Middle Ages 121
Middle East 142, 145
Mihailova, S. 17–18, 20
Mill, J.S. 231
mindfulness 179–90
misalignment 93–4
Mit Ghamr Savings Bank 137
Mitschow, M.C. 326
moderation 231
modernism 30–1
Monetary Authority of Singapore (MAS)
    142–4
monetary policy 157–9
money 120–1, 126, 144–5; supply 161
monitoring 207, 212–15
Monvoisin, V. 118–33
Moody's 155, 162
moral hazard 101, 110, 147–56, 160–2,
    164, 350, 354
moral philosophy 23, 29–31
moral practices 34–5
Morehouse University 263
motivation 340; motivational readiness 76
MRI *see* functional magnetic resonance
    imaging
mudarabah 136–7
multiculturalism 30–1
multinationals 28–9, 322, 324–9
Murphy, K.J. 101
Murphy, P.E. 257
musharakah 136, 142
Muslims 134, 137–9
mutualization of risk 128–9, 131
Myers, J.G. 260
Myrgorodski, B. 14–16

NASA 198
National Bank of Poland 150

national cultures 191, 193–5
Natural Symbols 195
Neck, C.P. 40
needs 272, 274
neoliberalism 227
Netherlands 95, 199, 281
neuromarketing 242–52
New York Times 217
New Zealand 209, 214
Newell, H. 11
Nicomachean Ethics 68, 172
Nielsen, R.P. 103
Nietzsche, F. 172
Nigeria 16–17
nihilism 31
Nill, A. 194
Nillès, J.-J. 169, 173
Nisbett, R.E. 242–4
non-governmental organizations (NGOs) 256–8, 269, 277, 281, 283
Nordstrom 175
normative discourse 6, 8, 23–6, 86, 103, 192, 207–8, 233, 288, 336, 350
North America 303, 336; typical approach 22, 24, 26
Northern Rock 107
Nowak, A.Z. 147–66
Nwachukwu, O. 193
nylon tights 242

Obama, B. 153
obesity 255, 259
OCBC Bank 143
Ogunoku, B. 16
oil tankers 13–14
opportunism 107–8, 110
organizational approach 39–41
Organizational Violence 65
Orientalism 229
Orlitzky, M. 51
O'Sullivan, P. 3–33, 147–66, 349–55
Oxfam 279

Packard, D. 216
Pakistan 283
Panama 13
panopticon 212
paradigms 63, 66, 245; protection 198; shift 52
Parmalat 171, 197, 202
Pascal's wager 177
Passet, R. 119
Patel, T. 191–205
Paulson, H. 153
Peery, N. 54–5

pension funds 162
performance 51–5, 78; employee relations 341, 343–4; finance/economics 102, 106, 111–12; organizational behaviour 185, 208–9, 212; *see also* high performance work systems
Perkins, T.J. 217
Perrow, C. 88
Perry, S. 54
Persian Gulf 138
Peters, T. 175
Petrograd 13–16, 20
petroleum 14–15
pharmaceuticals 326, 329
phenomenological data 67
philanthropy 270, 280
Philips Design 270, 274, 277, 280–3
Pirsch, J. 261
Pitesa, M. 206–20
plastic waste 269, 277–8
Pless, N.M. 80
pluralism 231
Poland 13, 20, 110, 150–1
political correctness 9–10
pollution 267, 269
Ponzi schemes 154
Popa, P. 17–18, 20
Popper, K. 169–70, 172, 176–7
Porter, A. 102
Porter, M.E. 27–8, 52
positivism 4, 23–5, 39, 337–8
Positron Emission Tomograph (PET) 246
postmodernism 29–30, 182
Powell, W.W. 88, 93
power 8, 10
Prahalad, C.K. 335
pre-employment testing 210
Pressley-Brown, S. 262
pretexting 217
prevention campaigns 255
Price Waterhouse Coopers (PwC) 293
principal-agent problem 148–9
prisons 207, 212
privacy 209–10, 212–15, 248
Proctor and Gamble 226
profit-sharing 136
profitability 26–9, 52, 106–7, 109, 111, 138, 197, 208, 275–6, 295
Protection Motivation Theory 255
Protestantism 180–1
psychological contracts 78–9
psychologization 310
puritanism 180–1, 351
pyramid of needs 272–3

qard hasan 136
qualifications 340, 343
quantitative easing 157
quantitative vs. qualitative data 66
Quran 138–41, 144

Rajan, R. 111
Rajgopal, S. 107
ranking 297
rating agencies 128, 155–6, 160, 162
rationalism 30, 173
rationality 196, 198–200
Ratnovski, L. 109, 112
Rawl, L. 200
Reagan, R. 353
real estate 126, 138, 142–3, 163
recklessness 148, 151, 160–1
recognition 74–82, 250
recruitment 317–29
recycling 263, 269, 277–8
reference systems 69–71
reflexiveness 182
regulation 3–4, 89–96, 112–13, 119, 161,
    163–4, 229
reification 74, 77–81, 319
relativism 29–31, 202, 228, 230, 326, 352
Renault 258
rent-seeking 110
reputation 53
research and development (R&D) 275, 326
reserve requirements 158
responsiveness 53, 55
revolution 8–9, 80–1
reward systems 78, 80, 111
Rhodeback, M. 193
riba 135, 140
Richelieu 303
Rio Declaration 5
risk 49, 101, 106–13, 118, 120–5, 127–32,
    158, 162, 244; absorption 200
Roche, L. 169–78
Roosevelt, F.D. 126
Ross, J.K. 260
Rossiter, J.R. 249
Roux, C. 277
Roux, L. 101–17
Royal Bank of Scotland (RBS) 101, 107
Royal Philips Electronics 270, 280
rubbish 279–80
Russell, B. 30
Russia 13, 49, 55

Sadowsky, J. 175
safety 28, 211
Sahni, N. 327–9

Sanders, W.M.G. 107
Sanséau, P.-Y. 332–45
Sarbanes-Oxley Act 36
Sartre, J.-P. 171
Saudi Arabia 137
scandals 19, 39, 42–3, 54, 118, 170–1,
    216–18, 349, 353–4
Scarborough, H. 11
Schlegelmilch, B.B. 325
Schmidt, H. 171–2
Schön, D. 182
Schwartz, M. 198
scientific management 288
Scott Paper Corporation 82–4
Securities and Exchange Commission
    155–6
securitization 109–10, 125, 127–9
Seiagustus 13–16, 19–20, 28
selection 319–29
self 34–5
self-actualization 273
self-leadership 40
Sengupta, S. 287–301
Serie A 91
service economy 273, 333
Sévérac, P. 170, 172
Sgherri, M.-S. 172
shadow banking 109
Shanley, M. 53
shareholders 26–8, 101–3, 105–9, 197,
    295, 340, 350–1, 354
Sharfman, B.S. 111
Shariah law 110, 135–8
Shariah-compliant finance (SCF) 135,
    143–4
Shevlin, T. 107
Shilon, N. 111
short-termism 107–8
Shrivastava, P. 52
Shultz, C. 194
Sierra Leone 13, 16
Silberstein, R.B. 249
sin industries 260
Singapore 134, 142–5
Singh, J. 325
Singhapakdi, A. 193
skills 302–4, 306
skin whitening 225–6
small and medium sized enterprises (SMEs)
    104
Smith, A. 350
Smith, M. 3–21, 317–31, 349–55
Smith, S.M. 260
smoking 255
sobriety 211–12

social marketing 255–6, 262
social networking 207
social responsibility 6, 24–7, 119, 142, 172, 193, 231–2 *see also* corporate social responsibility
societal marketing 254–66
Society of Human Resource Management 62
Socrates 9–10, 173, 176, 303
solidarity 80, 83–4
Sony 272
Soufani, K. 101–17
South Africa 49–50, 55, 258, 303
sovereign debt 156, 162, 353
Soviet Union 10, 25, 353
Spain 91–2, 95, 193
speculation 110, 135–6
Spicer, A. 324
Spinoza 169–73, 177
spirituality 187–8
spying 216–18
stakeholders 53, 105, 198–9, 230, 233, 339, 350–1; surveillance 208–10
Standard Chartered Bank 143
Standard and Poor's 155, 162
Stanford University 273
state 3–4, 87–8, 90–2, 94–5, 118–19, 125–6
Statue of Liberty 256
Steiler, D. 179–90
Stiglitz, J. 163–4
Stocker, M. 104
Stop Huntington Animal Cruelty (SHAC) 199–200, 202–3
Storey, J. 318
stoves 280–3
Strahilevitz, M. 260
Strandgaard, J. 93
Strategic Management 52, 349, 351, 354–5
strategies 39, 64–5, 87
streamlining 271–2
stress 171, 179–80, 184–6, 188, 290, 292–4
subjectivity 8, 35
subprime 3, 126, 150, 156
Suchman, M. 95
Suddaby, R. 88–9
suicides 344
sukuk 136, 138, 143
Sullivan, L. 270
sulphur 14–15
super-ego 170, 173–5, 177
Supreme Court of the United States 212
surveillance 206–10, 212–16
sustainability 37, 60–73, 275–6
Swaen, V. 260

Sweden 89, 198, 325
Sweeney, J. 193
Switzerland 111
Swords, D. 194
systemic violence 65

tail risks 111
takaful 137, 143
taken-for-grantedness 87–9, 93–6
takeovers 106
Tallinn 15–16
Tanzi, C. 197
targets 26
Tate, G. 108
tax 93, 95, 142–3, 159–60
Taylorism 82, 181, 288–90, 333, 335
team-based production 288
technology 207, 214–15, 243–4
telecommunications 342
Telegraph, The 106
teleology 230
telephone calls 207
television 227, 250
Teodoro CT 16, 19
Tepco 354
tests 210, 333
Thailand 193
Thatcher, M. 160, 353
Thomas, T. 184
Thompson, M. 198, 202
three-party contract 304–12
time and labour systems 214
tipping 234
tobacco 260
tolerance 30–1
too large to fail 164
Tornikoski, C. 317–31
Totocalcio 91
toxic waste 14–20
training 69, 187–9, 296, 298
travel insurance 149
Trinity System 65
triple bottom line 276
Troubled Asset Relief Program 105
trust 82–3, 216
Tsalikis, J. 193
Tse, T. 101–17
tuition fees 102
Tunis 15

UBS 111
Ukraine 354
ultra-liberalism 351–4
Unilever 226
unions 82–3, 320, 341–3